CAMBRIDGE LIBRARY COLLECTION

Books of enduring scholarly value

Classics

From the Renaissance to the nineteenth century, Latin and Greek were compulsory subjects in almost all European universities, and most early modern scholars published their research and conducted international correspondence in Latin. Latin had continued in use in Western Europe long after the fall of the Roman empire as the lingua franca of the educated classes and of law, diplomacy, religion and university teaching. The flight of Greek scholars to the West after the fall of Constantinople in 1453 gave impetus to the study of ancient Greek literature and the Greek New Testament. Eventually, just as nineteenth-century reforms of university curricula were beginning to erode this ascendancy, developments in textual criticism and linguistic analysis, and new ways of studying ancient societies, especially archaeology, led to renewed enthusiasm for the Classics. This collection offers works of criticism, interpretation and synthesis by the outstanding scholars of the nineteenth century.

Cornelii Taciti Annalium Libri V, VI, XI, XII

A lecturer at the University of Bristol, Pitman published this edition of Tacitus' *Annals* in Oxford in 1912. The title of the work derives from Tacitus's style of history, which he dealt with on a year-by-year basis. *Annals* covered the reigns of four Roman emperors, beginning after the death of Augustus. Of the 16 original books covering a period of 54 years, much of what Tacitus wrote has not survived. This edition of *Annals* includes four books: the incomplete Book 5 and Book 6, which cover the final years and death of Tiberius, and Books 11 and 12 which cover the the end of the reign of Claudius. (Books 7 to 10 are missing.) The text and introduction are from the 1894 edition by Henry Furneaux; Pitman's intention is 'to serve the needs of students requiring a less copious and advanced commentary' than that supplied by Furneaux.

T0370795

Cornelii Taciti
Annalium
Libri V, VI, XI, XII

With Introduction and Notes
Abridged from the Larger Work

EDITED BY HENRY FURNEAUX
AND H. PITMAN

CAMBRIDGE
UNIVERSITY PRESS

CAMBRIDGE UNIVERSITY PRESS

Cambridge, New York, Melbourne, Madrid, Cape Town, Singapore,
São Paolo, Delhi, Dubai, Tokyo

Published in the United States of America by Cambridge University Press, New York

www.cambridge.org
Information on this title: www.cambridge.org/9781108012393

© in this compilation Cambridge University Press 2010

This edition first published 1912
This digitally printed version 2010

ISBN 978-1-108-01239-3 Paperback

CORNELII TACITI

ANNALIUM

LIBRI V, VI, XI, XII

WITH INTRODUCTIONS AND NOTES
ABRIDGED FROM THE LARGER WORK
OF HENRY FURNEAUX, M.A., BY

H. PITMAN, M.A.,

LECTURER IN CLASSICS AT THE UNIVERSITY OF BRISTOL

OXFORD

AT THE CLARENDON PRESS

1912

HENRY FROWDE, M.A.

PUBLISHER TO THE UNIVERSITY OF OXFORD

LONDON, EDINBURGH, NEW YORK, TORONTO

MELBOURNE AND BOMBAY

PREFACE

This volume has been prepared on the same scale and with the same purpose as my edition of Books xiii–xvi of the *Annals*. It is designed to serve the needs of students requiring a less copious and advanced commentary than that given in Mr. Furneaux's large edition. In substance the Introductions and Notes are drawn from Mr. Furneaux's work, but I have ventured to give explanations or translations of my own in certain passages, left without comment by him, which seemed to me likely to present difficulty to students as yet unfamiliar with Tacitus' peculiarities of expression. I have endeavoured to make this volume as far as possible self-contained, by taking illustrations of Tacitus' diction mostly from passages in the books given in the text, and by stating the chief facts of importance that are related in any other part of the *Annals* about the personages mentioned in this part of the narrative.

The Text is that of Furneaux's edition, 1894. I have not thought it consistent with the plan of this book to give more than the briefest discussion of the points where his readings differ from those of other editors.

My best thanks are due to my friend and colleague, Professor F. Brooks, of the University of Bristol, for his kind help in the work of scrutinizing the proof-sheets for misprints or misstatements.

H. PITMAN.

University of Bristol,
July, 1912.

CONTENTS

INTRODUCTION:

INTRODUCTION

I

LIFE OF TACITUS

§ 1. OUR knowledge of the chief facts and dates in the life of Tacitus rests mainly on allusions in his own writings and those of his friend the younger Pliny, who addresses several letters to him and often speaks of him in others.

His praenomen is not mentioned in this correspondence, and is differently given by later authorities as Gaius or Publius. His family connexions are unknown; but he would appear to have been the first of his name to attain senatorial rank, though of sufficient position to have begun his 'cursus honorum' at the earliest, or almost the earliest, legal age; as he can hardly have been born earlier than 52–54 A. D., and must have been quaestor not later than 79 A. D., by which time he had also received in marriage the daughter of Agricola, who was already a consular, and one of the first men in the State.

His boyhood falls thus under the time of Nero; his assumption of the 'toga virilis' would coincide, or nearly so, with the terrible year of Galba, Otho, and Vitellius; his early manhood was spent under Vespasian and Titus; the prime of his life under Domitian; the memory of whose tyranny is seen in all his historical writings, which were composed at various dates in the great time of Trajan.

Most of his life may be supposed to have been spent in Rome, where he became one of the leaders of the Bar, and one of the best known literary names of Rome; so that a stranger sitting next to him at the games, and finding him to be a man of letters, asked whether he was speaking to Tacitus or to Pliny[1]. He is further known[2] as having been consul suffectus and in that capacity colleague with Nerva in 97 A. D., and as associated with Pliny in the prosecution of Marius Priscus, proconsul of Africa, in

---

[1] Plin. *Epp.* ix 23, 2. [2] Ib. ii 1, 6.

100 A.D.[1] This is the last fact in his life definitely known, and there is no evidence that he outlived Trajan.

§ 2. The *Annals*, more properly entitled 'Libri ab excessu divi Augusti,' comprising in sixteen Books the history of fifty-four years from the death of Augustus to that of Nero, are the latest in date of his writings, and are shown by an allusion to the Eastern conquests of Trajan (ii 61, 2) to have been published at some date not earlier than 115 A.D., and probably before the retrocession of the Eastern frontier under Hadrian in 117 A.D. The first six Books, comprising the principate of Tiberius, rest on a single manuscript, called the First Medicean, written probably in the tenth or eleventh century, and now preserved at Florence. The text of Books xi–xii, given in this volume, is based on a MS. known as the Second Medicean, which contains all that we have of Books xi–xvi, besides all the extant part of the Histories, with the exception of i 69–75 and i 86—ii 2. It is known to have been sent from Florence to Rome in 1427 A.D., but it was shortly afterwards returned to Florence, where it passed to the Convent of St. Mark, and thence to the Laurentian Library, where it still remains. Other existing MSS. cannot be proved to be of earlier date, and are generally regarded as based, if not on the Medicean MS. itself, at any rate on the same source as that from which it was taken, their variations being either attempted emendations or preserving the right text in places where the original letters of Med. have become illegible and been reproduced by a later hand.

Materials available to Tacitus.

§ 3. It is not Tacitus' usual practice to give the names of the authorities whom he followed, and in the case of the first six Books of the *Annals* he does so only twice, mentioning the history of the German wars by C. Plinius, in i 69, 3, and the memoirs of the younger Agrippina in iv 53, 3. In each of these cases it would appear that he is here giving something overlooked by the other authors whom he usually followed. As a rule his references are

---

[1] Plin. *Epp.* ii 11, 2.

made in merely general terms ; he speaks of 'auctores' and 'scriptores,' or introduces a statement by 'quidam tradidere,' 'ferunt,' or 'tradunt,' and the number of such expressions indicates that the sources from which he gathered his materials were abundant. Not many names of the historians who dealt with the period covered by the *Annals* remain, however. Of contemporary accounts of Tiberius' times all that is extant is now contained in a few passages of Valerius Maximus, and in the closing portion of Velleius Paterculus' history, published in 30 A.D., in which is a short sketch of the first sixteen years of Tiberius' reign. It is not known if any other histories of Tiberius' reign were produced in his lifetime, but soon after his death several works, now lost, came out. There was Tiberius' own autobiography, referred to by Suetonius (*Tib.* 61); there was a volume of memoirs by the younger Agrippina, giving an account of the inner history of the court and family of Tiberius, which probably supplied Suetonius with much of the scandal which he repeats, and may have greatly influenced the historians who preceded Tacitus, by whose time the book seems to have passed out of circulation ; and Claudius also wrote an autobiography, as well as a general history from the end of the civil wars onwards, a voluminous work in forty-three Books. It is also known that M. Seneca, the father of Nero's tutor, composed a history from the beginning of the civil wars to a time shortly before his own death : this took place early in the reign of Gaius, so that we may conjecture that his history went down to the death of Tiberius. Another famous historian, of a slightly later date, was M. Servilius Nonianus, who was consul in 35 A.D. and died in 59 A.D.; but it is not known what was the period with which he dealt. More information remains as to the work of Aufidius Bassus, who died in 60 A.D. ; he wrote a history of the wars of the Romans in Germany, as well as a general history, to which a continuation was written by the elder Pliny, and as Pliny called this continuation a 'history of his own times,' Bassus' work probably went to the time of Claudius. Pliny also wrote another work in twenty Books on the wars of the Romans in Germany, but with the exception of his *Natural History* his writings are lost to us.

All these would be available to Tacitus as material for the history contained in this volume. Later authors, to whom Tacitus refers

in his history of Nero's reign, were M. Cluvius Rufus, a companion
of Nero in Greece, author of a history (probably) from Gaius to
Vitellius, Fabius Rusticus, one of Tacitus' authorities for his treatment of Britain (*Agr.* 10, 3), and the general Corbulo (xiii 20 :
xv 16).

Other materials available for the *Annals* generally would be
biographies of famous men, such as that, produced later, of Thrasea
by Arulenus Rusticus, and those referred to by Tacitus as prece-
dents for his own work on Agricola (*Agr.* 1). From such a source
he probably drew his knowledge of the cases of victims of Tiberius,
which had been left unrecorded by his other authorities (see vi 7, 6).
There would also be funeral orations on public men, published
speeches, and collections of letters like that published later by the
younger Pliny. There were also the public records : 'acta' or
'commentarii senatus' had been kept since the first consulship
of Julius Caesar, who at the same time also started the 'acta diurna
urbis,' the daily gazette chronicling proceedings in the courts and
chief events of public importance ; and Tacitus made use of both ;
e. g. xv 74, 3 ; iii 3, 2. The events of which he wrote, too, were
sufficiently near to his own day for a considerable amount of tradition about them to be still existing and worth recording, as the
frequency of 'ferunt,' 'traditur,' &c., before stories cited by him
indicates.

Historical value of the Annals.

§ 4. As Dio complains, it was more difficult for historians to get
at the truth under the Empire than under the Republic. Politics
were no longer for the general public ; in jurisdiction, in the
administration of the provinces, and in the conduct of war, much
was done by the princeps and his private advisers that could only
become known from official versions issued at the time, or from
such reminiscences as generals or imperial officials cared to publish
subsequently. Persons outside government circles remained at the
mercy of the official version : reminiscences of a general might be
mere self-glorification. Tacitus believed himself to be writing

impartially, and was a diligent student and compiler of materials, aiming at basing his narrative on a 'consensus auctorum.' But like other ancient historians he probably had little sense of the necessity of correctly estimating the intrinsic merits of the authors from whom he drew his material. And in the earlier part of the *Annals* it is more than probable that his portrait of Tiberius is unfairly coloured, because he has drawn for his facts upon authorities violently prejudiced against that monarch. For such suspicions against the subject-matter of the four last books there is less foundation. The events there recorded took place in Tacitus' own childhood: as a young man he must have had frequent opportunity of meeting and talking with people who had lived under Nero, and in the light of what he heard from them he would be less likely to be misled by the writers whom he consulted, if they were guilty of misrepresentation. And these writers were certainly in a position to know the facts.

Tacitus' conception of the function of history.

§ 5. Tacitus' professed purpose in writing history is a moral one, 'to rescue virtue from oblivion, and that base words and deeds should have the fear of posthumous infamy' (iii 65, 1); he wishes, in fact, to influence men in the right direction by holding up examples of noble conduct for imitation, of base conduct for avoidance. At the same time it is his aim to point out the right political conduct for the subjects of the principate; 'how even under bad princes there can be good citizens' (*Agr.* 42, 5); that the best course is at the same time the safest, and is one of dignified moderation, such as that followed by Manius Lepidus under Tiberius, Memmius Regulus under Nero, and Agricola under Domitian, avoiding on the one hand the vile obsequiousness of the flatterers and tools, who after all were discarded by their master or punished by his successor, and on the other such truculent and ostentatious opposition as that of Helvidius Priscus, inviting and incurring destruction.

This point of view gives his work a wider range than that of a mere biographer like Suetonius. To Tacitus the general working of the Roman system is interesting as a field for the display of character, and events are selected and represented in illustration of the motives of the agents. This outlook makes him careless about exact details of strategy, geography, and chronology, such as are expected of a modern historian, and brings him into line with the satirists, whom he further resembles in his bold characterization, his vivid contrasts and tendencies to exaggeration, and the epigrammatic style of his diction.

II

ON THE SYNTAX AND STYLE OF TACITUS

Note—Most of what is here said is applicable to the writings of Tacitus as a whole, and especially to the *Annals*; but the instances given are almost wholly from the four Books contained in this volume.

By the time of Tacitus, Latin prose composition had already departed much from the standard of Cicero or Caesar, through the frequent adoption of words and forms of expression from the great classic poets, who had by that time become textbooks in every grammar-school; also through an increasing tolerance of Greek words and grammatical Graecisms, partly due to such study of Augustan poetry, partly to an increasing taste for what was Greek as such [1].

The special qualities of the style of Tacitus have been held to consist chiefly in rhetorical or poetical colouring, in the study of brevity, and in that of variety; all of which characteristics are no doubt due mainly to his professional career [2]. He has himself told us that the pleader in his day could no longer expatiate like Cicero, but was bound to be terse, epigrammatic, and striking, and to grace his style with poetic colouring from the treasury of Vergil and Horace, or even from more recent poets [3]. In falling in with this fashion, Tacitus draws the poetic element in his style almost exclusively from Vergil, to whom he is repeatedly and abundantly indebted; while his chief prose models are Sallust and Livy, his great predecessors in the field of

[1] Juvenal mentions (7, 226) the use of Horace and Vergil as school-books, and also dwells at length (3, 61 foll.) on the extent to which the Rome of his day had become Greek.

[2] See Intr. I, § I.   [3] *Dial. de Oratoribus*, 19, 20.

SYNTAX

history[1]. The effort at variety of expression, besides being natural in the case of an orator, is further due to the historian's desire to relieve what he feels to be the oppressive monotony of his subject[2], by saying the same thing with the utmost variety of expression, by often giving the sentence an unexpected turn, by inventing new words or new senses of words, or reviving such as had become somewhat obsolete.

Of the various usages noted in the following sections, comparatively few are altogether peculiar to Tacitus; but many are new in prose, and all are so far Tacitean that they are used by him with more boldness and freedom than by earlier prose authors.

A. SYNTAX

[The references in square brackets are to the paragraphs in the Introduction on Syntax in the large edition, Vol. I]

I. Substantives, Adjectives, and Pronouns.

1 [1, 3]. Abstract nouns are used for concrete, especially in the plural, as nobilitates, xii 20, 1 ; perhaps, dominationes, xii 30, 4. Notice also matrimonium = wife, xii 6, 3 ; servitium = slaves, xii 17, 1 ; senectutem Tiberii ut inermem despiciens, practically = senem Tiberium, vi 31, 1 ; so, also, pueritia Domitii = puer Domitius, xii 8, 3.

2 [4, 6]. Adjectives are used freely in the neuter with the force of substantives ; (a) in the plural, as novissima, vi 50, 8 ; suprema, vi 50, 3 ; xii 66, 2 ; summa imperii, xi 8, 2 ; so, laetus praesentium et inanium spe, v 10, 3 ; brevia litorum, vi 33, 5 ; (b) in the singular, as lubricum iuventae, vi 49, 3 ; in lubrico, vi 51, 3 ; intellegens falsi, xii 26, 2.

Adjectives are also used adverbially, as secondary predicates : pergit properus, vi 44, 1 ; secretus agitat, xi 21, 2. Neuter adjectives sometimes stand as adverbs : praeceps, vi 17, 4 ; aeternum, xii 28, 2.

---

[1] See below, § 68.　　　　　　　　[2] See iv 32 and 33.

INTRODUCTION

An adjective sometimes stands in agreement with a noun or pronoun to form a phrase which might have been expressed by a clause with quod : as nihil . . . novum, xii 2, 1 ; nihil nisi atrox . . . terrebat, xii 35, 1 ; nullae . . . litterae suspicionem dabant, vi 47, 4.

3 (*a*) [8, 9]. Pronouns of the third person are omitted, especially in the accusative, in spite of the harshness or obscurity involved. Se is omitted in vi 48, 3 ; v 5, 2 ; and many other places noted in the commentary. Eum is omitted in vi 46, 7 ; xi 4, 4 ; eam, in xii 65, 4.

(*b*) The indefinite quis is used in the phrase ut quis, for ut quisque, vi 7, 4, and elsewhere.

(*c*) Quis ille is used with a peculiar brachylogy in xi 7, 1 : xii 36, 2.

II. Cases.

A. *Accusative.*

4 [11]. The poetical or Greek accusative of the part concerned, not frequent in prose, is freely used : clari genus, vi 9, 5 ; adlevatur animum, vi 43, 3.

5 [10]. The accusative of the place towards which motion takes place is found without preposition : xii 31, 3 ; 51, 4 (perhaps).

6 [12]. Transitive accusatives are used

(*a*) in apposition to the sentence, i. e. in explanation of the action described, not of a single word in the sentence : auspicium prosperi transgressus, vi 37, 2 ; terrorem, xii 29, 2 ; so, too (probably), pretium festinandi, vi 29, 2 ; subsidium, xii 32, 4 ;

(*b*) after verbs expressing the feelings, as pavescere ;

(*c*) after compound verbs, where a dative or a repetition of the preposition with its case would be more usual : (genua) advolvi, vi 49, 3 ; accedere, xii 31, 3 ; erumpere, xii 63, 2 ; evadere, v 10, 4 ; exire, vi 49, 3 ; praeiacere, xii 36, 4 ; praeminere, xii 12, 1 ; praesidere, xii 14, 7.

7 [14]. The use of adverbial accusatives such as id temporis is extended to new expressions, as id auctoritatis, xii 18, 1.

SYNTAX

B. *Dative.*

8 (*a*) [15]. After compound verbs expressing deprivation, Tacitus follows poets and Livy in using a dative, rather than ablative with a preposition : extrahere, vi 23, 5 ; eximere, vi 9, 6.

(*b*) [21]. After compound verbs, Tacitus follows poets in using a dative rather than ad or in with the accusative : penatibus induxerit, v 1, 3 ; indicibus accessere, vi 7, 5.

9 [19]. The dative of a noun, so closely connected with another that a genitive would be expected, is frequent in poets and Livy, and still more so in Tacitus : ministri sceleribus, vi 36, 4 ; corpori custodes, ibid. ; rex Hiberis, xi 8, 2.

10 [18]. The Dative of Agent is used without restriction to the gerundive or adjectives in -bilis, and without any prominence of the idea of the 'interest' of the agent : possessa Cyro, vi 31, 2 ; mihi narratus, xi 29, 1 ; cui pars provinciae habebatur, xii 54, 3 : most of such expressions should be referred to this case rather than ablative, as Macedonibus sitae, vi 41, 2 ; audita scriptaque senioribus, xi 27, 2 ; quis . . . ultio . . . timebatur, xii 9, 2.

11 [22]. The Dative of Purpose or Work contemplated is very frequent, the gerund or gerundive in this case following a participle or a verb, in the sense of a final clause : componendis patrum actis delectus, v 4, 1 ; reciperandaeque Armeniae Hiberum Mithridaten deligit, vi 32, 5 ; quibus abluendis . . . egrediens, xi 2, 4 ; dissimulando metu digrediuntur, xi 32, 1 ; so also, xi 1, 1 ; xii 66, 1, and many other passages.

Sometimes it follows adjectives : accipiendis suspicionibus promptior, xii 4, 3 ; facilis capessendis inimicitiis, v 11, 1.

A noun may be used in this way : custodiae eius imponit, xii 41, 8 ; excubiis adest, xii 69, 1 ; diem locumque foederi accepit, xii 46, 6 ; coniugio accepit, vi 20, 1.

12 [23]. This should be distinguished from 'predicative' datives, showing that which a thing or person serves as or occasions, such as rubori, xi 17, 3 ; ostentui . . . dehonestamento, xii 14, 6 ; remedio quaesita, vi 17, 3 ; curae, vi 22, 2 ; exitio, xi 24, 5. In xi 14, 5 usui stands, in an unusual manner, attributively.

C. *Ablative.*

13 [24]. The Ablative of Place Whence is used freely, without preposition, both of proper names : Etruria Lucaniaque et omni Italia in senatum accitos, xi 24, 2 ; and of common names : ordine senatorio movetur, xii 4, 4 ; often also after compound verbs implying separation : depromptum sinu, vi 40, 1 ; so also, probably, exutum campis, xii 45, 3.

14 [25]. The Ablative of Place Where is used, without preposition, as freely as in poetry : domibus, vi 3, 3 ; terra caelove, vi 33, 3; campo, xii 36, 4.

15 [26]. The Ablative of Time may denote a whole period during which something took place (a post-Augustan use) : bellis civilibus, vi 11, 3 ; duodecim annis, vi 51, 4 ; secutis diebus, xi 38, 3. On the other hand, the preposition ' in ' is sometimes used to denote a point or a period of time : eo in tempore, xi 29, 1.

The following ablatives also may be referred to this heading, as denoting the occasion at which something happens : solita convivio, xi 38, 2 ; proelio solita, xii 56, 2 ; prosperis dubiisque sociam, xii 5, 3.

16 [27]. The Instrumental Ablative is used of persons, where the fact of the presence of a person, rather than the personality of the agent, is emphasized : Tiridates simul fama atque ipso Artabano perculsus, vi, 44 3.

This case is also used to describe the force with which military operations are conducted, like the Greek αἴρειν στρατῷ : multis equitum milibus in castra venit, vi 37, 4 ; multa manu . . . adventabat, vi 44, 3.

17. Tacitus sometimes affects the poetical collocation of an ablative of ' Respect ' with an adjective, as editam loco, xii 16, 3 ; rudem iuventa, xii 15, 1. (Cf. such expressions as curvam compagibus alvom, Verg. *Aen.* ii 51 ; saeva sonoribus arma, *Aen.* ix 651.)

18 [29]. The Ablative of Quality is used without the association of a common noun (such as ' vir ') : truci eloquentia habebatur, vi 48, 6 ; et quidam summis honoribus, vi 9, 5 ; Cotta Messalinus . . . inveterata invidia, vi 5, 1. Sometimes the epithet is omitted :

iuvenem nobilem dignitate formae, vi mentis, ac propinquo consulatu, xi 28, 1; with this may be compared the brachylogical ablative of material: moenia non saxo sed cratibus et vimentis, xii 16, 3.

19 [30]. The Causal Ablative is used with much freedom in the *Annals*, where a preposition, as 'propter', or 'causa' or 'gratia' with genitive, would be expected: regem . . . adversis proeliorum exitiosum, vi 36, 2; continuo abscessu velut exilium obiectando, vi 38, 2; amore, xi 26, 5; largitione aut spei magnitudine, xi 36, 2; caritate, xii 4, 3; defectione, xii 10, 1; qua necessitate, xii 46, 6.

20. Such an ablative is often associated with an adjective meaning famous: castellum insigne fama, xii 13, 2; egregium vita famaque, vi 51, 5.

21 [31]. Ablative Absolute. The following uses are characteristic:

(a) the neuter ablative singular of the participle stands by itself: multum certato, xi 10, 3; nec ultra expectato quam, xi 26, 7; this often introduces a substantival clause: non distincto sua an aliena manu (perisset), xi 38, 2; comperto Graecam quoque littera turam non simul coeptam absolutamque, xi 13, 3;

(b) the participle is used without any word in agreement, where it can easily be supplied from the sense of the passage: concedente (eo), vi 16, 5; invalido (imperatore), vi 47, 4;

(c) the participle is followed by a relative, without expression of the antecedent: additis quae ante deliquerant, vi 9, 1; missis qui ... pellicerent, xi 19, 3; excitis quorum de sententia petitus rex, xii 12, 3.

22. It should be remembered that the ablative has the wide general function of expressing the circumstances attendant on an action. This explains

(a) the frequent occurrence of a substantive and adjective in an ablative not definitely referable to the categories 'absolute,' 'causal,' 'descriptive,' &c., which are names for special developments of the general function. Besides ordinary 'absolute ablatives,' equivalent to a temporal clause, like caede continua, vi 29, 1, there are many for which 'ablative of attendant circumstance' would be a better name; some of these approach the 'causal' use, as certo si abnueret exitio et non nulla fallendi spe, simul magnis praemiis, xi 12, 3; Chauci nulla dissensione domi et morte Sanquinii alacres, xi 18, 1 ; some express 'manner,' as non nulla spe et aliquando ira, xi 37, 1 ; some are nearly 'descriptive,' as actae principi grates, quaesitiore in Domitium adulatione, xii 26, 1 ; suscipi bellum avio itinere, importuoso mari, xii 20, 2 ; ignobilem Hiberum mercennario milite disserebat, vi 34, 5, seems partly causal, partly descriptive. (See also v 10, 2 ; vi 45, 5 ; xi 36, 4 ; xii 5, 1 ; xii 13, 3 ; xii 18, 1 ; xii 30, 4.)

(*b*) the ablative of gerund or gerundive, as the equivalent of a present participle or temporal clause introduced by 'dum': adiciendo, v 6, 5 ; ordiendo, vi 8, 1 ; obiectando, vi 38, 2 ; ventitando, xii 3, 1 ; memorando, xii 44, 5.

D. *Genitive.*

23 [32]. Partitive and quasi-partitive genitives are abundant, and often there is no stress on the partitive notion, the phrase becoming equivalent, as in poetry (e. g. strata viarum, in Lucretius and Vergil), to a simple substantive and adjective.

(*a*) With neut. sing. : extremo anni, vi 27, 1 ; lubricum iuventae, vi 49, 3 ; per medium diei, xi 21, 2 ; post multum vulnerum, xii 56, 5 ; medio diei, xii 69, 1.

(*b*) With neut. plur.: simulationum falsa, vi 45, 5 ; castellorum ardua, xi 9, 1 ; incerta Oceani, xi 20, 2 ; montium edita, xii 56, 4.

(*c*) A substantive, accompanied by an adjective, is taken out of its natural case, and put in the partitive genitive : cunctis civium, xi 22, 4 ; adversis proeliorum (= adversis proeliis), vi 36, 3 ; so, probably, provinciarum vectigalibus = the tribute-paying provinces, xi 22, 8.

(*d*) Such a genitive may stand without any word expressing partition being expressed: Caninius Gallus quindecimvirum, vi 12, 1.

24 [33]. Objective Genitive.

(*a*) The elliptical genitive, common with verbs of accusing and judging, is extended to new examples : postulare, vi 9, 5 ; repetundarum teneri, xi 7, 8 ; urgere (if the reading is sound), vi 29, 3.

(*b*) It is frequent with participles, as retinens, v 11, 2 ; cupiens, vi 46, 2 ; casus prioris impatiens, xii 52, 1.

SYNTAX

(c) With adjectives, it expresses sometimes the direct object, as Praescium periculorum, vi 21, 5 ; often, a more remote object, as if in place of ' de ' and ablative ; matrimonii certa, xii 3, 2 ; sceleris certa, xii 66, 2 (cf. Aeneas . . . iam certus eundi, Verg. *Aen.* iv 554) ; and it is very frequently used, quite loosely, to denote in what respect an epithet is applied (Genitive of Reference) : trepidus admirationis et metus, vi 21, 4; occultos consilii, vi 36, 3: vetus regnandi, vi 44, 1 ; operum et laboris ignavas (legiones), xi 18, 2 ; atrox odii, xii 22, 1 ; oblatae occasionis propera, xii 66, 2 ; vitae manifestam, xii 51, 5 ; praecipuus olim circumveniendi Titii Sabini, vi 4, 1 ; absentium aequos (= fair-minded in regard to absent *persons*), vi 36, 5.

25 [34]. The Genitive of Quality is used with the same brachylogy as the corresponding ablative (18) : effusae clementiae, vi 30, 3 ; ademptae virilitatis, vi 31, 3.

26 [37]. In such phrases as the following, the genitive of gerund or gerundive shows a bold extension of the idea ' belonging to ' :

(a) defining a noun : cuius apiscendae otium apud Rhodum . . . habuit, vi 20, 3 ; pecunia omittendae delationis, vi 30, 1 ; spatium exuendi pacta, xi 43, 1 ;

(b) used predicatively : quae conciliandae misericordiae videbantur, xi 3, 1 ; so Sall. *Cat.* 6, regium imperium initio conservandae libertatis atque augendae reipublicae fuerat.

III. VERBS.

27 [38, 39]. Verbs of speaking, thinking, and even of motion are omitted with more freedom than in earlier classical Latin : haec (dixit), vi 2, 6 ; haec apud senatum (acta sunt), vi 10, 2.

Parts of esse, other than present indicative and infinitive, are omitted, even in dependent clauses : quae retinenda . . . (essent), xi 15, 3; quidquid Neronibus avitum (fuerit), xi 35, 2 ; also, in apodosis of conditional sentence, oppressa cunctantium dubitatio (erat), vi 43, 1 ; notice also the omission of fuisse after a future participle, periturum, xi 3, 2.

28 [40]. Simple verbs are often used for compound, as in poetry : noscere for cognoscere, vi 9, 7 ; xii 60, 3 ; firmare for confirmare, vi

6, 2 ; vi 50, 5 ; ferre for proferre, vi 49, 3 ; xii 4, 1 : venire for evenire, xii 32, 4 ; vertere (probably) for evertere, xii 45, 5.

29 [41]. Verbs, usually transitive, are found used intransitively : vertere, vi 19, 1 ; 46, 3 (so also, of things, in Livy, Sallust and Caesar) ; mutare, xii 29, 1 ; agere, xi 16, 4 ; agitare, xi 21, 2.

30 [42]. Intransitive verbs are found used personally, in the passive, as in poetry : triumphari, xii 19, 4.

IV. MOODS AND TENSES.

A. *Infinitive.*

31 [43]. Verbs of commanding, entreating, advising, and those which express effort and compulsion, which in earlier classical prose are usually followed by ' ut ' or ' ne ' with the subjunctive, are used in great numbers by Tacitus with an infinitive clause completing their sense : admonuit C. Cestium patrem dicere, vi 7, 3 ; Vibidiam . . . oravit . . . adire, xi 32, 5 ; hortatur . . . capessere, xi 16, 3 ; impule-rat uxorem suam iuvenem inlicere, vi 45, 5 ; inducunt sententiam expromere, xii 9, 1 ; perpulit . . . subire, xi 29, 3. The use of a passive infinitive in this way is noticeable : (liber) quem Gallus recipi inter ceteros . . . postulaverat, vi 12, 1 ; cieri Narcissum postulat, xi 30, 2 ; permitti Meherdaten . . . orabant, xi 10, 8 ; vete-ranos coloniamque deduci impetrat, xii 27, 1.

Other instances may be seen in vi 12, 4 ; vi 19, 4 ; vi 23, 5 ; vi 33, 1 ; xi 26, 1 ; xii 11, 4 ; xii 29, 2.

The somewhat doubtful ' instabat . . . aperire ' of xi 34, 2 may be referred to this use.

32 [44]. The accusative and infinitive, expressing an indirect statement, is found with verbs not usually associated with it, as eum . . . incolumem fore gratatur, vi 21, 5 : cf. Trebellenum incusans popularium iniurias inultas sinere, iii 38, 4.

33 [45]. A personal construction is often found where in earlier classical prose the impersonal construction would be usual ; this is specially common with verbs of accusing : incusabatur facile tole-raturus exilium, vi 3, 3 ; Sex. Marius defertur incestasse filiam,

vi 19, 1 ; so also, introspicere creditus, v 4, 1 ; see also vi 34, 4 ; 50, 7.

34 [46]. The Historic Infinitive is not only used in graphic narrative in main sentences, as in xii 51, 3, &c., but also occurs in subordinate clauses: ubi . . . non cremare quisquam, vi 19, 4; cum Tiridates . . . distrahi consiliis, vi 44, 3 ; so also, after cum, xi 34, 3; after ubi, xi 37, 3.

35 [47]. The 'Epexegetic' Infinitive, so common in Horace, is employed: perrumpere adgreditur, xii 31, 5.

B. *Indicative.*

36 [48]. The historic present is very common, and is hardly differentiated from a past tense : postulantur, et . . . adiciebatur, vi 9, 5 ; subicitur, vi 12, 5 ; renovat . . . contulit, xi 8, 6. It may have a subjunctive dependent upon it in the imperfect tense : impellit milites ut pacem flagitarent, xii 46, 5 ; see also vi 48, 6.

37 [49]. Explanatory clauses in the indicative are inserted in the midst of oratio obliqua : inde Phoenicas, quia mari praepollebant, intulisse Graeciae gloriamque adeptos tamquam reppererint quae acceperant, xi 14, 1.

38 [50]. The indicative is used vividly in place of the subjunctive, in the apodosis of conditional clauses, stating what might have happened as though it had actually occurred : contremuerant . . . ni . . . exemisset, vi 9, 6 ; ni caedem Narcissus properavisset, verterat pernicies in accusatorem, xi 37, 1 ; or an incomplete action or tendency, showing vividly what was on the point of happening : summum supplicium decernebatur, ni professus indicium foret, vi 3, 5 ; offerebantur . . . nisi . . . iussisset, xi 34, 4 (see also vi 36, 1 ; xii 42, 1); or what would have been, in contrast to what did happen : si statim interiora . . . petivisset, . . . omnes in unum cedebant, vi 43, 1 ; nec fugam sistebat, ni legiones proelium excepissent, xii 39, 1. In, reciperare avebat, ni . . . cohibitus foret, xi 10, 1, an ellipsis may be understood : 'he was eager to recover . . . , (and would have done so) if he had not been prevented.'

INTRODUCTION

C. *Subjunctive.*

39 [51]. The Hypothetical Subjunctive, with condition not formally expressed, or Potential Subjunctive is used : nec ideo adsequare, vi 8, 9 ; non omiserim, vi 20, 3 ; scias, xi 18, 5.

40 [53]. The subjunctive follows 'quamquam', even though expressing a fact: quamquam mater . . . transierit, vi 51, 1 ; quamquam multa simul offunderentur, xi 20, 1 ; so, too, quamvis : quamvis bellum negavisset, xi 20, 3 ; also donec, even where the notion of purpose or expectation is not implied : donec Carenem . . . globus circumveniret, xii 44, 4.

41 [52]. The subjunctive is frequently used in subordinate clauses, of cases frequently occurring : after nisi, v 11, 2 ; si, vi 1, 5 ; 30, 1 ; quantum, vi 19, 5 ; qui, vi 8, 4 ; quoties, vi 10, 3 ; 21, 1 ; xii 47, 3. The pluperfect indicative, preferred in such cases by Cicero and Caesar, is seen in vi 24, 2.

V. PARTICIPLES.

Cf. also § 21.

42 [54]. The 'aoristic' use of the present participle should be noticed

(*a*) in abl. abs. : praemonente Narcisso pauca verba fecit, xi 35, 3 ; so, hortante, vi 29, 7 ; accusante, vi 18, 2 ;

(*b*) in nom. : Quadratus cognoscens proditum Mithridaten, xii 48, 1 ;

(*c*) as equivalent to a relative clause with a past tense : gloriam trucidantium Crassum, ii 2, 4.

43 [54]. Participles are used in the place of subordinate clauses :

(*a*) causal : adnectebatur crimini Vibia . . . ut casus prioris impatiens, xii 52, 1 ; tamquam passus, xi 36, 5 ;

(*b*) final : auxiliis . . . contractis tamquam reciperaturus Armeniam, xii 49, 2 ;

(*c*) indirect statement : subdito rumore tamquam Mesopotamiam invasurus, vi 36, 1.

44 [55]. A participial construction is used, as in Livy, giving the sense of an abstract noun followed by a genitive : et non permissa provincia dignationem addiderat, vi 27, 2 ; see also vi 35, 5.

SYNTAX

VI. Prepositions.

See also, for their omission, §§ 5, 8, 13, 14, 19; anastrophe, § 55. 46 [56–63]. The following are some of the most characteristic usages in Tacitus:

Apud is often used with names of places and countries as well as with common names, in place of the locative or 'in' with ablative: apud Cycladas insulas, v 10, 1; apud oppidum Edessam, xii 12, 4; apud forum, xii 7, 3. In xii 1, 1 it is equivalent to 'inter'.

Ad often = 'in regard to': praecipuos ad scelera, vi 7, 3; ad honesta . . . (levis), xi 33, 1.

Circa, = 'concerning': publica circa artes bonas socordia, xi 15, 1; circa necem Gaii Caesaris narratus, xi 29, 1. (So in Seneca and Pliny mai.)

In, (a) with accusative, much used to express the effect intended or resulting, like ἐπί or πρός: in diversum, xi 19, 1; in speciem, xii 44, 6; in barbarum corrupta, vi 42, 1; also used boldly in place of a genitive or dative: amore in maritum, xi 26, 5; in fratrum filias coniugia, xii 6, 5; adoptio in Domitium, xii 25, 1; tristia in bonos... esse, vi 22, 2; in reliquos data venia, xii 32, 4;

(b) with ablative of a neuter adjective, used as alternative to the employment of an adverb, or an adjective predicate: maxime in lubrico egit, vi 51, 3; in incerto iudicium est, vi 22, 1.

Iuxta is used metaphorically, as a preposition, = 'next to,' 'close upon': laqueum iuxta, v 9, 3; populi imperium iuxta libertatem, vi 42, 3; and as an adverb in the sense of 'pariter': iuxta invisi, vi 4, 1.

Per is used in expressions of time, where ablative might be expected: per idem tempus, v 10, 1; per medium diei, xi 21, 2; or has the force of an instrumental or modal ablative: animus per libidines corruptus, xi 37, 5; per maerorem, v 6, 5; per deridiculum auditur, vi 2, 2; per silentium, xi 37, 5; see also magnas per opes, vi 22, 4.

Super, = de, frequently; vi 49, 3; xi 23, 1; xii 22, 1.

Simul is used as preposition, with ablative (like ἅμα), in vi 9, 5.

INTRODUCTION

VII. Adverbs and Conjunctions.

47 [64]. Comparative sentences are often abbreviated—

(*a*) by the omission of 'magis' or 'potius' before 'quam': mitem et recens repertam quam ex severitate prisca rationem adhibuit, xi 25, 5 ;

(*b*) by the use of the positive with 'quanto,' answering to a comparative with 'tanto': tanto acceptius ... quanto modicus, vi 45, 2 ; quanto ignota barbaris, tanto laetiora, xii 11, 2 ;

(*c*) by the omission of 'eo' (or 'tanto') 'magis,' in the apodosis: quantum saevitia glisceret, miseratio arcebatur, vi 19, 5 ; quantum introspiceret, magis ac magis trepidus, vi 21, 4 ; see also vi 26, 3.

48 [65]. The omission of conjunctions (asyndeton) is frequent, owing to Tacitus' rhetorical tendencies ; in lively narration : amplecti adlevare adhortari, xii 51, 3 ; in enumerations, often leading up to a climax : tempus preces satias, vi 38, 1 ; omnis sexus, omnis aetas, inlustres ignobiles, vi 19, 3 ; decus pudorem corpus cuncta regno viliora habere, xii 65, 4.

49 [66]. Adverbs are used as adjectives, attributively, as in Greek : nullis extrinsecus adiumentis, xii 61, 4 ; and even predicatively : multis coram, vi 42, 6 ; nullis palam . . . causis, xi 22, 1.

50 [67]. Tamquam, quasi, and (less frequently) velut are used—

(*a*) of something pretended or alleged to be the reason for the fact described : finem accepit quasi nescius exercendi, vi 11, 5 ; is velut propria ad negotia digrediens . . ., vi 50, 4 ; in exilium agitur quasi finem principis per Chaldaeos scrutaretur, xii 52, 1 ; gloriam adeptos tamquam reppererint, xi 14, 1 ;

(*b*) of a real reason, or one believed in by the person stating it : Rubrio Fabato, tamquam . . . Parthorum ad misericordiam fugeret, custodes additi, vi 14, 3 ; cupido auri immensa obtentum habebat quasi subsidium regno pararetur, xii 7, 7 ; so also, quasi . . . sacratum, xii 47, 3 ;

(*c*) sometimes these words simply introduce a reported reason or thought : nocturnae quietis species alteri obiecta, tamquam vidisset . . ., xi 4, 3 ; laetis hostibus tamquam ducem . . . bellum absumpsisset, xii 39, 5 ; primo tamquam dolus pararetur territus, vi 43, 3.

B. STYLE

I. INNOVATIONS IN VOCABULARY.

51 [69, 70]. Tacitus often prefers unusual forms, as claritudo, firmitudo, to the forms in -as ; cognomentum, vimentum, to the form in -men ; medicamen, tegumen, to the forms in -mentum ; besides introducing words not previously found, or found only in poets.

The following are some of the most noticeable :

(*a*) Many substantives in -tor and -sor are used in an unusual sense or are introduced by Tacitus : defector, xi 8, 5 ; cupitor, xii 7, 4 ; provisor, xii 4, 1 ; repertor (also in Sallust), xii 53, 6 ; auxiliator (also in Petronius and Quintilian), vi 37, 4. New forms in -us, as distinctus, vi 28, 3, are introduced.

(*b*) New negative adjectives : incelebratus, vi 7, 6 ; innumera, xii 29, 2.

(*c*) New intensive forms : perintempestiva, xii 26, 2.

(*d*) Frequentative are preferred to simple forms of verbs : advectare, vi 13, 2 ; auctitare, vi 16, 1 ; tractare, vi 44, 4 ; dissertare, xii 11, 1 ; coeptare, xii 32, 4.

Other new or unusual usages are—

adulatorius, vi 32, 7 ; nec . . . anquirendum quin, xii 6, 2 ; desolatus for privatus, xii 26, 2 ; emercari, xii 14, 1 ; gratibus, xii 37, 5 ; infensare, vi 34, 1 ; intendere, = augere, xii 35, 2 ; maturri-mum, xii 65, 5 ; praestruere, xii 33, 2 ; provixisse, vi 25, 1 ; proviso, xii 39, 3.

Note also gnarus, = notus, vi 35, 4 and elsewhere ; ignarus, = ignotus, vi 22, 5 and elsewhere.

II. RHETORICAL AND POETICAL COLOURING.

To this head belong many of the syntactical usages already noticed.

52 [74]. The following are some of the most striking metaphorical expressions : ardescere (in nuptias incestas), xi 25, 8 ; exuere (amicitiam), vi 8, 1 ; induere, with 'diem', vi 20, 1 ; with 'diversa', vi

33, 3 ; with 'adulationem', vi 42, 1 ; with 'hostilia', xii 40, 3 ; inligare (veneno), vi 32, 3; provolvere, = dispossess, vi 17, 4; resolvere (venas), vi 48, 5 ; so also, exsolvere, xi 3, 2 ; rumpere (vocem), vi 20, 1 ; vergere, applied to time, xi 4, 4.

Notice also ambiguus, xi 15, 2 ; lubricus, vi 49, 3.

53 [75]. Personification is employed to render expressions more forcible : adulto autumno, xi 31, 4 ; modestia hiemis, xii 43, 3 ; idem annus gravi igne urbem adfecit, vi 45, 1 ; so, tulere illa tempora, vi 7, 4 ; locorum fraus, xii 33, 2.

54 [76]. Hendiadys, or the co-ordination of two words in the same case, of which the one defines the other like an adjective or genitive : quasi valetudine et contactu, vi 7, 4 ; scientiae caerimoniarumque vetus, vi 12, 2 ; famam et posteros, xi 6, 1 ; per insectationes et nuntios, xii 14, 1 ; veteranos coloniamque, xii 27, 1.

55 [77]. Anastrophe

(a) of prepositions is frequent in the case of ab, ad, apud, ex, in, and inter, but not found with circa, praeter, prope, sine, supra, and pro : note also iuxta, v 9, 3 ; xii 21, 2 ; intra, xi 10, 5 ; infra, xi 20, 4 ;

(b) of conjunctions : 'ut' occurs fifth word of clause, xi 49, 3 ; note also anastrophe of 'quamquam', v 9, 1 ; vi 30, 7.

56. Anaphora : multa, xii 33, 1 ; non, xii 32, 4 ; per, xii 39, 3 ; quod, xii 46, 1.

57. The following expressions may be also noticed here :

(a) instead of using a concrete substantive qualified by adjective or participle, Tacitus often uses an abstract substantive coupled with a concrete in the 'defining' genitive : iniectu multae vestis (= multis vestibus iniectis), vi 50, 9 ; concursu plurium (= concurrentibus pluribus), xii 47, 4 ; abscessu suorum et incursantibus barbaris, xii 49, 2. Notice also, egressibus adhaerescere, xi 12, 4 ; egit gratis benevolentiae patrum, vi 2, 5 ; and other similar uses of abstract nouns in vi 21, 1 ; xii 45, 5 ; xii 66, 1.

(b) an adjective is sometimes put in agreement with a word to which it does not seem properly to belong ('Hypallage') : rudes et informes saxorum compages, xii 35, 5; novas litterarum formas, xi 13, 3. This figure is common in Horace, as Graia victorum manus, Epod. x 12, and in Greek drama, as νεῖκος ἀνδρῶν ξύναιμον, and is due to treating the substantive with its qualifying genitive as a single notion.

STYLE

III. INFLUENCE OF THE STUDY OF BREVITY.

58 [80]. Ellipses have already been noticed, in the case of verbs, § 27, prepositions, §§ 5, 8, 13, 14, 19, and other particles, § 48. Observe also the omission of annus, xi 11, 1; filia, xii 1, 3, and the curious conciseness of expression in xii 18, 3. See also vi 26, 3.

59 [82]. Parenthetical remarks are sometimes introduced concisely by a word apparently in apposition in the nominative, and equivalent to a relative clause: rarum, vi 10, 3; incertum an . . ., xi 22, 2 (like δῆλον ὅτι). This use is to be distinguished from that in § 6 a. A pure parenthesis may be seen in xii 42, 4.

60 [83]. Zeugma, or the reference to two objects of a verb strictly applicable only to the nearest, is common in Tacitus : see the use of fore, vi 21, 5; nequibat, xii 64, 6; peritus, xi 29, 2. In vi 24, 3, quemadmodum nurum filiumque fratris et nepotes domumque omnem caedibus complevisset, 'necasset' must be supplied with the first group of objects. Verbs also are used with two objects in different senses, by 'syllepsis': struere, xi 12, 1; moliri, xii 22, 1; intentare, xii 47, 5. So, too, a masculine noun may be applied to persons of both sexes : pronepotes, v 1, 4; filii, xi 38, 3; fratres, xii 4, 2.

61 [84]. 'Pregnant' constructions may be seen in xii 18, 3 (quoted above, § 58); and in the use of infantiam, xi 34, 1; gratia, xii 7, 4; Chaldaeos, xii 22, 1; maiora, xii 9, 1.

IV. INFLUENCE OF THE STUDY OF VARIETY.

62 [85]. The form of words is varied ; thus, Eastern names vary in declension, as Artaxata, which is sometimes fem. sing., sometimes neut. plur. ; so also Tigranocerta ; Vologeses is sometimes Vologesus.

Similarly, Tacitus uses both alioqui and alioquin ; balneae and balneum ; dein and deinde ; grates and gratias agere ; inermis and inermus ; senecta and senectus, &c.

63 [86]. Names often mentioned are varied ; either by inversion of usual order, as Scauro Mamerco, vi 9, 5, or by use of one part of

the name when it has been given in full before, as Appius Silanus vi 9, 5, and then simply Appius; notice also the names in vi 10.

64 [87–91]. The following are some of the most characteristic methods whereby Tacitus effects variety in corresponding clauses—

(i) A preposition is varied to one of similar meaning: apud . . . in, v 10, 1 ; vi 22, 2 ; so, elsewhere, per . . . in; inter . . . apud.

(ii) Cases are varied in appositional phrases : subsidio victis et terrorem adversus victores, xii 29, 2 ; subsidium . . . et imbuendis sociis, xii 32, 4.

(iii) A participle is varied by a corresponding adjective : modo virtutem admirans, modo timore aeger, xii 51, 3 ; or an ablative of description by an adjective : adversus superiores tristi adulatione, adrogans minoribus, xi 21, 4 ; so also, clari genus . . . summis honoribus, vi 9, 5.

(iv) An instrumental ablative is varied by an ablative absolute : vi militis Romani . . . simul Hibero exercitu campos persultante, xi 9, 1 ; see also xi 10, 2 ; or a causal ablative by a clause: non amore in maritum, sed ne Silius . . . sperneret, xi 26, 5. So also a clause with ut corresponds to a participle : rata . . ., utque . . . adolesceret, xii 8, 3 ; and a prepositional phrase balances a participle : adstititque tribunus per silentium, at libertus increpans, xi 37, 5.

(v) Variation from substantive to a clause : constantia orationis, et quia repertus erat qui . . ., eo usque potuere, vi 9, 1 ; and from infinitive to substantive : ne dubia tentare armis quam incruentas condiciones mallet, xii 46, 2.

(vi) Numbers varied : cui non iudicium, non odium erat, nisi indita et iussa, xii 3, 3 ; eques . . . pedites, vi 35, 3 ; pedites, eques, xii 29, 4.

(vii) Voice varied : quo ambiguos inliceret, prompti firmarentur, vi 44, 2.

(viii) Asyndeton—varied with conjunctions: cum arma munimenta impediti vel eminentes loci . . . perrumperentur, xii 17, 2 ; inlustres ignobiles dispersi aut aggerati, vi 19, 3.

Other instances of Tacitus' fondness for variety in expression may be seen in xii 33 ; 39, 3 ; 46, 1.

65 [93]. The expression of facts that have to be stated often is carefully varied; the great number of different phrases used by

Tacitus for such events as accusation, banishment, suicide, death, will be readily noticed on reading the text.

V. INFLUENCE OF IMITATION.

66 [95]. The Graecisms in Tacitus are chiefly such as had already become naturalized in Latin, and most have been noticed in previous paragraphs. To these may be added immunire, $= \dot{\epsilon}\nu\tau\epsilon\iota\chi\acute{\iota}\zeta\epsilon\iota\nu$, xi 19, 1; quae . . . revincebatur, vi 5, 2, where the passive may be regarded as equivalent to a middle voice: et alia clarum, $= \tau\acute{a} \tau\epsilon$ $\ddot{a}\lambda\lambda a \lambda a\mu\pi\rho\acute{o}\nu$, xii 3, 2.

67 [96]. Some archaic usages are affected, as potiri with accusative, xi 10, 8; dissertare, xii 11, 1.

68 [97]. The debt of Tacitus to his chief predecessors in historical writing and to the great classical poets may be illustrated here by a few instances; others can be gathered from previous sections (e. g. 26 b), and many are pointed out in the notes on the text.

(1) Sallust : *Annals.*
    Fr. genua patrum advolvuntur . . . . . vi 49 3
    Jug. 21, 2 uno die . . . coeptum atque patratum
        bellum . . . . xii 16, 4
    Jug. 70, 2 carum acceptumque popularibus suis . xii 29, 1

(2) Livy :
    iii 27, 7 puncto saepe temporis maximarum rerum
        momenta verti . . . . v 4, 2

(3) Horace :
    Od. ii. 6, 125 laetus in praesens . . . . xi 15, 1

(4) Vergil :
    Aen. i 288 a magno *demissum* nomen Iulo . . xii 58, 1
    „ i 111 in *brevia* et syrtis urget . . . vi 33, 5
    ,, vi 617 sedet *aeternumque* sedebit . . xii 28, 2
    „ vii 628 *ingruit* Aeneas . . . . xii 12, 2
    ,, x 669 expendere poenas . . . . xii 19, 4
    „ ix 397 fraude loci . . . . . xii 33, 2

III

THE CONSTITUTION OF THE EARLY PRINCIPATE

§ 1. In the constitution solemnly inaugurated by his acceptance
of the title of 'Augustus' at the beginning of B. C. 27, Octavian
was content to be designated not as 'king' or 'dictator,' but only
as 'prince.' If this term is, as has been commonly supposed,
shortened from 'princeps senatus,' it implied only that (as was
no doubt the fact) his name stood first on the roll of senators, and
would convey no idea of his relation to the state. The fact,
however, that he is always spoken of not as 'princeps senatus' but
as simply 'princeps' seems, together with many other considera-
tions, to point to the conclusion that the term, if an abbreviation
of any kind, is rather that of some such an expression as 'princeps
civitatis,' and was intended to designate his general position as first
citizen of the Republic, which he claimed to have in other respects
restored in its entirety.

Thus understood, the title conveys no monarchical idea, and
does not even imply magistracy; though certain powers always
held with it made the princeps first magistrate of the state.

§ 2. Of these, the first and most important was the 'imperium
proconsulare,' whereby, in contrast to those holding a more
limited 'imperium,' he was distinctively the sole 'imperator[1],' or
'emperor,' of the Roman empire, and commander-in-chief of all
its fleets and armies. Not only the 'legati' of his own special
provinces, but also the proconsuls of those left to the senate,
ranked as his subordinates; and all military operations were held
by a fiction to be conducted under his 'auspicia'; while, by
a further extension, this power was valid also in Italy and even
within the walls of Rome, giving him not only the supreme
command of the home army and police, but also power of life and
death over all citizens, even of senatorial rank, and a special juris-

---

[1] The use of this title, as commemorative of victories (see ii 18 and
Intr. p. lii), is distinct from its use to denote supreme command.

diction, whereby he could either try in person criminal and civil charges of every description, or remit them, as he thought fit, to other tribunals.

§ 3. Hardly less important was the 'tribunitia potestas.' In the later time of the Republic, the office of tribune had been generally the most powerful urban magistracy, as that of proconsul had been the chief title of military command ; and the princeps was as much above ordinary tribunes as above ordinary proconsuls. He held office for life, was hampered by the veto of no colleague [1], and was known to be able, if need be, to support any coercive action by military force. From this office he derived personal inviolability ; it was through it that he could summon the senate and propose questions to it, as well as intervene to forbid or modify any decree displeasing to him. Also, in this capacity, he seems to have so far represented the people, that the old civic right of 'provocatio ad populum' from the sentence of the magistrate passes into an appeal to Caesar, and the whole prerogative of pardon is thus vested in him [2].

§ 4. By a third power, that of the 'regimen legum et morum,' he retained to himself the most important powers belonging to the ancient censorship [3], such as the revision of the lists of senators and knights, and the expulsion of unworthy members of those bodies.

§ 5. Another office, regularly held by the princeps from and after B. C. 12, was that of 'pontifex maximus,' whereby he became the supreme authority in many of the chief religious questions belonging to the state.

§ 6. It will be seen that the form of the Roman Republic was preserved ; that the Caesars professedly derived their power from their tenure of republican magistracies or modifications of such, and were supreme by a combination of such offices, and by such extension of their functions as would not seem inconsistent with

[1] The suggestion of a tribune, to veto a decision of the senate known to be in accordance with Nero's wishes, was scouted as futile, xvi 26, 6.

[2] iv 31, 1 ; vi 5, 2.

[3] The censorship itself was allowed to drop after B. C. 22, and was very rarely revived by subsequent emperors. Claudius held it in 47 A. D., xi 13.

their original idea. Not unfrequently the princeps also filled one of the consulships[1], rather as a recognition of the dignity of the office than as deriving any additional power from it. Otherwise, the annual magistracies existed on their ancient footing, and discharged their usual duties of routine; the most important being those of the consuls, as the regular presidents of the senate, and of the praetors, as presiding over and regulating the 'iudicia publica.' Side by side with them were important new officers directly appointed by the princeps; of whom the 'praefectus praetorio' and 'praefectus vigilum' were his military and police vicegerents in Rome, while the 'praefectus urbi' and 'praefectus annonae' must have encroached on some functions of the republican magistrates[2].

§ 7. Passing from the magistrates to the senate and the comitia, we find that one of the first acts of Tiberius was practically to annihilate the latter body, by transferring the election of magistrates to the senate[3]. The people may probably have felt that the substance of power had long since departed from them, and that only the shadow had now followed it: at any rate, the change took place without serious opposition, and the populace were left with nothing henceforth to care for but their bread and their amusements[4].

§ 8. With the senate it was outwardly far otherwise. In place of the 'senatus populusque Romanus,' in whose name the acts of Rome used to run, this august body alone remained, with apparently still more than its ancient majesty. 'Affairs that concerned the state, and the most important affairs which concerned individuals[5],' were still handled by it with apparent freedom; its decrees come to differ only in form from laws; in choosing magistrates, who by virtue of such magistracy become senators[6], it is formally a self-elective body; in form even the right of choosing the princeps himself devolves upon it[7]; the whole narrative of

[1] Tiberius was consul with Seianus in the early months of 31 A.D. For one of Claudius' consulships see xii 41, 1.

[2] An attempt to bring a criminal before a praetor rather than the praefectus urbi is noticed in xiv 41, 2.

[3] i 15, 1.   [4] 'Panem et circenses,' Juv. 10, 81.   [5] iv 6, 2.

[6] As a rule, the senate was entered through the quaestorship.

[7] Thus after the death of Claudius the senate confirmed the soldiers' choice of Nero, xii 69, 3.

THE EARLY PRINCIPATE

Tacitus is full of its debates and decisions. As of old, it awards triumphal honours and other recognition of victories[1], and sends its thanks or rewards to allied kings as representative of the state ; it decrees public funerals[2] and other honours to the dead[3] ; it makes regulations to repress disorder[4], and curb extravagance and immorality[5], and to deal stringently with the abuses of religious or superstitious practices ; while, abroad, all important questions appertaining to the administration of its own provinces are referred to it. Besides all this, the senate has supplanted the praetor's tribunal as the great high court of criminal justice, before which culprits of rank are almost always arraigned, especially on the constantly recurring charge of ' maiestas[6].'

§ 9. Those, however, who could look below the surface knew well that, not the senate, but the emperor through the senate, governed ; and that it acted rather as representative of him than of the state. Every magistrate was really so far his nominee that only such candidates as had his recommendation, or at least his approval[7], could be chosen ; and as the entry to the senate itself was through magistracy[8] or by the direct nomination of the princeps[9], every senator must have felt that he owed his position to the emperor ; who, besides the powers formally conferred on him, had all the advantage arising from the general recognition that, who-ever was master of the legions, was master of as much else as he thought fit to claim.

§ 10. If we look to the practical working of the imperial ad-ministration, the chief difference felt by the inhabitants of Rome must have consisted in the greater maintenance of order. Seven thousand ' vigiles ' were distributed over the city ; a more distinctly

[1] xii 38, 2. [2] vi 11, 6. [3] v 2. [4] vi 13, 3.
[5] xii 53, 1. [6] v 3 ; vi 5 ; &c.
[7] The princeps ' commended ' two out of the twenty quaestors annually elected, four out of the twelve praetors, and ' nominated ' the consuls. The consulship was rarely held for a full year : the two consuls who gave their name to the year retired after a few months, and were succeeded by ' consules suffecti.' Two months eventually became the ordinary length of tenure of this office, so that there were twelve consuls per annum.
[8] i.e. by the quaestorship (see above, § 8).
[9] Some senators are styled ' adlecti a principe.'

military police force of three urban cohorts, each a thousand strong, enforced the summary jurisdiction of the city praefect; and nine praetorian cohorts of similar strength were at hand, if needed. This security must have been in itself no small boon to trade and industry; and even the poorest class must have found their gain in the more systematic regulation of the corn supply.

§ 11. In the empire outside, the most important change to notice is the division of provinces made in B.C. 27 between Augustus and the senate, whereby only the more peaceful were retained by the latter; those lately acquired, or otherwise needing the presence of military force, being taken over by the emperor.

§ 12. Of the senatorial provinces, the two chief were Asia and Africa. The former, comprising a large triangular tract with its base on the western coast of Asia Minor, included generally Mysia, Lydia, Caria, and nearly all Phrygia, with most of the islands in the Aegean, and had its metropolis and seat of government at Ephesus. The latter would coincide in modern geography with the western part of Tripoli, the whole of Tunis, and a considerable portion of Algeria, its chief cities being Utica and the new Julian colony of Carthage.

§ 13. For the proconsulship of these two great provinces lots were drawn annually by the two senior consulars who had not previously held either. The other senatorial provinces, eight or nine in number[1], were similarly allotted to annual governors, also styled proconsuls, though usually only of praetorian rank. Their duties, as a rule, were civil only, nor are any soldiers, except a few by way of police, to be found generally in these provinces[2]. Besides the assistance of one or more legati of high senatorial rank, each proconsul was attended by a quaestor, who received all sums due to the aerarium.

§ 14. The Caesarian provinces, whose revenues formed the main support of the fiscus, comprised all those fronting the enemies

---

[1] Those usually so reckoned were Sicily, Sardinia (with Corsica), Hispania Baetica, Gallia Narbonensis, Macedonia, Achaia, Bithynia, Cyprus, and Crete (with Cyrene); but some of these were at times given over to Caesar.

[2] Africa formed an exception to this rule, having a regular force of one legion.

of the empire, and many other important countries. Their governors, appointed directly by the princeps, held office during his pleasure, usually for from three to five years, but often for much longer periods [1], and, like proconsuls of senatorial provinces, had the assistance of 'legati,' as also of a 'procurator fisci,' whose duties answered to those of the quaestor. Holding often the command of large armies, and having much fuller power of life and death [2], these governors were in a far higher real position than that of a senatorial proconsul; although, in recognition of the sole 'proconsulare imperium' of the emperor, none had a higher title than that of 'legatus Augusti propraetore.'

§ 15. To the greatest provinces, in which large forces were stationed, legati of consular rank were always sent [3]. Foremost among these are Upper and Lower Germany and Syria, each with its garrison of four legions, those of the German armies fully organized and trained by war against the unsubdued tribes beyond the Rhine, and those of Syria charged with maintaining the prestige of Rome against Parthia.

§ 16. Another class, corresponding to the second class of senatorial provinces, comprised those in which only a single legion, or even a smaller force, was stationed. In these the legatus was usually only of praetorian rank, but had otherwise the same status as in the greater provinces. As an example of such may be taken the three divisions of Gaul, Gallia Belgica, Lugdunensis, and Aquitania, for all of which insignificant forces seem ordinarily to have sufficed, with the German legions in reserve in case of a rising.

§ 17. In a third class of provinces of still less importance, the procurator, of only equestrian rank, instead of being placed under a legatus, is himself the acting governor, perhaps usually in some subordination to the legatus of a neighbouring province. One well-known instance of such a government in the time of Tiberius, that

---

[1] Cf. the case of Poppaeus Sabinus, vi 39, 3.

[2] Senatorial proconsuls could not (except in Africa) execute a soldier; and any citizen, under a capital charge, could appeal from any governor to Caesar. A well-known instance is that of St. Paul (Acts xxv. 11).

[3] Besides those here mentioned, Hispania Tarraconensis, Moesia, Pannonia, and Dalmatia, belonged to this class.

of Pontius Pilatus in Judaea, shows that an officer even of this rank might have command of at least a cohort[1].

§ 18. Egypt, as the great granary of Rome, had an exceptional position, and, though held by a considerable force, was entrusted to no legatus, but jealously retained by the princeps under his own control, with a vicegerent of equestrian rank styled 'praefectus.'

§ 19. All governors of provinces had fixed salaries from the treasury; and cruelty and extortion, though by no means things of the past, enjoyed far less impunity than such as collusive accusers, or judges interested in connivance, had often secured for the culprit in former times. From this cause, probably also from the more equitable assessment of tribute through a systematic census, the provinces are admitted to have been gainers by the fall of the Republic, and there is evidence that those placed under the emperor were more economically governed than the senatorial.

§ 20. Several states and kingdoms not formally reduced to provinces, but left semi-independent under native rulers, helped to strengthen the empire against hostile nations[2].

§ 21. The great military force of the empire was massed along its north-eastern frontier, formed, roughly speaking, by the Rhine, Danube, and Euphrates. The eight legions of Germany and the four of Syria have been already mentioned; the line of the Danube was secured by five in Moesia and Pannonia, supported by two more in Dalmatia; to these are to be added two in Egypt, one in Africa, and three in Spain, making up the whole standing force of twenty-five legions. Italy had no other garrison than the praetorian and urban cohorts (whose head quarters were in Rome), and the fleets of Misenum and Ravenna.

§ 22. The legion, commanded by a legatus of senatorial, often even of praetorian rank, consisted of ten cohorts, each subdivided into three maniples, each of which contained two centuries. All its soldiers, though recruited freely from all parts of the empire, were Roman citizens; but a large auxiliary or non-citizen force was always attached to it, supplementing it chiefly with light troops and cavalry: the whole corps being thus made up to a strength of about 10,000 of all arms and descriptions. The main armies may

[1] St. Matt. xxvii 27, &c.
[2] e. g. Commagene under Antiochus, xii 55; Ituraea and Judaea, xii 23.

THE EARLY PRINCIPATE

thus be rated in the aggregate at about 250,000 men ; to which perhaps 100,000 may be added for the troops of Italy, the marines of the fleets, and the detached bodies stationed in peaceful provinces.

§ 23. This organization as a whole dates from Augustus, and was maintained by Tiberius as he found it, without other change of importance than the transference of the election of magistrates to the senate, and the concentration of the praetorian guard in Rome.

On alterations under Claudius and Nero.

§ 24. Under Claudius more and more of the work of the State passed out of the hands of the senate and its magistrates ; and knights or freedmen, as ministers of the emperor, responsible to him alone, were appointed over new departments of administration at home and abroad. Nero professed to restore to the senate and law-courts functions that had been usurped by his predecessor's creatures (xiii 4, 3). But this restoration, even if sincerely intended at the outset, was out of harmony with the natural trend of events : the old-fashioned, cumbrous machinery of the senate made it a hindrance rather than a help in the work of government. Again, from its quasi-independent status, the senate was, in the emperor's eyes, a perpetual source of possible rebellion. And so in the course of his reign Nero's original attitude of professed respect for the senate changed to one of fear and suspicion. He exterminated its noblest and most eminent members, and it is recorded that he even threatened at one time to abolish the whole order and govern solely through knights and freedmen (Suet. *Ner.* 37).

§ 25. As the breach between the emperor and the aristocracy continually widened, he was brought into closer relation with the populace. The transference of the cost of the corn dole from the aerarium to the fiscus, whether actually the work of Claudius or Nero, seems to have borne its chief fruit under the latter. The mass, who now thus, in the most direct way, looked to the princeps for their food, dispensed in his name and by his officers, and supplemented by gifts of various kinds and by constant and gratuitous amusements, formed a vast and increasing 'clientela Caesaris,' in comparison with which the adherents of the shattered and impoverished aristocratic houses could have been no more than a handful.

xxxv   C 2

INTRODUCTION

IV

THE CAREER AND CHARACTER OF TIBERIUS

At the close of the sixth book of the *Annals*, Tacitus gives his view of Tiberius' career and character, the consideration of which involves some account of his life as a whole, including the period prior to that which falls within this volume.

Tacitus' estimate of Tiberius is wholly condemnatory. His character is represented as bad and vicious, not allowed full play while pressure of circumstances required its repression and while his position was not absolutely secure. Towards the end of his life, however, when all external restraints were removed, he is declared to have come out in his true colours as a monster of cruelty and vice.

The facts of Tiberius' early life make it evident that such a description must not be accepted without qualification. Even Tacitus does not refuse to him a measure of commendation in regard to his early career, calling him 'egregium vita famaque quoad privatus vel in imperiis sub Augusto fuit' (vi 51, 5). Now this period of his life extends to Tiberius' fifty-sixth year, an age by which a person's character is usually developed and can be seen in its true nature. So far, however, no allegations of such debauchery as is attributed to him at the close of his life by Tacitus can be made ; on the contrary, his character was by all accounts temperate and austere ; and the sentence just quoted invalidates the charge of drunkenness made against him by Suetonius. The occupations, moreover, in which these years were spent were not such as could possibly have been given to, or undertaken by, a man of bad character and vicious life. We find Tiberius all through this period engaged in public affairs of great importance, and conducting them honourably and efficiently. He entered on the 'cursus honorum,' with Augustus' sanction, at an earlier age than was customary except for members of the imperial family, and when only twenty-two years old received the important commission of settling the affairs of the East, in 20 B.C., when, on the occasion of the Parthian agreement with Rome, he received from Phraates the standards captured from Crassus in 53 B.C., and instituted Artaxias on the

throne of Armenia. After this he was constantly employed by
Augustus in his great work of securing the northern frontiers of the
empire. In 15 B. C., being in command among the Helvetii, he
co-operated with his brother Drusus in the subjugation of the tribes
to the north of Italy, bringing Rhaetia and Vindelicia under the
Roman rule. Then, from the years 12 to 10 B.C., he conducted
three campaigns in Pannonia, the effect of which was to secure the
frontiers of the Illyrian province. After this, upon the death of
Drusus in Germany in 9 B. C., he took up the work of the extension
of Roman influence in that quarter, and brought the tribes between
the Elbe and the Rhine into submission. All this was work that
only a general of real capacity and energy could have accomplished
with success, and Augustus showed how much he valued his powers
by associating him in the 'tribunicia potestas' for five years from
6 B. C., and by sending him out again from the years 4 to 11 A. D.,
when serious troubles again broke out in Germany and Pannonia.
But in spite of this career of honour the circumstances of his
private life were not happy : he was exposed to sorrows and disap-
pointments that must have soured his character. He was treated
by Augustus as a useful instrument for forwarding the imperial
policy and was honoured as such ; but to the emperor's convenience
his own personal inclinations must always be subordinated. About
15 B. C. he was married to Vipsania, daughter of Agrippa, but soon
after Agrippa's death, in 12 B.C., he was forced to put away the wife
for whom he had a deep affection, and to marry Julia the daughter
of Augustus, Agrippa's widow. In regard to the succession, too,
his position was unsatisfactory. Had Augustus died at this stage,
he would have been content that Tiberius, a man of tried ability
and experience, should be his successor. But when Tiberius
returned from his work in Germany, it became evident that it was
Augustus' ambition that his heir should be one of his own blood,
and that he would be found in the person of one of his grandsons,
Gaius, or Lucius, Caesar, who were now respectively thirteen and
ten years old. Tiberius, then, after spending his best energies in
Augustus' service and sacrificing his own domestic happiness at the
emperor's bidding, found that he must now yield up the prospect of
further advancement to his young rivals. Realizing this, and dis-
gusted at Julia's infidelities, he resolved to retire from public life,

and went into retirement at Rhodes, in 6 B. C., persisting in this determination even against the express wish of Augustus, who wanted him to undertake the settlement of the Eastern provinces, where the disturbances in Armenia were a danger to the continuance of peace. His refusal brought upon him the displeasure of Augustus, and when the tribunician power which he had received for five years expired, his position was by no means safe, and his retirement came to amount very nearly to banishment. He obtained leave to return to Rome in 2 A. D., but continued in seclusion until the death of Gaius Caesar in 4 A. D. Then, Lucius Caesar being already dead, Tiberius was admitted once more to the emperor's favour; he was now adopted into the family of the Caesars, was associated with Augustus in the 'tribunicia potestas,' and was displayed as the heir before the greatest armies of the state (i 3, 3). A second period of military activity now ensued. Tiberius conducted campaigns in Germany in 4 and 5 A. D., then he had to deal with the great rebellion which broke out in Pannonia in 6 A. D., and he remained in that country until the disaster suffered by Varus in Germany in 9 A. D. required his presence there. He then reorganized the army acting in defence of the Rhine frontier, in 10 A.D., and advanced into Germany in 11 A. D., re-establishing order, and finally returning to Rome for a triumph in the following year. He was then rewarded with a renewal of the 'tribunicia potestas,' and was further associated with the emperor in his 'proconsulare imperium.' At the time of Augustus' last illness he had set forth for the Illyrian province, whence he returned to succeed to the principate.

At the time of his accession Tiberius was in his fifty-sixth year. The events of his life so far, alternating between military activity and retirement, high honour and obscurity, and bringing bereavement and disappointment, left him austere and reserved, prone to take a cynical view of society and to set small store on the deference now paid him. A sentence in Tacitus (i 80, 3), that his penetration was keen but his resolution weak, seems to be borne out by the facts, and this mixture of weakness and strength, clear insight coupled with irresolution in action, affords the key to much of the conduct of the new ruler.

In a passage where Tacitus reviews the first eight years of

TIBERIUS

Tiberius' reign (iv 6), this period is admitted to have been one of good and upright administration. So far, the Senate was continually being consulted and was treated with respect; the Republican magistrates continued to exercise their functions, and the worthiest men were selected for office; in the provinces, cruelty and extortion were repressed; at home, the laws, with the exception of that dealing with 'maiestas,' were uprightly administered; in his private life the emperor was frugal and moderate, and disputes about property between citizens and himself were settled in the ordinary courts. For all this, however, Tacitus, in his final account of Tiberius, allows him no credit at all: it is merely 'a show of virtue,' hypocritically assumed, and mainly prompted by fear and jealousy of his son Drusus and his nephew Germanicus.

Much, however, upon which Tacitus bases his strictures is capable of a more favourable interpretation. Great stress is laid on the hypocrisy of Tiberius' professed diffidence in accepting the principate at the outset. But it should be remembered that there was as yet no precedent for the succession of a 'princeps,' and, to make the new ruler's position that of a constitutional monarch and not that of a despot, it was important to emphasize that his elevation was by the full consent of the governed. This was what the Senate's invitation to Tiberius to take up Augustus' powers implied.

Neither is it fair to regard Tiberius' treatment of Germanicus as attributable to none but jealous and malicious motives. Tiberius actually strengthened the powers given to Germanicus by Augustus (i 3, 5; 14, 4), and rewarded him with a triumph and the title of 'imperator' (i 55; 58). His recall from Germany can be accounted for on other grounds than the jealousy of the 'princeps'; his expeditions were not producing any real profit, but were on the contrary inflicting severe burdens on Gaul (ii 5, 3), and Tiberius' own acquaintance with the conditions prevalent in Germany might well justify his decision to discontinue further campaigns in that country. Nor can Tacitus' statement be accepted that Tiberius sent Germanicus to the East with the sinister intention of compassing his destruction ('amoliri specie honoris,' ii 42, 1). There is no evidence that Germanicus' death was due to other than natural causes. Some indeed ascribed it to witchcraft! Others declared that he had been poisoned, but the evidence for this broke down completely. Piso, who had thwarted Germanicus by all means in his power when in the East, was put on trial for his misbehaviour, and felt so sure of condemnation that he committed suicide; there was a rumour that his interference with Germanicus had been prompted by Tiberius (iii 16), but Tacitus does not vouch for it as a fact. We can believe that Tiberius had no great affection for Germanicus, whom at one time he must have regarded as a possible rival, and whose wife, Agrippina, was of an aggressive disposition and personally obnoxious to him; there is absolutely no evidence, and not much likelihood, that he schemed his destruction. It is possible that he put Piso in charge of Syria, during Germanicus' mission to the East, knowing him to be a man of independent character, and wishing that there should be some counterpoise to Germanicus' power: he did not, however, foresee the lengths to which Piso, through sheer personal dislike of Germanicus, would carry his opposition, and he showed no signs of condoning Piso's actions or attempting to shield him, but solemnly charged the Senate at his trial to sift the charges against him with the utmost impartiality and without any consideration of what they might fancy to be the emperor's view of the case or his wishes in the matter (iii 12).

It has been mentioned that Tacitus cited the cases tried under the law of 'maiestas' as the exception to the equitable administration of justice. It was under Tiberius that trials of this sort first became frequent, and this is one of Tacitus' strongest reasons for his unfavourable view of him. The statute under which such cases were tried was one capable of wide interpretation: Tacitus declares that under the Republic, persons guilty of treachery in the field or sedition at home were actionable for 'maiestas,' and that then deeds alone, not words, made them liable (i 72, 2). As a matter of fact, however, it was possible even under the Republic to prosecute under this count for libels and slanders: such a view is to be seen in Cicero (*ad Fam.* iii 11, 2), and it was enforced by Augustus in the case of libellous publications, though under him trials for 'maiestas' occurred but seldom. In the course of Tiberius' reign there was a plentiful crop of prosecutions of this sort in which words as well as deeds were charged, and there arose the odious profession

TIBERIUS

of the 'delatores,' the informers who worked up evidence of guilty
words or acts against the Emperor, obtaining rewards when they
effected a conviction.

Now, we may notice that at the outset the practice of bringing
these accusations was not encouraged by Tiberius, nor did he
allow it to be exercised without moderation. In this first period of
his rule twelve cases are recorded by Tacitus, in two of which[1] the
acts (if proved) would have been indictable for treason under any
government ; in three cases the charge of 'maiestas' was dismissed
by the emperor himself; and in three more instances the result was
acquittal (i 74; iii 49; iii 70; i 74; ii 50). On another occasion of
such a prosecution, for an offence of words, death was inflicted by
the Senators without consulting Tiberius, and he expostulated with
them for their precipitate action (iii 51).

We see, then, that at first Tiberius was not eager that these
prosecutions should be multiplied, or that condemnation should
follow accusation as a matter of course. At the same time, Tiberius,
in not repressing them altogether, was responsible for their introduction, and encouraged their extension by permitting a share of
the property of those condemned to go to the accusers. Nor was
this a time when strong measures were necessary as a precaution
against insurrection ; there was a general submissiveness to his
rule ; the Senators, from amongst whom most of the victims of the
prosecutions for 'maiestas' were drawn, were, as he scornfully
said of them, 'willing to be slaves' (iii 65, 3). That he permitted
these prosecutions was due, probably, not to the thirst for blood
which Tacitus would ascribe to him, but rather to a certain timidity
of nature which led him to think that his own security might be
the better maintained through the intimidation by this means of
possible opponents to his domination.

We now come to the third of the periods into which our historian
divides Tiberius' life. For the next six years, while his mother
still lived, a period covering the ninth to the fifteenth year of his
reign, and the sixty-fourth to the seventieth of his life, he is said to
have been 'inter bona malaque mixtus'; some evil traits, that is,
such as cruelty and covetousness, began to escape from their disguise,

---

[1] Cn. Piso and Antistius Vetus, iii 38, 2.

xli

but an appearance of virtue was still kept up while his mother's eye was upon him.

This was the time when his great minister Seianus was at the height of his influence. Seianus held the office of 'praefectus urbis' as well as the command of the praetorian guards. These he had concentrated within a camp close to the city wall, and in virtue of his two appointments and his close connexion with the emperor, in whose 'imperium,' though he was only an eques, he was associated (iv 7, 2), he acquired an immense ascendancy in Rome, and became in effect the emperor's vicegerent. Nobles courted his favour as the necessary step towards obtaining office (iv 1, 4; 68, 2); an attack by one of his creatures was held to make condemnation certain (iv 32, 2). His ambition, according to Tacitus, was unbounded, and he schemed at removing all possible rivals that he might eventually succeed to the principate on Tiberius' death. To this end he contrived the murder of Tiberius' son Drusus, and then began intriguing against the family of Germanicus and Agrippina.

The whole of this period is described as one of 'cruel orders, incessant accusations, treacherous friendships' (iv 33, 3), and indeed the domestic history of this time is largely taken up with trials for state offences. The number of such cases rises to twenty in the course of six years, but analysis of them shows that they were by no means all unjustified, or the mere excesses of malicious autocracy. In four cases serious charges were proved, and acquittal would have been an abuse of justice[1]; some of those condemned were informers, as Firmius Catus (iv 31, 7); in three cases the result was acquittal[2]; another case was indefinitely adjourned (iv 66, 3); in another the emperor intervened to pardon (iv 31, 1); and in another the gravest charge was dropped (iv 21, 4). The remaining cases, however, do show a greater sensitiveness on the part of the emperor towards libels, and a more pronounced tendency to insist on condemnation. The attack on Cremutius Cordus (iv 34) for a passage in his history, eulogizing Brutus and Cassius the murderers of Julius Caesar, seems peculiarly harsh. Evidence was

[1] Silius iv 19, 5; Serenus iv 13, 2; Capito iv 15, 3; Suillius iv 31, 6.
[2] Carsidius Sacerdos and C. Gracchus iv 13, 3; Fonteius Capito iv 36, 4.

TIBERIUS

procured by disgraceful means against Titus Sabinus (iv 69) ; confiscation for the benefit of the exchequer was enforced (iv 20) ;
informers had their rewards assured to them even when the accused
anticipated condemnation by suicide (iv 30). Towards the close of
this period, too, began the ominous dispatches from the emperor at
Capreae (iv 70); the emperor's absence from Rome became permanent, and the evils prevalent became intensified, with Seianus in
charge at Rome and working upon his master's timidity to further
his own ends. And so we find that the house of Germanicus has
now fallen into danger of destruction, though at the beginning of
this period it was still in favour (iv 8).

The last stage opens with the death of Livia Augusta, whom
Tacitus at this point represents as having afforded protection to
the house of Germanicus against the murderous plots of Seianus, in
spite of previous insinuations that she was the 'terrible step-mother,'
to blame for all the deaths that had occurred in the house of the
Caesars. Now, however, her death is said to remove the restraint
upon Tiberius' resentment against Agrippina and her sons; and
Tiberius and Seianus in consequence immediately effect the banishment of Agrippina and Nero, and a year later Drusus is imprisoned
also. But Seianus' influence still had its limits ; Agrippina's third
son, Gaius, was in Tiberius' favour, and was regarded as his heir,
and Nero survived two years more. Seianus was not permitted to
make the hoped-for marriage which would have united him to the
imperial family, and was not associated in the tribunician power.
Soon Tiberius, ever prone to suspicion, when other grounds for it
were removed, turned against his minister, and Seianus was destroyed as guilty of plotting against the emperor and Gaius. It is
not certain whether this plot really existed : it seems inherently
probable from what we know of the character and career of Seianus ;
but though its existence was believed in by Tacitus and Suetonius,
and it is related as a fact by Josephus, it does not appear to have
been formally proved in the Senate which condemned him, and the
account in Dio suggests that no conspiracy was ever matured [1].

In Tacitus' account, at the beginning of Book vi, of the events
following the downfall of Seianus, we read of a very reign of terror.

[1] With this, too, the words in Juvenal x 75 seem to agree.

xliii

INTRODUCTION

Tiberius was never weary of accusations and executions; men perished for old offences as well as recent ones, for words as well as deeds; a very plague of 'delation' broke out; an 'immensa strages,' of all who were accused of complicity with Seianus, was perpetrated (vi 19, 3). A closer view shows that such a description exaggerates the facts. There are cases still of pardon and acquittal (vi 5, 2 ; 9, 1 ; 7, 1); some escape by giving information (vi 3, 5; 7, 5), others by adjournment or by being ignored (vi 9, 7 ; 14, 4) ; others receive a less sentence than death (vi 3, 3; 18, 2-3), and amid the horrors of the time prudent men, such as M'. Lepidus, L. Piso, Aelius Lamia, Poppaeus Sabinus, can still hold their own in honour (vi 27, 4; 10, 3; 27, 2 ; 39, 3). Of course, even after such deduction is made, there is still a long list of victims, amounting to some forty in number, and there must have been many others whose destruction was narrated in the lost part of the *Annals*. The 'immensa strages' of vi 19, 3 may refer to the execution of twenty in one day as reported in Suetonius (*Tib.* 61). But when all allowance is made, not less than eighty persons must have perished in the last six years of Tiberius' reign, and for most of these deaths the emperor was responsible, though at the end they were directly brought about by Macro acting in his master's name.

Some of these victims would be creatures of Seianus, and, if his conspiracy was a fact, would be guilty of complicity with him, and were justly executed; but there were circumstances of horrible cruelty in the execution of Seianus' children and the old mother of Fufius Geminus (vi 10, 1), and in the accusation of the descendants of Theophanes (vi 18, 5). Finally, in regard to the closing years of Tiberius' life, both Tacitus and Suetonius charge him with the constant practice of abominable sensuality in his retirement at Capreae. The references to Tiberius in earlier authors, as Philo, Josephus, Seneca, and the elder Pliny, do not offer any confirmation of these charges; even Juvenal, who, one might suppose, would take up such a subject with avidity, represents his companions at Capreae as no worse than astrologers (x 93), and even in Tacitus' description of the emperor's retinue when he set forth from Rome to Capreae there is no indication that he is preparing to retire to scenes of vicious self-indulgence; his attendants are chiefly Greek men of letters, chosen for their interesting conversation (iv 58).

TIBERIUS

Intrinsically, it is most improbable that a man of seventy should, after a life of austerity and self-control, enter upon a course of gross and unnatural sensuality, and prolong his life in spite of it to the age of nearly seventy-eight. While there is no positive evidence available for the refutation of these charges, they are, however, distinctly 'not proven'; and inasmuch as they are of just the kind that ancient malice would invent against an unpopular person living in close retirement, it is only fair to give Tiberius the benefit of the doubt in the matter.

It remains to offer some explanation of the cause of Tacitus' uncompromising hostility to Tiberius. It seems partly accountable by the fact that Tacitus' political sympathies were with the 'noble' opposition to the principate at its inception ; he regarded the old days of republican 'liberty' as representing a higher condition of political life, and could not help viewing the founders of the empire as the destroyers of a constitution that represented a more exalted ideal. Moreover, into his view of Tiberius there probably entered a considerable amount of the traditional ill-feeling entertained by the other 'nobiles' against the house of the Claudii, whose political conduct had often run counter to noble interests and whose independence, in fact, was characterized by their peers as arrogance.

Then Tacitus no doubt read the times of Tiberius very much in the light of his experience of Domitian's rule, and saw, or fancied he saw, prevalent under Tiberius the abuses that reached their height under Domitian, a reign of terror owing to the unchecked iniquities of the informers and the abject servility of the Senate. Nor had Tiberius the qualities shown by Trajan, the emperor whose rule was so welcomed by Tacitus in contrast to all the oppression of Domitian. Trajan was a great conqueror, whose armies advanced beyond the Danube and the Euphrates, whereas Tiberius shrank timidly behind the frontiers bequeathed to him. Trajan's vast operations in engineering and building were in strong contrast to the parsimony that checked Tiberius from any such beneficent expenditure (vi 45, 2). And so Tiberius won no credit with Tacitus for the sound, though less dazzling, features of his administration, of which there is no doubt,—the preservation of peace and the equitable regulation of the provinces. This side of Tiberius' government must not be forgotten. Cruelty and extortion in the provinces were checked; liberality was shown to foreign subjects when in difficulty, as in the case of the bounties given to the cities of Asia when ruined by earthquakes (ii 47), and the gratitude of provincials, attested by temples and monuments in foreign countries, should be set against the complaints of nobles that liberty, which to them meant the licence to plunder, had been destroyed.

It is not the purpose of this essay to represent Tiberius as an ideal monarch; at his best, he did not rise above the level of a sound administrator; his reign is barren of great improvements or extensions of the imperial system; but it is desirable to give some indication of the points where Tacitus' prejudices lead to misrepresentation. Absolute power too often proves a burden beyond the power of human nature to support, and the words of Arruntius (vi 48), that Tiberius' character had broken down under the strain of it, offer a view more reasonable than that suggested by Tacitus. Tiberius was not strong in the qualities of courageous independence or quick and resolute decision; as age weakened him, his mother's strong will no longer exercised upon him its influence towards humane and moderate courses; then came the shock of the sense that the minister whom he had trusted had proved treacherous to him; left isolated and suspicious, he lost his grip even on the routine of administration, and came to see at every turn enemies who must be struck down to make life safe for him.

V

THE CHARACTER AND GOVERNMENT OF CLAUDIUS

We have no complete account of Claudius' life in Tacitus, whose narrative is lost until we come to the closing years of Claudius' reign, when he is represented as having sunk into a state of dotage, without will of his own, absent-minded and callous to the pitch of imbecility, and entirely dominated by his wife and his freedmen ministers. From other writers, however, enough material can be drawn to construct a fairly complete record of his life and character.

CLAUDIUS

We gather that in infancy and childhood Claudius suffered a succession of illnesses, which so intensified his natural defects that he was kept in the background and regarded with aversion and contempt even by his mother. While his gifted brother Germanicus was rapidly advanced to honour and office, Claudius remained in obscurity. Under Augustus he received nothing higher than an augurship, and under Tiberius merely the ' consularia ornamenta,' in spite of his desire for the actual consulship. From early years, however, he displayed a passion for literary and historical studies : a long list of his compositions is given by Suetonius, and in this field he was not without ability. This is acknowledged by Augustus in a letter to Livia which is quoted by Suetonius, who also tells us of Augustus wondering how one who conversed so badly could declaim so well. So also Tacitus says of him, ' nec in Claudio quoties meditata dissereret elegantiam requireres' (xiii 3,6). His intellectual pursuits, however, do not appear to have kept him from indulgence in coarse pleasures, and Suetonius states that he spent his leisure with low companions, in drinking, gambling, and debauchery. He may be compared to James I of England, ' the wisest fool in Christendom,' full of erudition, but lacking force of character and practical ability, ungainly, stammering, and undignified.

Under Gaius, Claudius, now in middle life, was promoted to higher rank, becoming a senator instead of being merely an equestrian, and receiving the consulship. But he suffered insults and was exposed to danger ; he was reprimanded for his acts as consul and was asked his ' sententia ' in the Senate last of all the ' consulares ' ; at Court he was the butt of practical jokes inflicted upon him by Gaius and his courtiers, and once, when sent on a deputation to Gaius in Gaul, he came near losing his life.

It is quite possible that during this period he may have purposely exaggerated his eccentricities and submitted to the emperor's insults, finding it safest to be despised, while secretly looking forward to the time of his own accession. It was not likely that Gaius' tyranny would be endured for any great length of time, and by his connexion with the imperial house Claudius was the most natural successor. And it was at this stage that he married Valeria Messalina, a woman of higher rank than either of his previous wives, Plautia Urgulanilla and Aelia Paetina, for she was a great-granddaughter of Octavia, the sister of Augustus, and this alliance must have improved his prospects of succession. Indeed, his sudden elevation to the principate may well have been due to some pre-concerted plan rather than the sudden half-humorous suggestion of the soldiers who found him hiding in the palace on the day of Gaius' murder. At any rate, the acts of the new government do not look like those of persons taken unawares, and it is those measures of Claudius' administration especially that fall in the early part of his reign that manifest creditable statesmanship, either in himself or in the advisers whom he had the good sense to follow.

Gaius had left the empire in a state of disorganization and confusion. His maniacal extravagances had depleted the treasury and brought the populace into the danger of famine, while his oppression had alienated the nobility and brought the principate into disfavour with the upper classes. Abroad, Gaul had been pillaged, the German tribes provoked to hostility, the Jews in Palestine were on the verge of rebellion, and in other regions, as Mauretania, Commagene, and Parthia, disturbances had been caused by Gaius' capricious interference with, or deposition of, native rulers.

The new administration proceeded to remedy these conditions, and showed a considerable measure of ability in dealing with the task. The finances were reorganized; the lavish expenditure of Gaius on shows and largesses was discontinued, and many of the taxes imposed in the last reign could in consequence be remitted. At this period we find the term 'fiscus' now first definitely applied to the fund into which the revenues from the imperial provinces went, and from which the expenses of their administration were met. A difference no doubt had previously been drawn between this fund and the income from the emperor's personal estates in different parts of the empire, but both had been included under the term 'res suae' or 'res familiaris.' The 'fiscus Caesaris' now became a separate and important department of the imperial administration, under the charge of the 'libertus a rationibus.' This official, in origin one of the servile staff of the emperor's household, rose under Claudius to increased dignity, which was enhanced by the prohibition of the use of this name for the freedman holding the corresponding functions in any other Roman household. Pallas, the 'libertus a rationibus' under Claudius, even received the insignia of the praetorship. Others also

CLAUDIUS

of the emperor's financial agents obtained increased dignity and power: his procurators were to have magisterial jurisdiction in suits affecting the fiscus, and the emperor's procurators, rather than quaestors, took the superintendence of the corn-ships at Ostia and the management of the emperor's domainlands in Cisalpine Gaul and South Italy (xii 60).

In dealing with the questions that called for settlement abroad, Claudius' measures, briefly stated, were as follows. National feeling in Judaea was conciliated by the withdrawal of the insignia of Roman rule from the country and by the appointment of a native prince, Agrippa, as king over all the dominions which his grandfather, Herod the Great, had held under Augustus.

In Armenia, Mithridates, originally appointed king by Tiberius, but summoned to Rome and imprisoned by Gaius (xi 8, 1), was restored to his kingdom, where he maintained his authority and reasserted Armenia's independence against Parthia. So, also, Antiochus, taken from Commagene by Gaius, was reinstated (xii 55, 1). Mauretania, which had been convulsed by a rising for national independence owing to Gaius' seizure and execution of its king, Ptolemaeus, was subjugated by Suetonius Paulinus and Hosidius Geta in 41 A.D., and reduced to two provinces, under procurators who were in charge of considerable military force.

In 46 A.D. we find the kingdom of Thrace brought within the Roman provincial system, on the death of Rhoemetalces, the king instituted by Gaius. For many years the country had been left under native rulers acting under Roman protection, but they had not succeeded in maintaining their authority satisfactorily, and now Thrace was put under a procurator, with 2,000 troops, subject to the higher authority of the legatus of Moesia. About the same time, the provinces of Macedonia and Achaia, which since 15 A.D. had been under the charge of the legatus of Moesia, were restored to senatorial control.

In Gaul, Druidism was suppressed, since it was a possible source of national insurrection, but the Romanized inhabitants received many privileges, and their country was regarded with special favour by Claudius as being his birthplace. In Germany, the safety of the frontier was secured by expeditions against the Chatti and the Chauci, and in one of the expeditions against the former, the last of the three eagles taken from Varus in 9 A. D. was recovered, as well as some captives surviving from his army ; and in dealing with the Chauci great success attended the operations of Corbulo (xi 18–20). The Roman garrisons were, however, drawn to the Gallic side of the Rhine, and attempts to annex the country to the east of the river were forbidden, in accordance with the precept of Augustus, though some of the German tribes nearest the Rhine acknowledged the suzerainty of Rome, and a strip of territory on the right bank was kept clear of Germans, and reserved for the use of the Roman troops (xiii 54, 2).

Claudius' chief military exploit, the invasion of Britain and reduction of a considerable part of it into a province, is described in a separate chapter (p. lx).

An important feature of Claudius' reign is the foundation of Roman colonies in the provinces, of which the most famous were Colonia Agrippinensis (Cologne) and Camulodunum (Colchester) : in Noricum, too, five ' municipia ' are mentioned by the elder Pliny as owing their status to the favour of Claudius. Seneca, in his satire on Claudius, taunts him with the indiscriminate bestowal of Roman citizenship upon provincials, but there is no positive evidence that this was really done on any large scale. Seneca probably exaggerates the effect of Claudius' admission of eminent Gauls to the Senate and magistracies in Rome. This concession, expressed in the oration of Claudius, of which a fragment has been found in an inscription at Lyons, and the gist of which seems to be condensed in Tacitus' report in xi 24, was a natural development of the policy pursued towards the chiefs of Gaul by both Augustus and Tiberius, who by honouring and trusting them as far as possible had sought to attach them firmly to their connexion with Rome. These chiefs already possessed the Roman citizenship, and the status of 'equites' ; they now received the 'right of the broad stripe,' entitling them to a seat in the Senate and to stand for the Roman magistracies. This wise and liberal measure was viewed with jealousy and alarm by the Roman nobles, and it was to such feelings that Seneca appealed in the reference which he made in his satire to Claudius' indulgence towards the provincials.

A general review, therefore, of Claudius' administration shows it to contain many favourable features. But it would be a mistake to lose sight of the imperfections in his system of government or of the abuses to which his defects of character gave rise. There was a sinister aspect in the method of his elevation to the position of princeps; he was a ruler imposed upon the state by the choice of the soldiers; and this military 'praerogativa,' to which the ratification of the Senate came second, was rewarded with lavish gifts to the troops. By a similar procedure Agrippina, at Claudius' death, was enabled to set her son on the throne, in spite of Britannicus' better right; the precedent had been set for what in later times proved so terrible an abuse, the acquirement of the imperial throne by purchase from the legions.

The intention, professed by Claudius, to restore the constitution as it had been under Augustus, when government was shared between the Senate and the princeps, was not actually realized, and was perhaps owing to the conditions of the time not practicable. For the past ten years, through the closing part of Tiberius' reign and the rule of Gaius, the Senate had been oppressed and intimidated: it was now reduced in numbers and its energies were impaired, so that it was not capable of resuming an effective grasp of public administration. We do not henceforward find the Senate making provision for current emergencies or new spheres of administration; rather than this, the emperor selects new ministers directly responsible to himself, from among the equites or the imperial freedmen, and his 'procuratores' are found in charge of new departments at home, and enjoy increased power and independence throughout the empire. Such a system might have worked satisfactorily enough under a ruler of strong character and practical ability. But Claudius was lacking in these qualities. In his early life he had had no such administrative training as had fallen to Augustus and Tiberius; till middle life his occupations, at best, had been those of the recluse and student. Nor was his learning worn 'lightly, like a flower,' but it made him diffuse and pedantic, unable to see facts in their true proportion, prone to give rambling and far-fetched reasons for his opinions, and to make much of fanciful 'reforms,' such as the introduction of new letters or the revival of ancient methods of spelling. Vanity of this sort, coupled with the desire to show himself like Augustus, led him to interfere to excess in judicial business. It is true that some of his decisions were shrewd, and some of the principles of law which he enunciated were afterwards quoted with approval by juristic writers, but, attempting to deal personally with too great a number of cases, he was often presented with an accumulation of business, which he attempted to meet by cutting short the full investigation of cases and making hasty and capricious decisions. Such methods gave to those who could catch his ear an opportunity of getting judgement in their own favour (xi 5, 1); Claudius was easily swayed by those around him, and they instituted a regular traffic with the parties in the suits heard by him. A great deal of this judicial work was dealt with by the emperor in private, and there was no appeal from his judgement: it became, therefore, one of the most popular acts of Claudius' successor to promise the discontinuance of this abuse of justice (xiii 4, 2).

His vanity and blindness to realities are also seen in his fondness for taking military honours without having achieved any actual military exploits. Not only did he celebrate a triumph for the conquest of Britain, though he was only present in the country for sixteen days, but he accepted the title of 'imperator' twenty-seven times, for victories many of which cannot now be identified at all, and showered triumphal distinctions broadcast upon his subordinates for wholly insufficient reasons (xi 20, 5).

Then the fact that the main departments of administration, comprising most of the duties that in a modern state would be assigned to a body of civil servants under state control, were in the hands of freedmen who were simply the emperor's own domestic officials, gave opportunities for intrigue and corruption within the palace. The freedmen began to exercise control over everything: candidates for office applied to them, and paid their price for recommendation to the princeps; misgovernment in the provinces might go on unchecked if the governors could get the freedmen to connive at the plunder (xii 54; cf. also xii 45, 5; 46, 5; xiii 1); and contracts for public works gave the directing freedmen other fruitful opportunities for peculation (xii 57). The 'avarice of the Claudian times' (*H.* v 12, 5) became a byword.

But the worst abuses of Claudius' reign arose from his timidity, coupled with the possession of absolute power. It was easy for

CLAUDIUS

his confidants, by working on his fears, to procure the destruction of those whose wealth excited their greed or whom they wished to remove for their own ends. A conspiracy against the emperor's life, detected in the second year of his reign, was met by widespread executions, directed at their pleasure by the freedmen and Messalina ; and the latter in particular was ever ready to compass the death of those who disdained her advances or crossed her path in any way. The early chapters of the eleventh book present a case, typical probably of many others, in which, to gratify her jealousy and satisfy her cupidity, four lives were sacrificed, the emperor was subdued to her will against his own inclinations, and men of the highest rank combined to contrive charges to coerce the emperor's judgement.

In recording the final event in Messalina's career of unbridled profligacy, the bigamous marriage with Silius, from which her own destruction resulted, Tacitus assures us that he has added nothing to the accounts of the authorities whom he followed (xi 27). The tale seems incredible indeed, but there are difficulties hardly less great in the variant mentioned by Suetonius, but rejected by him, to the effect that Claudius was a consenting party to Messalina's going through the form of marriage with Silius, in order that the ill effect of an omen portended to 'the husband of Messalina' might be averted from himself. This version leaves it unexplained how Narcissus had the power to turn the emperor's fears towards the political dangers of the new marriage almost immediately after he had been induced by his superstitious fears to consent to it, and whether the eminent and contemporary authorities whom Tacitus followed were ignorant of, or suppressed, so important a feature in the story as the emperor's cognizance of the marriage.

In the closing period of Claudius' reign, after the death of Messalina, the emperor is described by Tacitus as entirely dominated by her successor Agrippina. She had a strong confederate in the freedman Pallas, and won a position of even greater influence than that held by Livia in the time of Augustus. She obtained, as outward marks of her ascendancy, the title 'Augusta,' and a seat with the emperor on great public occasions (xii 37, 5 ; 56, 5) ; she amassed great wealth, procured the command of the praetorians for her own nominee (xii 42), and enabled her son by a

liii

INTRODUCTION

previous marriage to become the supplanter of Claudius' own
child Britannicus. There was a party in the Senate opposed to
her, as is witnessed by the attacks on her partisans, unsuccessful
in the case of Vitellius (xii 42), but successful in another, that of
Tarquitius Priscus (xii 59); and in the freedman Narcissus she
had a deadly enemy, who finally organized an intrigue for her
destruction and the restoration of Britannicus to the prospect of
succession. But she had so secured her position that she was able
to prevent this intrigue from coming to effect: she hastened the
emperor's death, procured her son's accession, and soon afterwards
compelled Narcissus to commit suicide.

It will be noticed that the best features of Claudius' administration are shown in the early part of his reign. Then, it would
seem, his powers were at their best, and the ministers who co-
operated with him aimed at producing a good impression by
efficient administration. Neither can the fulsome eulogy[1] nor the
scathing denunciation[2] of Seneca be accepted as affording the true
portrait of Claudius. The satire has undoubtedly much influenced
the accounts of subsequent historians, but when allowance has been
made for the satirist's extravagance, there remains a sufficiency of
concrete facts to render such an account as we have from Tacitus
credible enough. There are acts of senseless extravagance (xii 56),
the neglect to attend to the standing need of provisioning the city
(xii 43), failure to control misgovernment in the provinces (xii 54)
and gross abuse of justice (xi 1–3). Such are the evils that naturally arise under an absolute ruler whose character is in decay:
that of Claudius, we may conclude, had broken down within a
few years after his succession, as the routine of administration
wearied him and unrestrained sensuality exhausted his powers.

[1] The 'Consolatio ad Polybium,' written by Seneca before his recall from
exile.
[2] The 'Apocolocyntosis,' a satire written against Claudius, after his death,
for Nero's amusement.

liv

VI

PARTHIA AND ARMENIA

At the time of his assassination, Julius Caesar was preparing for a great expedition against Parthia, which seems to have been designed not only to avenge the disaster of Crassus at Carrhae in 53 B.C., but also to effect a great extension of Rome's possessions in the East. This scheme lapsed at his death, and advantage was taken of the unsettled state of things which ensued throughout the Roman world by the Parthian king Orodes, who sent an army of invasion into Syria, under his son Pacorus and the Roman exile Labienus. Decidius Saxa, legatus of Antony in Syria, was killed, and Syria, Palestine, and most of Asia Minor were overrun by the Parthians. This invasion seriously affected the power of Rome in the East for two years (41, 40 B.C.). But the campaigns of Ventidius Bassus, in 39 and 38 B.C., resulted in the recovery of the ground thus lost: Roman prestige was restored, and in Parthia itself there was a revolution, in which Orodes was murdered and his throne seized by his son Phraates.

Antony at this time, by his partition of the empire with Octavian, was in charge of the East, and was scheming to destroy the Parthian monarchy and build up for himself a great Oriental empire in its place. After lengthy preparations, he led a huge army of sixteen legions, late in 36 B.C., into Media; but his invasion was a complete failure, and he was in danger of utter disaster in the course of his retreat. Nor did he improve his prospects against Parthia by his action in Armenia in 34 B.C., when he seized its king Artavasdes, and took him prisoner to Alexandria on a charge of desertion in the previous year; for this thoroughly exasperated the Armenians whom he should have retained as allies, filling them with hatred and mistrust, and giving them ample grounds for that readiness which they showed for so long a period afterwards to intrigue with Parthia against Rome.

Antony never actively resumed his schemes against Parthia; his energies were becoming impaired, and the quarrel with Octavian was now developing. At the time of the Actian war internal

INTRODUCTION

disturbances in Parthia, fortunately for Rome, averted reprisals from that quarter; a temporary revolution had driven Phraates from his throne and had put a rival, Tiridates, in his place, and at the time of Octavian's success Phraates was only just recovering his position.

On succeeding to the undivided possession of the empire, Octavian took no steps to carry out Antony's grandiose schemes of conquest in the East, though circumstances made him heir to Antony's enmity with both Parthia and Armenia. But his army was in no condition to enter upon distant and difficult enterprises; the veterans were clamouring for their discharge and their rewards; while Octavian himself desired to settle his own position at home on a secure basis, and the questions arising on the European frontiers of his empire concerned him more nearly. He was content, for the present, to leave the states of Asia for the most part under the arrangements that he found prevailing: then he returned to Rome, and for several years was fully occupied with the settlement of the constitution, and the task of dealing with those parts of his European empire where Rome's hold was not fully secure[1].

At the same time, there was at the end of the Actian war a widespread feeling in Rome that the new ruler (now entitled Augustus) was to enter on a career of conquest in the East as well as the West. Passages in Vergil and Horace, published at this time, indicate a general expectation that Augustus was to bring both Parthia and Britain into the Roman empire[2]. However, so far as the East was concerned, Augustus avoided war; for the present there was no danger imminent, and he might later on improve Rome's position in the East by other means. There was always the prospect of sudden deposition, by internal revolution, of the Parthian and Armenian monarchs, and Augustus gave protection to refugee princes who might at some future occasion be installed in their stead and govern in the Roman interest. Thus he had,

[1] The formation of the province of Moesia, for the protection of Greece against the Dacians, the organization of Gaul, and campaigns in the Alps and in Spain, belong to this period.

[2] Hor. *Od.* iii 5, 4 ' praesens divus habebitur | Augustus adiectis Britannis | imperio gravibusque Persis.' Cf. also *Od.* i 2; 12; 29; ii 13; iii 2; 3; 6. Verg. *Georg.* iii 25.

apparently soon after Actium, received Tiridates in his flight from Phraates, and given him a home in the province of Syria. Other Eastern princes to whom Augustus gave asylum were the two sons of the late king Artavasdes, brothers of Artaxias now reigning in Armenia, whom he had found at Alexandria : these were Tigranes and another who is conjectured to be the Artavasdes mentioned in ii 4, 1. There was also Artavasdes the Median prince, who had supported Tiridates against Phraates, and had for a time been held in captivity by the latter. He escaped and fled to Augustus after Antony's downfall, and was set by him on the throne of Armenia Minor. A demand was made by Phraates in 23 B.C. that Tiridates should be given up to him, but Augustus refused to do this, though he sent back Phraates' own son, who when still an infant had been carried off by Tiridates in his flight. But in the year 20 B.C., Augustus visited Syria, and made with Phraates the agreement which his panegyrists represented as a virtual conquest of Parthia. Phraates restored the standards taken from Crassus, and became the friend of Rome, undertaking to give no support to neighbouring kingdoms in opposition to Rome. It was undoubtedly a triumph for Augustus' diplomacy, and brought Rome a great increase of prestige in Asia. Vergil and Horace celebrated the achievement in glowing terms, and Augustus himself represented Parthia as humbled and submissive [1].

At the same time Media was given to Ariobarzanes, son of the Median Artavasdes who had recently died at Rome. In regard to Armenia, Augustus had meant to invade that country and exact vengeance for the massacre of Romans perpetrated by Artaxias at the time of his accession, but no invasion in force proved necessary, as Artaxias was murdered by his relatives (ii 3, 3), and his brother Tigranes was accepted as king, and was instituted in his kingdom by Tiberius. This was represented by Augustus as equivalent to the capture of the country : coins bear the legend ' Armenia Capta ' or ' Recepta,' and he stated that though he might

---

[1] Verg. *Aen*. viii 726 ' Euphrates ibat iam mollior undis.' Cf. also *Aen.* vii 606. Hor. *Od.* iv 15, 7 ' (signa) derepta Parthorum superbis | postibus'; also *Od.* iv 5, 25; 14, 42. Augustus writes, ' Parthos . . . supplices amicitiam populi Romani petere coegi'; *Mon. Anc.* v 42.

have made Armenia a province he preferred to restore it to a native prince (*Mon. Anc.* v 24-8).

The settlement with Parthia proved fairly satisfactory. Phraates, Tacitus declares (ii 1, 2), henceforth showed marks of service and respect to Rome, and ten years later he sent his children to be brought up in Rome, an act which was of high importance, as providing a supply of Romanized princes for future vacancies on the throne of Parthia.

In Armenia, the rule of Tigranes seems to have been of but short duration. Evidently there was a strong body of resistance to Roman intervention, and it seems that, in spite of Augustus' agreement with Phraates, the anti-Roman factions in Armenia could obtain Parthian support. There were successive revolutions and changes of monarchs, the record of which is fragmentary and the chronology defective. It seems that Tigranes' rule soon came to an end, and then his son and daughter, Tigranes and Erato, married in the fashion of Oriental royalties, reigned as king and queen. They seem to have had support from Parthia, to the detriment of Artavasdes[1], whom the Romans favoured, and who for a short time took the throne at Augustus' bidding, but was again driven out, probably by Tigranes and Erato, on which occasion a number of Romans lost their lives (ii 4, 1). This may be the crisis which Tiberius was invited to go and settle, in 6 B.C., when he refused, insisting on going into retirement at Rhodes instead.

The situation in Armenia was not dealt with until 3 or 2 B.C., when Augustus began negotiating with the Parthians in protest against their intrigues in Armenia. About this time Artavasdes died, and then Tigranes requested Augustus to agree to his tenure of Armenia. Augustus told him to apply to Gaius Caesar, who was sent out to deal with affairs in the East in 1 B.C.; but before the meeting took place Tigranes died in a battle 'with barbarians' (Dio, lv 10, a), and, Erato abdicating, Gaius had to choose a new king. He appointed Ariobarzanes king of Media, son of the Median Artavasdes (see p. lvii), with the consent of the Armenians, as Tacitus states (ii 4, 2), but this consent was probably limited to the Romanizing party in Armenia, and there was armed opposition from the other,

---

[1] Perhaps the third son of the Artavasdes seized by Antony; see p. lv.

PARTHIA AND ARMENIA

the pro-Parthian, faction, and Gaius, trying to enforce his creation of Ariobarzanes by attacking his opponents at Artagira, incurred the wound which ended in his death in 4 A.D.

We learn from the 'Monumentum Ancyranum' that when Ariobarzanes died, the Armenians rebelled against his son, another Artavasdes, and killed him, on which Augustus nominated as their king the Tigranes who is mentioned in vi 40, 2. This Tigranes, however, was not able to maintain his position, and Erato became queen again, but not for long; the throne remained vacant until Vonones, driven from Parthia by Artabanus in 10 or 11 A.D., was for a short time accepted as their king by the Armenians.

This Vonones was one of the sons of Phraates who, as was mentioned above, had been sent to be brought up at Rome. Phraates had been murdered, and his throne taken, by his natural son Phraataces, about 2 B.C.: he was followed by Orodes, who was assassinated in 7 or 8 A.D., and then the Parthian nobles applied to Augustus to send them one of Phraates' sons, and it was in response to this that Vonones was made king of Parthia. But his Romanized ways made him unpopular with the leading nobles in his own country ; a plot was formed against him, and Artabanus was made king in his stead, in 10 or 11 A.D. This man on his mother's side was of the royal family of the Arsacidae, but on his father's side probably a Dahan (see vi 42, 4; 36, 5).

Artabanus enjoyed a long reign, ruling till 40 A.D., and soon after his accession insisted on the Romans withdrawing their support from Vonones. The latter was removed from Armenia, and given a home in Syria : but, at the time of Germanicus' mission to the East, in 18 A.D., he was sent away to Cilicia in deference to Artabanus' wishes, and, attempting to escape back to Armenia, was killed by his Roman guards.

Germanicus received from Artabanus a renewal of the agreement of Parthia with Rome, and, proceeding into Armenia, instituted on the throne Zeno, son of Polemo king of Pontus, a prince who was the object of the national choice of the Armenians, and who now, under the name of Artaxias, held till his death, some sixteen years later, the throne which had stood vacant since the removal of Vonones. During this time there are no troubles recorded between Rome and Armenia, but by the time of the death of Artaxias,

INTRODUCTION

Artabanus had abandoned his policy of deference to Rome, and now took occasion to challenge Rome's direction of the succession to the throne of Armenia by seizing it for his son Arsaces, arrogantly announcing his intention to reassert his authority as Parthian monarch over all the possessions 'once held by Cyrus and Alexander' (vi 31).

The events which followed need not be further described here, as the manner in which Tiberius dealt with the crisis is described towards the end of Book vi (chaps. 31-44). Mithridates, established by the Romans as king of Armenia, was able to maintain his position, and, before the death of Tiberius, Artabanus had been forced by Vitellius to make submission and homage, and to deliver his son as a hostage.

This settlement was upset by Gaius, who summoned Mithridates to Rome and imprisoned him, leaving Artabanus once more master of the situation in Armenia. However, on Artabanus' death civil war arose between his sons, and the whole Parthian empire was so much disturbed by this that Claudius was able to reinstate Mithridates in Armenia in the face of Parthian opposition, at some date not later than 43 A.D. (xi 8).

For subsequent events in the East reference should be made to the narrative in the text of Books xi and xii.

VII

THE CONQUEST OF BRITAIN UNDER CLAUDIUS

The conquest of Britain had undoubtedly been regarded by Julius Caesar as the natural complement of the subjugation of Gaul, since Britain was a source of reinforcement to the Gallic resistance to Rome, and Roman literature, about the time of the battle of Actium, shows that there was then a general idea that Augustus was meditating the achievement of this exploit as a legacy from the divine Julius. But as time went on, Augustus dropped the project : there was no serious danger now to be feared from Gaul, and work more pressing occupied him nearer home. Friendly relations, however, were secured by negotiation, and by the end of

CONQUEST OF BRITAIN

Augustus' reign the island had, according to Strabo, become entirely friendly to Rome. The same relations continued under Tiberius. This was due no doubt to the policy of Cunobelinus, king of the Catuvellauni, whose authority was paramount over the south-eastern portion of the island, and whose long reign continued from the latter years of Augustus to the beginning of the reign of Claudius.

Claudius' determination to annex Britain was occasioned by the unsettled state of things arising upon the death of Cunobelinus, when the chiefs who succeeded to his power were hostile to Rome. Adminius, one of the late king's sons, had fled to Gaius, and there was also Bericus, who was a suppliant to Claudius pressing for reinstatement. The imperial policy required either that Britain should be under a king acknowledging the protectorate of Rome, or that it should become a province. Caratacus, who had succeeded to Cunobelinus' position, was hostile to Roman dictation ; and the prospect of extending the Roman dominions across the Ocean and winning a triumph for the achievement had an irresistible appeal to Claudius' vanity.

The expedition, which was sent in the third year of Claudius' reign (43 A.D.), was well and adequately organized. The numbers and quality of the troops were such as to ensure success. Four seasoned legions were taken for the purpose, three from Germany and one from Pannonia : their numbers may be estimated as from twenty to twenty-five thousand, and the army would contain besides rather more than double that number of auxiliaries. The officers were eminent and able. At the head of the army was Aulus Plautius Silvanus, 'a senator of the highest reputation' (Dio), consul fourteen years before, at some time legatus of Delmatia, and now probably transferred from one of the highest provincial appointments. Among his subordinates was Vespasian, so far of only praetorian rank, and acting as legatus of the Second Legion, marked out for future eminence by his successes in the ensuing campaign ; there were also Flavius Sabinus, Vespasian's brother, the city prefect of 69 A.D., and Hosidius Geta, who had fought with success in Mauretania. In the personal train of Claudius came Servius Sulpicius Galba, the subsequent emperor, M. Licinius Crassus Frugi, a consular of long standing, the senator Valerius Asiaticus, and Ti. Plautius Silvanus Aelianus, distinguished subsequently for his achievements in Moesia.

INTRODUCTION

For the events of the invasion we have only the narrative in Dio, meagre in detail and vague in its geography. It appears that the British resistance was headed by Caratacus and Togodumnus, who had lately succeeded to their father's kingdom. Early in the campaign a tribe called the Boduni submitted, and received a Roman garrison in their midst. Then the Roman army in its onward march had to fight a two-days battle for the passage of a river[1] which barred their way, after which the barbarians fell back north of the Thames, where they still threatened a vigorous resistance under the leadership of Caratacus, Togodumnus having fallen.

Plautius halted on the bank of the Thames, where he waited for the emperor to come with reinforcements, no doubt occupying the interval in settling the districts through which he had marched. When Claudius arrived, the Roman army crossed the Thames, defeated the Britons and marched on to the chief city of the Catuvellauni, Camulodunum, which they occupied. Caratacus escaped, and we find him a few years later the leading spirit in the resistance of the Silures; but his dominion passed into the hands of the Romans, and in other places British princes made their submission. Among these was Prasutagus, king of the Iceni, who made a treaty with the Romans which would secure the new province from attack from the north; while in the south-east a native prince Cogidubnus was entrusted with a kingdom extending over the Regni (in Sussex) and including the town at Chichester.

In the remaining three years of his command, Plautius completed the subjugation of Cunobelinus' kingdom, while to Vespasian was given the task of settling its western portion. By Vespasian's operations the country from Hampshire, including the Isle of Wight (Vectis), was subdued as far as the Mendips; so that now the new province of Britain may be regarded as that part of England which lies south of a line from Gloucester to Colchester. These two places would be the main fortified camps on the frontier; Verulamium would be an intermediate post; and Londinium a place of support in the rear.

We recover the narrative of Tacitus for the events in Britain from

[1] This was probably the Medway. The Romans would have landed on the coast of Kent, and their march would be directed towards the Thames, with Camulodunum as their ultimate goal.

47 A. D., when P. Ostorius Scapula succeeded Plautius, but the subject is not presented in clear detail, and only a rough summary of the events can be made. On his arrival, the new legatus had to deal with raids upon the new province from the unsubdued parts of Britain, and to check these he annexed a further portion from what is now included in the Midland counties. This excited alarm among the Iceni on the east, the Brigantes in the north, and the Silures in the west; and in the last-named quarter a long and bitter struggle began. The Silures had now for their leader the fugitive Caratacus, and for three years he conducted a skilfu resistance to the Romans in the counties along the eastern borders of Wales. At the end of this period, in 51 A.D., the strife was ended by a great pitched battle (described in xii 33–35), the site of which is a matter of conjecture (xii 33, 2). This resulted in the complete defeat of the Britons, the capture of Caratacus' brothers, and the subsequent surrender of the person of Caratacus himself. But the resistance of the Silures was not finally overcome. A permanent camp for the Second Legion was now made at Isca Silurum (Caerleon-on-Usk), and the position was maintained with difficulty and at the cost of several reverses (xii 38–40). Moreover, the hostility of the Brigantes now became acute, and one of their princes, Venutius, came to the front as the Britons' most skilful national leader.

At an early stage in these renewed hostilities, Ostorius died, and during the next six years, under the government of Didius Gallus and then of Veranius, no accession of territory was effected, but in all probability the administration and the defence of the districts already gained were systematically organized. At the close of Claudius' reign, then, the condition of Roman Britain may be briefly described as follows : Isca and Venta (Caerwent) were held with strong garrisons as posts against the Silures ; Viroconium (Wroxeter), against the Ordovices who occupied North Wales ; Deva (Chester) and Lindum (Lincoln) confronted the Brigantes. Each of these places (except Venta) was the head-quarters of a legion, and all were connected with each other and with their bases of support in the south-east by the Foss Way[1] and the Watling

[1] The Watling Street ran from London to Viroconium; the Foss Way from Lindum to Aquae Sulis (Bath).

Street, with their subsidiary branches. The principal town of the province was Camulodunum, the former capital of Cunobelinus' kingdom. Here, in the period of Ostorius' government, a Roman colony was settled (xii 32, 5), and the place became the seat of a large and flourishing Romanized population. Further south, Londinium already enjoyed a considerable commercial importance.

VIII (1). A. DESCENDANTS OF AUGUSTUS.

C. Octavius $=$ Scribonia.
(Caesar Augustus)

M. Vipsanius Agrippa $=$ Julia I.

- C. Caesar, *d.* 4 A.D., L. Caesar, *d.* 2 A.D., Julia II, *m.* L. Aemilius Paullus.
  - M. Aemilius Lepidus.
  - Aemilia Lepida, *m.* M. Junius Silanus.
    - M. Silanus, *d.* 54 A.D.
    - L. Silanus, *d.* 49 A.D.
    - D. Silanus, *d.* 64 A.D.
    - Junia Calvina.
    - Junia Lepida.
      - L. Silanus, *d.* 65 A.D.
- Agrippina I, *m.* Germanicus II.
  - Nero Caesar, *m.* Julia, granddaughter of Tiberius.
  - Drusus Caesar, *m.* Aemilia Lepida.
  - Gaius, the Emperor 'Caligula.'
  - Agrippina II, *m.* Cn. Domitius Ahenobarbus.
    - L. Domitius, the Emperor **Nero.**
  - Drusilla.
  - Julia, or **Livilla.**
- Agrippa Postumus, *d.* 14 A.D.

B. DESCENDANTS OF OCTAVIA, SISTER OF AUGUSTUS.

Octavia $=$ M. Antonius (triumvir).

- Antonia ma. *m.* L. Domitius Ahenobarbus.
  - Cn. Domitius Ahenobarbus, *m.* Agrippina II.
    - **L. Domitius (the Emperor Nero).**
- Antonia mi. *m.* Claudius Drusus (Germanicus I).
  - Germanicus Caesar (Germanicus II) *m.* Agrippina I.
    - Three sons, including the Emperor **Gaius.** See Stem **A.**
    - Three daughters, including Agrippina II, mother of **Nero.**

VIII (2). C. THE CLAUDIAN CAESARS.

Ti. Claudius Caesar, descended from Appius Claudius Caecus, *d.* 33 B.C. = Livia Drusilla (afterwards and wife of Augustus).

Ti. Claudius Nero = Julia, daughter (the Emperor Tiberius) of Augustus.

Antonia mi. = Nero Claudius Drusus (Germanicus I)

Vipsania Agrippina = Ti. Claudius Nero (the Emperor Tiberius)

Drusus Caesar, *m.* Livia, dr. of Antonia mi.

Two sons who died young.

Julia,
m. (1). Nero Caesar, by whom she had no issue; see Stem A.
(2). C. Rubellius Blandus, by whom she was mother of Rubellius Plautus.

Germanicus Caesar (Germanicus II), *m.* Agrippina I. See Stem A.

Livia, *m.* Drusus, son of the Emperor Tiberius.

Ti. Claudius Drusus Nero Germanicus (the Emperor Claudius).

The Emperor Claudius married—
(1) Plautia Urgulanilla; mother of two children who died young.
(2) Aelia Paetina; mother of Claudia Antonia, *d.* 66 A.D.
(3) Valeria Messalina; mother of (*a*) Octavia, who married Nero, and was murdered by him in 62 A.D. (*b*) Ti. Claudius Britannicus, murdered by Nero in 55 A.D.
(4) Agrippina II.

SUMMARY OF CONTENTS

BOOK V

BOOK VI

to take refuge with the Scythians. 37. Advance of Tiridates, supported by Vitellius, into Mesopotamia.

Ch. 38. Death of Fulcinius Trio and other persons. 39. Tiberius near Rome ; death and character of Poppaeus Sabinus.

A. U. C. 789, A. D. 36. Q. Plautius, Sex. Papinius Allenius, coss.

40. Death of Tigranes, once king of Armenia, Aemilia Lepida, wife of Drusus, and others. 41. Suppression of a rising of the Cietae in Cappadocia.

Ch. 42-44. Further account of affairs in the East.
42. Tiridates received at Seleucia, and crowned king at Ctesiphon by the Surena. 43. Some of the nobles form a new plot to restore Artabanus. 44. Artabanus collects troops and advances rapidly ; retreat of Tiridates, who is deserted by all, and takes refuge in Syria.
45. Great loss by fire in Rome ; munificence of Tiberius.

A. U. C. 790, A. D. 37. Cn. Acerronius Proculus, C. Petronius Pontius Nigrinus, coss.

Ch. 46. Tiberius aware of the court paid by Macro to Gaius ; his hesitation to name an heir, and prediction to Gaius. 47. Albucilla charged with crimes in which Domitius, Vibius Marsus, and Arruntius are involved. 48. Suicide of Arruntius ; Albucilla imprisoned. 49. Suicide of Sex. Papinius.

Ch. 50, 51. Last moments and death of Tiberius.
50. His failing health and last journey to Misenum ; advice of Charicles, and measures taken by Gaius and Macro ; circumstances of his death (March 16) in the seventy-eighth year of his age. 15. Vicissitudes of his life ; his character at various periods.

BOOK XI

A. U. C. 800, A. D. 47. Ti. Claudius Caesar Aug. Germanicus IV, L. Vitellius III, coss.

Ch. 1-4. Persons destroyed through the influence of Messalina.
1-3. Valerius Asiaticus accused by Suillius and Sosibius : his acquittal prevented by a device of Vitellius : he commits suicide. 4. Two knights named Petra condemned on pretext of a dream : rewards given to the accusers.

Ch. 5-7. Discussion respecting the payment of fees to advocates : a limit of ten sestertia imposed.

SUMMARY OF CONTENTS

Ch. 8–10. Affairs in the East.

8. The Parthians, alienated by the cruelty of Gotarzes, call in Vardanes, who besieges Seleucia. 9. Mithridates, who had been imprisoned by Gaius, is sent out by Claudius and recovers Armenia : Gotarzes and Vardanes make terms, the former retiring in favour of the latter : Seleucia surrendered. 10. Gotarzes renews hostilities and is defeated, but returns to the throne on the death of Vardanes.

Ch. 11–15. Affairs at Rome.

11. Ludi saeculares held : young L. Domitius wins popular favour. 12. Messalina diverted from attacking Agrippina and Domitius by her new passion for Silius. 13. Censorial edicts of Claudius : new letters added by him to the alphabet. 14. Digression on the origin and history of letters. 15. A college of haruspices founded.

Ch. 16–21. Affairs in Germany.

16, 17. Italicus, son of Flavus, the brother of Arminius, sent from Rome to be king of the Cherusci : he meets with various fortune at their hands. 18. Corbulo, appointed legatus of Lower Germany, restores the discipline of the army, and repels the Chauci from the province. 19, 20. He imposes terms on the Frisii, and plans an expedition against the Chauci maiores, but is recalled by Claudius, and makes a canal between the Maas and Rhine. 21. Curtius Rufus opens mines in Upper Germany : his origin and history described.

Ch. 22. Nonius, a knight, found with arms in the emperor's presence : candidates for the quaestorship obliged to give gladiatorial shows : origin and history of that magistracy.

A. U. C. 801, A. D. 48. A. Vitellius, L. Vipstanus Poplicola, coss.

Ch. 23, 24. Debate on admitting citizens from Gallia Comata to the 'ius honorum' : speech of Claudius on the subject.

Ch. 25. New patrician families created : unworthy senators removed : a lustrum held, and the number of citizens enumerated.

Ch. 26–38. Last excesses and death of Messalina.

26, 27. Silius urges Messalina to celebrate marriage with him : opportunity taken of the emperor's absence at Ostia. 28, 29. Alarm of the chief freedmen : Narcissus alone takes immediate action. 30. Claudius informed of the marriage by two women and Narcissus. 31. Advice given to Claudius : representation by Messalina of a vintage festival. 32. News of the approach of Claudius disperses the guests, most of whom are arrested. 33. Bold course taken by Narcissus. 34. Claudius refuses to see Messalina and the children. 35, 36. Narcissus takes him to the house of Silius and thence to the praetorian camp ; where Silius and the other chief persons, also Mnester the actor, are executed. 37, 38. Messalina goes back to the gardens of Lucullus ; where her mother joins her. Narcissus, fearing a change of purpose in Claudius, gives orders in his name for her execution, and allows him to suppose that she had committed suicide. Her memory condemned by the senate, and Narcissus rewarded.

BOOK XII

SUMMARY OF CONTENTS

procurator of Cappadocia, bribed by Radamistus to support him in seizing Armenia. 50, 51. Vologeses sets up his brother Tiridates as king of Armenia, and invades the country. Radamistus at length forced to fly: his wife Zenobia saved from death and taken captive.

A. U. C. 805, A. D. 52.   Faustus Cornelius Sulla Felix, L. Salvius Otho Titianus, coss.

Ch. 52. Furius Camillus Scribonianus exiled: astrologers expelled from Italy. 53. Honours decreed to Pallas. 54. His brother Felix procurator of Judaea and Samaria. 55. Rebellion of the Clitae in Cilicia put down by king Antiochus. 56, 57. Ceremony of opening the tunnel made to drain lake Fucinus: Agrippina blames Narcissus for the failure of the work.

A. U. C. 806, A. D. 53.   D. Iunius Silanus, Q. Haterius Antoninus, coss.

Ch. 58. Marriage of Nero to Octavia: his speeches for Ilium and Bononia: freedom given back to Rhodes. 59. Suicide of Statilius Taurus under a false charge got up by Agrippina. 60. Judicial authority of procurators established: contrast with previous enactments. 61. Immunity given to the people of Cos. 62, 63. Remission of tribute granted to the Byzantines.

A. U. C. 807, A. D. 54.   M. Asinius Marcellus, M.' Acilius Aviola, coss.

Ch. 64–69. Agrippina resolves to kill Claudius.
64. Prodigies announced: Agrippina, conscious of her danger, causes the death of Domitia Lepida. 65. Narcissus boldly takes up the cause of Britannicus. 66, 67. He is obliged by illness to leave Rome: Agrippina profits by his absence to poison Claudius by the help of Locusta and Xenophon. 68, 69. Oct. 13. The death of Claudius kept secret till all arrangements were made: Nero saluted as imperator by the soldiers and confirmed by the senate: funeral and deification of Claudius.

BRITANNIA

Orkneys

CALEDONIA

Boresti

F. of Forth

F. of Clyde

Luguvallium

HIBERNIA

BRIGANTES

Monapia

Eburacum

Mona

Lindum

Deva

ORDOVICES

Viroconium

ICENI

Severn

SILURES

Glevum

Camulodunum

Isca

Verulamium

TRINOVANTES

Calleva

Thames

Aqua Sulis

Londinium
Durovernum

Rutupiae

Venta

Dubrae

CANTII

Portus Lemanae

Clausentum

GALLIC SEA

B. V. Darbishire, Oxford, 1907.

Scale

0   100   English Miles

Hispania

Hibernia

Caledonia

Britannia

Germania

Gallia

Britain and surrounding countries
as imagined by Tacitus

ANNALES

V, VI, XI, XII

LIBER V. FRAGMENTUM.

1. RUBELLIO ET FUFIO consulibus, quorum utrique Geminus cognomentum erat, Iulia Augusta mortem obiit, aetate extrema, nobilitatis per Claudiam familiam et adoptione 2 Liviorum Iuliorumque clarissimae. primum ei matrimonium et liberi fuere cum Tiberio Nerone, qui bello Perusino pro- 10 fugus, pace inter Sex. Pompeium ac triumviros pacta in 3 urbem rediit. exim Caesar cupidine formae aufert marito, incertum an invitam, adeo properus ut ne spatio quidem ad 4 enitendum dato penatibus suis gravidam induxerit. nullam posthac subolem edidit, sed sanguini Augusti per coniunc- 15 tionem Agrippinae et Germanici adnexa communes prone- 5 potes habuit. sanctitate domus priscum ad morem, comis ultra quam antiquis feminis probatum, mater inpotens, uxor facilis et cum artibus mariti, simulatione filii bene composita. 6 funus eius modicum, testamentum diu inritum fuit. laudata 20 est pro rostris a Gaio Caesare pronepote, qui mox rerum potitus est.

2. At Tiberius, quod supremis in matrem officiis defuisset, nihil mutata amoenitate vitae, magnitudinem negotiorum per

litteras excusavit, honoresque memoriae eius ab senatu large
decretos quasi per modestiam imminuit, paucis admodum
receptis et addito ne caelestis religio decerneretur : sic ipsam
maluisse.   quin et parte eiusdem epistulae increpuit ami- 2
5 citias muliebres, Fufium consulem oblique perstringens. is 3
gratia Augustae floruerat, aptus adliciendis feminarum
animis, dicax idem et Tiberium acerbis facetiis inridere
solitus, quarum apud praepotentes in longum memoria est.

3. Ceterum ex eo praerupta iam et urguens dominatio ;
10 nam incolumi Augusta erat adhuc perfugium, quia Tiberio
inveteratum erga matrem obsequium, neque Seianus audebat
auctoritati parentis antire : tunc velut frenis exsoluti pro- 2
ruperunt, missaeque in Agrippinam ac Neronem litterae, quas
pridem adlatas et cohibitas ab Augusta credidit vulgus ;
15 haud enim multo post mortem eius recitatae sunt.   verba 3
inerant quaesita asperitate ; sed non arma, non rerum
novarum studium, amores iuvenum et inpudicitiam nepoti
obiectabat.   in nurum ne id quidem confingere ausus, 4
adrogantiam oris et contumacem animum incusavit, magno
20 senatus pavore ac silentio, donec pauci, quis nulla ex
honesto spes (et publica mala singulis in occasionem gratiae
trahuntur), ut referretur postulavere, promptissimo Cotta
Messalino cum atroci sententia.   sed aliis a primoribus 5
maximeque a magistratibus trepidabatur : quippe Tiberius
25 etsi infense invectus cetera ambigua reliquerat.

4. Fuit in senatu Iunius Rusticus, conponendis patrum
actis delectus a Caesare, eoque meditationes eius introspicere creditus.   is fatali quodam motu (neque enim ante 2
specimen constantiae dederat) seu prava sollertia, dum im-
30 minentium oblitus incerta pavet, inserere se dubitantibus ac
monere consules ne relationem inciperent ; disserebatque
brevibus momentis summa verti ; posse quandoque *domus*
Germanici exitium paenitentiae *esse* seni.   simul populus 3

effigies Agrippinae ac Neronis gerens circumsistit curiam
faustisque in Caesarem ominibus falsas litteras et principe
4 invito exitium domui eius intendi clamitat.   ita nihil triste
illo die patratum. ferebantur etiam sub nominibus consularium fictae in Seianum sententiae, exercentibus plerisque 5
5 per occultum atque eo procacius libidinem ingeniorum. unde
illi ira violentior et materies criminandi : spretum dolorem
principis ab senatu, descivisse populum ; audiri iam et legi
novas contiones, nova patrum consulta ; quid reliquum nisi
ut caperent ferrum et, quorum imagines pro vexillis secuti 10
forent, duces imperatoresque deligerent ?

   5. Igitur Caesar repetitis adversum nepotem et nurum
probris increpitaque per edictum plebe, questus apud patres
quod fraude unius senatoris imperatoria maiestas elusa
2 publice foret, integra tamen sibi cuncta postulavit. nec ultra 15
deliberatum quo minus non quidem extrema decernerent
(id enim vetitum), sed paratos ad ultionem vi principis im-
pediri testarentur.

LIBER VI.

V. 6 (VI. 1). . . . . Quattuor et quadraginta orationes
super ea re habitae, ex quis ob metum paucae, plures adsuetudine . . . 'mihi pudorem aut Seiano invidiam adlaturum censui. versa est fortuna, et ille quidem, qui collegam 2
5 et generum adsciverat, sibi ignoscit : ceteri, quem per dedecora fovere, cum scelere insectantur. miserius sit ob 3
amicitiam accusari an amicum accusare, haud discreverim.
non crudelitatem, non clementiam cuiusquam experiar, sed 4
liber et mihi ipsi probatus antibo periculum. vos obtestor 5
10 ne memoriam nostri per maerorem quam laeti retineatis,
adiciendo me quoque iis qui fine egregio publica mala
effugerunt.'

V. 7 (VI. 2). Tunc singulos, ut cuique adsistere, adloqui
animus erat, retinens aut dimittens partem diei absumpsit,
15 multoque adhuc coetu et cunctis intrepidum vultum eius
spectantibus, cum superesse tempus novissimis crederent,
gladio quem sinu abdiderat incubuit. neque Caesar ullis 2
criminibus aut probris defunctum insectatus est, cum in
Blaesum multa foedaque incusavisset.

20 **V. 8** (VI. 3). Relatum inde de P. Vitellio et Pomponio
Secundo. illum indices arguebant claustra aerarii, cui praefectus erat, et militarem pecuniam rebus novis obtulisse ;
huic a Considio praetura functo obiectabatur Aelii Galli
amicitia, qui punito Seiano in hortos Pomponii quasi fidissi-
25 mum ad subsidium perfugisset. neque aliud periclitantibus 2
auxilii quam in fratrum constantia fuit, qui vades exstitere.
mox crebris prolationibus spem ac metum iuxta gravatus 3
Vitellius petito per speciem studiorum scalpro levem ictum

4 venis intulit vitamque aegritudine animi finivit. at Pomponius multa morum elegantia et ingenio inlustri, dum
adversam fortunam aequus tolerat, Tiberio superstes fuit.

V. 9 (VI. 4). Placitum posthac ut in reliquos Seiani
liberos adverteretur, vanescente quamquam plebis ira ac 5
2 plerisque per priora supplicia lenitis. igitur portantur in
carcerem, filius imminentium intellegens, puella adeo nescia,
ut crebro interrogaret, quod ob delictum et quo traheretur;
neque facturam ultra, et posse se puerili verbere moneri.
3 tradunt temporis eius auctores, quia triumvirali supplicio 10
adfici virginem inauditum habebatur, a carnifice laqueum
iuxta conpressam; exim oblisis faucibus id aetatis corpora
in Gemonias abiecta.

V. 10 (VI. 5). Per idem tempus Asia atque Achaia exter-
ritae sunt acri magis quam diuturno rumore, Drusum Ger- 15
manici filium apud Cycladas insulas, mox in continenti visum.
2 et erat iuvenis haud dispari aetate, quibusdam Caesaris
libertis velut adgnitus; per dolumque comitantibus adlicie-
bantur ignari fama nominis et promptis Graecorum animis ad
nova et mira. quippe elapsum custodiae pergere ad paternos 20
exercitus, Aegyptum aut Suriam invasurum, fingebant simul
3 credebantque. iam iuventutis concursu, iam publicis studiis
frequentabatur, laetus praesentibus et inanium spe, cum
auditum id Poppaeo Sabino: is Macedoniae tum intentus
4 Achaiam quoque curabat. igitur quo vera seu falsa antiret, 25
Toronaeum Thermaeumque sinum praefestinans, mox Eu-
boeam Aegaei maris insulam et Piraeum Atticae orae, dein
Corinthiense litus angustiasque Isthmi evadit; marique
Ionio Nicopolim Romanam coloniam ingressus, ibi demum
cognoscit sollertius interrogatum, quisnam foret, dixisse 30
M. Silano genitum, et multis sectatorum dilapsis ascendisse
5 navem tamquam Italiam peteret. scripsitque haec Tiberio,
neque nos originem finemve eius rei ultra comperimus.

V. 11 (VI. 6). Exitu anni diu aucta discordia consulum
erupit. nam Trio, facilis capessendis inimicitiis et foro
exercitus, ut segnem Regulum ad opprimendos Seiani ministros oblique perstrinxerat: ille, nisi lacesseretur, modestiae 2
5 retinens, non modo rettudit collegam, sed ut noxium coniurationis ad disquisitionem trahebat. multisque patrum 3
orantibus ponerent odia in perniciem itura, mansere infensi
ac minitantes, donec magistratu abirent.

VI. 1 (7). Cn. Domitius et Camillus Scribonianus con-
10 sulatum inierant, cum Caesar tramisso quod Capreas et
Surrentum interluit freto Campaniam praelegebat, ambiguus
an urbem intraret, seu, quia contra destinaverat, speciem
venturi simulans. et saepe in propinqua degressus, aditis 2
iuxta Tiberim hortis, saxa rursum et solitudinem maris
15 repetiit, pudore scelerum et libidinum, quibus adeo indomitis
exarserat, ut more regio pubem ingenuam stupris pollueret.
nec formam tantum et decora corpora, set in his modestam 3
pueritiam, in aliis imagines maiorum incitamentum cupidinis
habebat. praepositique servi, qui conquirerent pertraherent, 5
20 dona in promptos, minas adversum abnuentes, et si retinerent
propinquus aut parens, vim raptus suaque ipsi libita velut in
captos exercebant.

2 (8). At Romae principio anni, quasi recens cognitis
Liviae flagitiis ac non pridem etiam punitis, atroces sententiae
25 dicebantur, in effigies quoque ac memoriam eius, et bona
Seiani ablata aerario ut in fiscum cogerentur, tamquam
referret. Scipiones haec et Silani et Cassii isdem ferme aut 2
paulum inmutatis verbis, adseveratione multa censebant, cum
repente Togonius Gallus, dum ignobilitatem suam magnis
30 nominibus inserit, per deridiculum auditur. nam principem 3
orabat deligere senatores, ex quis viginti sorte ducti et ferro
accincti, quotiens curiam inisset, salutem eius defenderent

4 crediderat nimirum epistulae subsidio sibi alterum ex con-
5 sulibus poscentis, ut tutus a Capreis urbem peteret. Tiberius
tamen, ludibria seriis permiscere solitus, egit gratis benevolentiae patrum : sed quos omitti posse, quos deligi ? semperne
eosdem an subinde alios ? et honoribus perfunctos an iuvenes, 5
privatos an e magistratibus ? quam deinde speciem fore
sumentium in limine curiae gladios ? neque sibi vitam tanti,
6 si armis tegenda foret. haec adversus Togonium verbis
moderans, neque *ut* ultra abolitionem sententiae suaderet.

3 (9). At Iunium Gallionem, qui censuerat ut praetoriani 10
actis stipendiis ius apiscerentur in quattuordecim ordinibus
sedendi, violenter increpuit, velut coram rogitans, quid illi
cum militibus, quos neque dicta [imperatoris] neque praemia
2 nisi ab imperatore accipere par esset. repperisse prorsus
quod divus Augustus non providerit : an potius discordiam 15
et seditionem a satellite Seiani quaesitam, qua rudes animos
nomine honoris ad corrumpendum militiae morem pro-
3 pelleret ? hoc pretium Gallio meditatae adulationis tulit,
statim curia, deinde Italia exactus ; et quia incusabatur facile
toleraturus exilium delecta Lesbo, insula nobili et amoena, 20
retrahitur in urbem custoditurque domibus magistratuum.
4 isdem litteris Caesar Sextium Paconianum praetorium perculit
magno patrum gaudio, audacem, maleficum, omnium secreta
rimantem delectumque ab Seiano cuius ope dolus Gaio
5 Caesari pararetur. quod postquam patefactum, prorupere 25
concepta pridem odia, et summum supplicium decernebatur,
ni professus indicium foret.

4 (10). Ut vero Latinium Latiarem ingressus est, accusator
ac reus iuxta invisi gratissimum spectaculum praebebant.
Latiaris, ut rettuli, praecipuus olim circumveniendi Titii 30
2 Sabini et tunc luendae poenae primus fuit. inter quae
Haterius Agrippa consules anni prioris invasit, cur mutua

F

accusatione intenta nunc silerent: metum prorsus et noxae
conscientiam pro foedere haberi ; at non patribus reticenda
quae audivissent. Regulus manere tempus ultionis, seque 3
coram principe exsecuturum; Trio aemulationem inter
5 collegas et si qua discordes iecissent melius oblitterari
respondit. urguente Agrippa Sanquinius Maximus e con- 4
sularibus oravit senatum, ne curas imperatoris conquisitis
insuper acerbitatibus augerent: sufficere ipsum statuendis
remediis. sic Regulo salus et Trioni dilatio exitii quaesita.
10 Haterius invisior fuit, quia somno aut libidinosis vigiliis 5
marcidus et ob segnitiam quamvis crudelem principem non
metuens inlustribus viris perniciem inter ganeam ac stupra
meditabatur.

    5 (11). Exim Cotta Messalinus, saevissimae cuiusque
15 sententiae auctor eoque inveterata invidia, ubi primum
facultas data, arguitur pleraque *in* C. Caesarem quasi incertae virilitatis, et cum die natali Augustae inter sacerdotes
epularetur, novendialem eam cenam dixisse; querensque
de potentia M'. Lepidi ac L. Arruntii, cum quibus ob rem
20 pecuniariam disceptabat, addidisse: 'illos quidem senatus,
me autem tuebitur Tiberiolus meus.' quae cuncta a pri- 2
moribus civitatis revincebatur, iisque instantibus ad imperatorem provocavit. nec multo post litterae adferuntur,
quibus in modum defensionis, repetito inter se atque Cottam
25 amicitiae principio crebrisque eius officiis commemoratis, ne
verba prave detorta neu convivalium fabularum simplicitas
in crimen duceretur postulavit.

    6 (12). Insigne visum est earum Caesaris litterarum
initium ; nam his verbis exorsus est: 'quid scribam vobis,
30 patres conscripti, aut quo modo scribam aut quid omnino
non scribam hoc tempore, di me deaeque peius perdant
quam perire me cotidie sentio, si scio.' adeo facinora atque 2
flagitia sua ipsi quoque in supplicium verterant. neque

frustra praestantissimus sapientiae firmare solitus est, si
recludantur tyrannorum mentes, posse aspici laniatus et
ictus, quando ut corpora verberibus, ita saevitia, libidine,
3 malis consultis animus dilaceretur.   quippe Tiberium non
fortuna, non solitudines protegebant quin tormenta pectoris 5
suasque ipse poenas fateretur.

   7 (13). Tum facta patribus potestate statuendi de *C.*
Caeciliano senatore, qui plurima adversum Cottam prompserat, placitum eandem poenam inrogari quam in Aruseium
et Sanquinium, accusatores L. Arruntii; quo non aliud 10
honorificentius Cottae evenit, qui nobilis quidem, set egens
ob luxum, per flagitia infamis, sanctissimis Arruntii artibus
dignitate ultionis aequabatur.
2 Q. Servaeus posthac et Minucius Thermus inducti,
Servaeus praetura functus et quondam Germanici comes, 15
Minucius equestri loco, modeste habita Seiani amicitia;
3 unde illis maior miseratio.   contra Tiberius praecipuos ad
scelera increpans admonuit C. Cestium patrem dicere senatui
4 quae sibi scripsisset, suscepitque Cestius accusationem.   quod
maxime exitiabile tulere illa tempora, cum primores senatus 20
infimas etiam delationes exercerent, alii propalam, multi per
occultum; neque discerneres alienos a coniunctis, amicos
ab ignotis, quid repens aut vetustate obscurum: perinde in
foro, in convivio, quaqua de re locuti incusabantur, ut quis
praevenire et reum destinare properat, pars ad subsidium sui, 25
5 plures infecti quasi valetudine et contactu.   sed Minucius et
Servaeus damnati indicibus accessere.   tractique sunt in
casum eundem Iulius Africanus e Santonis Gallica civitate,
6 Seius Quadratus: originem non repperi.   neque sum ignarus
a plerisque scriptoribus omissa multorum pericula et poenas, 30
dum copia fatiscunt aut, quae ipsis nimia et maesta fuerant,
ne pari taedio lecturos adficerent verentur: nobis pleraque
digna cognitu obvenere, quamquam ab aliis incelebrata.

8 (14). Nam ea tempestate, qua Seiani amicitiam ceteri
falso exuerant, ausus est eques Romanus M. Terentius, ob
id reus, amplecti, ad hunc modum apud senatum ordiendo :
'fortunae quidem meae fortasse minus expediat adgnoscere **2**
5 crimen quam abnuere : sed utcumque casura res est, fatebor
et fuisse me Seiano amicum, et ut essem expetisse, et
postquam adeptus eram laetatum. videram collegam patris **3**
regendis praetoriis cohortibus, mox urbis et militiae munia
simul obeuntem. illius propinqui et adfines honoribus **4**
10 augebantur ; ut quisque Seiano intimus, ita ad Caesaris
amicitiam validus : contra quibus infensus esset, metu ac
sordibus conflictabantur. nec quemquam exemplo adsumo : **5**
cunctos, qui novissimi consilii expertes fuimus, meo unius
discrimine defendam. non enim Seianum Vulsiniensem, set **6**
15 Claudiae et Iuliae domus partem, quas adfinitate occupaverat,
tuum, Caesar, generum, tui consulatus socium, tua officia in
re publica capessentem colebamus. non est nostrum aesti- **7**
mare quem supra ceteros et quibus de causis extollas : tibi
summum rerum iudicium di dedere, nobis obsequii gloria
20 relicta est. spectamus porro quae coram habentur, cui ex **8**
te opes honores, quis plurima iuvandi nocendive potentia,
quae Seiano fuisse nemo negaverit. abditos principis sensus, **9**
et si quid occultius parat, exquirere inlicitum, anceps : nec
ideo adsequare. ne, patres conscripti, ultimum Seiani diem, **10**
25 sed sedecim annos cogitaveritis. etiam Satrium atque Pomponium venerabamur ; libertis quoque ac ianitoribus eius
notescere pro magnifico accipiebatur. quid ergo ? indistincta **11**
haec defensio et promisca dabitur ? immo iustis terminis divi-
datur. insidiae in rem publicam, consilia caedis adversum
30 imperatorem puniantur : de amicitia et officiis idem finis et
te, Caesar, et nos absolverit.'

9 (15). Constantia orationis, et quia repertus erat qui
efferret quae omnes animo agitabant, eo usque potuere, ut

accusatores eius, additis quae ante deliquerant, exilio aut
morte multarentur.

2 Secutae dehinc Tiberii litterae in Sex. Vistilium praetorium, quem Druso fratri percarum in cohortem suam trans-
3 tulerat.   causa offensionis Vistilio fuit, seu composuerat 5
quaedam in Gaium Caesarem ut impudicum, sive ficto
4 habita fides.   atque ob id convictu principis prohibitus cum
senili manu ferrum temptavisset, obligat venas ; precatusque
5 per codicillos, immiti rescripto venas resolvit.   acervatim ex
eo Annius Pollio, Appius Silanus Scauro Mamerco simul ac 10
Sabino Calvisio maiestatis postulantur, et Vinicianus Pollioni
patri adiciebatur, clari genus et quidam summis honoribus.
6 contremuerantque patres (nam quotus quisque adfinitatis aut
amicitiae tot inlustrium virorum expers erat?), ni Celsus
urbanae cohortis tribunus, tum inter indices, Appium et 15
7 Calvisium discrimini exemisset.   Caesar Pollionis ac Viniciani
Scaurique causam, ut ipse cum senatu nosceret, distulit, datis
quibusdam in Scaurum tristibus notis.

10 (16).   Ne feminae quidem exsortes periculi.   quia
occupandae rei publicae argui non poterant, ob lacrimas 20
incusabantur ; necataque est anus Vitia, Fufii Gemini mater,
2 quod filii necem flevisset.   haec apud senatum : nec secus
apud principem Vescularius Flaccus ac Iulius Marinus ad
mortem aguntur, e vetustissimis familiarium, Rhodum secuti
et apud Capreas individui, Vescularius insidiarum in Libonem 25
internuntius ; Marino participe Seianus Curtium Atticum
oppresserat.   quo laetius acceptum sua exempla in con-
sultores recidisse.

3 Per idem tempus L. Piso pontifex, rarum in tanta claritudine, fato obiit, nullius servilis sententiae sponte auctor, et 30
4 quotiens necessitas ingrueret, sapienter moderans.   patrem
ei censorium fuisse memoravi ; aetas ad octogensimum
annum processit ; decus triumphale in Thraecia meruerat.

sed praecipua ex eo gloria, quod praefectus urbi recens 5
continuam potestatem et insolentia parendi graviorem mire
temperavit.

11 (17). Namque antea, profectis domo regibus ac mox
5 magistratibus, ne urbs sine imperio foret, in tempus deli-
gebatur qui ius redderet ac subitis mederetur; feruntque
ab Romulo Dentrem Romulium, post ab Tullo Hostilio
Numam Marcium et ab Tarquinio Superbo Spurium Lucre-
tium inpositos. dein consules mandabant; duratque simu- 2
10 lacrum, quotiens ob ferias Latinas praeficitur qui consulare
munus usurpet. ceterum Augustus bellis civilibus Cilnium 3
Maecenatem equestris ordinis cunctis apud Romam atque
Italiam praeposuit: mox rerum potitus ob magnitudinem
populi ac tarda legum auxilia sumpsit e consularibus qui
15 coerceret servitia et quod civium audacia turbidum, nisi vim
metuat. primusque Messalla Corvinus eam potestatem et 4
paucos intra dies finem accepit, quasi nescius exercendi; tum 5
Taurus Statilius, quamquam provecta aetate, egregie toleravit;
dein Piso viginti per annos pariter probatus, publico funere 6
20 ex decreto senatus celebratus est.

12 (18). Relatum inde ad patres a Quintiliano tribuno
plebei de libro Sibullae, quem Caninius Gallus quindecimvirum recipi inter ceteros eiusdem vatis et ea de re senatus
consultum postulaverat. quo per discessionem facto misit
25 litteras Caesar, modice tribunum increpans ignarum antiqui
moris ob iuventam. Gallo exprobrabat, quod scientiae caeri- 2
moniarumque vetus incerto auctore, ante sententiam collegii,
non, ut adsolet, lecto per magistros aestimatoque carmine,
apud infrequentem senatum egisset. simul commonefecit, 3
30 quia multa vana sub nomine celebri vulgabantur, sanxisse
Augustum, quem intra diem ad praetorem urbanum deferrentur neve habere privatim liceret. quod a maioribus quo- 4
que decretum erat post exustum sociali bello Capitolium,

quaesitis Samo, Ilio, Erythris, per Africam etiam ac Siciliam
et Italicas colonias, carminibus Sibullae, una seu plures
fuere, datoque sacerdotibus negotio, quantum humana ope
5 potuissent, vera discernere. igitur tunc quoque notioni quindecimvirum is liber subicitur.   5

   13 (19). Isdem consulibus gravitate annonae iuxta seditionem ventum, multaque et plures per dies in theatro
licentius efflagitata quam solitum adversum imperatorem.
2 quis commotus incusavit magistratus patresque, quod non
publica auctoritate populum coercuissent, addiditque quibus 10
ex provinciis et quanto maiorem quam Augustus rei frumen-
3 tariae copiam advectaret. ita castigandae plebi compositum
senatus consultum prisca severitate, neque segnius consules
4 edixere. silentium ipsius non civile, ut crediderat, sed in
superbiam accipiebatur.   15

   14 (20). Fine anni Geminius, Celsus, Pompeius, equites
Romani, cecidere coniurationis crimine; ex quis Geminius
prodigentia opum ac mollitia vitae amicus Seiano, nihil ad
2 serium. et Iulius Celsus tribunus in vinclis laxatam catenam
et circumdatam in diversum tendens suam ipse cervicem 20
3 perfregit. at Rubrio Fabato, tamquam desperatis rebus
Romanis Parthorum ad misericordiam fugeret, custodes
4 additi. sane is repertus apud fretum Siciliae retractusque
per centurionem nullas probabiles causas longinquae pere-
grinationis adferebat: mansit tamen incolumis, oblivione 25
magis quam clementia.

   15 (21). Ser. Galba L. Sulla consulibus diu quaesito quos
neptibus suis maritos destinaret Caesar, postquam instabat
2 virginum aetas, L. Cassium, M. Vinicium legit. Vinicio
oppidanum genus: Calibus ortus, patre atque avo con- 30
sularibus, cetera equestri familia erat, mitis ingenio et
3 comptae facundiae. Cassius plebeii Romae generis, verum
antiqui honoratique, et severa patris disciplina eductus facili-

tate saepius quam industria commendabatur. huic Drusil- **4**
lam, Vinicio Iuliam Germanico genitas coniungit superque
ea re senatui scribit, levi cum honore iuvenum. dein redditis **5**
absentiae causis admodum vagis flexit ad graviora et offen-
5 siones ob rem publicam coeptas, utque Macro praefectus
tribunorumque et centurionum pauci secum introirent,
quotiens curiam ingrederetur, petivit. factoque large et sine **6**
praescriptione generis aut numeri senatus consulto ne tecta
quidem urbis, adeo publicum consilium numquam adiit,
10 deviis plerumque itineribus ambiens patriam et declinans.

    16 (22). Interea magna vis accusatorum in eos inrupit,
qui pecunias faenore auctitabant adversum legem dictatoris
Caesaris, qua de modo credendi possidendique intra Italiam
cavetur, omissam olim, quia privato usui bonum publicum
15 postponitur. sane vetus urbi faenebre malum et seditionum **2**
discordiarumque creberrima causa, eoque cohibebatur antiquis quoque et minus corruptis moribus. nam primo **3**
duodecim tabulis sanctum, ne quis unciario faenore amplius
exerceret, cum antea ex libidine locupletium agitaretur;
20 dein rogatione tribunicia ad semuncias redactum, postremo
vetita versura. multisque plebis scitis obviam itum fraudibus, **4**
quae totiens repressae miras per artes rursum oriebantur.
sed tum Gracchus praetor, cui ea quaestio evenerat, multi- **5**
tudine periclitantium subactus rettulit ad senatum, trepidique
25 patres (neque enim quisquam tali culpa vacuus) veniam a
principe petivere ; et concedente annus in posterum sexque
menses dati, quis secundum iussa legis rationes familiares
quisque componerent.

    17 (23). Hinc inopia rei nummariae, commoto simul
30 omnium aere alieno, et quia tot damnatis bonisque eorum
divenditis signatum argentum .fisco vel aerario attinebatur.
ad hoc senatus praescripserat, duas quisque faenoris partes **2**
in agris per Italiam conlocaret. sed creditores in solidum

3 appellabant, nec decorum appellatis minuere fidem.   ita
primo concursatio et preces, dein strepere praetoris tribunal,
eaque quae remedio quaesita, venditio et emptio, in con-
trarium mutari, quia faeneratores omnem pecuniam mer-
4 candis agris condiderant.   copiam vendendi secuta vilitate, 5
quanto quis obaeratior, aegrius distrahebant, multique for-
tunis provolvebantur ; eversio rei familiaris dignitatem ac
famam praeceps dabat, donec tulit opem Caesar disposito
per mensas miliens sestertio factaque mutuandi copia sine
usuris per triennium, si debitor populo in duplum praediis 10
5 cavisset.   sic refecta fides, et paulatim privati quoque creditores reperti.   neque emptio agrorum exercita ad formam
senatus consulti, acribus, ut ferme talia, initiis, incurioso fine.

   18 (24). Dein redeunt priores metus postulato maiestatis
Considio Proculo, qui nullo pavore diem natalem celebrans 15
raptus in curiam pariterque damnatus interfectusque est.
2 sorori eius Sanciae aqua atque igni interdictum accusante
Q. Pomponio.   is moribus inquies haec et huiusce modi a se
factitari praetendebat, ut parta apud principem gratia peri-
3 culis Pomponii Secundi fratris mederetur.   etiam in Pom- 20
peiam Macrinam exilium statuitur, cuius maritum Argolicum,
socerum Laconem e primoribus Achaeorum Caesar ad-
4 flixerat.   pater quoque inlustris eques Romanus ac frater
5 praetorius, cum damnatio instaret, se ipsi interfecere.   datum
erat crimini, quod Theophanen Mytilenaeum proavum eorum 25
Cn. Magnus inter intimos habuisset, quodque defuncto
Theophani caelestes honores Graeca adulatio tribuerat.

   19 (25). Post quos Sex. Marius Hispaniarum ditissimus
defertur incestasse filiam et saxo Tarpeio deicitur.   ac ne
dubium haberetur magnitudinem pecuniae malo vertisse, 30
aurarias *argentarias*que eius, quamquam publicarentur, sibi-
2 met Tiberius seposuit.   inritatusque suppliciis cunctos, qui
carcere attinebantur accusati societatis cum Seiano, necari

iubet. iacuit inmensa strages, omnis sexus, omnis aetas, 3
inlustres ignobiles, dispersi aut aggerati. neque propinquis 4
aut amicis adsistere, inlacrimare, ne visere quidem diutius
dabatur, sed circumiecti custodes et in maerorem cuiusque
5 intenti corpora putrefacta adsectabantur, dum in Tiberim
traherentur, ubi fluitantia aut ripis adpulsa non cremare
quisquam, non contingere. interciderat sortis humanae 5
commercium vi metus, quantumque saevitia glisceret, miseratio arcebatur.

10   **20** (26). Sub idem tempus Gaius Caesar, discedenti
Capreas avo comes, Claudiam, M. Silani filiam, coniugio
accepit, immanem animum subdola modestia tegens, non
damnatione matris, non exitio fratrum rupta voce; qualem
diem Tiberius induisset, pari habitu, haud multum distan-
15 tibus verbis. unde mox scitum Passieni oratoris dictum 2
percrebruit, neque meliorem umquam servum neque de-
teriorem dominum fuisse.

Non omiserim praesagium Tiberii de Servio Galba tum 3
consule; quem accitum et diversis sermonibus pertemptatum
20 postremo Graecis verbis in hanc sententiam adlocutus *est*
' et tu, Galba, quandoque degustabis imperium,' seram ac
brevem potentiam significans, scientia Chaldaeorum artis,
cuius apiscendae otium apud Rhodum, magistrum Thrasullum
habuit, peritiam eius hoc modo expertus.

25   **21** (27). Quotiens super tali negotio consultaret, edita
domus parte ac liberti unius conscientia utebatur. is litte- 2
rarum ignarus, corpore valido, per avia ac derupta (nam
saxis domus imminet) praeibat eum, cuius artem experiri
Tiberius statuisset, et regredientem, si vanitatis aut fraudum
30 suspicio incesserat, in subiectum mare praecipitabat, ne index
arcani exsisteret. igitur Thrasullus isdem rupibus inductus 3
postquam percontantem commoverat, imperium ipsi et futura
sollerter patefaciens, interrogatur an suam quoque genitalem

horam comperisset, quem tum annum, qualem diem haberet.
4 ille positus siderum ac spatia dimensus haerere primo, dein
pavescere, et quantum introspiceret, magis ac magis trepidus
admirationis et metus, postremo exclamat ambiguum sibi
5 ac prope ultimum discrimen instare.   tum complexus eum 5
Tiberius praescium periculorum et incolumem fore gratatur,
quaeque dixerat oracli vice accipiens inter intimos amicorum
tenet.

    22 (28). Sed mihi haec ac talia audienti in incerto iudicium
est, fatone res mortalium et necessitate immutabili an forte 10
2 volvantur. quippe sapientissimos veterum quique sectam
eorum aemulantur diversos reperias, ac multis insitam
opinionem non initia nostri, non finem, non denique homines
dis curae; ideo creberrime tristia in bonos, laeta apud de-
3 teriores esse.   contra alii fatum quidem congruere rebus 15
putant, sed non e vagis stellis, verum apud principia et
nexus naturalium causarum; ac tamen electionem vitae
nobis relinquunt, quam ubi elegeris, certum imminentium
4 ordinem.   neque mala vel bona quae vulgus putet: multos,
qui conflictari adversis videantur, beatos, at plerosque quam- 20
quam magnas per opes miserrimos, si illi gravem fortunam
5 constanter tolerent, hi prospera inconsulte utantur. ceterum
plurimis mortalium non eximitur quin primo cuiusque ortu
ventura destinentur, sed quaedam secus quam dicta sint
cadere, fallaciis ignara dicentium: ita corrumpi fidem artis, 25
cuius clara documenta et antiqua aetas et nostra tulerit.
6 quippe a filio eiusdem Thrasulli praedictum Neronis imperium in tempore memorabitur, ne nunc incepto longius
abierim.

    23 (29). Isdem consulibus Asinii Galli mors vulgatur, 30
quem egestate cibi peremptum haud dubium, sponte vel
2 necessitate, incertum habebatur. consultusque Caesar an
sepeliri sineret, non erubuit permittere ultroque incusare

casus, qui reum abstulissent, antequam coram convinceretur:
scilicet medio triennio defuerat tempus subeundi iudicium 3
consulari seni, tot consularium parenti. Drusus deinde 4
extinguitur, cum se miserandis alimentis, mandendo e cubili
5 tomento, nonum ad diem detinuisset. tradidere quidam 5
praescriptum fuisse Macroni, si arma ab Seiano temptarentur,
extractum custodiae iuvenem (nam in Palatio attinebatur)
ducem populo imponere. mox, quia rumor incedebat fore 6
ut nuru ac nepoti conciliaretur Caesar, saevitiam quam
10 paenitentiam maluit.

24 (30). Quin et invectus in defunctum probra corporis,
exitiabilem in suos, infensum rei publicae animum obiecit
recitarique factorum dictorumque eius descripta per dies
iussit, quo non aliud atrocius visum : adstitisse tot per annos 2
15 qui vultum, gemitus, occultum etiam murmur exciperent, et
potuisse avum audire, legere, in publicum promere vix fides,
nisi quod Attii centurionis et Didymi liberti epistulae servorum nomina praeferebant, ut quis egredientem cubiculo
Drusum pulsaverat, exterruerat. etiam sua verba centurio 3
20 saevitiae plena, tamquam egregium, vocesque deficientis
adiecerat, quis primo [alienationem mentis simulans] quasi
per dementiam funesta Tiberio, mox, ubi exspes vitae fuit,
meditatas compositasque diras inprecabatur, ut quem ad
modum nurum filiumque fratris et nepotes domumque omnem
25 caedibus complevisset, ita poenas nomini generique maiorum
et posteris exsolveret. obturbabant quidem patres specie 4
detestandi : sed penetrabat pavor et admiratio, callidum olim
et tegendis sceleribus obscurum huc confidentiae venisse, ut
tamquam dimotis parietibus ostenderet nepotem sub verbere
30 centurionis, inter servorum ictus, extrema vitae alimenta
frustra orantem.

25 (31). Nondum is dolor exoleverat, cum de Agrippina
auditum, quam interfecto Seiano spe sustentatam provixisse

reor, et postquam nihil de saevitia remittebatur, voluntate
exstinctam, nisi si negatis alimentis adsimulatus est finis, qui
2 videretur sponte sumptus.   enimvero Tiberius foedissimis
criminationibus exarsit, impudicitiam arguens et Asinium
Gallum adulterum, eiusque morte ad taedium vitae con- 5
3 pulsam. sed Agrippina aequi inpatiens, dominandi avida,
4 virilibus curis feminarum vitia exuerat. eodem die defunctam,
quo biennio ante Seianus poenas luisset, memoriaeque id
prodendum addidit Caesar, iactavitque quod non laqueo
5 strangulata neque in Gemonias proiecta foret. actae ob id 10
grates decretumque ut quintum decumum kal. Novembris,
utriusque necis die, per omnis annos donum Iovi sacraretur.

   26 (32). Haud multo post Cocceius Nerva, continuus
principi, omnis divini humanique iuris sciens, integro statu,
2 corpore inlaeso, moriendi consilium cepit. quod ut Tiberio 15
cognitum, adsidere, causas requirere, addere preces, fateri
postremo grave conscientiae, grave famae suae, si proximus
3 amicorum nullis moriendi rationibus vitam fugeret. aversatus
sermonem Nerva abstinentiam cibi coniunxit. ferebant
gnari cogitationum eius, quanto propius mala rei publicae 20
viseret, ira et metu, dum integer, dum intemptatus, honestum
finem voluisse.

4   Ceterum Agrippinae pernicies, quod vix credibile, Plancinam traxit. nupta olim Cn. Pisoni et palam laeta morte
Germanici, cum Piso caderet, precibus Augustae nec minus 25
5 inimicitiis Agrippinae defensa erat. ut odium et gratia
desiere, ius valuit ; petitaque criminibus haud ignotis, sua
manu sera magis quam inmerita supplicia persolvit.

   27 (33). Tot luctibus funesta civitate pars maeroris fuit,
quod Iulia Drusi filia, quondam Neronis uxor, denupsit in 30
domum Rubellii Blandi, cuius avum Tiburtem equitem
2 Romanum plerique meminerant. extremo anni mors Aelii
Lamiae funere censorio celebrata, qui administrandae Suriae

imagine tandem exsolutus urbi praefuerat. genus illi decorum, vivida senectus ; et non permissa provincia dignationem addiderat.   exim Flacco Pomponio Suriae pro 3
praetore defuncto recitantur Caesaris litterae, quis incusabat
5 egregium quemque et regendis exercitibus idoneum abnuere
id munus, seque ea necessitudine ad preces cogi, per quas
consularium aliqui capessere provincias adigerentur, oblitus
Arruntium, ne in Hispaniam pergeret, decumum iam annum
attineri.   obiit eodem anno et M'. Lepidus, de cuius modera- 4
10 tione atque sapientia in prioribus libris satis conlocavi. neque 5
nobilitas diutius demonstranda est : quippe Aemilium genus
fecundum bonorum civium, et qui eadem familia corruptis
moribus, inlustri tamen fortuna egere.

    28 (34). Paulo Fabio L. Vitellio consulibus post longum
15 saeculorum ambitum avis phoenix in Aegyptum venit prae-
buitque materiem doctissimis indigenarum et Graecorum
multa super eo miraculo disserendi.   de quibus congruunt, 2
et plura ambigua sed cognitu non absurda, promere libet.
sacrum Soli id animal et ore ac distinctu pinnarum a ceteris 3
20 avibus diversum consentiunt qui formam eius effinxere : de
numero annorum varia traduntur.   maxime vulgatum quin- 4
gentorum spatium : sunt qui adseverent mille quadringentos
sexaginta unum interici, prioresque alios tres Sesoside
primum, post Amaside dominantibus, dein Ptolemaeo, qui
25 ex Macedonibus tertius regnavit, in civitatem cui Heliopolis
nomen advolavisse, multo ceterarum volucrum comitatu novam
faciem mirantium.   sed antiquitas quidem obscura : inter 5
Ptolemaeum ac Tiberium minus ducenti quinquaginta anni
fuerunt.   unde nonnulli falsum hunc phoenicem neque 6
30 Arabum e terris credidere, nihilque usurpavisse ex iis, quae
vetus memoria firmavit.   confecto quippe annorum numero, 7
ubi mors propinquet, suis in terris struere nidum eique vim
genitalem adfundere, ex qua fetum oriri ; et primam adulto

curam sepeliendi patris, neque id temere, sed sublato murrae
pondere temptatoque per longum iter, ubi par oneri, par
meatui sit, subire patrium corpus inque Solis aram perferre
8 atque adolere.   haec incerta et fabulosis aucta : ceterum
aspici aliquando in Aegypto eam volucrem non ambigitur.   5

    29 (35). At Romae caede continua Pomponius Labeo,
quem praefuisse Moesiae rettuli, per abruptas venas sanguinem
2 effudit : aemulataque est coniunx Paxaea. nam promptas
eius modi mortes metus carnificis faciebat, et quia damnati
publicatis bonis sepultura prohibebantur, eorum qui de se 10
statuebant humabantur corpora, manebant testamenta, pretium
8 festinandi.   sed Caesar missis ad senatum litteris disseruit
morem fuisse maioribus, quotiens dirimerent amicitias, inter-
dicere domo eumque finem gratiae ponere : id se repetivisse
in Labeone, atque illum, quia male administratae provinciae 15
aliorumque criminum arguebatur, culpam invidia velavisse,
frustra conterrita uxore, quam etsi nocentem periculi tamen
4 expertem fuisse.   Mamercus dein Scaurus rursum postulatur,
5 insignis nobilitate et orandis causis, vita probrosus. nihil
hunc amicitia Seiani, sed labefecit haud minus validum ad 20
exitia Macronis odium, qui easdem artes occultius exercebat ;
detuleratque argumentum tragoediae a Scauro scriptae,
6 additis versibus qui in Tiberium flecterentur : verum ab
Servilio et Cornelio accusatoribus adulterium Liviae, magorum
7 sacra obiectabantur.   Scaurus, ut dignum veteribus Aemiliis, 25
damnationem anteiit, hortante Sextia uxore, quae incitamentum mortis et particeps fuit.

    30 (36). Ac tamen accusatores, si facultas incideret,
poenis adficiebantur, ut Servilius Corneliusque perdito Scauro
famosi, quia pecuniam a Vario Ligure omittendae delationis 30
ceperant, in insulas interdicto igni atque aqua demoti sunt.
2 et Abudius Ruso functus aedilitate dum Lentulo Gaetulico,
sub quo legioni praefuerat, periculum facessit, quod is Seiani

filium generum destinasset, ultro damnatur atque urbe ex-
igitur.   Gaetulicus ea tempestate superioris Germaniae 3
legiones curabat mirumque amorem adsecutus erat, effusae
clementiae, modicus severitate et proximo quoque exercitui
5 per L. Apronium socerum non ingratus. unde fama constans 4
ausum mittere ad Caesarem litteras, adfinitatem sibi cum
Seiano haud sponte sed consilio Tiberii coeptam ; perinde se
quam Tiberium falli potuisse, neque errorem eundem illi sine
fraude, aliis exitio habendum.   sibi fidem integram et, si 5
10 nullis insidiis peteretur, mansuram ; successorem non aliter
quam indicium mortis accepturum.   firmarent velut foedus, 6
quo princeps ceterarum rerum poteretur, ipse provinciam
retineret. ·haec, mira quamquam, fidem ex eo trahebant, quod 7
unus omnium Seiani adfinium incolumis multaque gratia
15 mansit, reputante Tiberio publicum sibi odium, extremam
aetatem, magisque fama quam vi stare res suas.

   31 (37). C. Cestio M. Servilio consulibus nobiles Parthi in
urbem venere, ignaro rege Artabano.   is metu Germanici 2
fidus Romanis, aequabilis in suos, mox superbiam in nos,
20 saevitiam in populares sumpsit, fretus bellis, quae secunda
adversum circumiectas nationes exercuerat, et senectutem
Tiberii ut inermem despiciens avidusque Armeniae, cui defuncto rege Artaxia Arsacen liberorum suorum veterrimum
inposuit, addita contumelia et missis qui gazam a Vonone
25 relictam in Suria Ciliciaque reposcerent ; simul veteres
Persarum ac Macedonum terminos, seque invasurum possessa primum Cyro et post Alexandro per vaniloquentiam ac
minas iaciebat.   sed Parthis mittendi secretos nuntios vali- 3
dissimus auctor fuit Sinnaces, insigni familia ac perinde
30 opibus, et proximus huic Abdus ademptae virilitatis.   non
despectum id apud barbaros ultroque potentiam habet.
ii adscitis et aliis primoribus, quia neminem gentis Arsacida- 4
rum summae rei inponere poterant, interfectis ab Artabano

plerisque aut nondum adultis, Phraaten regis Phraatis filium
Roma poscebant : nomine tantum et auctore opus, ut
sponte Caesaris [ut] genus Arsacis ripam apud Euphratis
cerneretur.

   32 (38). Cupitum id Tiberio : ornat Phraaten accingitque 5
paternum ad fastigium, destinata retinens, consiliis et astu
2 res externas moliri, arma procul habere. interea cognitis
insidiis Artabanus tardari metu, modo cupidine vindictae
3 inardescere. et barbaris cunctatio servilis, statim exsequi
regium videtur : valuit tamen utilitas, ut Abdum specie 10
amicitiae vocatum ad epulas lento veneno inligaret, Sinnacen
4 dissimulatione ac donis, simul per negotia moraretur. et
Phraates apud Suriam dum omisso cultu Romano, cui per
tot annos insueverat, instituta Parthorum sumit, patriis mori-
5 bus impar morbo absumptus est. sed non Tiberius omisit 15
incepta : Tiridatem sanguinis eiusdem aemulum Artabano,
reciperandaeque Armeniae Hiberum Mithridaten deligit con-
ciliatque fratri Pharasmani, qui gentile imperium obtinebat ;
et cunctis quae apud Orientem parabantur L. Vitellium
6 praefecit. eo de homine haud sum ignarus sinistram in 20
urbe famam, pleraque foeda memorari, ceterum *in* regendis
7 provinciis prisca virtute egit. unde regressus et formidine
Gai Caesaris, familiaritate Claudii turpe in servitium mutatus
exemplar apud posteros adulatorii dedecoris habetur, cesse-
runtque prima postremis, et bona iuventae senectus flagitiosa 25
oblitteravit.

   33 (39). At ex regulis prior Mithridates Pharasmanem
perpulit dolo et vi conatus suos iuvare, repertique corruptores
2 ministros Arsacis multo auro ad scelus cogunt ; simul Hiberi
magnis copiis Armeniam inrumpunt et urbe Artaxata po- 30
tiuntur. quae postquam Artabano cognita, filium Oroden
ultorem parat ; dat Parthorum copias, mittit qui auxilia
3 mercede facerent : contra Pharasmanes adiungere Albanos,

G

accire Sarmatas, quorum sceptuchi utrimque donis acceptis
more gentico diversa induere.   sed Hiberi locorum potentes 4
Caspia via Sarmatam in Armenios raptim effundunt.   at qui 5
Parthis adventabant, facile arcebantur, cum alios incessus
5 hostis clausisset, unum reliquum mare inter et extremos
Albanorum montes aestas impediret, quia flatibus etesiarum
implentur vada: hibernus auster revolvit fluctus pulsoque
introrsus freto brevia litorum nudantur.

   34 (40). Interim Oroden sociorum inopem auctus auxilio
10 Pharasmanes vocare ad pugnam et detrectantem incessere,
adequitare castris, infensare pabula ; ac saepe *in* modum
obsidii stationibus cingebat, donec Parthi contumeliarum in-
solentes circumsisterent regem, poscerent proelium.   atque 2
illis sola in equite vis: Pharasmanes et pedite valebat.   nam
15 Hiberi Albanique saltuosos locos incolentes duritiae patien-
tiaeque magis insuevere; feruntque se Thessalis ortos, qua 3
tempestate Iaso post avectam Medeam genitosque ex
ea liberos inanem mox regiam Aeetae vacuosque Colchos
repetivit.   multaque de nomine eius et oraclum Phrixi 4
20 celebrant ; nec quisquam ariete sacrificaverit, credito vexisse
Phrixum, sive id animal seu navis insigne fuit.   ceterum 5
derecta utrimque acie Parthus imperium orientis, claritudinem
Arsacidarum, contraque ignobilem Hiberum mercennario
milite disserebat; Pharasmanes integros semet a Parthico
25 dominatu, quanto maiora peterent, plus decoris victores aut,
si terga darent, flagitii atque periculi laturos ; simul horridam 6
suorum aciem, picta auro Medorum agmina, hinc viros, inde
praedam ostendere.

   35 (41). Enimvero apud Sarmatas non una vox ducis: se
30 quisque stimulant ne pugnam per sagittas sinerent: impetu
et comminus praeveniendum.   variae hinc bellantium species, 2
cum Parthus sequi vel fugere pari arte suetus distraheret
turmas, spatium ictibus quaereret, Sarmatae omisso arcu,

quo brevius valent, contis gladiisque ruerent; modo equestris
proelii more frontis et tergi vices, aliquando ut conserta acie
3 corporibus et pulsu armorum pellerent pellerentur. iamque
et Albani Hiberique prensare, detrudere, ancipitem pugnam
hostibus facere, quos super eques et propioribus vulneribus 5
4 pedites adflictabant. inter quae Pharasmanes Orodesque,
dum strenuis adsunt aut dubitantibus subveniunt, conspicui
eoque gnari, clamore telis equis concurrunt, instantius
5 Pharasmanes; nam vulnus per galeam adegit. nec iterare
valuit, praelatus equo et fortissimis satellitum protegentibus 10
saucium: fama tamen occisi falso credita exterruit Parthos
victoriamque concessere.

36 (42). Mox Artabanus tota mole regni ultum iit.
peritia locorum ab Hiberis melius pugnatum; nec ideo
abscedebat, ni contractis legionibus Vitellius et subdito 15
rumore, tamquam Mesopotamiam invasurus, metum Romani
2 belli fecisset. tum omissa Armenia versaeque Artabani res,
inliciente Vitellio desererent regem saevum in pace et ad-
3 versis proeliorum exitiosum. igitur Sinnaces, quem antea
infensum memoravi, patrem Abdagaesen aliosque occultos 20
consilii et tunc continuis cladibus promptiores ad defectionem
trahit, adfluentibus paulatim qui metu magis quam bene-
4 volentia subiecti repertis auctoribus sustulerant animum. nec
iam aliud Artabano reliquum quam si qui externorum
corpori custodes aderant, suis quisque sedibus extorres, quis 25
neque boni intellectus neque mali cura, sed mercede aluntur
5 ministri sceleribus. his adsumptis in longinqua et conter-
mina Scythiae fugam maturavit, spe auxilii, quia Hyrcanis
Carmaniisque per adfinitatem innexus erat: atque interim
posse Parthos absentium aequos, praesentibus mobiles, ad 30
paenitentiam mutari.

37 (43). At Vitellius profugo Artabano et flexis ad novum
regem popularium animis, hortatus Tiridaten parata capes-

sere, robur legionum sociorumque ripam ad Euphratis ducit.
sacrificantibus, cum hic more Romano suovetaurilia daret, **2**
ille equum placando amni adornasset, nuntiavere accolae
Euphraten nulla imbrium vi sponte et inmensum attolli,
5 simul albentibus spumis in modum diadematis sinuare orbes,
auspicium prosperi transgressus. quidam callidius inter- **3**
pretabantur, initia conatus secunda neque diuturna, quia
eorum quae terra caelove portenderentur certior fides, flumi-
num instabilis natura simul ostenderet omina raperetque.
10 sed ponte navibus effecto tramissoque exercitu primus Ornos- **4**
pades multis equitum milibus in castra venit, exul quondam
et Tiberio, cum Delmaticum bellum conficeret, haud in-
glorius auxiliator eoque civitate Romana donatus, mox
repetita amicitia regis multo apud eum honore, praefectus
15 campis qui Euphrate et Tigre inclutis amnibus circumflui
Mesopotamiae nomen acceperunt. neque multo post Sinnaces **5**
auget copias, et columen partium Abdagaeses gazam et
paratus regios adicit. Vitellius ostentasse Romana arma **6**
satis ratus monet Tiridaten primoresque, hunc, Phraatis avi
20 et altoris Caesaris quaeque utrobique pulchra meminerit,
illos, obsequium in regem, reverentiam in nos, decus quisque
suum et fidem retinerent. exim cum legionibus in Suriam
remeavit.

38 (44). Quae duabus aestatibus gesta coniunxi, quo
25 requiesceret animus a domesticis malis : non enim Tiberium,
quamquam triennio post caedem Seiani, quae ceteros mollire
solent, tempus preces satias mitigabant, quin incerta vel
abolita pro gravissimis et recentibus puniret. eo metu Ful- **2**
cinius Trio, ingruentis accusatores haud perpessus, supremis
30 tabulis multa et atrocia in Macronem ac praecipuos libertorum Caesaris conposuit, ipsi fluxam senio mentem et
continuo abscessu velut exilium obiectando. quae ab here- **3**
dibus occultata recitari Tiberius iussit, patientiam libertatis

alienae ostentans et contemptor suae infamiae, an scelerum
Seiani diu nescius mox quoquo modo dicta vulgari malebat
veritatisque, cui adulatio officit, per probra saltem gnarus fieri.
4 isdem diebus Granius Marcianus senator, a C. Graccho
maiestatis postulatus, vim vitae suae attulit, Tariusque Gra- 5
tianus praetura functus lege eadem extremum ad supplicium
damnatus.

39 (45). Nec dispares Trebelleni Rufi et Sextii Paconiani
exitus : nam Trebellenus sua manu cecidit, Paconianus in
carcere ob carmina illic in principem factitata strangulatus 10
2 est. haec Tiberius non mari, ut olim, divisus neque per
longinquos nuntios accipiebat, sed urbem iuxta, eodem ut
die vel noctis interiectu litteris consulum rescriberet, quasi
aspiciens undantem per domos sanguinem aut manus carni-
3 ficum. fine anni Poppaeus Sabinus concessit vita, modicus 15
originis, principum amicitia consulatum ac triumphale decus
adeptus maximisque provinciis per quattuor et viginti annos
inpositus, nullam ob eximiam artem, sed quod par negotiis
neque supra erat.

40 (46). Q. Plautius Sex. Papinius consules sequuntur. 20
eo anno neque quod L. Aruseius . . . morte adfecti forent,
adsuetudine malorum ut atrox advertebatur, sed exterruit
quod Vibulenus Agrippa eques Romanus, cum perorassent
accusatores, in ipsa curia depromptum sinu venenum hausit,
prolapsusque ac moribundus festinatis lictorum manibus in 25
carcerem raptus est, faucesque iam exanimis laqueo vexatae.
2 ne Tigranes quidem, Armenia quondam potitus ac tunc
3 reus, nomine regio supplicia civium effugit. at C. Galba
consularis et duo Blaesi voluntario exitu cecidere, Galba
tristibus Caesaris litteris provinciam sortiri prohibitus : Blaesis 30
sacerdotia, integra eorum domo destinata, convulsa distulerat,
tunc ut vacua contulit in alios, quod signum mortis intel-
4 lexere et exsecuti sunt. et Aemilia Lepida, quam iuveni

Druso nuptam rettuli, crebris criminibus maritum insectata,
quamquam intestabilis, tamen impunita agebat, dum super-
fuit pater Lepidus : post a delatoribus corripitur ob servum
adulterum, nec dubitabatur de flagitio : ergo omissa defen-
5 sione finem vitae sibi posuit.

41 (47). Per idem tempus Clitarum natio Cappadoci
Archelao subiecta, quia nostrum in modum deferre census,
pati tributa adigebatur, in iuga Tauri montis abscessit loco-
rumque ingenio sese contra imbelles regis copias tutabatur,
10 donec M. Trebellius legatus, a Vitellio praeside Suriae cum
quattuor milibus legionariorum et delectis auxiliis missus,
duos collis, quos barbari insederant (minori Cadra, alteri
Davara nomen est), operibus circumdedit et erumpere ausos
ferro, ceteros siti ad deditionem coegit.

15 At Tiridates volentibus Parthis Nicephorium et Anthemu- 2
siada ceterasque urbes, quae Macedonibus sitae Graeca
vocabula usurpant, Halumque et Artemitam Parthica oppida
recepit, certantibus gaudio qui Artabanum Scythas inter
eductum ob saevitiam exsecrati come Tiridatis ingenium
20 Romanas per artes sperabant.

42 (48). Plurimum adulationis Seleucenses induere, civitas
potens, saepta muris neque in barbarum corrupta, sed condi-
toris Seleuci retinens. trecenti opibus aut sapientia delecti
ut senatus, sua populo vis. et quotiens concordes agunt, 2
25 spernitur Parthus: ubi dissensere, dum sibi quisque contra
aemulos subsidium vocant, accitus in partem adversum omnes
valescit. id nuper acciderat Artabano regnante, qui plebem 3
primoribus tradidit ex suo usu : nam populi imperium iuxta
libertatem, paucorum dominatio regiae libidini propior est.
30 tum adventantem Tiridaten extollunt veterum regum honori- 4
bus et quos recens aetas largius invenit ; simul probra in
Artabanum fundebant, materna origine Arsaciden, cetera
degenerem. Tiridates rem Seleucensem populo permittit. 5

mox consultans, quonam die sollemnia regni capesseret,
litteras Phraatis et Hieronis, qui validissimas praefecturas
6 optinebant, accipit, brevem moram precantium. placitumque
opperiri viros praepollentis, atque interim Ctesiphon sedes
imperii petita : sed ubi diem ex die prolatabant, multis coram 5
et adprobantibus Surena patrio more Tiridaten insigni regio
evinxit.

43 (49). Ac si statim interiora ceterasque nationes petivisset, oppressa cunctantium dubitatio et omnes in unum
cedebant: adsidendo castellum, in quod pecuniam et paelices 10
2 Artabanus contulerat, dedit spatium exuendi pacta. nam
Phraates et Hiero et si qui alii delectum capiendo diademati
diem haut concelebraverant, pars metu, quidam invidia in
Abdagaesen, qui tum aula et novo rege potiebatur, ad Artabanum vertere ; isque in Hyrcanis repertus est, inluvie 15
3 obsitus et alimenta arcu expediens. ac primo tamquam
dolus pararetur territus, ubi data fides reddendae dominationi venisse, adlevatur animum et quae repentina mutatio
4 exquirit. tum Hiero pueritiam Tiridatis increpat, neque
penes Arsaciden imperium, sed inane nomen apud inbellem 20
externa mollitia, vim in Abdagaesis domo.

44 (50). Sensit vetus regnandi falsos in amore odia non
fingere. nec ultra moratus, quam dum Scytharum auxilia
conciret, pergit properus et praeveniens inimicorum astus,
amicorum paenitentiam; neque exuerat paedorem, ut vulgum 25
2 miseratione adverteret. non fraus, non preces, nihil omissum
3 quo ambiguos inliceret, prompti firmarentur. iamque multa
manu propinquans Seleuciae adventabat, cum Tiridates simul
fama atque ipso Artabano perculsus distrahi consiliis, iret
4 contra an bellum cunctatione tractaret. quibus proelium et 30
festinati casus placebant, disiectos et longinquitate itineris
fessos ne animo quidem satis ad obsequium coaluisse disserunt, proditores nuper hostesque eius, quem rursum foveant.

verum Abdagaeses regrediendum in Mesopotamiam censebat, **5**
ut amne obiecto, Armeniis interim Elymaeisque et ceteris
a tergo excitis, aucti copiis socialibus et quas dux Romanus
misisset fortunam temptarent.   ea sententia valuit, quia **6**
5 plurima auctoritas penes Abdagaesen et Tiridates ignavus ad
pericula erat.   sed fugae specie discessum; ac principio **7**
a gente Arabum facto ceteri domos abeunt vel in castra
Artabani, donec Tiridates cum paucis in Suriam revectus
pudore proditionis omnes exsolvit.

10   **45** (51). Idem annus gravi igne urbem adfecit, deusta
parte circi, quae Aventino contigua, ipsoque Aventino; quod
damnum Caesar ad gloriam vertit exsolutis domuum et insularum pretiis.   miliens sestertium in munificentia *ea* con- **2**
locatum, tanto acceptius in vulgum, quanto modicus privatis
15 aedificationibus ne publice quidem nisi duo opera struxit,
templum Augusto et scaenam Pompeiani theatri; eaque
perfecta, contemptu ambitionis an per senectutem, haud
dedicavit.   sed aestimando cuiusque detrimento quattuor **3**
progeneri Caesaris, Cn. Domitius, Cassius Longinus, M.
20 Vinicius, Rubellius Blandus delecti additusque nominatione
consulum P. Petronius.   et pro ingenio cuiusque quaesiti **4**
decretique in principem honores.   quos omiserit receperitve,
in incerto fuit ob propinquum vitae finem.   neque enim **5**
multo post supremi Tiberio consules, Cn. Acerronius C.
25 Pontius, magistratum occepere, nimia iam potentia Macronis,
qui gratiam Gai Caesaris numquam sibi neglectam acrius
in dies fovebat impuleratque post mortem Claudiae, quam
nuptam ei rettuli, uxorem suam Enniam imitando amorem
iuvenem inlicere pactoque matrimonii vincire, nihil abnuen-
30 tem, dum dominationis apisceretur; nam etsi commotus
ingenio simulationum tamen falsa in sinu avi perdidicerat.

   46 (52). Gnarum hoc principi, eoque dubitavit de tradenda
re publica, primum inter nepotes, quorum Druso genitus

sanguine et caritate propior, sed nondum pubertatem ingressus, Germanici filio robur iuventae, vulgi studia, eaque
2 apud avum odii causa. etiam de Claudio agitanti, quod is
conposita aetate bonarum artium cupiens erat, inminuta
3 mens eius obstitit. sin extra domum successor quaereretur, 5
ne memoria Augusti, ne nomen Caesarum in ludibria et con-
4 tumelias verterent metuebat: quippe illi non perinde curae
5 gratia praesentium quam in posteros ambitio. mox incertus
animi, fesso corpore, consilium, cui impar erat, fato permisit,
iactis tamen vocibus per quas intellegeretur providus futu- 10
6 rorum; namque Macroni non abdita ambage occidentem ab
7 eo deseri, orientem spectari exprobravit. et Gaio Caesari,
forte orto sermone L. Sullam inridenti, omnia Sullae vitia et
8 nullam eiusdem virtutem habiturum praedixit. simul crebris
cum lacrimis minorem ex nepotibus conplexus, truci alterius 15
9 vultu, ' occides hunc tu ' inquit ' et te alius.' sed gravescente
valetudine nihil e libidinibus omittebat, in patientia firmitu-
dinem simulans solitusque eludere medicorum artes atque
eos, qui post tricesimum aetatis annum ad internoscenda
corpori suo utilia vel noxia alieni consilii indigerent. 20

47 (53). Interim Romae futuris etiam post Tiberium
caedibus semina iaciebantur. Laelius Balbus Acutiam,
P. Vitellii quondam uxorem, maiestatis postulaverat; qua
damnata cum praemium accusatori decerneretur, Iunius
Otho tribunus plebei intercessit, unde illis odia, mox Othoni 25
2 exitium. dein multorum amoribus famosa Albucilla, cui
matrimonium cum Satrio Secundo coniurationis indice fuerat,
defertur inpietatis in principem; conectebantur ut conscii
et adulteri eius Cn. Domitius, Vibius Marsus, L. Arruntius.
3 de claritudine Domitii supra memoravi; Marsus quoque 30
4 vetustis honoribus et inlustris studiis erat. sed testium
interrogationi, tormentis servorum Macronem praesedisse
commentarii ad senatum missi ferebant, nullaeque in eos

imperatoris litterae suspicionem dabant, invalido ac fortasse ignaro ficta pleraque ob inimicitias Macronis notas in Arruntium.

48 (54). Igitur Domitius defensionem meditans, Marsus 5 tamquam inediam destinavisset, produxere vitam : Arruntius 2 cunctationem et moras suadentibus amicis, non eadem omnibus decora respondit : sibi satis aetatis, neque aliud 3 paenitendum quam quod inter ludibria et pericula anxiam senectam toleravisset, diu Seiano, nunc Macroni, semper 10 alicui potentium invisus, non culpa, sed ut flagitiorum inpatiens. sane paucos ad suprema principis dies posse vitari : quem ad modum evasurum imminentis iuventam ? an, cum 4 Tiberius post tantam rerum experientiam vi dominationis convulsus et mutatus sit, Gaium Caesarem vix finita pueritia, 15 ignarum omnium aut pessimis innutritum, meliora capessiturum Macrone duce ? qui ut deterior ad opprimendum Seianum delectus plura per scelera rem publicam conflictavisset. prospectare iam se acrius servitium, eoque fugere 5 simul acta et instantia. haec vatis in modum dictitans venas 20 resolvit. documento sequentia erunt bene Arruntium morte usum. Albucilla inrito ictu ab semet vulnerata iussu senatus 6 in carcerem fertur. stuprorum eius ministri, Carsidius Sacerdos praetorius ut in insulam deportaretur, Pontius Fregellanus amitteret ordinem senatorium, et eaedem poenae 25 in Laelium Balbum decernuntur, id quidem a laetantibus, quia Balbus truci eloquentia habebatur, promptus adversum insontes.

49 (55). Isdem diebus Sex. Papinius consulari familia repentinum et informem exitum delegit, iacto in praeceps 30 corpore. causa ad matrem referebatur, quae pridem repu- 2 diata adsentationibus atque luxu perpulisset iuvenem ad ea quorum effugium non nisi morte inveniret. igitur accusata 3 in senatu, quamquam genua patrum advolveretur luctumque

communem et magis inbecillum tali super casu feminarum
animum aliaque in eundem dolorem maesta et miseranda
diu ferret, urbe tamen in decem annos prohibita est, donec
minor filius lubricum iuventae exiret.

50 (56). Iam Tiberium corpus, iam vires, nondum dissi- 5
mulatio deserebat: idem animi rigor; sermone ac vultu
intentus quaesita interdum comitate quamvis manifestam
2 defectionem tegebat. mutatisque saepius locis tandem apud
promunturium Miseni consedit in villa, cui L. Lucullus
3 quondam dominus. illic eum adpropinquare supremis tali 10
modo compertum. erat medicus arte insignis, nomine
Charicles, non quidem regere valetudines principis solitus,
4 consilii tamen copiam praebere. is velut propria ad negotia
digrediens et per speciem officii manum complexus pulsum
5 venarum attigit. neque fefellit: nam Tiberius, incertum an 15
offensus tantoque magis iram premens, instaurari epulas
iubet discumbitque ultra solitum, quasi honori abeuntis amici
tribueret. Charicles tamen labi spiritum nec ultra biduum
6 duraturum Macroni firmavit. inde cuncta conloquiis inter
praesentes, nuntiis apud legatos et exercitus festinabantur. 20
7 septimum decimum kal. Aprilis interclusa anima creditus est
mortalitatem explevisse; et multo gratantum concursu ad
capienda imperii primordia Gaius Caesar egrediebatur, cum
repente adfertur redire Tiberio vocem ac visus vocarique qui
8 recreandae defectioni cibum adferrent. pavor hinc in omnes, 25
et ceteri passim dispergi, se quisque maestum aut nescium
fingere; Caesar in silentium fixus a summa spe novissima
9 expectabat. Macro intrepidus opprimi senem iniectu multae
vestis iubet discedique ab limine. sic Tiberius finivit, octavo
et septuagesimo aetatis anno.   30

51 (57). Pater ei Nero et utrimque origo gentis Claudiae,
quamquam mater in Liviam et mox Iuliam familiam adoptio-
2 nibus transierit. casus prima ab infantia ancipites; nam

proscriptum patrem exul secutus, ubi domum Augusti privignus introiit, multis aemulis conflictatus est, dum Marcellus et Agrippa, mox Gaius Luciusque Caesares viguere;
etiam frater eius Drusus prosperiore civium amore erat. sed **3**
5 maxime in lubrico egit accepta in matrimonium Iulia, inpudicitiam uxoris tolerans aut declinans. dein Rhodo regressus **4**
vacuos principis penates duodecim annis, mox rei Romanae
arbitrium tribus ferme et viginti obtinuit. morum quoque **5**
tempora illi diversa : egregium vita famaque, quoad privatus
10 vel in imperiis sub Augusto fuit; occultum ac subdolum
fingendis virtutibus, donec Germanicus ac Drusus super-
fuere; idem inter bona malaque mixtus incolumi matre, **6**
intestabilis saevitia, sed obtectis libidinibus, dum Seianum
dilexit timuitve, postremo in scelera simul ac dedecora
15 prorupit, postquam remoto pudore et metu suo tantum
ingenio utebatur.

LIBER XI.

1. . . . nam Valerium Asiaticum, bis consulem, fuisse
quondam adulterum eius credidit; pariterque hortis inhians,
quos ille a Lucullo coeptos insigni magnificentia extollebat,
2 Suillium accusandis utrisque immittit. adiungitur Sosibius
Britannici educator, qui per speciem benevolentiae mone- 5
ret Claudium cavere vim atque opes principibus infensas:
praecipuum auctorem Asiaticum interficiendi *Gai* Caesaris
non extimuisse contione in populi Romani fateri gloriamque facinoris ultro petere; clarum ex eo in urbe, didita
per provincias fama parare iter ad Germanicos exercitus, 10
quando genitus Viennae multisque et validis propinquitatibus
3 subnixus turbare gentiles nationes promptum haberet. at
Claudius nihil ultra scrutatus citis cum militibus tamquam
opprimendo bello Crispinum praetorii praefectum misit,
a quo repertus est apud Baias vinclisque inditis in urbem 15
raptus.

2. Neque data senatus copia: intra cubiculum auditur,
Messalina coram, et Suillio corruptionem militum, quos
pecunia et stupro in omne flagitium obstrictos arguebat,
exim adulterium Poppaeae, postremum mollitiam corpo- 20
2 ris obiectante. ad quod victo silentio prorupit reus.
3 ingressusque defensionem, commoto maiorem in modum
4 Claudio, Messalinae quoque lacrimas excivit. quibus abluendis cubiculo egrediens monet Vitellium, ne elabi reum
5 sineret: ipsa ad perniciem Poppaeae festinat, subditis qui 25
terrore carceris ad voluntariam mortem propellerent, adeo
ignaro Caesare, ut paucos post dies epulantem apud se
maritum eius Scipionem percontaretur, cur sine uxore dis-
cubuisset, atque ille functam fato responderet.

3. Sed consultanti super absolutione Asiatici flens Vitellius,
commemorata vetustate amicitiae utque Antoniam principis
matrem pariter observavissent, dein percursis Asiatici in
rem publicam officiis recentique adversus Britanniam militia,
5 quaeque alia conciliandae misericordiae videbantur, liberum
mortis arbitrium ei permisit; et secuta sunt Claudii verba
in eandem clementiam. hortantibus dehinc quibusdam 2
inediam et lenem exitum, remittere beneficium Asiaticus
ait : et usurpatis quibus insueverat exercitationibus, lauto
10 corpore, hilare epulatus, cum se honestius calliditate Tiberii
vel impetu Gai Caesaris periturum dixisset, quam quod
fraude muliebri et inpudico Vitellii ore caderet, venas
exsolvit, viso tamen ante rogo iussoque transferri partem
in aliam, ne opacitas arborum vapore ignis minueretur :
15 tantum illi securitatis novissimae fuit.

4. Vocantur post haec patres, pergitque Suillius addere
reos equites Romanos inlustres, quibus Petra cognomentum. at causa necis ex eo, quod domum suam Mnesteris 2
et Poppaeae congressibus praebuissent. verum nocturnae 3
20 quietis species alteri obiecta, tamquam vidisset Claudium
spicea corona evinctum, spicis retro conversis, eaque
imagine gravitatem annonae praedixisset. quidam pam- 4
pineam coronam albentibus foliis visam atque ita interpretatum tradidere, vergente autumno mortem principis
25 ostendi. illud haud ambigitur, qualicumque insomnio ipsi 5
fratrique perniciem adlatam. sestertium quindeciens et
insignia praeturae Crispino decreta. adiecit Vitellius ses- 6
tertium deciens Sosibio, quod Britannicum praeceptis, Claudium consiliis iuvaret. rogatus sententiam et Scipio, ' cum 7
30 idem' inquit ' de admissis Poppaeae sentiam quod omnes,
putate me idem dicere quod omnes,' eleganti temperamento
inter coniugalem amorem et senatoriam necessitatem.

5. Continuus inde et saevus accusandis reis Suillius

multique audaciae eius aemuli; nam cuncta legum et
magistratuum munia in se trahens princeps materiam prae-
2 dandi patefecerat. nec quicquam publicae mercis tam
venale fuit quam advocatorum perfidia, adeo ut Samius,
insignis eques Romanus, quadringentis nummorum milibus 5
Suillio datis et cognita praevaricatione ferro in domo eius
3 incubuerit. igitur incipiente C. Silio consule designato,
cuius de potentia *et* exitio in tempore memorabo, consurgunt
patres legemque Cinciam flagitant, qua cavetur antiquitus,
ne quis ob causam orandam pecuniam donumve accipiat.   10

6. Deinde obstrepentibus iis, quibus ea contumelia parabatur, discors Suillio Silius acriter incubuit, veterum oratorum
exempla referens, qui famam et posteros praemia eloquentiae
2 cogitavissent. pulcherrimam alioquin et bonarum artium
principem sordidis ministeriis foedari ; ne fidem quidem 15
integram manere, ubi magnitudo quaestuum spectetur.
3 quodsi in nullius mercedem negotia agantur, pauciora fore :
nunc inimicitias, accusationes, odia et iniurias foveri, ut
quo modo vis morborum pretia medentibus, sic fori tabes
4 pecuniam advocatis ferat. meminissent C. Asinii, M. Mes- 20
sallae ac recentiorum Arruntii et Aesernini : ad summa
5 provectos incorrupta vita et facundia. talia dicente consule
designato, consentientibus aliis, parabatur sententia, qua lege
repetundarum tenerentur, cum Suillius et Cossutianus et ceteri,
qui non iudicium, quippe in manifestos, sed poenam statui 25
videbant, circumsistunt Caesarem, ante acta deprecantes.

7. Et postquam adnuit, agere incipiunt : quem illum tanta
2 superbia esse, ut aeternitatem famae spe praesumat ? usui et
rebus subsidium praeparari, ne quis inopia advocatorum poten-
3 tibus obnoxius sit. neque tamen eloquentiam gratuito con- 30
tingere : omitti curas familiares, ut quis se alienis negotiis
4 intendat. multos militia, quosdam exercendo agros tolerare
vitam ; nihil a quoquam expeti, nisi cuius fructus ante

providerit. facile Asinium et Messallam, inter Antonium et 5
Augustum bellorum praemiis refertos, aut ditium familiarum
heredes Aeserninos et Arruntios magnum animum induisse.
prompta sibi exempla, quantis mercedibus P. Clodius aut 6
5 C. Curio contionari soliti sint. se modicos senatores, *qui* 7
quieta re publica nulla nisi pacis emolumenta peterent.
cogitaret plebem, quae toga enitesceret: sublatis studiorum
pretiis etiam studia peritura. ut minus decora haec, ita 8
haud frustra dicta princeps ratus, capiendis pecuniis *statuit*
10 modum usque ad dena sestertia, quem egressi repetundarum
tenerentur.

8. Sub idem tempus Mithridates, quem imperitasse Armeniis *iussuque Gai* Caesaris vinctum memoravi, monente
Claudio in regnum remeavit, fisus Pharasmanis opibus. is 2
15 rex Hiberis idemque Mithridatis frater nuntiabat discordare
Parthos summaque imperii ambigua, minora sine cura
haberi. nam Gotarzes inter pleraque saeva necem fratri 3
Artabano coniugique ac filio eius paraverat, unde metus [eius]
in ceteros, et accivere Vardanen. ille, ut erat magnis ausis 4
20 promptus, biduo tria milia stadiorum invadit ignarumque et
exterritum Gotarzen proturbat; neque cunctatur quin proximas praefecturas corripiat, solis Seleucensibus dominationem
eius abnuentibus. in quos, ut patris suique defectores, ira 5
magis quam ex usu praesenti accensus, inplicatur obsidione
25 urbis validae et munimentis obiecti amnis muroque et com-
meatibus firmatae. interim Gotarzes Daharum Hyrcanorum- 6
que opibus auctus bellum renovat, coactusque Vardanes
omittere Seleuciam Bactrianos apud campos castra contulit.

9. Tunc distractis Orientis viribus et quonam inclinarent
30 incertis, casus Mithridati datus est occupandi Armeniam, vi
militis Romani ad excindenda castellorum ardua, simul
Hibero exercitu campos persultante. nec enim restitere 2
Armenii, fuso qui proelium ausus erat Demonacte praefecto.

3 paululum cunctationis attulit rex minoris Armeniae Cotys,
versis illuc quibusdam procerum; dein litteris Caesaris
coercitus, et cuncta in Mithridaten fluxere, quamquam
4 atrociorem quam novo regno conduceret. at Parthi imperatores cum pugnam pararent, foedus repente iaciunt 5
cognitis popularium insidiis, quas Gotarzes fratri patefecit;
congressique primo cunctanter, dein complexi dextras apud
altaria deum pepigere fraudem inimicorum ulcisci atque
5 ipsi inter se concedere. potiorque Vardanes visus retinendo
regno : at Gotarzes, ne quid aemulationis exsisteret, penitus 10
6 in Hyrcaniam abiit. regressoque Vardani deditur Seleucia
septimo post defectionem anno, non sine dedecore Parthorum,
quos una civitas tam diu eluserat.

10. Exim validissimas praefecturas invisit; et reciperare
Armeniam avebat, ni a Vibio Marso, Suriae legato, bellum 15
2 minitante cohibitus foret. atque interim Gotarzes paenitentia
concessi regni et vocante nobilitate, cui in pace durius ser-
3 vitium est, contrahit copias. et huic contra itum ad amnem
Erinden; in cuius transgressu multum certato pervicit
Vardanes, prosperisque proeliis medias nationes subegit ad 20
4 flumen Sinden, quod Dahas Ariosque disterminat. ibi modus
rebus secundis positus : nam Parthi quamquam victores
5 longinquam militiam aspernabantur. igitur exstructis monimentis, quibus opes suas testabatur nec cuiquam ante
Arsacidarum tributa illis de gentibus parta, regreditur ingens 25
gloria atque eo ferocior et subiectis intolerantior ; qui dolo
ante conposito incautum venationique intentum interfecere,
primam intra iuventam, sed claritudine paucos inter senum
regum, si perinde amorem inter populares quam metum
6 apud hostes quaesivisset. nece Vardanis turbatae Partho- 30
7 rum res inter ambiguos, quis in regnum acciperetur. multi
ad Gotarzen inclinabant, quidam ad Meherdaten prolem
Phraatis, obsidio nobis datum : dein praevaluit Gotarzes.

H

potitusque regiam, per saevitiam ac luxum adegit Parthos 8
mittere ad principem Romanum occultas preces, quis permitti Meherdaten patrium ad fastigium orabant.

11. Isdem consulibus ludi saeculares octingentesimo post
5 Romam conditam, quarto et sexagensimo quam Augustus
ediderat spectati sunt. utriusque principis rationes praeter- 2
mitto, satis narratas libris quibus res imperatoris Domitiani
composui. nam is quoque edidit ludos saeculares iisque 3
intentius adfui sacerdotio quindecimvirali praeditus ac tunc
10 praetor, quod non iactantia refero, sed quia collegio quin- 4
decimvirum antiquitus ea cura et magistratus potissimum
exsequebantur officia caerimoniarum.   sedente Claudio 5
circensibus ludis, cum pueri nobiles equis ludicrum Troiae
inirent interque eos Britannicus imperatore genitus et L.
15 Domitius adoptione mox in inperium et cognomentum
Neronis adscitus, favor plebis acrior in Domitium loco
praesagii acceptus est. vulgabaturque adfuisse infantiae 6
eius dracones in modum custodum, fabulosa et externis
miraculis adsimilata : nam ipse, haudquaquam sui detractor,
20 unam omnino anguem in cubiculo visam narrare solitus est.

12. Verum inclinatio populi supererat ex memoria Germanici, cuius illa reliqua suboles virilis ; et matri Agrippinae
miseratio augebatur ob saevitiam Messalinae, quae semper
infesta et tunc commotior, quo minus strueret crimina et
25 accusatores, novo et furori proximo amore distinebatur.
nam in C. Silium, iuventutis Romanae pulcherrimum, ita 2
exarserat, ut Iuniam Silanam, nobilem feminam, matrimonio
eius exturbaret vacuoque adultero poteretur. neque Silius 3
flagitii aut periculi nescius erat : sed certo, si abnueret,
30 exitio et non nulla fallendi spe, simul magnis praemiis,
opperiri futura et praesentibus frui pro solacio habebat.
illa non furtim, sed multo comitatu ventitare domum, 4
egressibus adhaerescere, largiri opes, honores, postremo,

velut translata iam fortuna, servi liberti paratus principis
apud adulterum visebantur.

13. At Claudius matrimonii sui ignarus et munia censoria
usurpans, theatralem populi lasciviam severis edictis increpuit, quod in P. Pomponium consularem (is carmina 5
2 scaenae dabat) inque feminas inlustres probra iecerat. et lege
lata saevitiam creditorum coercuit, ne in mortem parentum
pecunias filiis familiarum faenori darent. fontesque aquarum
3 Simbruinis collibus deductos urbi intulit. ac novas litterarum formas addidit vulgavitque, comperto Graecam quo- 10
que litteraturam non simul coeptam absolutamque.

14. Primi per figuras animalium Aegyptii sensus mentis
effingebant—ea antiquissima monimenta memoriae humanae
inpressa saxis cernuntur,—et litterarum semet inventores
perhibent; inde Phoenicas, quia mari praepollebant, intulisse 15
Graeciae gloriamque adeptos, tamquam reppererint quae
2 acceperant. quippe fama est Cadmum classe Phoenicum
vectum rudibus adhuc Graecorum populis artis eius
3 auctorem fuisse. quidam Cecropem Atheniensem vel
Linum Thebanum et temporibus Troianis Palamedem 20
Argivum memorant sedecim litterarum formas, mox alios
4 ac praecipuum Simoniden ceteras repperisse. at in Italia
Etrusci ab Corinthio Demarato, Aborigines Arcade ab
Evandro didicerunt; et forma litteris Latinis quae veter-
rimis Graecorum. sed nobis quoque paucae primum fuere, 25
5 deinde additae sunt. quo exemplo Claudius tres litteras
adiecit, quae usui imperitante eo, post oblitteratae, as-
piciuntur etiam nunc in aere publico † dis plebiscitis per
fora ac templa fixo.

15. Rettulit deinde ad senatum super collegio haruspicum, 30
ne vetustissima Italiae disciplina per desidiam exolesceret;
saepe adversis rei publicae temporibus accitos, quorum
monitu redintegratas caerimonias et in posterum rectius

habitas; primoresque Etruriae sponte aut patrum Romanorum inpulsu retinuisse scientiam et in familias propagasse;
quod nunc segnius fieri publica circa bonas artes socordia,
et quia externae superstitiones valescant. et laeta quidem 2
5 in praesens omnia, sed benignitati deum gratiam referen-
dam, ne ritus sacrorum inter ambigua culti per prospera
oblitterarentur. factum ex eo senatus consultum, viderent 3
pontifices quae retinenda firmandaque haruspicum.

16. Eodem anno Cheruscorum gens regem Roma petivit,
10 amissis per interna bella nobilibus et uno reliquo stirpis
regiae, qui apud urbem habebatur nomine Italicus. pater- 2
num huic genus e Flavo fratre Arminii, mater ex Actumero
principe Chattorum erat; ipse forma decorus et armis
equisque in patrium nostrumque morem exercitus. igitur 3
15 Caesar auctum pecunia, additis stipatoribus, hortatur gentile
decus magno animo capessere: illum primum Romae
ortum nec obsidem, sed civem ire externum ad imperium.
ac primo laetus Germanis adventus, atque, eo quod nullis 4
discordiis imbutus pari in omnes studio ageret, celebrari,
20 coli, modo comitatem et temperantiam, nulli invisa, saepius
vinolentiam ac libidines, grata barbaris, usurpans. iamque 5
apud proximos, iam longius clarescere, cum potentiam eius
suspectantes, qui factionibus floruerant, discedunt ad conter-
minos populos ac testificantur adimi veterem Germaniae
25 libertatem et Romanas opes insurgere. adeo neminem 6
isdem in terris ortum, qui principem locum impleat, nisi
exploratoris Flavi progenies super cunctos attollatur? frustra 7
Arminium praescribi: cuius si filius hostili in solo adultus
in regnum venisset, posse extimesci, infectum alimonio,
30 servitio, cultu, omnibus externis: at si paterna Italico mens 8
esset, non alium infensius arma contra patriam ac deos
penates quam parentem eius exercuisse.

17. His atque talibus magnas copias coëgere; nec pau-

2 ciores Italicum sequebantur : non enim inrupisse ad invitos,
sed accitum memorabat, quando nobilitate ceteros anteiret :
virtutem experirentur, an dignum se patruo Arminio, avo
3 Actumero praeberet.   nec patrem rubori, quod fidem adversus
Romanos volentibus Germanis sumptam numquam omisisset. 5
4 falso libertatis vocabulum obtendi ab iis, qui privatim degeneres, in publico exitiosi, nihil spei nisi per discordias
5 habeant.   adstrepebat huic alacre vulgus ; et magno *ut* inter
barbaros proelio victor rex, dein secunda fortuna ad superbiam prolapsus pulsusque, ac rursus Langobardorum opibus 10
refectus per laeta per adversa res Cheruscas adflictabat.

18. Per idem tempus Chauci, nulla dissensione domi, et
morte Sanquinii alacres, dum Corbulo adventat, inferiorem
Germaniam incursavere duce Gannasco, qui natione Canninefas, auxiliare stipendium meritus, post transfuga, levibus 15
navigiis praedabundus Gallorum maxime oram vastabat,
2 non ignarus dites et inbelles esse.   at Corbulo provinciam
ingressus magna cum cura et mox gloria, cui principium
illa militia fuit, triremes alveo Rheni, ceteras navium, ut
quaeque habiles, per aestuaria et fossas adegit ; luntribusque 20
hostium depressis et exturbato Gannasco, ubi praesentia
satis composita sunt, legiones operum et laboris ignavas,
populationibus laetantes, veterem ad morem reduxit, ne quis
3 agmine decederet nec pugnam nisi iussus iniret.   stationes,
vigiliae, diurna nocturnaque munia in armis agitabantur. 25
4 feruntque militem, quia vallum non accinctus, atque alium,
5 quia pugione tantum accinctus foderet, morte punitos.   quae
nimia et incertum an falso iacta originem tamen e severitate
ducis traxere ; intentumque et magnis delictis inexorabilem
scias, cui tantum asperitatis etiam adversus levia credebatur. 30

19. Ceterum is terror milites hostesque in diversum
adfecit : nos virtutem auximus, barbari ferocim infregaere.
2 et natio Frisiorum, post rebellionem clade L. Apronii

coeptam infensa aut male fida, datis obsidibus consedit apud
agros a Corbulone descriptos : idem senatum, magistratus,
leges inposuit. ac ne iussa exuerent, praesidium immunivit, 3
missis qui maiores Chaucos ad deditionem pellicerent, simul
5 Gannascum dolo adgrederentur. nec inritae aut degeneres 4
insidiae fuere adversus transfugam et violatorem fidei. sed 5
caede eius motae Chaucorum mentes, et Corbulo semina
rebellionis praebebat, ut laeta apud plerosque, ita apud
quosdam sinistra fama. cur hostem conciret? adversa in 6
10 rem publicam casura : sin prospere egisset, formidolosum
paci virum insignem et ignavo principi praegravem. igitur 7
Claudius adeo novam in Germanias vim prohibuit, ut referri
praesidia cis Rhenum iuberet.

20. Iam castra in hostili solo molienti Corbuloni eae
15 litterae redduntur. ille re subita, quamquam multa simul
offunderentur, metus ex imperatore, contemptio ex barbaris,
ludibrium apud socios, nihil aliud prolocutus quam 'beatos
quondam duces Romanos,' signum receptui dedit. ut tamen 2
miles otium exueret, inter Mosam Rhenumque trium et
20 viginti milium spatio fossam perduxit, qua incerta Oceani
vitarentur. insigne tamen triumphi indulsit Caesar, quamvis 3
bellum negavisset.

Nec multo post Curtius Rufus eundem honorem adipis- 4
citur, qui in agro Mattiaco recluserat specus quaerendis
25 venis argenti ; unde tenuis fructus nec in longum fuit : at
legionibus cum damno labor, effodere rivos, quaeque in
aperto gravia, humum infra moliri. quis subactus miles, et 5
quia plures per provincias similia tolerabantur, componit
occultas litteras nomine exercituum, precantium imperatorem
30 ut, quibus permissurus esset exercitus, triumphalia ante
tribueret.

21. De origine Curtii Rufi, quem gladiatore genitum
quidam prodidere, neque falsa prompserim et vera exsequi

2 pudet. postquam adolevit, sectator quaestoris cui Africa
obtigerat, dum in oppido Adrumeto vacuis per medium diei
porticibus secretus agitat, oblata ei species muliebris ultra
modum humanum et audita est vox 'tu es, Rufe, qui in
3 hanc provinciam pro consule venies.' tali omine in spem 5
sublatus degressusque in urbem largitione amicorum, simul
acri ingenio quaesturam et mox nobiles inter candidatos
praeturam principis suffragio adsequitur, cum hisce verbis
Tiberius dedecus natalium eius velavisset: 'Curtius Rufus
4 videtur mihi ex se natus.' longa post haec senecta, et 10
adversus superiores tristi adulatione, adrogans minoribus,
inter pares difficilis, consulare imperium, triumphi insignia
ac postremo Africam obtinuit; atque ibi defunctus fatale
praesagium implevit.

    22. Interea Romae, nullis palam neque cognitis mox 15
causis, Cn. Nonius eques Romanus ferro accinctus reperitur
2 in coetu salutantum principem. nam postquam tormentis
dilaniabatur, de se non *infitiatus* conscios non edidit, incertum an occultans.

3   Isdem consulibus P. Dolabella censuit spectaculum gladia- 20
torum per omnes annos celebrandum pecunia eorum, qui
4 quaesturam adipiscerentur. apud maiores virtutis id praemium fuerat, cunctisque civium, si bonis artibus fiderent,
licitum petere magistratus; ac ne aetas quidem distingue-
batur, quin prima iuventa consulatum et dictaturas inirent. 25
5 sed quaestores regibus etiam tum imperantibus instituti sunt,
6 quod lex curiata ostendit ab L. Bruto repetita. mansitque
consulibus potestas deligendi, donec eum quoque honorem
7 populus mandaret. creatique primum Valerius Potitus et
Aemilius Mamercus sexagensimo tertio anno post Tarquinios 30
8 exactos, ut rem militarem comitarentur. dein gliscentibus
negotiis duo additi, qui Romae curarent: mox duplicatus
numerus, stipendiaria iam Italia et accedentibus provinciarum

vectigalibus: post lege Sullae viginti creati supplendo senatui, 9
cui iudicia tradiderat. et quamquam equites iudicia reci- 10
peravissent, quaestura tamen ex dignitate candidatorum aut
facilitate tribuentium gratuito concedebatur, donec sententia
5 Dolabellae velut venundaretur.

23. A. Vitellio L. Vipstano consulibus cum de supplendo
senatu agitaretur primoresque Galliae, quae Comata appel-
latur, foedera et civitatem Romanam pridem adsecuti, ius
adipiscendorum in urbe honorum expeterent, multus ea
10 super re variusque rumor. et studiis diversis apud prin- 2
cipem certabatur, adseverantium non adeo aegram Italiam,
ut senatum suppeditare urbi suae nequiret. suffecisse olim 3
indigenas consanguineis populis, nec paenitere veteris rei
publicae. quin adhuc memorari exempla quae priscis
15 moribus ad virtutem et gloriam Romana indoles prodiderit.
an parum quod Veneti et Insubres curiam inruperint, nisi 4
coetu alienigenarum velut captivitas inferatur? quem ultra 5
honorem residuis nobilium, aut si quis pauper e Latio
senator foret? oppleturos omnia divites illos, quorum avi 6
20 proavique hostilium nationum duces exercitus nostros ferro
vique ceciderint, divum Iulium apud Alesiam obsederint.
recentia haec: quid si memoria eorum oreretur, qui *sub* 7
Capitolio et arce Romana manibus eorundem prostrati
sint? fruerentur sane vocabulo civitatis: insignia patrum,
25 decora magistratuum ne vulgarent.

24. His atque talibus haud permotus princeps et statim
contra disseruit et vocato senatu ita exorsus est: 'maiores
mei, quorum antiquissimus Clausus origine Sabina simul
in civitatem Romanam et in familias patriciorum adscitus
30 est, hortantur uti paribus consiliis *in* re publica capessenda,
transferendo huc quod usquam egregium fuerit neque 2
enim ignoro Iulios Alba, Coruncanios Camerio, Porcios
Tusculo, et ne vetera scrutemur, Etruria Lucaniaque et

omni Italia in senatum accitos, postremo ipsam ad Alpes
promotam, ut non modo singuli viritim, sed terrae, gentes
3 in nomen nostrum coalescerent. tunc solida domi quies et
adversus externa floruimus, cum Transpadani in civitatem
recepti, cum specie deductarum per orbem terrae legionum 5
additis provincialium validissimis fesso imperio subventum
4 est. num paenitet Balbos ex Hispania nec minus insignes
viros e Gallia Narbonensi transivisse? manent posteri eorum
5 nec amore in hanc patriam nobis concedunt. quid aliud
exitio Lacedaemoniis et Atheniensibus fuit, quamquam armis 10
6 pollerent, nisi quod victos pro alienigenis arcebant? at con-
ditor nostri Romulus tantum sapientia valuit, ut plerosque
7 populos eodem die hostes, dein cives habuerit. advenae in
nos regnaverunt: libertinorum filiis magistratus mandare non,
ut plerique falluntur, repens, sed priori populo factitatum est. 15
8 at cum Senonibus pugnavimus: scilicet Vulsci et Aequi
9 numquam adversam nobis aciem instruxere. capti a Gallis
sumus: sed et Tuscis obsides dedimus et Samnitium iugum
subiimus. ac tamen, si cuncta bella recenseas, nullum breviore spatio quam adversus Gallos confectum: continua inde 20
10 ac fida pax. iam moribus artibus adfinitatibus nostris mixti
aurum et opes suas inferant potius quam separati habeant.
11 omnia, patres conscripti, quae nunc vetustissima creduntur,
nova fuere: plebeii magistratus post patricios, Latini post
plebeios, ceterarum Italiae gentium post Latinos. invete- 25
rascet hoc quoque, et quod hodie exemplis tuemur, inter
exempla erit.'

25. Orationem principis secuto patrum consulto primi
2 Aedui senatorum in urbe ius adepti sunt   datum id foederi
antiquo, et quia soli Gallorum fraternitatis nomen cum populo 30
Romano usurpant.

3   Isdem diebus in numerum patriciorum adscivit Caesar
vetustissimum quemque e senatu aut quibus clari parentes

fuerant, paucis iam reliquis familiarum, quas Romulus maiorum et L. Brutus minorum gentium appellaverant, exhaustis
etiam quas dictator Caesar lege Cassia et princeps Augustus
lege Saenia sublegere; laetaque haec in rem publicam munia 4
5 multo gaudio censoris inibantur. famosos probris quonam 5
modo senatu depelleret anxius, mitem et recens repertam
quam ex severitate prisca rationem adhibuit, monendo, secum
quisque de se consultaret peteretque ius exuendi ordinis:
facilem eius rei veniam. et motos senatu excusatosque 6
10 simul propositurum, ut iudicium censorum ac pudor sponte
cedentium permixta ignominiam mollirent. ob ea Vipstanus 7
consul rettulit patrem senatus appellandum esse Claudium:
quippe promiscum patris patriae cognomentum; nova in rem
publicam merita non usitatis vocabulis honoranda: sed ipse
15 cohibuit consulem ut nimium adsentantem. condiditque 8
lustrum, quo censa sunt civium quinquagiens noviens centena
octoginta quattuor milia septuaginta duo. isque illi finis
inscitiae erga domum suam fuit: haud multo post flagitia
uxoris noscere ac punire adactus, ut deinde ardesceret in
20 nuptias incestas.

26. Iam Messalina facilitate adulteriorum in fastidium
versa ad incognitas libidines profluebat, cum abrumpi dissimulationem etiam Silius, sive fatali vaecordia an imminentium
periculorum remedium ipsa pericula ratus, urguebat: quippe 2
25 non eo ventum, ut senectam principis opperirentur. insontibus
innoxia consilia, flagitiis manifestis subsidium ab audacia
petendum. adesse conscios paria metuentes. se caelibem, 3
orbum, nuptiis et adoptando Britannico paratum. mansuram 4
eandem Messalinae potentiam, addita securitate, si prae-
30 venirent Claudium, ut insidiis incautum, ita irae properum.
segniter eae voces acceptae, non amore in maritum, sed ne 5
Silius summa adeptus sperneret adulteram scelusque inter
ancipitia probatum veris mox pretiis aestimaret. nomen tamen 6

matrimonii concupivit ob magnitudinem infamiae, cuius apud
7 prodigos novissima voluptas est.   nec ultra exspectato quam
dum sacrificii gratia Claudius Ostiam proficisceretur, cuncta
nuptiarum sollemnia celebrat.

   27. Haud sum ignarus fabulosum visum iri tantum ullis 5
mortalium securitatis fuisse in civitate omnium gnara et nihil
reticente, nedum consulem designatum cum uxore principis,
praedicta die, adhibitis qui obsignarent, velut suscipiendorum
liberorum causa convenisse, atque illam audisse auspicum
verba, subisse, sacrificasse apud deos; discubitum inter 10
convivas, oscula complexus, noctem denique actam licentia
2 coniugali.   sed nihil compositum miraculi causa, verum
audita scriptaque senioribus tradam.

   28. Igitur domus principis inhorruerat, maximeque quos
penes potentia et, si res verterentur, formido, non iam secretis 15
conloquiis, sed aperte fremere, dum histrio cubiculum principis insultaverit, dedecus quidem inlatum, sed excidium procul
afuisse: nunc iuvenem nobilem dignitate formae vi mentis ac
propinquo consulatu maiorem ad spem adcingi; nec enim
2 occultum, quid post tale matrimonium superesset.   subibat 20
sine dubio metus reputantes hebetem Claudium et uxori de-
3 vinctum multasque mortes iussu Messalinae patratas: rursus
ipsa facilitas imperatoris fiduciam dabat, si atrocitate criminis
praevaluissent, posse opprimi damnatam ante quam ream;
sed in eo discrimen verti, si defensio audiretur, utque clausae 25
aures etiam confitenti forent.

   29. Ac primo Callistus, iam mihi circa necem *Gai* Caesaris
narratus, et Appianae caedis molitor Narcissus flagrantissima-
que eo in tempore gratia Pallas agitavere, num Messalinam
secretis minis depellerent amore Silii, cuncta alia dissimulantes. 30
2 dein metu, ne ad perniciem ultro traherentur, desistunt, Pallas
per ignaviam, Callistus prioris quoque regiae peritus et
potentiam cautis quam acribus consiliis tutius haberi: perstitit

Narcissus, set solum id immutans, ne quo sermone praesciam criminis et accusatoris faceret. ipse ad occasiones intentus, 3 longa apud Ostiam Caesaris mora, duas paelices, quarum is corpori maxime insueverat, largitione ac promissis et uxore
5 deiecta plus potentiae ostentando perpulit delationem subire.

30. Exim Calpurnia (id paelici nomen), ubi datum secretum, genibus Caesaris provoluta nupsisse Messalinam Silio exclamat; simul Cleopatram, quae id opperiens adstabat, an 2 comperisset interrogat, atque illa adnuente cieri Narcissum
10 postulat. is veniam in praeteritum petens, quod ei Vettios, 3 Plautios dissimulavisset, nec nunc adulteria obiecturum ait, nedum domum servitia et ceteros fortunae paratus reposceret. frueretur immo his, set redderet uxorem rumperetque tabulas 4 nuptiales. 'an discidium' inquit 'tuum nosti? nam matrimo- 5
15 nium Silii vidit populus et senatus et miles; ac ni propere agis, tenet urbem maritus.'

31. Tum potissimum *quemque* amicorum vocat, primumque rei frumentariae praefectum Turranium, post Lusium Getam praetorianis inpositum percontatur. quis fatentibus 2
20 certatim ceteri circumstrepunt; iret in castra, firmaret praetorias cohortes, securitati ante quam vindictae consuleret. satis constat eo pavore offusum Claudium, ut identidem 3 interrogaret, an ipse imperii potens, an Silius privatus esset. at Messalina non alias solutior luxu, adulto autumno 4
25 simulacrum vindemiae per domum celebrabat. urgueri prela, 5 fluere lacus; et feminae pellibus accinctae adsultabant ut sacrificantes vel insanientes Bacchae; ipsa crine fluxo thyrsum quatiens, iuxtaque Silius hedera vinctus, gerere cothurnos, iacere caput, strepente circum procaci choro. ferunt Vettium 6
30 Valentem lascivia in praealtam arborem conisum, interrogantibus quid aspiceret, respondisse tempestatem ab Ostia atrocem, sive coeperat ea species, seu forte lapsa vox in praesagium vertit.

32. Non rumor interea, sed undique nuntii incedunt, qui
gnara Claudio cuncta et venire promptum ultioni adferrent.
2 igitur Messalina Lucullianos in hortos, Silius dissimulando
3 metu ad munia fori digrediuntur. ceteris passim dilabentibus
adfuere centuriones, inditaque sunt vincla, ut quis reperiebatur 5
4 in publico aut per latebras. Messalina tamen, quamquam
res adversae consilium eximerent, ire obviam et aspici a
marito, quod saepe subsidium habuerat, haud segniter
intendit, misitque ut Britannicus et Octavia in complexum
5 patris pergerent. et Vibidiam, virginum Vestalium vetus- 10
tissimam, oravit pontificis maximi aures adire, clementiam
6 expetere. atque interim, tribus omnino comitantibus—id
repente solitudinis erat—spatium urbis pedibus emensa,
vehiculo, quo purgamenta hortorum excipiuntur, Ostiensem
viam intrat, nulla cuiusquam misericordia, quia flagitiorum 15
deformitas praevalebat.

33. Trepidabatur nihilo minus a Caesare : quippe Getae
praetorii praefecto haud satis fidebant, ad honesta seu prava
2 iuxta levi. ergo Narcissus, adsumptis quibus idem metus,
non aliam spem incolumitatis Caesaris adfirmat, quam si 20
ius militum uno illo die in aliquem libertorum transferret,
3 seque offert suscepturum. ac ne, dum in urbem revehitur,
ad paenitentiam a L. Vitellio et Largo Caecina mutaretur,
in eodem gestamine sedem poscit adsumiturque.

34. Crebra post haec fama fuit, inter diversas principis 25
voces, cum modo incusaret flagitia uxoris, aliquando ad
memoriam coniugii et infantiam liberorum revolveretur, non
aliud prolocutum Vitellium quam 'o facinus! o scelus!'
2 instabat quidem Narcissus aperiret ambages et veri copiam
faceret : sed non ideo pervicit, quin suspensa et quo ducerentur 30
inclinata responderet exemploque eius Largus Caecina
3 uteretur. et iam erat in aspectu Messalina clamitabatque
audiret Octaviae et Britannici matrem, cum obstrepere

accusator, Silium et nuptias referens ; simul codicillos
libidinum indices tradidit, quis visus Caesaris averteret. nec 4
multo post urbem ingredienti offerebantur communes liberi,
nisi Narcissus amoveri eos iussisset. Vibidiam depellere 5
5 nequivit, quin multa cum invidia flagitaret, ne indefensa
coniunx exitio daretur. igitur auditurum principem et fore
diluendi criminis facultatem respondit: iret interim virgo et
sacra capesseret.

35. Mirum inter haec silentium Claudi, Vitellius ignaro
10 propior: omnia liberto oboediebant. patefieri domum adulteri
atque illuc deduci imperatorem iubet. ac primum in vestibulo 2
effigiem patris Silii consulto senatus abolitam demonstrat,
tum quidquid avitum Neronibus et Drusis in pretium probri
cessisse. incensumque et ad minas erumpentem castris infert, 3
15 parata contione militum ; apud quos praemonente Narcisso
pauca verba fecit: nam etsi iustum dolorem pudor impediebat.
continuus dehinc cohortium clamor nomina reorum et poenas 4
flagitantium ; admotusque Silius tribunali non defensionem,
non moras temptavit, precatus ut mors adceleraretur. eadem 5
20 constantia et inlustres equites Romani cupidi maturae necis
fuerunt. Titium Proculum, custodem a Silio Messalinae 6
datum et indicium offerentem, Vettium Valentem confessum
et Pompeium Urbicum ac Saufeium Trogum ex consciis
tradi ad supplicium iubet. Decrius quoque Calpurnianus 7
25 vigilum praefectus, Sulpicius Rufus ludi procurator, Iuncus
Vergilianus senator eadem poena adfecti.

36. Solus Mnester cunctationem attulit, dilaniata veste
clamitans aspiceret verberum notas, reminisceretur vocis,
qua se obnoxium iussis Messalinae dedisset: aliis largitione 2
30 aut spei magnitudine, sibi ex necessitate culpam ; nec
cuiquam ante pereundum fuisse, si Silius rerum poteretur.
commotum his et pronum ad misericordiam Caesarem 3
perpulere liberti, ne tot inlustribus viris interfectis histrioni

consuleretur : sponte an coactus tam magna peccavisset,
4 nihil referre. ne Trauli quidem Montani equitis Romani
defensio recepta est. is modesta inventa, sed corpore insigni,
accitus ultro noctemque intra unam a Messalina proturbatus
5 erat, paribus lasciviis ad cupidinem et fastidia. Suillio 5
Caesonino et Plautio Laterano mors remittitur, huic ob
patrui egregium meritum : Caesoninus vitiis protectus est,
tamquam in illo foedissimo coetu passus muliebria.

37. Interim Messalina Lucullianis in hortis prolatare vitam,
componere preces, nonnulla spe et aliquando ira : tantum 10
inter extrema superbiae gerebat. ac ni caedem eius Nar-
2 cissus properavisset, verterat pernicies in accusatorem. nam
Claudius domum regressus et tempestivis epulis delenitus,
ubi vino incaluit, iri iubet nuntiarique miserae (hoc enim
verbo usum ferunt) dicendam ad causam postero die adesset. 15
3 quod ubi auditum et languescere ira, redire amor ac, si
cunctarentur, propinqua nox et uxorii cubiculi memoria
timebantur, prorumpit Narcissus denuntiatque centurionibus
et tribuno, qui aderat, exsequi caedem ; ita imperatorem
4 iubere. custos et exactor e libertis Euodus datur. isque 20
raptim in hortos praegressus repperit fusam humi, adsidente
matre Lepida, quae florenti filiae haud concors supremis
eius necessitatibus ad miserationem evicta erat suadebatque
ne percussorem opperiretur : transisse vitam neque aliud
5 quam morti decus quaerendum. sed animo per libidines 25
corrupto nihil honestum inerat; lacrimaeque et questus
inriti ducebantur, cum impetu venientium pulsae fores adstititque tribunus per silentium, at libertus increpans multis
et servilibus probris.

38. Tunc primum fortunam suam introspexit ferrumque 30
accepit, quod frustra iugulo aut pectori per trepidationem
admovens ictu tribuni transigitur. corpus matri concessum.
2 nuntiatumque Claudio epulanti perisse Messalinam, non

distincto sua an aliena manu. nec ille quaesivit, poposcit-
que poculum et solita convivio celebravit. ne secutis quidem 3
diebus odii gaudii, irae tristitiae, ullius denique humani
adfectus signa dedit, non cum laetantes accusatores as-
5 piceret, non cum filios maerentes. iuvitque oblivionem eius 4
senatus censendo nomen et effigies privatis ac publicis locis
demovendas. decreta Narcisso quaestoria insignia, levis- 5
simum fastidio eius, cum supra Pallantem et Callistum
ageret, † honesta quidem, sed **ex** quis deterrima orerentur
10 [tristitiis multis].

LIBER XII.

1. CAEDE Messalinae convulsa principis domus, orto apud
libertos certamine, quis deligeret uxorem Claudio, caelibis
2 vitae intoleranti et coniugum imperiis obnoxio. nec minore
ambitu feminae exarserant: suam quaeque nobilitatem formam opes contendere ac digna tanto matrimonio ostentare. 5
3 sed maxime ambigebatur inter Lolliam Paulinam M. Lollii
consularis et Iuliam Agrippinam Germanico genitam:
huic Pallas, illi Callistus fautores aderant; at Aelia Paetina
4 e familia Tuberonum Narcisso fovebatur. ipse huc modo,
modo illuc, ut quemque suadentium audierat, promptus, 10
discordantes in consilium vocat ac promere sententiam et
adicere rationes iubet.

2. Narcissus vetus matrimonium, filiam communem (nam
Antonia ex Paetina erat), nihil in penatibus eius novum
disserebat, si sueta coniunx rediret, haudquaquam nover- 15
calibus odiis visura Britannicum, Octaviam, proxima suis
2 pignora. Callistus inprobatam longo discidio, ac si rursum
adsumeretur, eo ipso superbam; longeque rectius Lolliam
induci, quando nullos liberos genuisset, vacuam aemulatione
3 et privignis parentis loco futuram. at Pallas id maxime in 20
Agrippina laudare, quod Germanici nepotem secum traheret,
dignum prorsus imperatoria fortuna: stirpem nobilem et
familiae *Iuliae* Claudiaeque posteros coniungeret, ne femina
expertae fecunditatis, integra iuventa, claritudinem Caesarum
aliam in domum ferret. 25

3. Praevaluere haec adiuta Agrippinae inlecebris: ad eum
per speciem necessitudinis crebro ventitando pellicit patruum,
ut praelata ceteris et nondum uxor potentia uxoria iam
2 uteretur. nam ubi sui matrimonii certa fuit, struere maiora

I

nuptiasque Domitii, quem ex Cn. Ahenobarbo genuerat, et
Octaviae Caesaris filiae moliri; quod sine scelere perpetrari
non poterat, quia L. Silano desponderat Octaviam Caesar
iuvenemque et alia clarum insigni triumphalium et gladiatorii
5 muneris magnificentia protulerat ad studia vulgi. sed nihil 3
arduum videbatur in animo principis, cui non iudicium, non
odium erat nisi indita et iussa.

4. Igitur Vitellius, nomine censoris serviles fallacias ob-
tegens ingruentiumque dominationum provisor, quo gratiam
10 Agrippinae pararet, consiliis eius implicari, ferre crimina in
Silanum, cuius sane decora et procax soror, Iunia Calvina,
haud multo ante Vitellii nurus fuerat. hinc initium accusa- 2
tionis; fratrumque non incestum, sed incustoditum amorem
ad infamiam traxit. et praebebat Caesar aures, accipiendis 3
15 adversus generum suspicionibus caritate filiae promptior. at 4
Silanus insidiarum nescius ac forte eo anno praetor,
repente per edictum Vitellii ordine senatorio movetur,
quamquam lecto pridem senatu lustroque condito. simul 5
adfinitatem Claudius diremit, adactusque Silanus eiurare
20 magistratum, et reliquus praeturae dies in Eprium Mar-
cellum conlatus est.

5. C. Pompeio Q. Veranio consulibus pactum inter
Claudium et Agrippinam matrimonium iam fama, iam amore
inlicito firmabatur; necdum celebrare sollemnia nuptiarum
25 audebant, nullo exemplo deductae in domum patrui fratris
filiae: quin et incestum ac, si sperneretur, ne in malum
publicum erumperet metuebatur. nec ante omissa cunc- 2
tatio quam Vitellius suis artibus id perpetrandum sumpsit.
percontatusque Caesarem an iussis populi, an auctoritati 3
30 senatus cederet, ubi ille unum se civium et consensui imparem respondit, opperiri intra palatium iubet. ipse curiam 4
ingreditur, summamque rem publicam agi obtestans veniam
dicendi ante alios exposcit orditurque: gravissimos principis

labores, quis orbem terrae capessat, egere adminiculis, ut
5 domestica cura vacuus in commune consulat. quod porro
honestius censoriae mentis levamentum quam adsumere coniugem, prosperis dubiisque sociam, cui cogitationes intimas,
cui parvos liberos tradat, non luxui aut voluptatibus adsue- 5
factus, sed qui prima ab iuventa legibus obtemperavisset.

6. Postquam haec favorabili oratione praemisit multaque
patrum adsentatio sequebatur, capto rursus initio, quando
maritandum principem cuncti suaderent, deligi oportere
2 feminam nobilitate puerperiis sanctimonia insignem. nec 10
diu anquirendum quin Agrippina claritudine generis anteiret :
datum ab ea fecunditatis experimentum et congruere artes
3 honestas. id vero egregium, quod provisu deum vidua
iungeretur principi sua tantum matrimonia experto. audivisse a parentibus, vidisse ipsos abripi coniuges ad libita 15
4 Caesarum : procul id a praesenti modestia. statueretur immo
documentum, quo uxorem imperator *a patribus* acciperet.
5 at enim nova nobis in fratrum filias coniugia : sed aliis
gentibus sollemnia, neque lege ulla prohibita ; et sobrinarum
diu ignorata tempore addito percrebruisse. morem accom- 20
modari, prout conducat, et fore hoc quoque in iis quae mox
usurpentur.

7. Haud defuere qui certatim, si cunctaretur Caesar, vi
2 acturos testificantes erumperent curia. conglobatur promisca
multitudo populumque Romanum eadem orare clamitat. 25
3 nec Claudius ultra exspectato obvius apud forum praebet se
gratantibus, senatumque ingressus decretum postulat, quo
iustae inter patruos fratrumque filias nuptiae etiam in pos-
4 terum statuerentur. nec tamen repertus est nisi unus talis
matrimonii cupitor, Alledius Severus eques Romanus, quem 30
5 plerique Agrippinae gratia inpulsum ferebant. versa ex eo
civitas et cuncta feminae oboediebant, non per lasciviam, ut
6 Messalina, rebus Romanis inludenti. adductum et quasi

virile servitium: palam severitas ac saepius superbia; nihil
domi inpudicum, nisi dominationi expediret.   cupido auri im- 7
mensa obtentum habebat, quasi subsidium regno pararetur.

    8. Die nuptiarum Silanus mortem sibi conscivit, sive eo
5 usque spem vitae produxerat, seu delecto die augendam ad
invidiam.   Calvina soror eius Italia pulsa est.   addidit Claudius 2
sacra ex legibus Tulli regis piaculaque apud lucum Dianae per
pontifices danda, inridentibus cunctis, quod poenae procura-
tionesque incesti id temporis exquirerentur.   at Agrippina, ne 3
10 malis tantum facinoribus notesceret, veniam exilii pro Annaeo
Seneca, simul praeturam impetrat, laetum in publicum rata
ob claritudinem studiorum eius, utque Domitii pueritia tali
magistro adolesceret et consiliis eiusdem ad spem dominationis uterentur, quia Seneca fidus in Agrippinam memoria
15 beneficii et infensus Claudio dolore iniuriae credebatur.

    9. Placitum dehinc non ultra cunctari, sed designatum
consulem Memmium Pollionem ingentibus promissis inducunt
sententiam expromere, qua oraretur Claudius despondere
Octaviam Domitio; quod aetati utriusque non absurdum et
20 maiora patefacturum erat.   Pollio haud disparibus verbis 2
ac nuper Vitellius censet; despondeturque Octavia, ac super
priorem necessitudinem sponsus iam et gener Domitius
aequari Britannico studiis matris, arte eorum, quis ob ac-
cusatam Messalinam ultio ex filio timebatur.

25   **10.** Per idem tempus legati Parthorum ad expetendum,
ut rettuli, Meherdaten missi senatum ingrediuntur mandataque
in hunc modum incipiunt: non se foederis ignaros nec
defectione a familia Arsacidarum venire, set filium Vononis,
nepotem Phraatis accersere adversus dominationem Gotarzis
30 nobilitati plebique iuxta intolerandam.   iam fratres, iam 2
propinquos, iam longius sitos caedibus exhaustos: adici
coniuges gravidas, liberos parvos, dum socors domi, bellis
infaustus ignaviam saevitia tegat.   veterem sibi ac publice 3

coeptam nobiscum amicitiam, et subveniendum sociis virium
4 aemulis cedentibusque per reverentiam.   ideo regum liberos
obsides dari, ut, si domestici imperii taedeat, sit regressus
ad principem patresque, quorum moribus adsuefactus rex
melior adscisceretur.   5

11. Ubi haec atque talia dissertavere, incipit orationem
Caesar de fastigio Romano Parthorumque obsequiis, seque
divo Augusto adaequabat, petitum ab eo regem referens,
2 omissa Tiberii memoria, quamquam is quoque miserat. addidit praecepta (etenim aderat Meherdates), ut non domina- 10
tionem et servos, sed rectorem et cives cogitaret, clemen-
tiamque ac iustitiam, quanto ignota barbaris, tanto laetiora
3 capesseret.   hinc versus ad legatos extollit laudibus alumnum
urbis, spectatae ad id modestiae : ac tamen ferenda regum
4 ingenia, neque usui crebras mutationes.   rem Romanam 15
huc satietate gloriae provectam, ut externis quoque gentibus
quietem velit.   datum posthac C. Cassio, qui Suriae praeerat,
deducere iuvenem ripam ad Euphratis.

12. Ea tempestate Cassius ceteros praeminebat peritia
legum : nam militares artes per otium ignotae, industrios- 20
2 que aut ignavos pax in aequo tenet.   ac tamen quantum sine
bello dabatur, revocare priscum morem, exercitare legiones,
cura provisu perinde agere ac si hostis ingrueret : ita dignum
maioribus suis et familia Cassia *ratus* per illas quoque gentes
3 celebrata.   igitur excitis quorum de sententia petitus rex, 25
positisque castris apud Zeugma, unde maxime pervius amnis,
postquam inlustres Parthi rexque Arabum Acbarus advenerat,
monet Meherdaten, barbarorum impetus acres cunctatione
languescere aut in perfidiam mutari : ita urgueret coepta.
4 quod spretum fraude Acbari, qui iuvenem ignarum et sum- 30
mam fortunam in luxu ratum multos per dies attinuit apud
5 oppidum Edessam.   et vocante Carene promptasque res
ostentante, si citi advenissent, non comminus Mesopotamiam,

sed flexu Armeniam petunt, id temporis inportunam, quia
hiems occipiebat.

13. Exim nivibus et montibus fessi, postquam campos
propinquabant, copiis Carenis adiunguntur, tramissoque
5 amne Tigri permeant Adiabenos, quorum rex Izates societatem Meherdatis palam induerat, in Gotarzen per occulta et
magis fida inclinabat. sed capta in transitu urbs Ninos, 2
vetustissima sedes Assyriae, *et* castellum insigne fama, quod
postremo inter Darium atque Alexandrum proelio Persarum
10 illic opes conciderant. interea Gotarzes apud montem, cui 3
nomen Sanbulos, vota dis loci suscipiebat, praecipua religione
Herculis, qui tempore stato per quietem monet sacerdotes,
ut templum iuxta equos venatui adornatos sistant. equi ubi 4
pharetras telis onustas accepere, per saltus vagi nocte de-
15 mum vacuis pharetris multo cum anhelitu redeunt. rursum
deus, qua silvas pererraverit, nocturno visu demonstrat,
reperiunturque fusae passim ferae.

14. Ceterum Gotarzes, nondum satis aucto exercitu, flumine
Corma pro munimento uti, et quamquam per insectationes et
20 nuntios ad proelium vocaretur, nectere moras, locos mutare et
missis corruptoribus exuendam ad fidem hostes emercari. ex 2
quis Izates Adiabeno, mox Acbarus Arabum cum exercitu
abscedunt, levitate gentili, et quia experimentis cognitum est
barbaros malle Roma petere reges quam habere. at Meher- 3
25 dates validis auxiliis nudatus, ceterorum proditione suspecta,
quod unum reliquum, rem in casum dare proelioque experiri
statuit. nec detrectavit pugnam Gotarzes deminutis hosti- 4
bus ferox; concursumque magna caede et ambiguo eventu,
donec Carenem profligatis obversis longius evectum integer
30 a tergo globus circumveniret. tum omni spe perdita Meher- 5
dates, promissa Parracis paterni clientis secutus, dolo eius
vincitur traditurque victori. atque ille non propinquum 6
neque Arsacis de gente, sed alienigenam et Romanum

increpans, auribus decisis vivere iubet, ostentui clementiae
7 suae et in nos dehonestamento. dein Gotarzes morbo obiit,
8 accitusque in regnum Vonones Medos tum praesidens. nulla
huic prospera aut adversa, quis memoraretur: brevi et
inglorio imperio perfunctus est, resque Parthorum in filium 5
eius Vologesen translatae.

15. At Mithridates Bosporanus amissis opibus vagus, postquam Didium ducem Romanum roburque exercitus abisse
cognoverat, relictos in novo regno Cotym iuventa rudem et
paucas cohortium cum Iulio Aquila equite Romano, spretis 10
utrisque concire nationes, inlicere perfugas; postremo exercitu coacto regem Dandaridarum exturbat imperioque eius
2 potitur. quae ubi cognita et iam iamque Bosporum invasurus
habebatur, diffisi propriis viribus Aquila et Cotys, quia Zorsines Siracorum rex hostilia resumpserat, externas et ipsi 15
gratias quaesivere missis legatis ad Eunonen, qui Aorsorum
3 genti *praesidens opibus* praecellebat. nec fuit in arduo
societas potentiam Romanam adversus rebellem Mithridaten
ostentantibus. igitur pepigere, equestribus proeliis Eunones
certaret, obsidia urbium Romani capesserent.   20

16. Tunc composito agmine incedunt, cuius frontem et
terga Aorsi, media cohortes et Bosporani tutabantur nostris
2 in armis. sic pulsus hostis, ventumque Sozam, oppidum
Dandaricae, quod desertum a Mithridate ob ambiguos
popularium animos optineri relicto ibi praesidio visum. 25
3 exim in Siracos pergunt, et transgressi amnem Pandam
circumveniunt urbem Uspen, editam loco et moenibus ac
fossis munitam, nisi quod moenia non saxo sed cratibus et
vimentis ac media humo adversum inrumpentes invalida
erant; eductaeque altius turres facibus atque hastis turbabant 30
4 obsessos. ac ni proelium nox diremisset, coepta patrataque
expugnatio eundem intra diem foret.

17. Postero misere legatos, veniam liberis corporibus

orantes : servitii decem milia offerebant. quod aspernati sunt victores, quia trucidare deditos saevum, tantam multitudinem custodia cingere arduum : belli potius iure caderent, datumque militibus, qui scalis evaserant, signum caedis. excidio 2
5 Uspensium metus ceteris iniectus, nihil tutum ratis, cum arma, munimenta, impediti vel eminentes loci amnesque et urbes iuxta perrumperentur. igitur Zorsines, diu pensitato 8 Mithridatisne rebus extremis an patrio regno consuleret, postquam praevaluit gentilis utilitas, datis obsidibus apud effigiem
10 Caesaris procubuit, magna gloria exercitus Romani, quem incruentum et victorem tridui itinere afuisse ab amne Tanai constitit. sed in regressu dispar fortuna fuit, quia 4 navium quasdam (quippe mari remeabant) in litora Taurorum delatas circumvenere barbari, praefecto cohortis et plerisque
15 auxiliarium interfectis.

18. Interea Mithridates nullo in armis subsidio consultat, cuius misericordiam experiretur. frater Cotys, proditor olim, deinde hostis, metuebatur : Romanorum nemo id auctoritatis aderat, ut promissa eius magni penderentur. ad Eunonen 2
20 convertit, propriis odiis *non* infensum et recens coniuncta nobiscum amicitia validum. igitur cultu vultuque quam 3 maxime ad praesentem fortunam comparato regiam ingreditur genibusque eius provolutus ‘ Mithridates ’ inquit ‘ terra marique Romanis per tot annos quaesitus sponte adsum : utere,
25 ut voles, prole magni Achaemenis, quod mihi solum hostes non abstulerunt.’

19. At Eunones claritudine viri, mutatione rerum et prece haud degeneri permotus, adlevat supplicem laudatque quod gentem Aorsorum, quod suam dextram petendae veniae
30 delegerit. simul legatos litterasque ad Caesarem in hunc 2 modum mittit : populi Romani imperatoribus, magnarum nationum regibus primam ex similitudine fortunae amicitiam, sibi et Claudio etiam communionem victoriae esse. bellorum 3

egregios fines, quotiens ignoscendo tarnsigatur : sic Zorsini
4 victo nihil ereptum.   pro Mithridate, quando gravius
mereretur, non potentiam neque regnum precari, sed ne
triumpharetur neve poenas capite expenderet.

20. At Claudius, quamquam nobilitatibus externis mitis, 5
dubitavit tamen, accipere captivum pacto salutis an repetere
2 armis rectius foret.   hinc dolor iniuriarum et libido vindictae
adigebat : sed disserebatur contra suscipi bellum avio itinere,
inportuoso mari ; ad hoc reges feroces, vagos populos,
solum frugum egenum, taedium ex mora, pericula ex pro- 10
perantia, modicam victoribus laudem ac multum infamiae, si
3 pellerentur.   quin arriperet oblata et servaret exulem, cui
4 inopi quanto longiorem vitam, tanto plus supplicii fore.   his
permotus scripsit Eunoni, meritum quidem novissima exempla
Mithridatem, nec sibi vim ad exsequendum deesse : verum 15
ita maioribus placitum, quanta pervicacia in hostem, tanta
beneficentia adversus supplices utendum ; nam triumphos de
populis regnisque integris acquiri.

21. Traditus posthac Mithridates vectusque Romam per
Iunium Cilonem, procuratorem Ponti, ferocius quam pro 20
fortuna disseruisse apud Caesarem ferebatur, elataque vox eius
in vulgum hisce verbis, ' non sum remissus ad te, sed reversus :
2 vel si non credis, dimitte et quaere.'   vultu quoque interrito
permansit, cum rostra iuxta custodibus circumdatus visui
populo praeberetur.   consularia insignia Ciloni, Aquilae 25
praetoria decernuntur.

22. Isdem consulibus atrox odii Agrippina ac Lolliae
infensa, quod secum de matrimonio principis certavisset, molitur crimina et accusatorem, qui obiceret Chaldaeos, magos
interrogatumque Apollinis Clarii simulacrum super nuptiis 30
2 imperatoris.   exim Claudius inaudita rea multa de claritudine
eius apud senatum praefatus, sorore L. Volusii genitam,
maiorem ei patruum Cottam Messalinum esse, Memmio quon-

dam Regulo nuptam (nam de Gai Caesaris nuptiis consulto
reticebat), addidit perniciosa in rem publicam consilia et materiem sceleri detrahendam : proin publicatis bonis cederet Italia.
ita quinquagiens sestertium ex opibus immensis exuli re- 3
5 lictum. et Calpurnia inlustris femina pervertitur, quia formam
eius laudaverat princeps, nulla libidine, sed fortuito sermone,
unde ira Agrippinae citra ultima stetit. in Lolliam mittitur 4
tribunus, a quo ad mortem adigeretur. damnatus et lege
repetundarum Cadius Rufus accusantibus Bithynis.

10 **23.** Galliae Narbonensi ob egregiam in patres reverentiam
datum, ut senatoribus eius provinciae non exquisita principis
sententia, iure quo Sicilia haberetur, res suas invisere
liceret. Ituraeique et Iudaei defunctis regibus, Sohaemo 2
atque Agrippa, provinciae Suriae additi. Salutis augu- 3
15 rium quinque et septuaginta annis omissum repeti ac deinde
continuari placitum. et pomerium urbis auxit Caesar, more 4
prisco, quo iis qui protulere imperium etiam terminos urbis
propagare datur. nec tamen duces Romani, quamquam 5
magnis nationibus subactis, usurpaverant, nisi L. Sulla et
20 divus Augustus.

24. Regum in eo ambitio vel gloria varie vulgata : sed
initium condendi, et quod pomerium Romulus posuerit,
noscere haud absurdum reor igitur a foro boario, ubi 2
aereum tauri simulacrum aspicimus, quia id genus animalium
25 aratro subditur, sulcus designandi oppidi coeptus, ut mag-
nam Herculis aram amplecteretur ; inde certis spatiis in- 3
teriecti lapides per ima montis Palatini ad aram Consi,
mox curias veteres, tum ad sacellum Larum, inde forum
Romanum ; forumque et Capitolium non a Romulo, sed
30 a Tito Tatio additum urbi credidere. mox pro fortuna
pomerium auctum. et quos tum Claudius terminos posuerit, 4
facile cognitu et publicis actis perscriptum.

25. C. Antistio M. Suillio consulibus adoptio in Domitium

auctoritate Pallantis festinatur, qui obstrictus Agrippinae ut
conciliator nuptiarum et mox stupro eius inligatus, stimu-
labat Claudium, consuleret rei publicae, Britannici pueritiam
2 robore circumdaret : sic apud divum Augustum, quamquam
nepotibus subnixum, viguisse privignos ; a Tiberio super 5
propriam stirpem Germanicum adsumptum : se quoque
3 accingeret iuvene partem curarum capessituro. his evictus
biennio maiorem natu Domitium filio anteponit, habita apud
senatum oratione *in* eundem quem a liberto acceperat
4 modum. adnotabant periti nullam antehac adoptionem 10
inter patricios Claudios reperiri, eosque ab Atto Clauso
continuos duravisse.

    26. Ceterum actae principi grates, quaesitiore in Domi-
tium adulatione ; rogataque lex qua in familiam Claudiam et
nomen Neronis transiret. augetur et Agrippina cognomento 15
2 Augustae. quibus patratis nemo adeo expers misericordiae
fuit, quem non Britannici fortuna maerore adficeret. desolatus paulatim etiam servilibus ministeriis puer intempestiva
3 novercae officia in ludibrium vertebat, intellegens falsi. neque enim segnem ei fuisse indolem ferunt, sive verum, seu 20
periculis commendatus retinuit famam sine experimento.

    27. Sed Agrippina quo vim suam sociis quoque natio-
nibus ostentaret, in oppidum Ubiorum, in quo genita erat,
veteranos coloniamque deduci impetrat, cui nomen inditum
2 e vocabulo ipsius. ac forte acciderat ut eam gentem Rhenum 25
transgressam avus Agrippa in fidem acciperet.
3 Isdem temporibus in superiore Germania trepidatum
adventu Chattorum latrocinia agitantium. dein P. Pomponius legatus auxiliares Vangionas ac Nemetas addito
equite alario *inmittit,* monitos ut anteirent populatores vel 30
4 dilapsis inprovisi circumfunderentur. et secuta consilium
ducis industria militum, divisique in duo agmina, qui laevum
iter petiverant, recens reversos praedaque per luxum

usos et somno graves circumvenere. aucta laetitia, quod
quosdam e clade Variana quadragensimum post annum
servitio exemerant.

28. At qui dextris et propioribus compendiis ierant, obvio
5 hosti et aciem auso plus cladis faciunt, et praeda famaque onusti ad montem Taunum revertuntur, ubi Pomponius
cum legionibus opperiebatur, si Chatti cupidine ulciscendi
casum pugnae praeberent. illi metu, ne hinc Romanus, inde 2
Cherusci, cum quis aeternum discordant, circumgrederentur,
10 legatos in urbem et obsides misere; decretusque Pomponio
triumphalis honos, modica pars famae eius apud posteros, in
quis carminum gloria praecellit.

29. Per idem tempus Vannius Suebis a Druso Caesare
inpositus pellitur regno, prima imperii aetate carus acceptus-
15 que popularibus, mox diuturnitate in superbiam mutans
et odio accolarum, simul domesticis discordiis circumventus.
auctores fuere Vibilius Hermundurorum rex et Vangio ac 2
Sido sorore Vannii geniti. nec Claudius, quamquam saepe
oratus, arma certantibus barbaris interposuit, tutum Vannio
20 perfugium promittens, si pelleretur; scripsitque Palpellio
Histro, qui Pannoniam praesidebat, legionem ipsaque e
provincia lecta auxilia pro ripa componere, subsidio victis
et terrorem adversus victores, ne fortuna elati nostram
quoque pacem turbarent. nam vis innumera, Lugii aliaeque 3
25 gentes, adventabant, fama ditis regni, quod Vannius triginta
per annos praedationibus et vectigalibus auxerat. ipsi 4
manus propria pedites, eques e Sarmatis Iazygibus erat,
impar multitudini hostium, eoque castellis sese defensare
bellumque ducere statuerat.

30 **30.** Sed Iazyges obsidionis impatientes et proximos per
campos vagi necessitudinem pugnae attulere, quia Lugius
Hermundurusque illic ingruerant. igitur degressus castellis 2
Vannius funditur proelio, quamquam rebus adversis laudatus,

quod et pugnam manu capessivit et corpore adverso vulnera
3 excepit. ceterum ad classem in Danuvio opperientem
perfugit; secuti mox clientes et acceptis agris in Pannonia
4 locati sunt. regnum Vangio ac Sido inter se partivere,
egregia adversus nos fide, subiectis, suone an servitii ingenio, 5
dum adipiscerentur dominationis, multa caritate, et maiore
odio, postquam adepti sunt.

31. At in Britannia P. Ostorium pro praetore turbidae res
excepere, effusis in agrum sociorum hostibus eo violentius,
quod novum ducem exercitu ignoto et coepta hieme iturum 10
2 obviam non rebantur. ille gnarus primis eventibus metum
aut fiduciam gigni, citas cohortes rapit, et caesis qui restite-
rant, disiectos consectatus, ne rursus conglobarentur infensa-
que et infida pax non duci, non militi requiem permitteret,
detrahere arma suspectis † cunctaque castris Antonam et 15
3 Sabrinam fluvios cohibere parat. quod primi Iceni abnuere,
valida gens nec proeliis contusi, quia societatem nostram
4 volentes accesserant. hisque auctoribus circumiectae nationes
locum pugnae delegere, saeptum agresti aggere et aditu
5 angusto, ne pervius equiti foret. ea munimenta dux 20
Romanus, quamquam sine robore legionum sociales copias
ducebat, perrumpere adgreditur et distributis cohortibus
6 turmas quoque peditum ad munia accingit. tunc dato signo
perfringunt aggerem suisque claustris impeditos turbant.
7 atque illi conscientia rebellionis et obsaeptis effugiis multa 25
et clara facinora fecere, qua pugna filius legati M. Ostorius
servati civis decus meruit.

32. Ceterum clade Icenorum compositi qui bellum inter
et pacem dubitabant; et ductus in Decangos exercitus.
2 vastati agri, praedae passim actae, non ausis aciem hostibus, 30
vel si ex occulto carpere agmen temptarent, punito dolo.
3 iamque ventum haud procul mari quod Hiberniam insulam
aspectat, cum ortae apud Brigantas discordiae retraxere

ducem, destinationis certum, ne nova moliretur nisi prioribus
firmatis. et Brigantes quidem, paucis qui arma coeptabant 4
interfectis, in reliquos data venia, resedere : Silurum gens non
atrocitate, non clementia mutabatur, quin bellum exerceret
5 castrisque legionum premenda foret. id quo promptius 5
veniret, colonia Camulodunum valida veteranorum manu
deducitur in agros captivos, subsidium adversus rebelles et
inbuendis sociis ad officia legum.

33. Itum inde in Siluras, super propriam ferociam
10 Carataci viribus confisos, quem multa ambigua, multa
prospera extulerant, ut ceteros Britannorum imperatores
praemineret. sed tum astu locorum fraude prior, vi militum 2
inferior, transfert bellum in Ordovicas, additisque qui pacem
nostram metuebant, novissimum casum experitur, sumpto ad
15 proelium loco, ut aditus, abscessus, cuncta nobis inportuna
et suis in melius essent, hinc montibus arduis, et si qua
clementer accedi poterant, in modum valli saxa praestruit.
et praefluebat amnis vado incerto, catervaeque armatorum 3
pro munimentis constiterant.

20 34. Ad hoc gentium ductores circumire, hortari, firmare
animos minuendo metu, accendenda spe aliisque belli incita-
mentis : enimvero Caratacus huc illuc volitans illum diem, 2
illam aciem testabatur aut reciperandae libertatis aut ser-
vitutis aeternae initium fore : vocabatque nomina maiorum, 3
25 qui dictatorem Caesarem pepulissent, quorum virtute vacui
a securibus et tributis intemerata coniugum et liberorum
corpora retinerent. haec atque talia dicenti adstrepere vulgus, 4
gentili quisque religione obstringi, non telis, non vulneribus
cessuros.

30 35. Obstupefecit ea alacritas ducem Romanum; simul
obiectus amnis, additum vallum, inminentia iuga, nihil nisi
atrox et propugnatoribus frequens terrebat. sed miles 2
proelium poscere, cuncta virtute expugnabilia clamitare ;

praefectique *et* tribuni paria disserentes ardorem exercitus
3 intendebant. tum Ostorius circumspectis quae inpenetrabilia
quaeque pervia, ducit infensos amnemque haud difficulter
4 evadit. ubi ventum ad aggerem, dum missilibus certabatur,
5 plus vulnerum in nos et pleraeque caedes oriebantur : post- 5
quam facta testudine rudes et informes saxorum conpages
distractae parque comminus acies, decedere barbari in iuga
6 montium. sed eo quoque inrupere ferentarius gravisque miles,
illi telis adsultantes, hi conferto gradu, turbatis contra
Britannorum ordinibus, apud quos nulla loricarum galearumve 10
tegmina ; et si auxiliaribus resisterent, gladiis ac pilis legionariorum, si huc verterent, spathis et hastis auxiliarium
7 sternebantur. clara ea victoria fuit, captaque uxor et filia
Carataci fratresque in deditionem accepti.

36. Ipse, ut ferme intuta sunt adversa, cum fidem Carti- 15
manduae reginae Brigantum petivisset, vinctus ac victoribus
traditus est, nono post anno, quam bellum in Britannia
2 coeptum. unde fama eius evecta insulas et proximas provincias pervagata per Italiam quoque celebrabatur, avebantque visere, quis ille tot per annos opes nostras sprevisset. 20
3 ne Romae quidem ignobile Carataci nomen erat ; et Caesar
4 dum suum decus extollit, addidit gloriam victo. vocatus
quippe ut ad insigne spectaculum populus : stetere in armis
5 praetoriae cohortes campo qui castra praeiacet. tunc
incedentibus regiis clientelis phalerae, torques quaeque bellis 25
externis quaesiverat traducta, mox fratres et coniunx et
6 filia, postremo ipse ostentatus. ceterorum preces degeneres
fuere ex metu : at non Caratacus aut vultu demisso aut
verbis misericordiam requirens, ubi tribunali adstitit, in hunc
modum locutus est. 30

37. ' Si quanta nobilitas et fortuna mihi fuit, tanta rerum
prosperarum moderatio fuisset, amicus potius in hanc urbem
quam captus venissem, neque dedignatus esses, claris maioribus

ortum, pluribus gentibus imperitantem foedere *in* pacem
accipere. praesens sors mea ut mihi informis, sic tibi 2
magnifica est. habui equos viros, arma opes: quid mirum,
si haec invitus amisi? nam si vos omnibus imperitare vultis, 3
5 sequitur ut omnes servitutem accipiant? si statim deditus 4
traherer, neque mea fortuna neque tua gloria inclaruisset;
et supplicium mei oblivio sequeretur: at si incolumem
servaveris, aeternum exemplar clementiae ero.' ad ea Caesar 5
veniam ipsique et coniugi et fratribus tribuit. atque illi
10 vinclis absoluti Agrippinam quoque, haud procul alio
suggestu conspicuam, isdem quibus principem laudibus
gratibusque venerati sunt. novum sane et moribus veterum 6
insolitum, feminam signis Romanis praesidere: ipsa semet
parti a maioribus suis imperii sociam ferebat.

15 **38.** Vocati posthac patres multa et magnifica super
captivitate Carataci disseruere, neque minus id clarum quam
quod Syphacem P. Scipio, Persen L. Paulus, et si qui alii
vinctos reges populo Romano ostendere. censentur Ostorio 2
triumphi insignia, prosperis ad id rebus eius, mox ambiguis,
20 sive amoto Carataco, quasi debellatum foret, minus intenta
apud nos militia fuit, sive hostes miseratione tanti regis
acrius ad ultionem exarsere. praefectum castrorum et 3
legionarias cohortes exstruendis apud Siluras praesidiis re-
lictas circumfundunt. ac ni cito nuntiis ex castellis proximis 4
25 subventum foret copiarum obsidio, occidione obcubuissent:
praefectus tamen et octo centuriones ac promptissimus
quisque e manipulis cecidere. nec multo post pabulantis 5
nostros missasque ad subsidium turmas profligant.

39. Tum Ostorius cohortes expeditas opposuit; nec ideo
30 fugam sistebat, ni legiones proelium excepissent: earum
robore aequata pugna, dein nobis pro meliore fuit. effugere 2
hostes tenui damno, quia inclinabat dies. crebra hinc proelia, 3
et saepius in modum latrocinii per saltus per paludes, ut

cuique sors aut virtus, temere proviso, ob iram ob praedam,
iussu et aliquando ignaris ducibus, ac praecipua Silurum
4 pervicacia. quos accendebat vulgata imperatoris Romani
vox, ut quondam Sugambri excisi aut in Gallias traiecti
5 forent, ita Silurum nomen penitus extinguendum. igitur 5
duas auxiliares cohortes avaritia praefectorum incautius
populantes intercepere; spoliaque et captivos largiendo
ceteras quoque nationes ad defectionem trahebant, cum
taedio curarum fessus Ostorius concessit vita, laetis hostibus,
tamquam ducem haud spernendum etsi non proelium, at 10
certe bellum absumpsisset.

40. At Caesar cognita morte legati, ne provincia sine
rectore foret, A. Didium suffecit. is propere vectus non
tamen integras res invenit, adversa interim legionis pugna,
cui Manlius Valens praeerat, auctaque et apud hostes eius 15
rei fama, quo venientem ducem exterrerent, atque illo augente
audita, ut maior laus compositi vel, si duravissent, venia iustior
2 tribueretur. Silures id quoque damnum intulerant lateque
3 persultabant, donec adcursu Didii pellerentur. sed post
captum Caratacum praecipuus scientia rei militaris Venutius, 20
e Brigantum civitate, ut supra memoravi, fidusque diu et
Romania armis defensus, cum Cartimanduam reginam
matrimonio teneret; mox orto discidio et statim bello
4 etiam adversus nos hostilia induerat. sed primo tantum
inter ipsos certabatur, callidisque Cartimandua artibus fra- 25
5 trem ac propinquos Venutii intercepit. inde accensi hostes,
stimulante ignominia, ne feminae imperio subderentur,
valida et lecta armis iuventus regnum eius invadunt.
6 quod nobis praevisum, et missae auxilio cohortes acre
proelium fecere, cuius initio ambiguo finis laetior fuit. 30
7 neque dispari eventu pugnatum a legione, cui Caesius
Nasica praeerat; nam Didius, senectute gravis et multa
copia honorum, per ministros agere et arcere hostem

satis habebat. haec, quamquam a duobus pro praeto- **8**
ribus plures per annos gesta coniunxi, ne divisa haud
perinde ad memoriam sui valerent: ad temporum ordinem
redeo.

5 **41.** Ti. Claudio quintum Servio Cornelio Orfito consulibus virilis toga Neroni maturata, quo capessendae rei
publicae habilis videretur. et Caesar adulationibus senatus **2**
libens cessit, ut vicensimo aetatis anno consulatum Nero
iniret atque interim designatus proconsulare imperium extra
10 urbem haberet ac princeps iuventutis appellaretur. additum **3**
nomine eius donativum militi, congiarium plebei. et ludicro **4**
circensium, quod adquirendis vulgi studiis edebatur, Britannicus in praetexta, Nero triumphali veste travecti sunt:
spectaret populus hunc decore imperatorio, illum puerili
15 habitu, ac perinde fortunam utriusque praesumeret. simul **5**
qui centurionum tribunorumque sortem Britannici misera-
bantur, remoti fictis causis et alii per speciem honoris;
etiam libertorum si quis incorrupta fide, depellitur tali
occasione. obvii inter se Nero Britannicum nomine, ille **6**
20 Domitium salutavere. quod ut discordiae initium Agrippina **7**
multo questu ad maritum defert: sperni quippe adoptionem,
quaeque censuerint patres, iusserit populus, intra penates
abrogari: ac nisi pravitas tam infensa docentium arceatur,
eruptura in publicam perniciem. commotus his quasi crimi- **8**
25 nibus optimum quemque educatorem filii exilio aut morte
adficit datosque a noverca custodiae eius inponit.

42. Nondum tamen summa moliri Agrippina audebat, ni
praetoriarum cohortium cura exsolverentur Lusius Geta et
Rufrius Crispinus, quos Messalinae memores et liberis eius
30 devinctos credebat. igitur distrahi cohortes ambitu duorum **2**
et, si ab uno regerentur, intentiorem fore disciplinam
adseverante uxore, transfertur regimen cohortium ad Burrum
Afranium, egregiae militaris famae, gnarum tamen cuius

3 sponte praeficeretur. suum quoque fastigium Agrippina
extollere altius : carpento Capitolium ingredi, qui honos
sacerdotibus et sacris antiquitus concessus venerationem
augebat feminae, quam imperatore genitam, sororem eius
qui rerum potitus sit et coniugem et matrem fuisse, unicum 5
4 ad hunc diem exemplum est. inter quae praecipuus propug-
nator eius Vitellius, validissima gratia, aetate extrema (adeo
incertae sunt potentium res) accusatione corripitur, deferente
5 Iunio Lupo senatore. is crimina maiestatis et cupidinem
imperii obiectabat; praebuissetque aures Caesar, nisi Agrip- 10
pinae minis magis quam precibus mutatus esset, ut accusatori
aqua atque igni interdiceret. hactenus Vitellius voluerat.

43. Multa eo anno prodigia evenere. insessum diris
avibus Capitolium, crebris terrae motibus prorutae domus,
ac dum latius metuitur, trepidatione vulgi invalidus quisque 15
obtriti ; frugum quoque egestas et orta ex eo fames in
2 prodigium accipiebatur. nec occulti tantum questus, sed
iura reddentem Claudium circumvasere clamoribus turbidis,
pulsumque in extremam fori partem vi urguebant, donec
3 militum globo infensos perrupit. quindecim dierum alimenta 20
urbi, non amplius, superfuisse constitit, magnaque deum
benignitate et modestia hiemis rebus extremis subventum.
4 at hercule olim Italia legionibus longinquas in provincias
commeatus portabat, nec nunc infecunditate laboratur, sed
Africam potius et Aegyptum exercemus, navibusque et 25
casibus vita populi Romani permissa est.

44. Eodem anno bellum inter Armenios Hiberosque
exortum Parthis quoque ac Romanis gravissimorum inter
2 se motuum causa fuit. genti Parthorum Vologeses imperita-
bat, materna origine ex paelice Graeca, concessu fratrum 30
regnum adeptus ; Hiberos Pharasmanes vetusta possessione,
Armenios frater eius Mithridates optinebat opibus nostris.
3 erat Pharasmani filius nomine Radamistus, decora proceritate,

vi corporis insignis et patrias artes edoctus, claraque inter
accolas fama. is modicum Hiberiae regnum senecta patris 4
detineri ferocius crebriusque iactabat, quam ut cupidinem
occultaret. igitur Pharasmanes iuvenem potentiae promptum 5
5 et studio popularium accinctum, vergentibus iam annis suis
metuens, aliam ad spem trahere et Armeniam ostentare,
pulsis Parthis datam Mithridati a semet memorando: sed
vim differendam et potiorem dolum, quo incautum oppri-
merent. ita Radamistus simulata adversus patrem discordia 6
10 tamquam novercae odiis impar pergit ad patruum, multaque ab eo comitate in speciem liberum cultus primores
Armeniorum ad res novas inlicit, ignaro et ornante insuper
Mithridate.

45. Reconciliationis specie adsumpta regressusque ad
15 patrem, quae fraude confici potuerint, prompta nuntiat, cetera
armis exsequenda. interim Pharasmanes belli causas con- 2
fingit: proelianti sibi adversus regem Albanorum et Romanos
auxilio vocanti fratrem adversatum, eamque iniuriam excidio
ipsius ultum iturum; simul magnas copias filio tradidit. ille 3
20 inruptione subita territum exutumque campis Mithridaten
compulit in castellum Gorneas, tutum loco ac praesidio
militum, quis Caelius Pollio praefectus, centurio Casperius
praeerant. nihil tam ignarum barbaris quam machinamenta 4
et astus oppugnationum: at nobis ea pars militiae maxime
25 gnara est. ita Radamistus frustra vel cum damno temptatis 5
munitionibus obsidium incipit; et cum vis neglegeretur,
avaritiam praefecti emercatur, obtestante Casperio ne socius
rex, ne Armenia donum populi Romani scelere et pecunia
verterentur. postremo quia multitudinem hostium Pollio, 6
30 iussa patris Radamistus obtendebant, pactus indutias abscedit, ut, nisi Pharasmanem bello absterruisset, Ummidium
Quadratum praesidem Suriae doceret quo in statu Armenia
foret.

46. Digressu centurionis velut custode exsolutus praefectus
hortari Mithridaten ad sanciendum foedus, coniunctionem
fratrum ac priorem aetate Pharasmanen et cetera necessitudinum nomina referens, quod filiam eius in matrimonio
2 haberet, quod ipse Radamisto socer esset: non abnuere 5
pacem Hiberos, quamquam in tempore validiores; et satis
cognitam Armeniorum perfidiam, nec aliud subsidii quam
castellum commeatu egenum: ne dubia tentare armis quam
3 incruentas condiciones mallet. cunctante ad ea Mithridate
et suspectis praefecti consiliis, quod paelicem regiam polluerat 10
inque cmnem libidinem venalis habebatur, Casperius interim
ad Pharasmanen pervadit, utque Hiberi obsidio decedant
4 expostulat. ille propalam incerta et saepius molliora respondens, secretis nuntiis monet Radamistum obpugnationem
5 quoquo modo celerare. augetur flagitii merces, et Pollio oc- 15
culta corruptione inpellit milites, ut pacem flagitarent seque
6 praesidium omissuros minitarentur. qua necessitate Mithridates diem locumque foederi accepit castelloque egreditur.

47. Ac primo Radamistus in amplexus eius effusus
simulare obsequium, socerum ac parentem appellare; adicit 20
2 ius iurandum, non ferro, non veneno vim adlaturum. simul
in lucum propinquum trahit, provisum illic sacrificii paratum
3 dictitans, ut dis testibus pax firmaretur. mos est regibus,
quotiens in societatem coëant, implicare dextras pollicesque
inter se vincire nodoque praestringere: mox ubi sanguis 25
in artus *se* extremos suffuderit, levi ictu cruorem eliciunt
atque invicem lambunt. id foedus arcanum habetur quasi
4 mutuo cruore sacratum. sed tunc qui ea vincla admovebat,
decidisse simulans genua Mithridatis invadit ipsumque pro-
5 sternit; simulque concursu plurium iniciuntur catenae. ac 30
compede, quod dedecorum barbaris, trahebatur; mox quia
vulgus duro imperio habitum, probra ac verbera intentabat.
6 et erant contra qui tantam fortunae commutationem mise-

rarentur; secutaque cum parvis liberis coniunx cuncta
lamentatione complebat. diversis et contectis vehiculis 7
abduntur, dum Pharasmanis iussa exquirerentur. illi cupido
regni fratre et filia potior animusque sceleribus paratus;
5 visui tamen consuluit, ne coram interficeret. et Radamistus, 8
quasi iuris iurandi memor, non ferrum, non venenum in
sororem et patruum expromit, sed proiectos in humum et
veste multa gravique opertos necat. filii quoque Mithridatis, 9
quod caedibus parentum inlacrimaverant, trucidati sunt.

10 **48.** At Quadratus cognoscens proditum Mithridaten et
regnum ab interfectoribus optineri, vocat consilium, docet
acta et an ulcisceretur consultat. paucis decus publicum 2
curae, plures tuta disserunt: omne scelus externum cum
laetitia habendum; semina etiam odiorum iacienda, ut saepe
15 principes **Romani** eandem Armeniam specie largitionis
turbandis barbarorum animis praebuerint: poteretur Rada- 3
mistus male partis, dum invisus, infamis, quando id magis
ex usu quam si cum gloria adeptus foret. in hanc sententiam
itum. ne tamen adnuisse facinori viderentur et diversa 4
20 Caesar iuberet, missi ad Pharasmanen nuntii, ut abscederet
a finibus Armeniis filiumque abstraheret.

49. Erat Cappadociae procurator Iulius Paelignus, ignavia
animi et deridiculo corporis iuxta despiciendus, sed Claudio
perquam familiaris, cum privatus olim conversatione scurrarum
25 iners otium oblectaret. is Paelignus auxiliis provincialium 2
contractis tamquam reciperaturus Armeniam, dum socios
magis quam hostes praedatur, abscessu suorum et incursantibus barbaris praesidii egens ad Radamistum venit; donis-
que eius evictus ultro regium insigne sumere cohortatur su-
30 mentique adest auctor et satelles. quod ubi turpi fama 3
divulgatum, ne ceteri quoque ex Paeligno coniectarentur,
Helvidius Priscus legatus cum legione mittitur, rebus turbidis
pro tempore ut consuleret. igitur propere montem Taurum 4

transgressus moderatione plura quam vi composuerat, cum
rediret in Suriam iubetur, ne initium belli adversus Parthos
existeret.

50. Nam Vologeses casum invadendae Armeniae obvenisse
ratus, quam a maioribus suis possessam externus rex flagitio 5
optineret, contrahit coplas fratremque Tiridaten deducere in
regnum parat, ne qua pars domus sine imperio ageret.
2 incessu Parthorum sine acie pulsi Hiberi, urbesque Arme-
3 niorum Artaxata et Tigranocerta iugum accepere. deinde
atrox hiems seu parum provisi commeatus et orta ex utroque 10
4 tabes perpellunt Vologesen omittere praesentia. vacuamque
rursus Armeniam Radamistus invasit, truculentior quam antea,
5 tamquam adversus defectores et in tempore rebellaturos. atque
illi, quamvis servitio sueti, patientiam abrumpunt armisque
regiam circumveniunt.   15

51. Nec aliud Radamisto subsidium fuit quam pernicitas
2 equorum, quis seque et coniugem abstulit. sed coniunx
gravida primam utcumque fugam ob metum hostilem et
mariti caritatem toleravit ; post festinatione continua orare ut
3 morte honesta contumeliis captivitatis eximeretur. ille primo 20
amplecti adlevare adhortari, modo virtutem admirans, modo
4 timore aeger, ne quis relicta poteretur. postremo violentia
amoris et facinorum non rudis destringit acinacen vulneratam-
que ripam ad Araxis trahit, flumini tradit, ut corpus etiam
auferretur : ipse praeceps Hiberos ad patrium regnum 25
5 pervadit. interim Zenobiam (id mulieri nomen) placida in
eluvie spirantem ac vitae manifestam advertere pastores, et
dignitate formae haud degenerem reputantes obligant vulnus,
agrestia medicamina adhibent cognitoque nomine et casu
in urbem Artaxata ferunt ; unde publica cura deducta ad 30
Tiridaten comiterque excepta cultu regio habita est.

52. Fausto Sulla Salvio Othone consulibus Furius Scribo-

nianus in exilium agitur, quasi finem principis per Chaldaeos
scrutaretur. adnectebatur crimini Vibia mater eius, ut casus
prioris (nam relegata erat) inpatiens. pater Scriboniani 2
Camillus arma per Delmatiam moverat; idque ad clementiam
5 trahebat Caesar, quod stirpem hostilem iterum conservaret.
neque tamen exuli longa posthac vita fuit : morte fortuita 3
an per venenum extinctus esset, ut quisque credidit, vul-
gavere. de mathematicis Italia pellendis factum senatus
consultum atrox et inritum. laudati dehinc oratione principis 4
10 qui ob angustias familiares ordine senatorio sponte cederent,
motique qui remanendo inpudentiam paupertati adicerent.

53. Inter quae refert ad patres de poena feminarum quae
servis coniungerentur; statuiturque, ut ignaro domino ad id
prolapsae in servitute, sin consensisset, pro libertis haberentur.
15 Pallanti, quem repertorem eius relationis ediderat Caesar, 2
praetoria insignia et centiens quinquagiens sestertium censuit
consul designatus Barea Soranus. additum a Scipione 3
Cornelio grates publice agendas, quod regibus Arcadiae ortus
veterrimam nobilitatem usui publico postponeret seque inter
20 ministros principis haberi sineret. adseveravit Claudius 4
contentum honore Pallantem intra priorem paupertatem
subsistere. et fixum est aere publico senatus consultum, 5
quo libertinus sestertii ter miliens possessor antiquae parsi-
moniae laudibus cumulabatur.

25 **54.** At non frater eius, cognomento Felix, pari moderatione agebat, iam pridem Iudaeae inpositus et cuncta
malefacta sibi inpune ratus tanta potentia subnixo. sane 2
praebuerant Iudaei speciem motus orta seditione, postquam
* * * cognita caede eius haud obtemperatum esset, manebat
30 metus ne quis principum eadem imperitaret. atque interim 3
Felix intempestivis remediis delicta accendebat, aemulo ad
deterrima Ventidio Cumano, cui pars provinciae habebatur,
ita divisis, ut huic Galilaeorum natio, Felici Samaritae pare-

rent, discordes olim et tum contemptu regentium minus
4 coercitis odiis. igitur raptare inter se, immittere latronum
globos, componere insidias et aliquando proeliis congredi,
5 spoliaque et praedas ad procuratores referre. hique primo
laetari, mox gliscente pernicie cum arma militum inter- 5
iecissent, caesi milites ; arsissetque bello provincia, ni Quad-
6 ratus Suriae rector subvenisset. nec diu adversus Iudaeos,
qui in necem militum proruperant, dubitatum quin capite
poenas luerent ; Cumanus et Felix cunctationem adferebant,
quia Claudius causis rebellionis auditis ius statuendi etiam de 10
7 procuratoribus dederat. sed Quadratus Felicem inter iudices
ostentavit, receptum in tribunal, quo studia accusantium de-
terrerentur ; damnatusque flagitiorum quae duo deliquerant
Cumanus, et quies provinciae reddita.

55. Nec multo post agrestium Cilicum nationes, quibus 15
Clitarum cognomentum, saepe et alias commotae, tunc
Troxobore duce montes asperos castris cepere atque inde
decursu in litora aut urbes vim cultoribus et oppidanis ac
2 plerumque in mercatores et navicularios audebant. obsessa-
que civitas Anemuriensis, et missi e Suria in subsidium 20
equites cum praefecto Curtio Severo turbantur, quod duri
circum loci peditibusque ad pugnam idonei equestre proe-
3 lium haud patiebantur. dein rex eius orae Antiochus blandimentis adversum plebem, fraude in ducem cum barbarorum
copias dissociasset, Troxobore paucisque primoribus inter- 25
fectis ceteros clementia composuit.

56. Sub idem tempus inter lacum Fucinum amnemque
Lirim perrupto monte, quo magnificentia operis a pluribus
viseretur, lacu in ipso navale proelium adornatur, ut quondam
Augustus structo trans Tiberim stagno, sed levibus navigiis 30
2 et minore copia ediderat. Claudius triremes quadriremesque
et undeviginti hominum milia armavit, cincto ratibus ambitu,
ne vaga efiugia forent, ac tamen spatium amplexus ad vim

remigii, gubernantium artes, impetus navium et proelio
solita. in ratibus praetoriarum cohortium manipuli turmae- 3
que adstiterant, antepositis propugnaculis, ex quis catapultae
ballistaeque tenderentur. reliqua lacus classiarii tectis navi-
5 bus obtinebant. ripas et colles montiumque edita in modum 4
theatri multitudo innumera complevit, proximis e municipiis
et alii urbe ex ipsa, visendi cupidine aut officio in principem.
ipse insigni paludamento neque procul Agrippina chlamyde 5
aurata praesedere. pugnatum quamquam inter sontes fortium
10 virorum animo, ac post multum vulnerum occidioni exempti
sunt.

57. Sed perfecto spectaculo apertum aquarum iter. incuria
operis manifesta fuit, haud satis depressi ad lacus ima vel
media. eoque, tempore interiecto, altius effossi specus, et 2
15 contrahendae rursus multitudini gladiatorum spectaculum
editur, inditis pontibus pedestrem ad pugnam. quin et 3
convivium effluvio lacus adpositum magna formidine cunctos
adfecit, quia vis aquarum prorumpens proxima trahebat,
convulsis ulterioribus aut fragore et sonitu exterritis. simul 4
20 Agrippina trepidatione principis usa ministrum operis Narcissum incusat cupidinis ac praedarum. nec ille reticet, 5
inpotentiam muliebrem nimiasque spes eius arguens.

58. D. Iunio Q. Haterio consulibus sedecim annos natus
Nero Octaviam Caesaris filiam in matrimonium accepit.
25 utque studiis honestis *et* eloquentiae gloria enitesceret, causa
Iliensium suscepta, Romanum Troia demissum et Iuliae
stirpis auctorem Aeneam aliaque haud procul fabulis vetera
facunde exsecutus perpetrat, ut Ilienses omni publico munere
solverentur. eodem oratore Bononiensi coloniae igni haustae 2
30 subventum centiens sestertii largitione. reddita Rhodiis
libertas, adempta saepe aut firmata, prout bellis externis
meruerant aut domi seditione deliquerant; tributumque Apamensibus terrae motu convolsis in quinquennium remissum.

59. At Claudius saevissima quaeque promere adigebatur
eiusdem Agrippinae artibus, quae Statilium Taurum opibus
inlustrem hortis eius inhians pervertit accusante Tarquitio
2 Prisco. legatus is Tauri Africam imperio proconsulari re-
gentis, postquam revenerant, pauca repetundarum crimina, 5
3 ceterum magicas superstitiones obiectabat. nec ille diutius
falsum accusatorem, indignas sordes perpessus, vim vitae
4 suae attulit ante sententiam senatus. Tarquitius tamen
curia exactus est, quod patres odio delatoris contra ambitum
Agrippinae pervicere.   10

60. Eodem anno saepius audita vox principis, parem vim
rerum habendam a procuratoribus suis iudicatarum ac si
2 ipse statuisset. ac ne fortuito prolapsus videretur, senatus
quoque consulto cautum plenius quam antea et uberius.
3 nam divus Augustus apud equestres, qui Aegypto praesi- 15
derent, lege agi decretaque eorum proinde haberi iusserat,
ac si magistratus Romani constituissent; mox alias per
provincias et in urbe pleraque concessa sunt, quae olim
4 a praetoribus noscebantur.   Claudius omne ius tradidit, de
quo totiens seditione aut armis certatum, cum Semproniis 20
rogationibus equester ordo in possessione iudiciorum loca-
retur, aut rursum Serviliae leges senatui iudicia redderent,
5 Mariusque et Sulla olim de eo vel praecipue bellarent. sed
tunc ordinum diversa studia, et quae evicerant publice
valebant. C. Oppius et Cornelius Balbus primi Caesaris 25
opibus potuere condiciones pacis et arbitria belli tractare.
6 Matios posthac et Vedios et cetera equitum Romanorum
praevalida nomina referre nihil attinuerit, cum Claudius
libertos, quos rei familiari praefecerat, sibique et legibus
adaequaverit.   30

61. Rettulit dein de inmunitate Cois tribuenda, multaque
super antiquitate eorum memoravit: Argivos vel Coeum
Latonae parentem vetustissimos insulae cultores; mox

adventu Aesculapii artem medendi inlatam maximeque inter
posteros eius celebrem fuisse, nomina singulorum referens et
quibus quisque aetatibus viguissent. quin etiam dixit Xeno- 2
phontem, cuius scientia ipse uteretur, eadem familia ortum,
5 precibusque eius dandum, ut omni tributo vacui in posterum
Coi sacram et tantum dei ministram insulam colerent. neque 3
dubium habetur multa eorundem in populum Romanum merita
sociasque victorias potuisse tradi : set Claudius, facilitate solita 4
quod uni concesserat, nullis extrinsecus adiumentis velavit.

10   **62.** At Byzantii data dicendi copia, cum magnitudinem
onerum apud senatum deprecarentur, cuncta repetivere.
orsi a foedere quod nobiscum icerant, qua tempestate bella- 2
vimus adversus regem Macedonum, cui ut degeneri Pseudo-
philippi vocabulum inpositum, missas posthac copias in
15 Antiochum, Persen, Aristonicum, et piratico bello adiutum
Antonium memorabant, quaeque Sullae aut Lucullo aut
Pompeio obtulissent, mox recentia in Caesares merita, quando
ea loca insiderent, quae transmeantibus terra marique ducibus
exercitibusque, simul vehendo commeatu opportuna forent.

20   **63.** Namque artissimo inter Europam Asiamque divortio
Byzantium in extremo Europae posuere Graeci, quibus
Pythium Apollinem consulentibus, ubi conderent urbem,
redditum oraculum est, quaererent sedem caecorum terris
adversam. ea ambage Chalcedonii monstrabantur, quod 2
25 priores illuc advecti, praevisa locorum utilitate, peiora
legissent. quippe Byzantium fertili solo, fecundo mari, quia
vis piscium inmensa, Pontum erumpens et obliquis subter
undas saxis exterrita, omisso alterius litoris flexu hos ad
portus defertur. unde primo quaestuosi et opulenti ; post 3
30 magnitudine onerum urguente finem aut modum orabant,
adnitente principe, qui Thraecio Bosporanoque bello recens
fessos iuvandosque rettulit. ita tributa in quinquennium
remissa.

64. M. Asinio M'. Acilio consulibus mutationem rerum in
2 deterius portendi cognitum est crebris prodigiis.   signa ac
tentoria militum igni caelesti arsere.   fastigio Capitolii examen
apium insedit.   biformes hominum partus et suis fetum
3 editum, cui accipitrum ungues inessent.   numerabatur inter 5
ostenta deminutus omnium magistratuum numerus, quaestore,
aedili, tribuno ac praetore et consule paucos intra menses
4 defunctis.   sed in praecipuo pavore Agrippina, vocem Claudii,
quam temulentus iecerat, fatale sibi ut coniugum flagitia
ferret, dein puniret, metuens, agere et celerare statuit, perdita 10
prius Domitia Lepida muliebribus causis, quia Lepida minore
Antonia genita, avunculo Augusto, Agrippinae sobrina prior
ac Gnaei mariti eius soror, parem sibi claritudinem credebat.
5 nec forma aetas opes multum distabant; et utraque inpudica,
infamis, violenta, haud minus vitiis aemulabantur, quam si 15
6 qua ex fortuna prospera acceperant.   enimvero certamen
acerrimum, amita potius an mater apud Neronem praevaleret:
nam Lepida blandimentis ac largitionibus iuvenilem animum
devinciebat, truci contra ac minaci Agrippina, quae filio dare
imperium, tolerare imperitantem nequibat.   20

65. Ceterum obiecta sunt, quod coniugem principis devotionibus petivisset quodque parum coercitis per Calabriam
2 servorum agminibus pacem Italiae turbaret.   ob haec mors
indicta, multum adversante Narcisso, qui Agrippinam magis
magisque suspectans prompsisse inter proximos ferebatur 25
certam sibi perniciem, seu Britannicus rerum seu Nero
poteretur; verum ita de se meritum Caesarem, ut vitam usui
3 eius inpenderet.   convictam Messalinam et Silium; pares
iterum accusandi causas esse, si Nero imperitaret; Britannico
successore nullum principi metum: at novercae insidiis 30
domum omnem convelli, maiore flagitio quam si inpudicitiam
4 prioris coniugis reticuisset.   quamquam ne inpudicitiam
quidem nunc abesse Pallante adultero, ne quis ambigat decus

pudorem corpus, cuncta regno viliora habere. haec atque 5
talia dictitans amplecti Britannicum, robur aetatis quam
maturrimum precari, modo ad deos, modo ad ipsum tendere
manus, adolesceret, patris inimicos depelleret, matris etiam
5 interfectores ulcisceretur.

66. In tanta mole curarum valetudine adversa corripitur,
refovendisque viribus mollitia caeli et salubritate aquarum
Sinuessam pergit. tum Agrippina, sceleris olim certa et ob- 2
latae occasionis propera nec ministrorum egens, de genere
10 veneni consultavit, ne repentino et praecipiti facinus pro-
deretur ; si lentum et tabidum delegisset, ne admotus supremis
Claudius et dolo intellecto ad amorem filii rediret. exquisitum 3
aliquid placebat, quod turbaret mentem et mortem differret.
deligitur artifex talium vocabulo Locusta, nuper veneficii 4
15 damnata et diu inter instrumenta regni habita. eius mulieris 5
ingenio paratum virus, cuius minister e spadonibus fuit
Halotus, inferre epulas et explorare gustu solitus.

67. Adeoque cuncta mox pernotuere, ut temporum illorum
scriptores prodiderint infusum delectabili cibo boleto vene-
20 num, nec vim medicaminis statim intellectam, socordiane an
Claudii vinolentia; simul soluta alvus subvenisse videbatur.
igitur exterrita Agrippina et, quando ultima timebantur, 2
spreta praesentium invidia, provisam iam sibi Xenophontis
medici conscientiam adhibet. ille tamquam nisus evomentis 3
25 adiuvaret, pinnam rapido veneno inlitam faucibus eius de-
misisse creditur, haud ignarus summa scelera incipi cum
periculo, peragi cum praemio.

68. Vocabatur interim senatus votaque pro incolumitate
principis consules et sacerdotes nuncupabant, cum iam
30 exanimis vestibus et fomentis obtegeretur, dum quae forent
firmando Neronis imperio componuntur. iam primum 2
Agrippina, velut dolore victa et solacia conquirens, tenere
amplexu Britannicum, veram paterni oris effigiem appellare

3 ac variis artibus demorari, ne cubiculo egrederetur. Antoniam
  quoque et Octaviam sorores eius attinuit, et cunctos aditus
  custodiis clauserat, crebroque vulgabat ire in melius valetu-
  dinem principis, quo miles bona in spe ageret tempusque
  prosperum ex monitis Chaldaeorum adventaret.   5

  69. Tunc medio diei tertium ante Idus Octobris, foribus
  palatii repente diductis, comitante Burro Nero egreditur ad
  cohortem, quae more militiae excubiis adest. ibi monente
2 praefecto faustis vocibus exceptus inditur lecticae. dubita-
  visse quosdam ferunt, respectantes rogitantesque ubi Britan- 10
  nicus esset : mox nullo in diversum auctore quae offerebantur
3 secuti sunt. inlatusque castris Nero et congruentia tempori
  praefatus, promisso donativo ad exemplum paternae largitionis, imperator consalutatur. sententiam militum secuta
4 patrum consulta, nec dubitatum est apud provincias. caele- 15
  stesque honores Claudio decernuntur et funeris sollemne
  perinde ac divo Augusto celebratur, aemulante Agrippina
5 proaviae Liviae magnificentiam. testamentum tamen haud
  recitatum, ne antepositus filio privignus iniuria et invidia
  animos vulgi turbaret.   20

NOTES

BOOK V

Chapter 1, § 1. C. Fufius Geminus is mentioned again in 1 ch. 2, 2; his father was a legatus of Caesar in Pannonia in 34 B.C. Of the other consul, L. Rubellius Geminus, nothing is known but the name.

Iulia Augusta: she received this name after Augustus' death, 14 A.D., when, by his will, 'Livia in familiam Iuliam nomenque Augustum adsumebatur', i 8, 2.

aetate extrema: at the age of 86 (Dio lviii 2, 1).

per Claudiam familiam: Livia's father was probably one of the sons of C. Claudius, consul in 130 B.C.; he was adopted by Livius Drusus, the famous tribune of 91 B.C.

§ 2. Tiberius Nero: he had been both quaestor and praetor before the Perusine War (40 B.C.), in which he actively supported L. Antonius against Octavian. After the fall of Perusia he escaped with Livia and their infant son Tiberius to Sextus Pompeius, from whom he went over to M. Antonius. The peace of Misenum (39 B.C.) made it possible for him to return to Rome, and he agreed with Octavian to divorce Livia, and himself acted the part of her father at the marriage ceremony, giving her to her new husband.

§ 3. ad enitendum: she was within three months of the birth of her second son Drusus.

§ 4. Agrippina, the daughter (by Agrippa) of Augustus' daughter Julia, married Germanicus, son of the Drusus just mentioned.

§ 5. sanctitate, &c.: an ablat. of description (Intr. II 18), 'pure in her home life, in the old style', (or a verb implying 'she approximated' may be supplied with 'priscum ad morem').

impotens, 'as a mother, imperious': the word denotes absence of restraint over one's impulses.

facilis, 'compliant'.

artibus, 'subtilty'.

bene composita, 'well matched', a metaphor from the arena.

The verdict of history has acquitted her of Tacitus' unfavourable imputations; she is generally acknowledged to have had a moderating influence, and one wholly for the better, on both her husband and her son.

§ 6. diu: until the accession of Gaius, who paid all legacies under her will, 'quod Tiberius suppresserat' (Suet. *Cal.* 16).

Chapter 2, § 1. amoenitate, 'luxury'. The word is usually 2 applied to the charms of scenery.

excusavit, 'pleaded in excuse'.

imminuit, 'reduced', as he had also done on the occasion of Augustus' death, i 14.

addito: Intr. II 21, a.

ne, &c.: she was subsequently deified after the accession of Claudius (Dio lx 5, 2), and shared a temple with Augustus in the Palatium.

§ 2. amicitias: Suetonius (*Tib.* 51) states that he soon struck down all her friends.

§ 3. oblique perstringens, 'with an implied censure of'.

Tiberium, 'having often made Tiberius the butt of his sarcastic witticisms'.

3 Chapter 3, § 1. praerupta: the word is applied to a cliff with a precipitous face; here = 'unmitigated'. Cf. 'praerupta audacia', sheer, *or* headlong, recklessness, Cic. *pro Rosc. Amer.* xxiv 68.

urgens, 'crushing'. So 'urgentium malorum suffugium', iv 66, 3.

§ 2. Neronem: eldest son of Germanicus and Agrippina. As a result of these charges he was banished to Pontia, and was put to death or forced to suicide shortly before the fall of Seianus, 31 A.D. He is called 'nepos' (§ 3), as Germanicus had been adopted as son by Tiberius, i 3, 5.

adlatas: sc. 'ad consules'.

§ 4. oris, 'of speech'.

ut referretur, 'that the question be put'.

Cotta Messalinus, son of Messalla Corvinus, who had been next in command under Brutus and Cassius at Philippi, and subsequently became a faithful subject of Augustus, whose colleague he was in the consulship in the year of Actium. (See also vi 11, 4.) Messalinus Cotta is represented by Tacitus as obsequious in furthering Tiberius' cruelty in the senate; cf. ii 32, 2 and vi 5, 1.

§ 5. magistratibus: they were anxious because the responsibility of a 'relatio' rested with them, and they were not clear as to what Tiberius really wished to be done.

4 Chapter 4, § 1. Iunius Rusticus: probably father of Arulenus Rusticus, who, as tribune of the plebs, was prepared to veto the trial of Thrasea when attacked by Nero, in 66 A.D. (xvi 26, 6), and who subsequently suffered death, under Domitian, for his biography of Thrasea.

componendis patrum actis: his office would be that of 'curator actorum senatus' or 'ab actis senatus'. The publication of a record of the proceedings of the senate was instituted by Julius Caesar in his first consulship (59 B.C.), but the practice was discontinued by Augustus (Suet. *Aug.* 36); and it is not certain when it was revived.

eoque . . . creditus: it would appear that minutes of the senate's proceedings were submitted to the emperor before publication.

§ 2. fatali quodam motu, 'through some (inexplicable) prompting of destiny'. Tacitus elsewhere also uses 'fatum' as a cause of something which he cannot explain; cf. iii 30, 7 'fato potentiae raro sempiternae'.

prava, 'misguided', explained by the next clause, 'while he lost sight of the immediate peril in his terror of future contingencies '.

brevibus, &c., 'small things turn the scale in great events'.

§ 3. **effigies . . . gerens**: in the same way the populace, when protesting against Nero's divorce of Octavia, in 62 A.D., carried her images in procession, and threw down those of her rival Poppaea (xiv 61, 1).

faustisque, &c., 'and with expressions of devotion to Caesar kept shouting that the letter (ch. 3, 2) was forged'.

§ 4. **ferebantur**, 'were reported', outside the senate.

libidinem ingeniorum, 'their licence of imagination'; i.e. in regard to the persons to whom they attributed these declarations against Seianus.

§ 5. **novas**, 'seditious', as in the phrase 'novae res'.

legi: said as though these expressions had been entered in the 'acta populi'; Intr. p. viii.

Chapter 5, § 1. imperatoria, &c., 'the imperial dignity had suffered public insult'. 'Imperatorius is usually applied to the emperor's power over the soldiers rather than over the senate.

integra, &c., 'that the decision should be left entirely in his own hands'.

§ 2. **nec**, &c., 'and in their deliberations they went no further than passing, not indeed a decree of condemnation (for that had been forbidden), but one testifying that they were prepared to punish but were compulsorily checked by the emperor'.

testarentur: the MS. here shows a small gap, beginning another line with 'quattuor', which belongs to the narrative of the latter part of 31 A.D. The history of the events of the rest of 29 A.D. to the point where the text begins again was probably missing in the MS. from which the extant MS. was copied. A summary of the chief events of this lost period is given in the Appendix following.

APPENDIX TO BOOK V

SUMMARY OF EVENTS BETWEEN V 5 AND V 6 [VI 1].

The history of this period is drawn chiefly from the writings of Dio and Suetonius; some light upon it is also afforded by references in Philo, Josephus, and Juvenal.

In 29 A.D., shortly after the events mentioned in the opening chapters of Book V, both Agrippina and Nero were sent into banishment, the former to Pandateria, and the latter to Pontia.

In 30 A.D., Tiberius, influenced by Seianus, had Drusus (son of Germanicus) accused, pronounced a public enemy, and imprisoned in the Palatium. Seianus was now at the summit of his power, and Tiberius appears even to have affianced him by betrothal to a member of his house, though to whom is unknown (v 6, 2; vi 8, 6).

In 31 A.D., Tiberius and Seianus were colleagues in the consulship for the early part of the year. His office entailed the removal of Seianus to Rome, and Tiberius never again admitted him to his presence, although he added to his honours, giving him a priesthood and a share in his 'proconsulare imperium'. Seianus too was still strong enough to procure the execution of Curtius Atticus, one of the emperor's 'cohors amicorum' at Capreae, of Fufius Geminus, friend of Livia Augusta, and perhaps the death of Nero also, as well as the appointment of one of his own creatures, Fulcinius Trio, as 'consul suffectus' in July.

Gaius, however, was generally regarded as the heir, and indications of the emperor's growing coldness alarmed Seianus, so that he formed a conspiracy [1] to assassinate Tiberius and Gaius. This was revealed, apparently, by Satrius Secundus (vi 47, 2) to Antonia (mother of Claudius), and by her, through her freedman Pallas, to Tiberius. He appointed a man of proved loyalty, Memmius Regulus, as 'consul suffectus', on Oct. 1, and before long, on Oct. 18, came the 'long wordy letter from Capreae' (Juvenal x 71), which contained the emperor's denunciation of Seianus to the senate and the appointment of Naevius Sertorius Macro over the praetorian guards in his place. The 'vigiles', over whom Seianus had no influence, guarded the senate, and carried out his arrest and execution. Sentence of death was shortly afterwards executed on his eldest son, his uncle Iunius Blaesus (v 7, 2), and others. Then followed the exposure by Apicata, the divorced wife of Seianus, of Livia (or 'Livilla'), widow of Tiberius' son Drusus; she was denounced as guilty of conspiring with Seianus for her husband's destruction, eight years before, and was put to death or forced to suicide. Further investigations into the circumstances of Drusus' death took place before the emperor himself and were conducted with atrocities of torture.

BOOK VI

6   **V 6 (vi 1), § 1.** The account of most of the year 29 A.D., all 30 A.D., and the first ten months of 31 A.D. is lost. The traditional division, making Book VI begin with the year 32 A.D., is that of Lipsius; most editors however, following Haase, now consider that the early part of Bk. VI, as well as the latter part of V, has been lost, and that V ended with the death of Seianus. The two systems of the numbering of the chapters are given in the text for convenience of reference.

[1] On the doubts as to the fact of this see Intr. p. xliii.

super ea re : the subject is conjectured to be the punishment of Livia for her complicity with Seianus in the murder of her husband Drusus, Tiberius' son, in 23 A.D. (iv. 3, 3 and foll.). This sentence is a mere fragment, quite disconnected from § 2, where the continuous narrative begins with the concluding words of an address made to his friends by some person unknown, attacked as a friend of Seianus.

§ 2. collegam : the word may refer to more than his association with Tiberius in the consulship of 31 A.D., and may imply that latterly he had even been 'collega imperii', filling a position comparable to that of Tiberius in the latter years of Augustus. [Even in 23 A.D. Drusus complained that he was called 'adiutor imperii', iv 7, 2.]

generum : in 25 A.D., Seianus had asked the emperor for permission to marry Livia (iv 39), but the emperor's reply, while offering promise of some connexion by marriage with the imperial house (iv 40, 11), discouraged him from pressing his suit (iv 41, 1).

The word 'gener' used here in reference to Seianus indicates that Tiberius had announced his betrothal to some member of the imperial family ; to whom is not known.

sibi ignoscit, 'excuses his own error'.

cum scelere insectantur, 'shrink from no wickedness in attacking' ; because they accuse the innocent.

§ 3. amicum accusare : an allusion perhaps to Satrius Secundus (vi 8, 10 ; 47, 2), the follower and subsequent accuser of Seianus.

§ 5. per maerorem : Intr. p. xxi.

quam laeti : for the omission of 'potius' see Intr. II 47.

adiciendo : Intr. II 22, b.

V 7 (vi 2), § 1. superesse, &c., 'that there was yet time to spare 7 before the end'. For 'novissima' = 'end of life', cf. vi 50, 8.

§ 2. Blaesus, uncle of Seianus, executed after his fall. He was in charge of Pannonia at the time of the death of Augustus (iii 16, 2), when his relaxation of discipline prompted the mutiny of the legions there. Thanks to Seianus' influence he subsequently became 'extra sortem' proconsul of Africa in 21 A.D., and gained the 'triumphalia insignia', and the title of 'imperator'.

V 8 (vi 3), § 1. P. Vitellius, the uncle of the subsequent emperor, 8 is often mentioned in the earlier books of the *Annals* as companion and subordinate officer of Germanicus. He became proconsul of Bithynia, probably in 18 A.D., and was one of the most vehement accusers of Cn. Piso at his trial for the alleged murder of Germanicus in 20 A.D.

Pomponius Secundus, a distinguished poet and tragedian of his day, and a personal friend of the elder Pliny.

aerarii : the 'aerarium militare', a fund for providing soldiers with pension on discharge, instituted in 6 A.D. by Augustus, supported chiefly by the tax 'centesima rerum venalium'. The fund was administered by three 'praefecti' of praetorian rank.

Aelii Galli : this is believed to be the name of the eldest son of

5

Seianus. Seianus himself was son of an 'eques' named Seius Strabo, and was adopted by an 'eques' Aelius Gallus.

§ 2. **fratrum**: the best known of these is L. Vitellius, father of the emperor ; for whom see vi 28, 1.

vades exstitere: they undertook their custody till their appeal should be heard by Caesar. Delivery into the charge of 'vades' or 'fideiussores' was one of the recognized kinds of 'custodia'; cf. vi 3, 3.

§ 3. **spem ac metum**: governed by 'gravatus'; cf. 'sane gravaretur aspectum civium', iii 59, 6.

§ 4. **Tiberio superstes fuit**: he was released from imprisonment, apparently by Gaius, and subsequently rose to the consulship. In 50 A. D. he gained 'ornamenta triumphalia' as legatus of the army of Upper Germany (xii 28, 2).

9   **V 9** (vi 4), § 1. **placitum**: the expression shows that the sentence was passed by the senate.

reliquos: there were three, of whom the eldest (c. 8, 1) appears to have perished at the same time as his father.

adverteretur : here and in ii 32, 5 used in the sense of 'punishing'; usually it = 'notice'.

plebis ira: at the fall of Seianus the populace had massacred those of his creatures whom they saw in the streets (Dio lviii 12, 1).

§ 2. **intellegens**: so with genit. in xii 26, 2.

puella : she may have been eleven or twelve years old. She had been betrothed in infancy to Claudius' son, Drusus, who died in childhood (Suet. *Cl.* 27).

neque, &c., 'she would not do so any more, and she could be corrected with a child's chastisement'.

verbere : the sing. is a poetical use; so in vi 24, 4.

§ 3. **triumvirali supplicio**: the 'tresviri capitales' continued, as under the Republic, to superintend the custody of the convicted and the execution of capital punishment.

iuxta, 'just before'.

compressam = 'violatam'.

oblisis faucibus, 'after being strangled'. This was the form of execution inflicted on the free ; slaves were crucified.

id aetatis: a classical use (cf. 'id aetatis duo filii', Cic. *pro Rosc. Am.* 64), extended by Tacitus to other phrases ; cf. xii 18, 1 'nemo id auctoritatis'.

Gemonias: the 'scalae Gemoniae', leading down from the Capitol to the forum, near the 'Tullianum' (state prison).

10   **V 10** (vi 5), § 1. **Asia**, &c., 'there was a scare in Asia and Achaia, causing intense excitement, but soon dying away'.

Drusum: he was really at this time a prisoner in the Palatine (vi 23, 5).

§ 2. **velut**, 'as they professed '.

per dolumque, &c.: supply 'iis' from 'libertis' above ; cf. a similar construction in vi 47, 4 : 'And while they fraudulently gave him their support, the ignorant also were attracted to his cause'.

fama: abl. of cause, followed by abl. abs.; cf. Intr. II 64, iv.

paternos: the armies of the East, commanded by Germanicus in his last years, 17-19 A. D. (ii 43 and foll.).

§ 3. **iuventutis,** &c., 'he was thronged by crowds of able-bodied followers and assured of the devotion of various communities (' publicis ') '.

inanium spe, 'hopefulness as to his visionary schemes '.

Poppaeus Sabinus: grandfather of Poppaea who became wife of Nero.   He received triumphal honours for crushing a rebellion in Thrace, in 26 A. D. (iv 46) ; his death, 35 A. D., is recorded in vi 39, where it is said that he had governed important provinces for twenty-four years.

Macedoniae, &c.: Macedonia and Achaia had been transferred from the senate to the emperor in 15 A. D. (i 76, 4), and, to lessen the expense of government, these two provinces were put in charge of a single 'legatus'.   For some time, as in the case of Sabinus [i 80], this legatus had also the charge of Moesia.   Achaia and Macedonia were restored to the senate by Claudius in 44 A. D.

§ 4. **Nicopolis** was founded by Augustus, opposite to Actium, on the north side of the Ambracian Gulf, where his camp had stood before the battle.   The town was not really a ' colony ', but had the status of an autonomous Greek city, like Athens and Sparta.

M. Silano: probably the person mentioned in vi 20, 1 as the father-in-law of Gaius.   He is mentioned in iii 24, 5 as having prevailed upon Tiberius and the senate, in 20 A. D., to permit the return of his brother, D. Silanus, who had been exiled by Augustus as the paramour of his grand-daughter Julia.

V 11 (vi 6), § 1. **consulum.**   These were ' suffecti ', L. Fulcinius 11 Trio, appointed in July, and P. Memmius Regulus, appointed in October of this year.

Trio had made his mark as a 'delator', and was a creature of Seianus.   He was forced to suicide in 35 A. D. (vi 38).

Regulus succeeded, in 35 A. D., to the governments held by Poppaeus Sabinus, and died in 61 A. D.   So highly was he esteemed that at one time Nero spoke of appointing him as his successor (xiv 47, 1).

facilis, &c., 'ready to take up enmities'.

oblique perstrinxerat: cf. v 2, 2.

§ 2. **nisi lacesseretur:** the subjunctive is frequentative. Intr. II 41.

noxium coniurationis, 'guilty of complicity', in Seianus' plot.

infensi: see also vi 4, 2.

VI 1 (vi 7), § 1. **Cn. Domitius,** husband of Agrippina, and father 1 of Nero.   He was related by marriage to Augustus, since his father was husband of Antonia daughter of Octavia.   He is described by Suet. (*Ner.* 5) as ' omni parte vitae detestabilis '.   He died about three years after the birth of Nero, which took place in 37 A. D.

Camillus Scribonianus: his name properly was M. Furius Camillus Arruntius, his father having been apparently adopted by

L. Arruntius, whose death is described in ch. 48. The name Scribonianus was subsequently acquired, but is given here, as that by which he is best known through the rebellion which he started in 42 A.D., when legatus of Dalmatia (xii 52, 2).

§ 2. degressus, 'landing', perhaps used like καταγεσθαι.

hortis: probably those bequeathed to the people by Julius Caesar.

saxa et solitudinem maris : probably referring to Capreae.

regio: the term is due to the conception of the oriental Macedonian despotisms.

§ 5. dona: a verb must be supplied, by zeugma, from 'exercebant'. Intr. II 60.

si retinerent: frequentative subjunctive. Intr. II 41.

libita: a rare substantival use; so in xii 6, 3; cf. 'moram cupitis adferebant', iv 3, 1.

2   Chapter 2, § 1. Liviae: she had been put to death at the time of Seianus' downfall, towards the end of the previous year, for her complicity in the poisoning of Drusus in 23 A.D.

in effigies, &c.: cf. the similar procedure in the case of Messalina, xi 38, 4.

in fiscum : this term had probably not yet become current, the first use of it being found in Seneca. 'Res', or 'bona, Caesaris' were used. Cf. also ch. 19, 1. All 'publicata bona' properly went into the 'aerarium', but Caesar could alter this arrangement, especially if the condemned had previously received imperial bounties. Later, confiscated property always went to the emperor, and 'confiscare' and 'publicare' became synonymous terms.

tamquam referret, 'as if it made any difference'. Caesar could control the 'aerarium' by originating 'senatus consulta' to deal with its funds.

§ 2. Scipiones, &c.: the plurals are probably used of single persons = 'men like S.', &c. A Scipio is mentioned in xi 2, 5: Silanus, v 10, 4; Cassius, ch. 15, 1.

adseveratione, 'seriousness'.

Togonius Gallus: unknown, apart from this 'sententia'.

§ 3. orabat deligere : Intr. II 31.

§ 4. epistulae: the letter in which Tiberius had denounced Seianus. In accordance with it the consul Regulus had presented himself at Capreae, but had been refused an audience.

§ 5. iuvenes: the only senators who had as yet gone through no magistracy would be those actually holding the quaestorship; these would be twenty-five years old or more.

§ 6. neque ut, &c., 'and without advising anything beyond the cancelling of the proposal'; i. e. its omission from the 'acta', without punishment of the proposer.

3   Chapter 3, § 1. Iunius Gallio, a famous orator of the time. Ovid addressed to him a condolence on the death of his wife (ex P. 4, 11). He adopted one of Seneca's brothers, who took the name

Iunius Gallio and was the proconsul of Achaia mentioned in Acts xviii 12.

actis stipendiis: they served sixteen years.

in quattuordecim ordinibus: the 'lex Roscia theatralis', carried by the tribune L. Roscius Otho in 67 B.C., assigned to the equites the fourteen rows of seats in the theatre next to the senators. Gallio's measure would raise discharged praetorians to equestrian dignity. This was already the privilege of a 'primipilaris'.

increpuit: the rebuke was administered in a letter.

dicta, 'orders'. If 'imperatoris' is read, it must go with 'dicta', 'orders of a commanding officer'; but this is very awkward, as the word is used immediately afterwards in the sense of 'emperor'.

§ 2. **ad corrumpendum, &c.,** 'to a breach of discipline'. Gallio's proposal might lead the praetorians to look to the senate, and not only to the emperor, for rewards.

§ 3. **incusabatur ... toleraturus:** Intr. II 33.

domibus: Intr. II 14. For such custody cf. the proposal of Julius Caesar as to the treatment of the Catilinarian conspirators; Sall. *Cat.* xlvii 3.

§ 4. **Paconianum:** for his death see ch. 39, 1. For the conspiracy in which he was implicated see App. to Book V, p. 4.

§ 5. **decernebatur, ni professus ... foret:** Intr. II 38.

indicium: cf. v 8, 1.

Chapter 4, § 1. ingressus est, 'proceeded to deal with'; cf. 'ingredi defensionem' (xi 2, 3), and the use of 'loqui' with a personal accusative, as 'etiam Catilinam loquebantur', Cic. *pro Mil.* xxiii 63.

Latinius Latiaris: his part in the overthrow of Titius Sabinus, a friend of Germanicus, at the instance of Seianus in 28 A.D., is described in iv 68 and foll.

circumveniendi ... luendae: cf. Intr. II 24, c.

§ 2. **Haterius Agrippa:** mentioned in the *Annals* (as a relative of Germanicus) as tribune in 15 A.D., praetor in 17 A.D., and consul in 22 A.D.

consules: see v 11.

intenta: so 'intento mortis metu', i 39, 4.

noxae conscientiam, 'complicity in guilt'.

§ 3. **si qua discordes iecissent,** 'any taunts which they had uttered in their quarrel'.

§ 4. **Sanquinius Maximus:** he had been cos. suff., probably in 23 A.D., was 'praefectus urbis' and again cos. suff. in 39 A.D., and died legatus of Lower Germany in 47 A.D. (xi 18, 1).

acerbitatibus, 'troubles'.

dilatio exitii: for his death see ch. 38, 2.

§ 5. **somno, &c.,** 'enervated by somnolence or nights spent in debauchery'.

Chapter 5, § 1. Cotta Messalinus: see v 3, 4.

9

die natali Augustae: this was Jan. 30.

novendialem. This name was given to a feast for the dead, held on the ninth day after a funeral.

M'. Lepidus: see note on ch. 27, 4.

L. Arruntius: another eminent senator and pleader. He had been mentioned by Augustus as a possible successor (i 13). He was appointed in 15 A.D. as one of the commissioners whose duty it was to prevent the flooding of the river Tiber. In ch. 27 it is mentioned that Tiberius prevented his tenure of the province of Spain for which he was qualified. Chapters 47 and 48 record his accusation and death in 37 A.D.

§ 2. **quae cuncta:** possibly accusative as object of ' revince-batur' used with the force of a middle voice.

simplicitas, ' frankness '.

in crimen duceretur: cf. xi 34, 2 'quo ducerentur inclina-tura '.

6   **Chapter 6, § 1. his verbis:** the letter was probably extant in the 'acta senatus'. Its opening words are quoted also by Sueto-nius (*Tib.* 67).

§ 2. **ipsi quoque,** i.e. 'ut et aliis tyrannis' [or perhaps the words mean that his wickedness brought unhappiness upon himself as well as causing suffering to the victims of his cruelty].

praestantissimus sapientiae: for the genitive see Intr. II 24, c. The term is applied to Socrates in allusion to his having been pronounced wisest of men by the Delphic oracle (Plato, *Apol.* v *ad fin.*). The sentiment quoted may be found in the *Gorgias* (524 E), but the words 'solitus est' imply that more than one passage is referred to.

firmare: so in ch. 50, 5 ; see Intr. II 28.

malis consultis, ' evil designs'.

§ 3. **fortuna,** 'rank', 'position'.

7   **Chapter 7, § 1. C. Caeciliano:** not known, apart from this passage.

prompserat, 'had uttered', 'stated'; so also xii 65, 2.

Aruseium et Sanquinium: these persons, and their accusation of Arruntius, must have been mentioned in the lost part of the *Annals.* Aruseius is, perhaps, again mentioned in ch. 40, 1 : this Sanquinius is not the same as the person in ch. 4, 4.

nobilis: he was son of Messalla Corvinus (ch. 11, 4).

sanctissimis, &c., ' was, by the honour of the vengeance exacted for him, set on a par with the stainless accomplishments of Arrun-tius '. The penalty inflicted on his accuser was probably exile.

§ 2. **Q. Servaeus:** he had been the first governor of Commagene, 18 A.D., and was one of the witnesses against Piso in 20 A.D.

Minucius Thermus: father, perhaps, of the praetor mentioned in xvi 20, 2 as victim of Tigellinus in 66 A.D.

modeste habita, &c., ' both of whom had enjoyed, without abusing it, the friendship of Seianus '.

§ 3. **increpans,** 'denouncing them as foremost in crime '.

admonuit ... dicere: Intr. II 31.

C. Cestium patrem : consul in 35 A. D., ch. 31, 1 ; probably father of the Cestius who was legatus of Syria, under Nero, in 63 A. D. (xv 25, 5).

§ 4. repens = ' recens ' ; so in xi 24, 7.

perinde, &c., ' men were attacked alike for language used in the forum, at a private repast, and on any subject whatever'.

destinare, ' to mark down' for destruction.

quasi valetudine ac contactu, 'by the contagion of some disease'. Hendiadys ; Intr. II 54.

§ 5. indicibus accessere : cf. ch. 3, 5.

Iulius Africanus : probably father of the orator of the name, famous in the next generation (*Dial.* 15, 3).

Santonis, the people of Saintonge, north of the Lower Garonne.

§ 6. obvenere, ' have come to my notice ' ; i. e. in research among memoirs or other sources.

Chapter 8, § 1. Nam : this introduces one of the stories referred 8 to at the end of the last chapter, omitted by other authors but regarded by Tacitus as worthy of record.

falso, ' disloyally '.

amplecti, ' to cling to ', ' profess ', ' acknowledge '.

ordiendo : Intr. II 22, b.

§ 3. patris : Lucius Seius Strabo, afterwards praefect of Egypt. The association of Seianus with his father in the command of the praetorian guard is mentioned as early as 14 A. D. (i 24, 3).

urbis et militiae munia : these words describe Seianus' virtual control of all departments of State through his influence with the princeps.

§ 4. propinqui : e. g. Iunius Blaesus, uncle of Seianus, who was appointed proconsul of Africa in 21 A. D. (iii 35, 1).

metu ac sordibus, ' danger and the suppliant's garb'. (Cf. xii 59, 3.)

§ 5. novissimi consilii : the ' coniuratio '; see p. 4.

§ 6. Vulsiniensem : he was born at Vulsinii in Etruria.

Claudiae : a daughter of Seianus was to have married Claudius' son Drusus, who, however, died in childhood.

Iuliae : Seianus is called ' gener ' by Tiberius in v 6, 2.

quas, &c., ' families into which he had been admitted by marriage connexions '.

consulatus socium : in the early part of 31 A. D.

officia ... capessentem : see note on ' collegam ', v 6, 2.

§ 8. quae coram habentur, 'arrangements that exist openly '. Cf. 'non in obscuro habentur', xv 16, 3.

quis : dat. plur.

§ 9. ideo = ' si exquiras ', 'nor if you should make the inquiry would you succeed in it '.

§ 10. sedecim : from the accession of Tiberius to the fall of Seianus, without counting the year in which each of these events happened.

Satrius Secundus is mentioned as a 'cliens Seiani' and accuser of Cremutius Cordus in 25 A.D. (iv 34, 2). See also ch. 47, 2.

Pomponium: not one of the distinguished Pomponii mentioned in the earlier books, but another satellite of Seianus, of whom probably mention was made in the lost part.

§ 11. **indistincta ... et promisca,** 'without discrimination or reserve'.

de amicitia, &c., 'as to our friendship and attentions to him, we as much as you shall be clear of blame since we ended them at the same time.

9 **Chapter 9, § 1. constantia,** 'courage'; cf. v 4, 2.

et quia, &c.: this clause is co-ordinate with 'constantia' as subject to 'potuere'.

efferret, 'utter'.

quae ante deliquerant, 'their previous misdeeds'. Cf. xii 54, 7.

additis, 'acting as additional grounds' for their punishment.

§ 2. **cohortem**: a 'cohors amicorum' attended the princeps or members of his family when travelling, just as under the Republic a provincial governor was attended by a 'cohors praetoria', a staff of personal friends.

§ 3. **seu,** &c., 'either that he had invented stories ... or the allegation (that he had done so) won credence'.

§ 4. **convictu ... prohibitus**: cf. ch. 29, 3.

When the emperor notified regular 'renuntiatio amicitiae', a form of banishment was often inflicted besides, or was understood (cf. iii 24, 5) to be implied.

§ 5. **Annius Pollio,** an ex-consul, perhaps grandfather of the Annius Pollio of xv 56, 4.

Appius Iunius Silanus was consul in 28 A.D.; he perished under Claudius; see xi 29, 1.

Mamercus Scaurus: great-grandson of the 'princeps senatus' prominent in the Jugurthine scandal. Cf. ch. 29, 4.

C. Calvisius Sabinus was consul in 26 A.D.; he became legatus of Pannonia under Gaius, but was accused, and committed suicide (Dio lix 18, 4).

L. Annius Vinicianus is mentioned by Dio as having been regarded as a possible successor to Gaius, and as an adherent of the conspiracy of Camillus Scribonianus (xii 52, 2).

simul: here used as preposition with abl. Intr. II 46.

§ 6. **Celsus**: cf. ch. 14, 2.

§ 7. **nosceret**: Intr. II 28.

tristibus notis, 'marks of his disfavour'.

10 **Chapter 10, § 1. occupandae reipublicae,** 'of usurping power in the State'.

Vitia: the name is not found elsewhere. 'Vibia', 'Vittia', and 'Fufia' are suggested emendations. For Fufius Geminus see v 1, 1; 2, 2.

§ 2. **haec**: sc. 'acta sunt'. All the cases, from ch. 2 to this point, are meant.

12

apud principem: the trial of these persons was held in the emperor's private court (Intr. III 2). In such cases the actual condemnation was usually pronounced by the senate, on report from the emperor; cf. ch. 47, 4.

Vescularius Flaccus, an 'eques' (ii 28), who received from Firmius Catus, and passed on to the emperor, information against Libo Drusus, which led to the latter's suicide.

Iulius Marinus: otherwise unknown. Curtius Atticus, an 'illustris eques', addressed by Ovid (*ex P.* ii 4), is mentioned in iv 58 as one of those in the retinue of Tiberius when he finally retired from the city, in 26 A.D. His destruction was probably described in the lost part.

individui, 'inseparable from him'.

sua exempla, &c., 'that the punishments prompted by them had recoiled on the contrivers'.

§ 3. L. Piso: consul in 15 B.C., son of L. Calpurnius Piso Caesoninus, the consul of 58 B.C. and censor of 50 B.C., who was a supporter of Clodius, an enemy of Cicero, and father of Julius Caesar's wife Calpurnia.

rarum: in apposition to the verbal notion of the sentence; Intr. II 59.

et quotiens, &c., 'and behaving with a wise moderation when the force of circumstances was overwhelming'. For the subjunctive cf. Intr. II 41.

§ 4. memoravi: this mention is lost.

decus triumphale: the 'triumphalia ornamenta' (cf. xi 20, 3), won by Piso in 11 B.C. after a three years' war.

§ 5. recens: adverb, qualifying 'continuam'; 'he exercised with wonderful moderation an office which had but recently been made permanent and was the more irksome owing to the habitual insubordination (of the people)'.

Chapter 11, § 1. Namque, &c.: the expression 'recens continuam' prompts Tacitus to give an account of the office of 'praefectus urbi'. This, existing originally in the regal period and then for a time under the Republic, for the purposes described in § 1, became unnecessary and disappeared after the institution of the 'praetor urbanus' in 367 B.C. Its shadow ('simulacrum', § 2), however, continued to exist in the appointment of a 'praefectus' who represented the consuls during the few days when they left Rome to attend the 'feriae Latinae' on the Alban Mount, nor was this 'simulacrum' abolished under the Empire: we find Drusus, son of Germanicus, holding it in 25 A.D. (iv 36, 1). The regular 'praefectura urbis', a more substantial office, independent of this 'simulacrum', arose out of the appointment by the 'princeps' of a vicegerent in Rome and Italy when he himself was obliged to be absent, as was Augustus in 36 B.C. during the war against Sextus Pompeius, and again during the Actian war, on both of which occasions Maecenas was left in charge of Rome. The actual title of 'praefectus urbi' was first held by Messalla Corvinus, in 26 A.D. (§ 4). The widest powers

13

of this 'praefectus' were naturally in abeyance when the princeps returned to Rome, and were limited as described in § 3. This jurisdiction, however, evidently soon became extended; it is found to clash with the praetor's under Nero (xiv 41, 2), and in later times the office became still more important.

in tempus, here, 'temporarily'.

subitis, 'emergencies' (substantival) ; Intr. II 2, a.

Romulius Denter: otherwise unknown.

Numa Marcius: the first pontiff under King Numa, according to Livy, and father of Ancus Marcius, according to Plutarch.

Spurius Lucretius: mentioned in Livy i 59, 12 as left in charge of the city, at the time of the expulsion of Tarquin by Brutus, when the latter marched out to the camp at Ardea.

§ 2. **feriae Latinae:** an annual festival held on Mons Albanus in honour of Jupiter Latiaris, being originally the religious part of the federal assembly of the towns of Latium. Rome assuming the leadership of the league, the consuls took the presidency of the festival, and after the dissolution of the league (338 B.C.) the ceremony was still continued. The time of year at which it was held varied. The 'feriae' lasted four days.

§ 3. **qui coerceret,** &c.: these duties had previously belonged to the 'tresviri capitales', but during the last period of the Republic it had been out of their power to check disorder at Rome.

§ 4. **Messalla Corvinus:** see v 3, 4.

accepit: for a few days in 26 B.C., during Augustus' absence in Gaul and Spain, 27–24 B.C.

§ 5. **Statilius Taurus:** he held this office in 16 B.C. He had been 'consul suffectus' in 37 B.C. A descendant of his is mentioned in xii 59, 1.

toleravit, 'sustained its duties'.

publico funere: burial at the public cost.

12   **Chapter 12,** § 1. **de libro Sibullae.** The books containing the Sibylline prophecies had been burnt with the Capitoline temple in 83 B.C., but the prophecies had been collected again, and Augustus had ordered their revision and had stored them in the temple of Apollo on the Palatine.

Caninius Gallus: besides being one of the 'quindecimviri', he had been 'triumvir monetalis' in 18 B.C. and 'consul suffectus' in 2 B.C.

quindecimvirum: partit. genit. The abl. with 'e' would be more usual (cf. ch. 4, 4).

The 'quindecimviri' had charge of the Sibylline Books and of the 'ludi saeculares', cf. xi 11, 4. Their number, originally two, was raised to ten when the office was opened to plebeians, in 367 B.C., and to fifteen by Sulla. Five of these, termed 'magistri' (§ 2), were superior to the rest.

recipi: Intr. II 31.

per discessionem: the senators moved over to the side of the house where the proposer sat, and the motion was carried without discussion.

§ 2. **scientiae caerimoniarumque**: hendiadys; Intr. II 54.
For the genit. with 'vetus' cf. ch. 44, 1 'vetus regnandi', and Intr.
II 24, c.

§ 3. **deferrentur**: the subject must be supplied from 'multa
vana' above, i.e. the prophecies of unrecognized validity, as yet
in private hands.

§ 4. **sociali bello**: a mistake. The occasion was the Civil War
between Marius and Sulla; the destruction of the temple occurred
in 83 B.C.

Samo, &c.: ablatives of place whence.

Italicas colonias: the cities of Magna Graecia. A Sibyl (pro-
phetess inspired by Apollo) was attributed to a great number of places
in the ancient world; the most famous was the Sibyl of Cumae.

discernere: this unusual infinitive, after 'dato negotio', may be
referred to the usages noted in Intr. II 31.

§ 5. **notioni**: the word is used by Cic. (*ad Att.* xi 20, 2) = 'co-
gnitio'; cf. 'noscere' for 'cognoscere' in ch. 9, 7.

Chapter 13, § 1. iuxta, &c., 'things came almost to an insur- **13**
rection'.

in theatro: such gatherings were now the chief occasions on which
popular demands or grievances found expression. On the occasion
of another dearth, Claudius was mobbed in the forum (xii 43, 2).

§ 2. **quod**, &c., 'for not having repressed the populace by the
weight of their official action'.

advectaret: rare, and poetical; see Intr. II 51, d.

§ 3. **consules**: specified here as the promulgators of the edict,
as such proclamations were more usually in the emperor's name.

§ 4. **in superbiam accipiebatur**, 'was taken not as a sign of
constitutional temper, but arrogance'; cf. 'in prodigium accipiebatur', xii 43, 1.

Chapter 14, § 1. Geminius, &c.: these three persons are all **14**
unknown.

coniurationis: that of Seianus; cf. v 11, 2.

nihil ad serium, '(his friend) in no matter of serious import'.

§ 2. **Iulius Celsus tribunus**: see ch. 9, 6.

circumdatam, &c., 'putting it round his neck and straining
against it'.

§ 3. **Rubrius Fabatus**: it is implied that he was a senator,
arrested for meditating a distant journey without leave. Senators
had to get permission to travel out of Italy, except to Sicily and
(after 49 A.D.) Gallia Narbonensis.

tamquam, &c.: Intr. II 50.

§ 4. **probabiles**, 'convincing'.

longinquae, 'distant', applying not to the place where he was
captured, but to his destination.

Chapter 15, § 1. Servius Sulpicius Galba: subsequently prin- **15**
ceps for a short time, in 69 A.D.; cf. ch. 20, 3.

Lucius Sulla: an inscription gives his cognomen 'Felix', showing him to have been a descendant of the dictator.

15

neptibus: the daughters of Germanicus, Drusilla and Julia, aged respectively sixteen and fifteen. Agrippina was already married (to Cn. Domitius Ahenobarbus, iv 75).

L. Cassius Longinus was consul in 30 A.D., and proconsul of Asia in 41 A.D., when he was put to death by Gaius. He was brother of C. Cassius the jurist (xii 12, 1).

M. Vinicius: consul with Cassius in 30 A.D., and again consul in 45 A.D. He was poisoned by Messalina in 46 A.D. (according to Dio).

§ 2. **oppidanum**: the term refers to an Italian municipality.

patre: P. Vinicius, consul in 2 A.D., mentioned in iii 11 as one of the ' patroni' asked for by Cn. Piso at his trial in 20 A.D.

avo: M. Vinicius, ' consul suffectus' in 19 B.C.

cetera: cf. xii 3, 2.

§ 3. **plebeii generis**: the 'gens Cassia' was originally patrician. The ' Cassii Longini' appear among distinguished plebeian families from the time of the Second Punic War.

patris: L. Cassius Longinus, ' consul suffectus' in 11 A.D.

facilitate, ' agreeable', or ' complaisant, nature'.

§ 4. **iuvenum**: both were ex-consuls. For the term cf. vi 2, 5 ; xi 12, 2.

§ 5. **vagis**, 'indefinite'.

offensiones, &c., 'the hatred incurred by him in the work of government'. For 'coeptas' cf. ch. 30, 4.

Naevius Sertorius Macro had been appointed successor to Seianus in the command of the praetorian troops in October, 31 A.D. He was eventually forced to suicide by Gaius, 38 A.D.

§ 6. **large**, &c., 'in comprehensive terms, without specification of the kind or the number (of his bodyguard)'. Such a guard for the emperor in the senate is mentioned in the time of Gaius and Claudius, and later.

publicum consilium: a phrase applied to the senate by Cicero and other previous authors.

deviis, &c.: cf. ch. 1, 2 ; 39, 2.

declinans: prob. transit., as in ch. 51, 3.

16   Chapter 16, § 1. **auctitabant**: Intr. II 51, d.

legem dictatoris Caesar: by an ordinance passed in 49 or 48 B.C. the interest paid, or in arrear, was struck off from the principal, and creditors had to take in lieu of payment the real and personal property of the debtor, estimated at what it had been worth before the Civil War. This was a temporary measure, and there was also a permanent law, imperfectly known to us, limiting the amount of money that might be legally held in private hands or loaned (' de modo credendi possidendique intra Italiam '). Its regulations doubtless aimed at forcing capitalists to place out on loan or invest a certain amount of their property, and probably required a definite proportion to be invested in Italian land, so as to encourage expenditure of capital on the soil and by giving capitalists a stake in the country to discourage mere money-lending.

omissam, 'which had fallen into abeyance'.

§ 2. creberrima causa: the early history of the Republic provides many instances, and the question of debt and usury was one of the most prominent in the struggle of plebeians against patricians.

§ 3. duodecim tabulis: published in 449 B.C. Tacitus is our only authority for assigning the law to this code. Livy ascribes it to the tribunes Duilius and Maenius in 357 B.C.

unciario faenore: interpreted by Niebuhr and Mommsen as 8⅓ per cent. for the year of ten months, 10 per cent. for twelve months. Others have taken it as one-twelfth per cent. per month.

agitaretur: sc. 'faenus'.

ad semuncias: in 347 B.C. (Livy vii 27, 3).

vetita versura: a 'lex Genucia', 'ne faenerare liceret', forbidding loans on interest in general, is chronicled by Livy, as passed in 342 B.C. 'Versura' strictly = payment by fresh loan. This law does not seem to have ever been formally repealed, though it was disregarded in practice.

§ 4. obviam itum fraudibus: one method of evasion was to make a 'socius', who was not bound by Roman law, the nominal creditor; against this a plebiscite was carried by M. Sempronius in 195 B.C., placing ' socii ' and ' Latini ' on the same footing as citizens in this respect.

§ 5. Gracchus: perhaps the same as the person mentioned in ch. 38, 4.

tali culpa: senators themselves generally derived a great deal of their wealth from money-lending: thus Seneca had invested large amounts in loans in Britain (xiii 42, 7).

concedente: Intr. II 21, b.

quis, &c., 'within which time each one was to bring his financial arrangements into conformity with the requirements of the law'.

Chapter 17, § 1. commoto, 'disturbed'; because creditors, **17** having broken the law, had to call in their loans.

attinebatur: the supply of cash in circulation had been diminished by its influx into the treasury, owing to the confiscation of the property of the numerous persons condemned in the previous year.

§ 2. ad hoc, 'to meet this difficulty' (not, as elsewhere, 'besides').

duas faenoris partes, 'two-thirds of the capital lent'. The object of the decree was probably to increase the demand for land, to the advantage of debtors who had estates to sell; but the creditors, as the next sentence relates, instead of leaving one-third still out on loan, called in the whole sum (' in solidum appellabant '), and as they had eighteen months in which to comply with the 'lex' against them, they could take their time in making the requisite purchase of land, whereas the debtors had to realize their estates at a time when the market was flooded with property for sale and money was scarce.

§ 3. concursatio: men applied in vain here and there for loans or extension of time for payment.

strepere, &c.: the praetor's court rang with notices of suits for debt.

condiderant, 'held in reserve'.

mercandis: dat. of purpose.

§ 4. **copiam,** with gerund, usually = 'opportunity'; here, 'abundance of sales'.

aegrius distrahebant, 'had more difficulty in selling'. The verb usually denotes sale in small parcels.

provolvebantur, 'were ejected'.

dignitatem: the rank of senator or 'eques' depended on 'census'.

praeceps: here used as an adverb; so also in iv 62, 3 'praeceps trahit'. The phrase 'in praeceps' is more usual.

per mensas, 'in banks'. The emperor thus brought into circulation the money which was locked up in the treasury, § 1.

si debitor, &c., 'if the debtor gave security to the State on landed property for double the amount of the loan'. 'Populo' implies that the loan came from the 'aerarium'; cf. ch. 2, 1, and note.

§ 5. **ad formam,** 'in compliance with the terms'.

18   **Chapter 18,** § 1. **Considio Proculo:** unknown apart from this passage.

pariter: = simul, 'there and then'. Ordinarily there was an interval of ten days between the passing and the execution of a sentence pronounced by the senate (iii 51, 3).

§ 2. **Q. Pomponius** was 'consul suffectus' in 41 A. D., on the death of Gaius, when he exhorted the senate to re-establish the Republic or to set up a worthy emperor. He was one of the adherents of Camillus Scribonianus in the conspiracy of 42 A. D.

fratris: see v 8.

§ 3. **Argolicum, . . . Laconem:** personal cognomina.

§ 4. **inlustris eques:** i. e. an eques possessed of senatorial census, but remaining within the equestrian rank from choice. See also note on xi 4, 1.

frater: Pompeius Macer, praetor 15 A. D.

§ 5. **Theophanes** was a distinguished citizen of Mitylene, who received the 'civitas' from Pompeius Magnus, and also won from him for Mitylene the privileges of a free city. He wrote a history of his patron's campaigns in the East. His son 'Macer Pompeius' was one of Augustus' procurators in Asia, and was the father of the 'inlustris eques' here mentioned. 'Eorum' refers to Pompeia and her brother.

caelestes honores: probably attributed to him in gratitude for the privilege granted for his sake to the city. There is an inscription extant to him as σωτῆρι καὶ εὐεργέτᾳ καὶ κτίστᾳ δευτέρῳ τῆς πατρίδος.

19   **Chapter 19,** § 1. **Sextus Marius:** mentioned in iv 36, 1 as the object of an accusation, in 25 A. D., before Drusus, son of Germanicus, when Tiberius stopped the proceedings and banished the accuser.

defertur incestasse: Intr. II 33.

vertisse: intrans. So 'convertit' xii 18, 2.

sibimet: i. e. the confiscated property went into the 'fiscus'; cf. ch. 2, 1.

§ 2. **inritatus**: like a wild beast that has tasted blood.

cunctos: Paconianus (ch. 3, 4 and 39, 1) would appear to be an exception.

carcere, 'in custody' (not necessarily in the 'Tullianum', which was too small to contain prisoners in any number).

§ 3. **iacuit**, &c., 'a vast heap of corpses lay exposed'. Tacitus represents the scene almost as a battlefield. Suetonius (*Tib.* 61), probably describing the same event, speaks of twenty persons executed in one day and exposed on the 'scalae Gemoniae'.

§ 4. **dabatur**: with infin.; cf. Intr. II 31.

ubi: for historic infin. in a subordinate sentence see Intr. II 34.

§ 5. **sortis humanae commercium**: lit. = 'the sharing of human fortune', i. e. 'sympathy for human trouble'.

quantum glisceret: Intr. II 41.

Chapter 20, § 1. discedenti Capreas: probably on the occasion **20** described in ch. 1, 2. At that time he would be twenty years old. He had been made pontifex in 31 A. D., and he was quaestor for this year, 33 A. D.

Claudiam: Iunia Claudilla, daughter of the M. Silanus mentioned in v 10, 4. She soon died (in childbirth, according to Suet. *Cal.* 12): her death is referred to in ch. 45, 5.

immanem animum: cf. also chs. 45, 46.

damnatione matris: see Appendix, p. 3.

exitio fratrum: Nero had perished in 31 A. D.; Drusus was still alive, but in prison. Tacitus is describing the demeanour of Gaius through this whole period of his association with Tiberius.

qualem . . . induisset, 'whatever mood he had assumed for the day'. Cf. 'animum induere', xi 7, 5; 'qualem diem haberet', ch. 21, 3.

habitu, 'deportment'. (The abl. may be regarded as absolute, parallel with 'rupta voce'.)

§ 2. **mox**, 'subsequently' (after he became princeps).

Passieni oratoris: C. Passienus Crispus, twice consul, the second time being in 44 A. D. He married first Domitia, sister of Agrippina's first husband, and after divorcing her was married to Agrippina herself, who was said to have poisoned him. Nero inherited his property.

§ 3. **Chaldaeorum**: astrologers, known also, in Tacitus, as 'mathematici', and 'periti caelestium'.

cuius apiscendae, &c., 'for acquiring which he had leisure at Rhodes, and employed Thrasullus as his teacher'. For the genit. see Intr. II 26, a. Thrasullus received freedom or 'civitas' from Tiberius, owing to his association with him at Rhodes, as is shown by the form of his name in an inscription, which has 'Ti. Claudius' before 'Thrasullus'. He returned with Tiberius to Rome, lived constantly with him, and died a year before him.

21   **Chapter 21. § 1. quotiens . . . consultaret:** frequentative; cf. Intr. II 41. So in **§ 2** 'statuisset', whereas the next verb, which is also frequentative, is in plupf. indic., for variety.

liberti unius conscientia : Intr. II 57, a.

§ 2. per avia ac derupta, 'by a wild and precipitous path '.

ne, &c., 'that there should be no one available to tell the secret '.

§ 3. isdem, &c., ' by way of the same cliffs'.

commoverat, ' had made a great impression on him '.

quem tum, &c., ' what was the aspect of the year, and of the day, which he was now passing '.

§ 4. positus, &c., 'the positions of the stars and their relative distances'.

quantum : cf. ch. 19, 5.

trepidus, 'excited by surprise and fear'; for the gen. see Intr. II 24, c.

ultimum, ' fatal '.

§ 5. praescium: supply ' esse ' from ' fore ' below. Here ' gratatur ' has the construction of a verb of speaking.

22   **Chapter 22, § 1. in incerto, &c.,** ' I find it hard to pronounce whether the fortunes of mankind are shaped by destiny and an unchangeable necessity or by chance '.

forte = τύχη, here ' chance ', as opposed to fate or law. Sometimes the word denotes the ordinary course of nature; thus, a ' natural' death is '‘fortuita', xii 52, 3.

§ 2. sapientissimos . . . quique . . . aemulantur: i. e. the founders of philosophy and their schools.

diversos, ' at variance '.

multis : the Epicureans.

in . . . apud: Intr. II 64, (i).

§ 3. contra alii : the Stoics. Thus, Seneca (*Nat. Qu.* ii 36) defines ' fatum' as the power of invariable causation manifested in nature, and in another place (*de Ben.* iv 7, 2) identifies this power with God ; ' hunc eundem (Deum) et fatum si dixeris non mentieris. Nam cum fatum nihil aliud sit quam series implexa causarum, ille est prima omnium causa unde ceterae pendent'.

fatum, &c., ' that fate is in harmony with events ', an inversion for ' that events proceed in accordance with fate '; cf. ' ignaviam alia ad vocabula transferri ', iii 34, 7.

sed non, &c., ' not in dependence on the wandering stars, but as determined by the foundations and sequences of natural causation '. Stoicism did not, however, altogether reject the possibility of ascertaining the will of heaven through astrology, as a mode of divination (Cic. *Div.* ii 42, 88).

quam ubi, &c., ' and when this choice has been made, there is (they say) a fixed series of consequences '.

§ 4. per, ' in the midst of '.

§ 5. ceterum, &c. : the popular belief is here stated, in contrast with the tenets of the two leading schools of philosophy : ' there is no ridding the majority of men of the conviction that a man's future is determined for him at the hour of his birth '.

fallaciis, 'through the frauds of those who speak without knowledge'. 'Ignara' = 'ignota': so 'gnara' = 'nota', xi 32, 1.

§ 6. **in tempore**, 'at the proper time', referring perhaps to xiv 9, 5, which recounts the prophecy given 'by the Chaldaeans' to Agrippina, that Nero should be emperor and kill his mother; to which she replied 'occidat dum imperet'.

Chapter 23, § 1. Asinius Gallus, son of Asinius Pollio. He was consul in 8 B. C., proconsul of Asia in 6 B. C., and was well known as an orator and man of letters. He is often mentioned in the early books of the *Annals*, usually as the author of some servile 'sententia' against a victim of Tiberius. He married Vipsania, daughter of Agrippa, after Tiberius had been obliged to divorce her in order to marry Julia, and by her was the father of several sons who rose to the consulship (see § 3). He had been denounced by a secret missive to Tiberius at Capreae, in 30 A. D., and was condemned in absence by the senate, after which he was detained in custody at the house of a magistrate.

§ 2. **sepeliri**: it was not necessary to get permission for burial except in the case of a person executed after formal sentence. It was not clear whether Gallus' death was to be regarded as an execution or a natural end.

non erubuit, &c.: Gallus, according to Dio, had been condemned by the senate at the time of his arrest, but had been reserved as if on appeal till Caesar's return to Rome. The hypocrisy attributed by Tacitus to the emperor consisted in professing regret for a delay which he himself had caused.

§ 3. **consulari**: his rank might have secured him an early hearing of his appeal.

tot consularium: the names of five of his sons known to us are Asinius Saloninus, C. Asinius, M. Asinius Agrippa (mentioned in the earlier books of the *Annals*), Asinius Gallus, banished for a conspiracy against Claudius in 46 A. D. (Dio), Asinius Celer, a noted gourmand (Pliny ma.), put to death by Claudius (Seneca, *Lud.* 13, 4): of these, the second, third, and fifth are known to have been consuls.

§ 4. **tomentum**, 'stuffing'; hay or straw.

§ 5. **praescriptum . . . imponere**: Intr. II 31.

§ 6. **maluit**: probably Drusus was killed to prevent another such plot as that mentioned in v 10, 1.

Chapter 24, § 1. probra corporis, 'gross unchastity'.

exitiabilem in suos: in iv 60 Tacitus says that Seianus worked on Drusus' dislike of his brother Nero and his jealousy of Agrippina's preference for him, and drew him into his plot for compassing Nero's ruin, holding out to him the prospect of becoming emperor if his elder brother was destroyed.

infensum rei publicae: Drusus had been declared 'hostis publicus'; Suet. *Tib.* 4.

descripta per dies, 'the account kept day by day'. The participle is here used as a substantive.

§ 2. **nisi quod**, &c.: the phrase qualifies 'vix fides'; all the foregoing facts were barely credible were it not that still worse was positively attested.

epistulae: letters to Tiberius read before the senate.

§ 3. **egregium**: Intr. II 2.

exspes: a poetical word ; Intr. II 51.

nurum, &c. : supply 'necasset', by zeugma, from 'caedibus complevisset'; Intr. II 60. Agrippina was not yet dead, but in banishment at Pandateria (App. p. 3): Drusus evidently anticipated her execution.

§ 4. **obturbabant**, 'interrupted'.

tegendis sceleribus : cf. ch. 51, 5 'occultum ac subdolum fingendis virtutibus'. It is not clear whether the case is ablat. of respect or dat. of purpose.

verbere: the singular is a poetic usage ; so in v 9, 2.

extrema, &c., 'the barest sustenance necessary to support life'.

25 Chapter 25, § 1. **provixisse**, 'had lived on'. The compound seems to be one coined by Tacitus: Intr. II 51.

nisi si, '(I think so) except on the supposition that', 'unless possibly'.

qui videretur: amplifying 'adsimulatus est', 'by the withholding of food her death was made to assume the appearance of one self-inflicted'.

§ 2. **enimvero**: the particle marks a transition from the less to the more important consideration.

impudicitiam: no such charge was made at her arrest (v 3, 4). Gallus, moreover, was old enough to be her father, and so far from ever appearing as her partisan is mentioned in iv 71, 3 as encouraging Tiberius to proceed against her.

§ 3. **aequi** : used as a substantive, 'a position of equality', i. e. with other subjects. The phrase is apparently from Statius (*Theb.* 3, 602) 'superum contemptor et aequi impatiens'.

exuerat, 'had put off feminine vices by assuming masculine interests'.

§ 4. **iactavit**, 'prided himself on the fact that'.

§ 5. **quintum decimum** : usually 'ante' precedes the ordinal number in such expressions. It is similarly omitted in ch. 50, 7.

26 Chapter 26, § 1. **Cocceius Nerva**: mentioned in iv 58, 1 as accompanying Tiberius on his final departure from Rome to Capreae in 26 A. D. He had already been 'consul suffectus', and was 'curator aquarum' for some years before his death.

principi: the case is· uncertain, the MS. reading 'principis', 'constant in his attendance on the emperor'.

divini iuris, pontifical law.

§ 2. **grave conscientiae**, 'a blow to his self-esteem'.

§ 3. **abstinentiam cibi coniunxit**, 'persisted in abstention from food' ; cf. 'sex annos coniunxit' ('spent six consecutive years') iv 57, 2.

ira et metu : sc. 'tanto magis commotus'.

§ 4. **Plancinam traxit**, 'involved Plancina also'. Her behaviour in aiding and abetting Piso in his opposition to Germanicus and in his violent resistance to his deposition from his province of Syria (17–19 A. D.) is told in the latter part of Bk. II.

cum Piso caderet: at his trial in 20 A. D. (iii 15, 3 ; 17, 2).

Chapter 27, § 1. Iulia Drusi filia: the daughter of Tiberius' **27** son Drusus, by Livia, sister of Germanicus. Her death (43 A. D.) is mentioned as due to Messalina, in xiii 32, 5 ; and the death of her son Rubellius Plautus in 62 A. D., owing to Nero's jealousy, is described in xiv 58, 59.

C. Rubellius Blandus is mentioned in an inscription of the time of Gaius as having been quaestor, tribune, praetor, consul, proconsul, and pontifex. The date of his consulship is not certain, but was some time before 21 A. D. [iii 51].

avum: mentioned by M. Seneca as the first ' eques ' to be a teacher of rhetoric ; the profession having been till then confined to freedmen.

Tiburtem equitem Romanum, ' a Roman knight from Tibur '.

§ 2. Aelius Lamia: probably the person mentioned in Horace, *Od.* i 26, 8. He was consul in 3 A. D., and served in Germany, Illyricum, and Africa. He was proconsul of Africa some time during the early part of the war with Tacfarinas, 17–19 A. D.

funere censorio: (1) ' a public funeral ', so-called because its expense would be met by the censors, or (2) better, ' the funeral of a censor ', i. e. the most honourable kind of public funeral, such as that given to one who had held the censorship, the highest magistracy.

administrandae Suriae imagine : his case was similar to that of Arruntius mentioned below.

The last legatus of Syria mentioned was Cn. Sentius, appointed in 19 A. D., who does not appear to have had a long tenure. Lamia probably succeeded him, but the province was actually administered by a 'legatus legionis' named Pacuvius (ii 79, 3).

urbi praefuerat: as successor to L. Piso (ch. 10, 3).

genus decorum: his father was praetor, but up to that time the family was merely equestrian, apparently of Formiae, tracing a mythical ancestry to ' Lamus ' (Hor. *Od.* iii 17, 1).

§ 3. Flaccus Pomponius: consul in 17 A. D., afterwards legatus of Moesia, and subsequently of Syria, after Lamia had become ' praefectus urbi '.

abnuere id munus: the reason may well have been that Tiberius was a stern repressor of extortion, not only that high position exposed its holders to charges of ' maiestas '.

Hispaniam : the Caesarian province of Hispania Citerior. For Arruntius cf. vi 7, 1.

decumum annum: the period is stated in round numbers ; the last governor of Hispania Citerior, L. Piso, died in 25 A. D.

§ 4. M'. Lepidus: an eminent senator who enjoyed the respect and favour of Tiberius in spite of the independent line taken by him at times (iv 20, 4). He was consul in 11 A. D., and proconsul of Asia in 26 A. D. He was nominated, with Iunius Blaesus, by

23

Tiberius for the government of Africa in 21 A. D. ; the senate were to select which of the two was to be appointed, but Lepidus withdrew. He defended Cn. Piso, and also his own sister Lepida, in 20 A. D. His father was Q. Aemilius Lepidus, consul in 21 B. C. On his mother's side he was related both to Cn. Pompeius Magnus and Sulla the dictator; for his mother Cornelia was the daughter of the dictator's son Faustus Cornelia Sulla, who married a daughter of Pompey. His relationship to Lepidus the triumvir is uncertain.

§ 5. **bonorum civium**: e.g. the consul who fell at Cannae, the conqueror of Macedonia, and the younger Scipio Africanus.

et qui, &c.: such persons as the triumvir and his father, consul in 78 B. C.

28   Chapter 28, § 1. **Paulus Fabius Persicus,** probably son of Paulus Fabius Maximus, who was husband of a cousin of Augustus. This Fabius is mentioned by Seneca as a profligate friend of Claudius, and was proconsul of Asia some time during his reign.

L. Vitellius is the proconsul of Syria in ch. 32, 5 and foll., and the well-known courtier of Claudius (xi 3, 1), under whom he held a second and third consulship and a censorship. He was father of the emperor A. Vitellius.

phoenix: its appearance is also recorded by Dio and Pliny ma., but is dated by them two years later.

§ 3. **ore**: probably the front of the head is meant.

distinctu: a poetical word.

effinxere, 'have depicted'; so in xi 14, 1. Herodotus (ii 73) describes it as in form an eagle, but with gold and red feathers.

de numero annorum: the phoenix was seen to be the symbol of a cycle of time, but its period was very differently given. That of 1461 years is the Egyptian 'annus magnus', being that in which the year of 365 days agrees with that of $365\frac{1}{4}$; 1461 of the one being equal to 1460 of the other. Those who take the period to be 500 years (Hdt., Ov., Sen., Mela) possibly take it as a round number for one-third of the above cycle, or as itself a period of correction of the calendar.

§ 4. **Sesoside**: the name 'Sesosis' represents the 'Sesostris' of Herodotus (ii 60, 4), being 'Sestûra' or Rameses II, who reigned in the fourteenth century B. C.

Amasis: circa 570–526 B. C.

Ptolemaeo: if Alexander himself is to be reckoned as the first Macedonian monarch of Egypt, this would be the second Ptolemy ('Philadelphus'), who reigned 284–247 B. C. Otherwise, this would be the third Ptolemy ('Euergetes'), 247–222 B. C., and the statement of § 5 points to this being the one meant by Tacitus.

§ 5. **antiquitas**: i. e. the date of 'Sesosis' and Amasis.

§ 6. **non nulli**: elsewhere in Tacitus used adjectivally, as in xi 12, 3.

§ 7. **struere nidum,** &c.: Herodotus gives much the same account (ii 73). The essential idea is the allegory describing the beginning of one period at the close of another.

temptato . . . ubi: Intr. II 21.

subire: cf. Verg. *Aen.* ii 708.

Solis aram: at Heliopolis ('Matarieh') about six miles north-east of Cairo.

§ 8. haec incerta, &c. : Tacitus rejects the fables, but believes in the appearance, at times, of a bird of unusual kind, in consequence of which the myth of the phoenix was developed.

Chapter 29, § 1. caede continua: Intr. II 22.   29

Pomponius Labeo, mentioned in iv 47, 1 as legatus of Moesia in 26 A. D., when he co-operated with Poppaeus Sabinus in putting down a rebellion in Thrace.

§ 2. damnati, &c. ; cf. ch. 23, 2.

testamenta, &c. : there were exceptions to this, as in the case of C. Silius, who was attacked on a charge of 'maiestas' in 24 A. D., and committed suicide, after which his property was confiscated (iv 20, 1).

§ 3. morem, &c. : so Germanicus renounced Piso's friendship (19 A. D., ii 70, 3). When the princeps acted so. some form of banishment was pronounced ('domo et provinciis suis interdixit', Suet. *Aug.* 66), or was taken to be implied, as in the case of Decimus Silanus, who went into exile on receiving Augustus' repudiation of friendship, and returned under Tiberius in 20 A. D. (iii 24), after appealing to Tiberius and the senate for permission.

culpam, &c., 'sought to cover his own guilt by bringing him into odium'.

§ 4. Mamercus Scaurus: cf. ch. 9, 5.

§ 5. detulerat, &c., 'made matter of information out of the subject of a tragedy written by Scaurus'; according to Dio (lviii 24, 4), the tragedy was 'Atreus', and contained a line, imitated from Eur. *Phoen.* 393 τὰς τῶν κρατούντων ἀμαθίας φέρειν χρεών, which Tiberius took as an allusion to himself, and said Αἴαντα αὐτὸν ποιήσω ; after which he forced him to commit suicide.

flecterentur, 'which might be applied '.

§ 6. Servilio et Cornelio: as they are mentioned by one name only, they may have already occurred in the lost portion. Their fate is given in the next chapter.

Liviae: ch. 2, 1.

magorum sacra: the practice of witchcraft, the use of spells and incantations (cf. Verg. *Ecl.* 8 ; Hor. *Od.* i 27, 21 ; *Epod.* v).

Chapter 30, § 1. si . . . incideret: Intr. II 41.   30

Varius Ligur: the name occurs in iv 42, 3, in a case of adultery.

§ 2. Abudius Ruso: otherwise unknown.

Cn. Lentulus Gaetulicus was consul in 26 A. D.

ultro: i. e. besides failing in the prosecution.

§ 3. L. Apronius is mentioned in the earlier books as an officer of Germanicus in 15 A. D. and proconsul of Africa in 20 A. D. He was governor of Lower Germany in 28 A. D., and appears to have retained his command in spite of his lack of success against the Frisii (iv 73).

§ 4. sine fraude, ' harmless '.

§ 5. indicium mortis, ' sentence of death '.

§ 7. unus: there is reason to think that even among those more nearly related, the destruction was not so universal ; for L. Seianus is noticed by Dio as spared at the same time as Terentius (ch. 8).

31   Chapter 31, § 1. C. Cestius: see ch. 7, 3.

M. Servilius Nonianus: Tacitus records his death in the year 59 A. D. (xiv 19), and speaks of his celebrity as a historian in his later years, after a successful forensic career.

Artabanus had taken possession of the throne of Parthia about the year 11 A. D., expelling Vonones who had succeeded in 7 or 8 A. D. Artabanus sent envoys to Germanicus in 18 A. D., and renewed with him the alliance of Parthia with Rome, and showed marks of respect after Germanicus' death in 19 A. D. (ii 58 and 72).

§ 2. aequabilis, ' without caprice '.

Artaxias: he was the son of Polemo king of Pontus, and was originally named Zeno, but took the name Artaxias at the ceremony of his investiture as king of Armenia by Germanicus in 18 A. D. (ii 56). His death is mentioned in this chapter as a recent occurrence, and may be attributed to 34 A. D.

contumelia : the insult consisted not only in this demand itself, but in the other contents of the letter, in which Artabanus inveighed against Tiberius as a murderer and debauchee, and called upon him to commit suicide (Suet. *Tib.* 66).

a Vonone, &c. : on his expulsion from Parthia (see above) Vonones for a time reigned in Armenia, but was threatened by Artabanus, and the Roman governor of Syria, Creticus Silanus, removed him from Armenia for the sake of peace with Parthia, and detained him first in Syria and then in Cilicia ; Vonones attempted to escape and was killed by a Roman veteran in 19 A. D. (ii 68).

veteres, &c., ' he spoke boastfully of the old boundaries of Persia and Macedonia, and uttered vainglorious threats of overrunning what first Cyrus and afterwards Alexander had held '. Such a claim would comprehend Greece itself, as well as Syria and Asia Minor.

Cyro . . . Alexandro: dative. Intr. II 10.

§ 3. ac perinde opibus : supply ' insignibus '.

id, ' this condition ', viz. ' ademptae virilitatis esse '.

§ 4. Phraaten regis Phraatis filium : this would be one of the four sons (of whom the Vonones of § 2 was another) sent by Phraates IV to Rome. Phraates IV ruled from 37 to 2 B.C. He was the king who inflicted a reverse on Antony in 36 B. C., and restored the standards taken from Crassus to Augustus in 20 B.C. ; the cession of his sons was made some time between 11 and 7 B.C.

nomine, &c., ' the (royal) name and the (imperial) sanction alone were needed to ensure that there should be seen on the bank of the Euphrates a descendant of Arsaces, there by Caesar's will '.

[The repetition of ' ut ', if retained, serves to emphasize ' sponte Caesaris ' and ' genus Arsacis ' as explanatory of ' auctore ' and ' nomine ' respectively, the terms being inverted by ' chiasmus '.]

Chapter 32, § 1. ornat ... accingitque: i. e. he gave him the **32** insignia of royalty, and the means of enforcing his claim by arms; cf. 'auctum pecunia additis stipatoribus', xi 16, 3.

destinata retinens, 'adhering to his determination'.

§ 2. tardari, modo ... inardescere: the first clause denotes the prevalent state, the second the occasional.

§ 3. inligaret, 'enfeebled', 'crippled'; cf. 'morbo implicata', iv 53, 1.

per negotia, 'by (constant) employment'.

§ 4. cultu, 'way of life', 'habits'.

impar, 'too delicate for'.

patriis moribus: a hard open-air life, with much riding and hunting.

§ 5. sanguinis eiusdem: a grandson of Phraates IV (ch. 37, 6), and probably a son of one of the princes sent to Rome; see note on ch. 31, 4.

reciperandae Armeniae: dative. Intr. II 11.

Hiberum. The Hiberi lived south of the Caucasus, north of Armenia, between Albania and Colchis.

gentile, 'of his own nation'; so xi 16, 3.

Vitellium: see ch. 28, 1. As Syria had been vacated in 33 A.D. (ch. 27, 3), it is probable that Vitellius had been already sent out as legatus of that province, and now received an extension of power similar to that given to Germanicus in 17 A.D. (ii 43, 2).

§ 7. regressus: he was recalled by Gaius in 40 A.D. to answer an accusation, and escaped by abject servility. On his conduct towards Claudius, Messalina, and Agrippina see xi 2, 4; 3, 1; xii 4, 1; 42, 4.

adulatorii: this adj. is not found elsewhere.

Chapter 33, § 1. perpulit ... iuvare: Intr. II 31.   **33**

ministros: personal attendants.

ad scelus, 'to poison him'; cf. 'sceleris certa', xii 66, 2.

§ 2. Artaxata: on the Araxes, near Erivan. The word is here fem. sing.; elsewhere it is sometimes used as a neut. plur.

auxilia facerent: i. e. 'auxiliares compararent'.

§ 3. Albanos: on the east of the Hiberi, separated on the south from Armenia maior by the river Cyrus; they extended to the Caspian Sea on the north and north-east. Their relation to Rome was that of a client-state.

Sarmatas: a general name, so also 'Sauromatae', for many tribes north of the Caucasus both in Europe and Asia.

quorum: referring to the Sarmatae only.

sceptuchi, 'wand-bearers'; the term in Greek writers usually designates the chief personal attendants on the Persian king; here it seems to denote rather 'satraps', governors placed by a monarch over parts of his kingdom.

diversa induere, 'took opposing sides'.

§ 4. Caspia via: the pass meant is that which Pliny (*N. H.* vi 11, 30: 13, 40) says should properly be termed the 'Caucasiae portae', a pass in the centre of the Caucasian range, the modern pass of Dariel, connecting the Iberian town Hermasta (Tiflis) with the upper valley of the Terek.

§ 5. qui: i.e. those Sarmatians who sided with the Parthians.

unum reliquum: the route along the western shore of the Caspian.

etesiarum: winds blowing from the north for thirty days from about July 20.

pulsoque introrsus freto, 'the sea being driven back upon itself'.

brevia: probably taken from Verg. *Aen.* i 111.

34   Chapter 34, § 1. infensare pabula, 'ravaged their foraging ground'.

regem, 'the prince'; probably Orodes had assumed also the title of king of Armenia.

§ 3. feruntque: so a legend quoted by Justin (xlii 2, 11) states that Jason was driven out of Thessaly by the daughters of Pelias, that he became reconciled to Medea and reinstated Aeetes, whom he found in exile, on the throne of Colchis; that he gained great victories and assigned territory from his conquests to his followers from Greece.

The real origin of the Hiberi and Albani was Scythic, and the Albani were akin to and sometimes confused with the Alauni or Alani.

inanem ... vacuos: the words seem to imply that the story followed by Tacitus was that Aeetes was dead when Jason returned to Colchis.

§ 4. de nomine eius, 'called after his name' (cf. Verg. *Aen.* i 277). Legends of Jason were widely spread in Albania and Iberia, and their extension was stimulated by the Thessalians who had followed Alexander (Grote, i ch. 13, p. 328 and foll.).

§ 5. mercennario milite: an ablative of accompanying circumstance, hardly needing further definition either as 'absolute', or 'ablative of quality' (Intr. II 22).

§ 6. Medorum: the word is used for the whole Parthian army; so Horace often interchanges the names 'Mede', 'Persian', and 'Parthian'. The word is here the more appropriate as the Parthians had adopted the 'perlucida ac fluida vestis' of the Medes (Just. xli 2, 4).

35   Chapter 35, § 1. non una, &c., 'their leader's was not the only speech heard'.

ne ... sinerent, 'not to permit an archer's battle'. The use of 'sinere' with accus. is found in Pliny ma. and poets.

§ 2. sequi vel fugere ... suetus: for 'Parthian tactics' cf. Verg. *G.* iii 31 'fidentemque fuga Parthum versisque sagittis'; Hor. *Od.* i 19, 11 'versis animosum equis Parthum'; also *Od.* ii 13, 17.

distraheret turmas, 'would spread out his squadrons'.

ictibus, 'shots' (of arrows).

quo brevius valent, 'with which their range is shorter'.

ruerent, 'charged to the fray'; the Sarmatae were mounted.

modo, &c., 'now, in the style of a cavalry engagement, there would be alternations of advance and retreat, again, as if the lines were locked in close fight, they won or lost ground by brute force and the shock of arms'. The subjunctives follow 'cum'. 'Ut conserta acie' balances 'equestris proelii more'; the Parthians aimed at maintaining cavalry tactics, the Sarmatae (though on horseback) at the close fighting more suited to infantry.

§ 3. iamque: now that it became a standing fight, those who were in great part foot-soldiers (ch. 34, 2) came into action.

detrudere: sc. 'ex equis'.

ancipitem, 'double', as the next sentence explains.

super, 'from above' (cf. Verg. *Aen.* v 697 'implenturque super puppes').

§ 4. gnari = 'noti'. Cf. xi 32, 1.

§ 5. praelatus = 'praeterlatus'.

Chapter 36, § 1. Mox: probably in the following year; see **36** ch. 38, 1.

ideo abscedebat . . . ni fecisset: Intr. II 38.

tamquam . . . invasurus: so, like ὡς with fut. partic., in xii 49, 2.

§ 2. adversis proeliorum: cf. 'castellorum ardua', xi 9, 1 and Intr. II 23. The abl. is causal: 'ruinous through his ill-success in the field'.

§ 3. occultos consilii, 'who had so far kept their determination secret'. For the genitive cf. 'non occultus odii', iv 7, 2 and Intr. II 24.

adfluentibus . . . qui: Intr. II 21.

sustulerant animum, 'had plucked up courage'.

§ 4. intellectus: in xiii 16, 4 ; 38, 4 the word means 'insight', 'knowledge'. 'Quis', &c., 'men who do not concern themselves about the goodness or badness of their mental outlook, but live as the hireling instruments of crime'.

§ 5. Scythiae: the Scythians east of the Caspian are meant.

Hyrcanis: a tribe at the south-east angle of the Caspian, next to whom were the Dahae, among whom Artabanus had been brought up.

Carmaniis: on the south-east of the Empire, near the entrance of the Persian Gulf.

per adfinitatem innexus: Artabanus had probably taken wives from each of the above races.

absentium aequos: the genitive here is similar to the Greek genitive used with a word expressing desire or affection ; see also Intr. II 24, c.

praesentibus mobiles: cf. 'nobilitatibus externis mitis', xii 20, 1 ; 'adrogans minoribus', xi 21, 4.

Chapter 37, § 1. hortatus . . . capessere: Intr. II 31.   **37**

ripam ad: cf. xii 51, 4 and Intr. II 55.

§ 2. suovetaurilia: the sacrifice of a pig, sheep, and bull to Mars. The 'suovetaurilia' originated in the Italian ritual of the 'lustration' of a farm, when the victims were first driven round the farm and then sacrificed to Mars. It was extended to acts of worship on the part of the community, as in the lustration of the people in the Campus Martius after the census had been taken, and it was especially used in the religious ceremonies in which the army was concerned, for Mars, originally an agricultural divinity, developed a warlike aspect which eventually became his principal characteristic.

placando amni: this applies only to 'ille ... adornasset'. For the dative see Intr. II 11.

equum: the usual Persian victim, offered to the Sun (Xen. *Anab.* iv 5, 35).

diadematis: the original form of the diadem is that of a white band tied in a bow behind, as represented on the heads of Dionysus.

§ 3. terra caelove: local ablatives; see Intr. II 14.

quia, &c., 'because omens signified on the earth or in the sky were more firmly to be relied on, whereas the changeable character of rivers no sooner showed signs than it swept them away'.

§ 4. multis equitum milibus ... venit: the ablat. is similar to the Greek dative in αἴρειν στρατῷ; so 'duabus legionibus Armeniam intrat', xv 7, 2. (Intr. II 16.)

auxiliator: Intr. II 51, a.

Delmaticum bellum: in connexion with the great Pannonian rebellion, 6–9 A.D. (See Intr. p. xxxviii.)

circumflui: a poetical word.

§ 5. columen: either (1) 'summit', 'crown' (of an edifice), or (2) 'pillar' (supporting the top of a building).

partium, 'of his cause'.

§ 6. Phraatis avi: see ch. 32, 5.

quae utrobique pulchra, 'all the noble qualities in either'.

38 Chapter 38, § 1. duabus aestatibus: 35 and part of 36 A.D.; cf. ch. 36, 1. The events in the East of 36 A.D. are resumed in ch. 41.

triennio: the real interval was rather more, Seianus having been executed in Oct., 31 A.D.

incerta, &c., 'exacted punishment in cases that were not proven and things of the past, as if they were most serious and immediate dangers'.

§ 2. Fulcinius Trio: see v 11, 1.

haud perpessus: from these and the next words it must be inferred that he committed suicide.

praecipuos libertorum: Tiberius' freedmen did not become influential till the closing years of his life; cf. 'modesta servitia, intra paucos libertos domus' (written of the year 23 A.D.), iv 6, 7.

fluxam, 'decayed'. obiectando: Intr. II 22, b.

abscessu, for 'absentia', causal ablat., explaining 'exilium'.

§ 3. vulgari: supply 'scelera'.

§ 4. senator: the term thus applied probably denotes a 'pedarius senator', i.e. one who had not held a curule office.

C. Graccho: see ch. 16, 5.

Tarius Gratianus: probably son of L. Tarius Rufus, who was cos. suff. in 16 B.C. 'curator aquarum' 23 A.D., and is mentioned by

Pliny (*N. H.* xviii 6, 7, 37) as having risen by military service to rank and wealth.

damnatus: sc. 'est'.

Chapter 39, § 1. Trebellenus Rufus: mentioned in ii 67 as **39** 'praetura functus', and put in charge of Thrace in 19 A.D., during the minority both of the children of Cotys and of Rhoemetalces, between whom the kingdom was divided upon the deposition of Rhescuporis, father of the latter.

Sextius Paconianus: ch. 3, 4.

§ 2. **per domos sanguinem:** referring to the cases of suicide at home.

manus, 'the work'.

§ 3. **Poppaeus Sabinus:** see v 10, 3.

modicus originis: Intr. II 24.

neque supra: i.e. he had not the 'eminentes virtutes' (i 80, 3) which might be dangerous in the eyes of the princeps.

Chapter 40, § 1. Q. Plautius, probably brother of Plautius **40** Silvanus, praetor in 24 A.D. (iv 22), and son of M. Plautius Silvanus, consul in 2 B.C.

Sex. Papinius: known from an inscription to have borne the cognomen 'Allenius', and to have filled the usual magistracies in succession besides being 'quindecimvir sacris faciundis'.

L. Aruseius: cf. ch. 7, 1.

A lacuna follows this name. Presumably some indulgence to Aruseius, as restoration from banishment, was recorded, and then followed a second 'neque quod' with the names of the persons who are subjects of 'adfecti forent'.

advertebatur: so this verb is used for 'animadvertere' also in xii 51, 5.

laqueo vexatae: the form of execution in the 'Tullianum' was carried out, so as to ensure the confiscation of his property (cf. ch. 29, 2).

§ 2. **Tigranes:** the fourth of the name, of those who were kings of Armenia. He was grandson of Herod the Great, and was nominated king of Armenia by Augustus, though it is doubtful if he ever actually reigned. His appointment was made at a period, between 1 B.C. and 11 A.D., about which information is scanty and confusing. Ariobarzanes, a Mede, had been appointed king of Armenia by Gaius Caesar during his mission to the East 1 B.C.–4 A.D.; he was followed by his son Artavasdes (III), against whom the Armenians rebelled; then followed this Tigranes (IV), who seems to have been recalled to Rome on an accusation and there detained till now. Vonones had occupied the throne, after Tigranes IV was removed, until removed by Metellus Creticus in deference to Artabanus king of Parthia (ch. 31, 2).

§ 3. **C. Galba:** called C. Sulpicius in iii 52, where his consulship in 22 A.D. is recorded. He was the elder brother of the Galba who subsequently was emperor for part of 68 A.D. on the death of Nero.

provinciam: Asia or Africa. He had ruined himself by extravagance (Suet. *Gal.* 3), which may well have been Tiberius' reason for his exclusion from the government of a province.

Blaesis: sons of Blaesus, uncle of Seianus (see v 2).

convulsa: abl. with ' domo '; their house was ' shaken to its foundations ' by the father's death.

quod, &c., ' which they understood to be the signal for their death and accordingly carried it out '.

§ 4. **rettuli**: in the lost portion.

Druso: see v 3, 2.

intestabilis, ' detestable '. She is stated by Dio (lviii 3, 8) to have intrigued with Seianus against her husband.

Lepidus: Marcus Aemilius Lepidus, sent as proconsul to Asia in 21 A.D. (iii 32); he is also mentioned in iii 72 as repairing at his own expense the ' Basilica Pauli', founded by his grandfather Aemilius Paulus, the consul of 50 B.C. He evidently was a favourite of Tiberius, as in 17 A.D. Tiberius made over to him the property of a woman who died intestate, instead of letting it pass into the ' fiscus ' (ii 48).

41 Chapter 41, § 1. **Clitarum**: the same form of the name occurs in xii 55, where mention is made of their king Antiochus. Coins of the period give the name as KIHTΩN. Their territory, extending over a considerable part of Western Cilicia, formed part of the kingdom of Cappadocia, and when that became a Roman province, 18 A.D., in the year after the death of Archelaus (ii 42, 6 ; 56, 4), this part was allowed to remain to his son.

deferre, ' to make a return of their property ', regularly, for the assessment of the tribute to be paid. The native king was organizing the taxation of his dominions on the Roman model.

ingenio = ' natura '; so ' servitii ingenio ', xii 30, 4.

legatus: sc. ' legionis '.

praeside Suriae: see xii 45, 6. Cilicia was administered as part of Syria.

ferro, ' by force of arms '.

§ 2. **At Tiridates**, &c. : here the narrative is resumed from the end of ch. 37.

Nicephorium et Anthemusiada: Anthemusias is near Edessa, and, if Tiridates crossed the Euphrates at Zeugma (the usual point), would be reached before Nicephorium, which lies further south, nearer to Thapsacus.

Macedonibus: dative; see Intr. II 10.

Halus: not otherwise known.

Artemita: beyond the Tigris, 500 stadia north-east of Seleucia.

Scythas: the Dahae (ii 3, 1).

42 Chapter 42, § 1. **Plurimum**, &c., ' the greatest show of adulation was put on by the men of Seleucia'. This city was on the Tigris, 300 stadia north-east of Babylon, a little below the modern Bagdad. It had been founded a little before 300 B.C. by Seleucus Nicator, one of Alexander's generals, the founder of the Syrian monarchy of the Seleucidae.

neque in barbarum corrupta, 'one that had not degenerated into barbarism'. The phrase is like such a Greek expression as εἰς τὸ βαρβαρικὸν διεφθαρμένη.

retinens : with genitive ; so, 'modestiae retinens', v 11, 2.

opibus aut sapientia : causal ablatives, equivalent to accusatives after 'propter'.

sua populo vis, 'the people have their own proper power'. This, in a free Greek state, would mean that the people formed the sovereign assembly, with power to pass or reject laws, and to elect magistrates and the 'senatus'; the latter being concerned with the details of executive.

§ 2. quotiens concordes agunt, 'whenever the citizens live in harmony'.

accitus, &c., 'called to aid one side, prevails over the whole body'.

§ 3. nam, &c., 'for popular government is closely associated with liberty, while oligarchy is more in harmony with kingly dictation'.

§ 4. degenerem, 'of low birth' ; so in xii 51, 5. On his father's side he was probably a Dahan (xii 3, 1).

§ 5. sollemnia regni, 'the ceremonials of accession to the throne'.

praefecturas, 'provinces', like the satrapies of the old Persian empire ; see xi 8, 4.

§ 6. Ctesiphon : fronting Seleucia, on the opposite bank of the Tigris.

coram et adprobantibus : to be taken as predicates ; cf. xi 22, 1 'nullis palam neque cognitis mox causis'.

Surena : title of the commander-in-chief of the armies of the Parthian empire.

insigni regio : the tiara and diadem (cf. ch. 37, 2).

Chapter 43, § 1. si . . . petivisset, . . . cedebant : Intr. II 38. **43**

oppressa : supply 'erat'.

in unum cedebant, 'would have come under his sole authority'.

spatium exuendi pacta, 'an interval in which they could disclaim their pledges'. The genitive is due to the notion of 'opportunity' conveyed by 'spatium'.

§ 2. concelebraverant, 'joined in celebrating'.

Abdagaesen : cf. ch. 36, 3 ; 37, 5.

in Hyrcanis : cf. ch. 36, 5.

§ 3. tamquam, &c. : Intr. II 50.

reddendae dominationi venisse : Intr. II 11.

animum : see Intr. II 4.

§ 4. inane, &c., 'the empty name (of king) was held by one rendered unwarlike through effeminacy learned abroad'.

vim, 'real power'.

Chapter 44, § 1. vetus regnandi : cf. ch. 12, 2 and Intr. II 24. **44**

falsos, &c., 'that false as they might be in their affection (for himself), they were not simulating hatred (towards his rivals)'.

Scytharum: Dahae and Sacae.

paenitentiam, 'change of mind'.

paedorem, 'signs of neglect'; he remained 'inluvie obsitus' (ch. 43, 3).

adverteret, 'attract'.

§ 3. simul fama, &c., 'terrified by the news as well as his rival's presence'. The omission of the preposition marks the effect of the verb as produced by the presence of the person rather than the actual agency of the person: so 'repentinis hostibus circumventi' (xv 4, 4).

distrahi: for historic infin. following a conjunction see Intr. II 34.

§ 4. ne animo quidem, 'had not yet sufficiently combined even in the will to obey', still less in readiness to act.

§ 5. amne: the Tigris, which he had crossed to Ctesiphon.

Elymaeis: they lived on the coast at the head of the Persian Gulf, and could not be 'a tergo' to Tiridates, as were the Armenians. Very probably their position was misapprehended by Tacitus: (there may, however, have been a branch of the tribe in another district). It is possible also to apply 'a tergo' to 'Elymaeis et ceteris' only, understanding that these were to harass Artabanus in the rear when he advanced against Tiridates.

§ 7. Arabum: those of Osrhoene, round Edessa in NW. Mesopotamia, are meant (cf. xii 12, 3).

exsolvit, 'relieved all his adherents from any shame at deserting him'. Affairs in the East are resumed in xi 8, 1. In the interval, Mithridates secured the kingdom of Armenia, Artabanus regained Parthia and made peace with Vitellius, and died in possession of the kingdom in 40 A. D.

45 Chapter 45, § 1. circi: the Circus Maximus, in the valley between the Palatine and the Aventine.

ipsoque Aventino: sc. 'deusto'; so 'deusto monte Caelio', iv 64, 1.

domuum, 'mansions' of the rich. insularum, 'blocks' of houses, let out in tenements to the poor.

§ 2. publice, 'on behalf of the state': so xii 10, 3.

templum Augusto: mentioned as decreed in 14 A. D. (i 10, 8). Livia was associated with Tiberius in its construction. It was built at the side of the Palatine near the Forum.

scaenam Pompeiani theatri, 'the stage of Pompey's theatre'. Its destruction by fire, in 22 A. D., is mentioned in iii 72, 4. This theatre was constructed in the Campus Martius by Pompey in his second consulship, 55 B. C., and was the first permanent structure of the kind in Rome.

§ 3. quattuor progeneri: for Cn. Domitius see vi 1, 1; for Cassius and Vinicius see ch. 15, 1; for Rubellius Blandus ch. 27, 1.

P. Petronius: from inscriptions he is known to have been 'consul suffectus' in 19 A. D., and proconsul of Asia for the unusual period of six years, after which he was legatus of Syria under Gaius. He was a friend of Claudius, in whose reign he died; his son was consul in 60 A. D. (xiv 29, 1), and his daughter was the first wife of Vitellius.

§ 5. **Cn. Acerronius Proculus**: afterwards proconsul of Achaia.
C. Pontius: an inscription gives his full name as C. Petronius Pontius Nigrinus.

impulerat, with infin. ; see Intr. II 31.

rettuli: ch. 20, 1.

vincire: in spite of this both Ennia and Macro were forced to commit suicide in the second year of Gaius' reign (38 A. D.).

apisceretur: here alone used with genitive ; so 'adipisci' in iii 55, 1 ; xii 30, 4 ; probably in imitation of τυγχάνειν.

commotus, 'passionate' : he was not yet insane.

simulationum falsa: Intr. II 23.

Chapter 46, § 1. **gnarum**: so in vi 35, 4 ; Intr. II 51.   46

dubitavit, ' he hesitated whom to designate as his successor '.

nepotes: Tiberius Gemellus, his own grandson, the son of Drusus, and Gaius, his grandson by adoption.

nondum pubertatem ingressus: he was in his eighteenth year, but had not yet taken the toga virilis (Suet. *Cal.* 15).

robur iuventae: Gaius was in his twenty-fifth year.

§ 2. **agitanti**: so, without the more usual accompaniment of 'animo ', in xi 23, 1.

composita aetate: Claudius was in his forty-sixth year.

bonarum artium: history and literature. Claudius was an industrious student, but was regarded as stupid ('hebes', xi 28, 2) and of weak intellect.

§ 4. **illi**, &c., ' he cared not so much for winning popularity with his own generation as for making a favourable impression upon posterity '.

§ 5. **fato permisit**, 'he left the decision in the hands of fate ', i. e. he left events to take their own course.

§ 6. **non abdita ambage**, ' in a riddle plain to read '. For ' ambage ' cf. xii 63, 2.

occidentem: sc. 'solem'.

§ 7. **habiturum**: sc. 'eum '. Intr. II 3.

§ 8. **truci alterius vultu**: abl. abs.

occides, &c.: Tiberius Gemellus was named by Tiberius in his will as joint heir with Gaius, who adopted him, but put him to death in the course of the first year of his reign. Gaius was himself assassinated in Jan., 41 A. D.

§ 9. **in patientia**: not ' in ', or ' by ', his ' endurance ', which would be expressed rather by a simple ablative, but ' amidst his sufferings '.

Chapter 47, § 1. **Laelius Balbus**: mentioned by Quintilian 47
(x 1, 24) as a famous orator of the time. See also ch. 48, 6.

P. Vitellii: see v 8, 1.

praemium: in iv 20, 2 one quarter of the property of a person condemned for ' maiestas ' is said to be the reward due to the accusers ' secundum necessitudinem legis ' (the ' lex Iulia de maiestate ', passed by Augustus). This would be the legal minimum : the senate could grant more, at its discretion.

Iunius Otho: perhaps son of the praetor of 22 A. D. (iii 66, 2).

illis : Balbus and Otho.

mox : probably under Gaius.

§ 2. **Albucilla :** see ch. 48, 6.

Satrius Secundus, mentioned in iv 34, 2 as a ' cliens Seiani ' and one of the accusers of the historian Cremutius Cordus. (The tense here and in ch. 8, 10 suggests that he was now dead.)

coniurationis : that of Seianus ; see p. 4.

Cn. Domitius : husband of Agrippina.

Vibius Marsus : see also xi 10, 1. He was ' consul suffectus in 17 A. D., proconsul of Africa 27–29 A. D., and legatus of Syria (xi 10, 1) about 42–44 A. D.

L. Arruntius : see vi 7, 1.

§ 4. **commentarii,** ' the record ', the minutes of the proceedings : in such cases as this the emperor sent a written account of the trial held in his private court to the senate, for them to pass sentence. (Cf. ch. 10, 2.) Here the trial had been conducted by Macro, and Tiberius himself had not sent the usual announcement of condemnation.

ferebant, ' showed '.

nullaeque, &c., ' the absence of any letter from the emperor against them '. Intr. II 2.

invalido : supply ' eo ', from ' imperatoris ' above.

48 **Chapter 48, § 1. produxere vitam :** Domitius died in 40 A. D., three years after the birth of Nero. Marsus was still alive in 44 A. D. ; see note on ch. 47, 2.

§ 3. **ludibria :** such as that mentioned in ch. 27, 3.

pericula : cf. ch. 7, 1.

suprema : so ch. 50, 2 ; xi 66, 2.

evasurum : ' supply ' se '. (Intr. II 3.)

§ 4. **convulsus,** ' ruined ' or ' demoralized '.

dominationis, ' absolute power '.

§ 6. **Albucilla :** she probably outlived Tiberius and died in prison, her death being one of those alluded to in the opening words of ch. 47.

Carsidius Sacerdos : mentioned in iv 13, 3 as charged in 23 A. D. with supplying Tacfarinas with provisions but acquitted. He was praetor in 27 A. D.

49 **Chapter 49, § 1. Sex. Papinius :** probably son of the consul of the preceding year (ch, 40, 1).

in praeceps : from an upper window.

§ 2. **repudiata,** ' divorced '.

adsentationibus, &c., ' by encouraging him in vicious practices '.

§ 3. **genua :** for the accusative instead of the more usual dative see Intr. II 6.

communem : common to men and women alike, at the loss of their children.

in eundem dolorem, ' to the same piteous effect ' ; cf. ' verba in eandem clementiam ', xi 3, 1.

diu, ' at length '. ferret : equivalent to ' proferret '. Intr. II 28.

lubricum iuventae : Intr. II 23.

Chapter 50, § 1. idem animi rigor, ' the same unbending will '. **50**
intentus, ' energetic '.

quaesita comitate, ' with forced gaiety '.

§ 2. villa : its situation is described by Phaedrus (ii 5, 9), ' prospectat Siculum et respicit Tuscum mare '.

§ 3. supremis, ' his last hour ', as in ch. 48, 3.

consilii copiam, ' opportunity of consulting him '.

§ 4. per speciem officii, ' as a mark of respect ' ; he was taking his hand to kiss it.

§ 5. neque fefellit (Tiberium), ' Tiberius noticed it '.

instaurari, ' to be renewed '.

discumbit, &c., ' remained at table longer than usual '.

firmavit : Intr. II 28.

§ 7. septimum decimum : for a similar omission of ' ante ' see ch. 25, 5.

interclusa anima, ' respiration being checked ' ; a natural death is meant.

creditus est : so ' introspicere creditus ', v 4, 1 ; Intr. II 33.

mortalitatem, ' the conditions of mortality ', i. e. liability to die.

explevisse, ' to have fulfilled ' ; so ' vestram meamque vicem explete ', iv 8, 7.

concursu : Intr. II 57, a.

§ 8. maestum aut nescium, ' concerned (for Tiberius) or unconscious (of anything unusual on foot) '.

Caesar : i. e. Gaius.

a summa, &c., ' fell from the highest hopes to the apprehension of his own doom '. For ' novissima ' cf. v 7, 1.

§ 9. opprimi senem, &c. : Suetonius (*Tib.* 73) states that Tiberius made as if he would give up his ring, and put it on again ; and then, after calling for assistance, tried to rise and fell lifeless by the bed. This story is quoted as from the history of M. Seneca (father of Nero's tutor), and is probably the version circulated by Gaius at the time.

iniectu multae vestis : Intr. II 57, a.

octavo et septuagesimo : he was born Nov. 17, 42 B. C.

Chapter 51, § 1. On Tiberius' father and mother see notes on v 1. **51**
familiam : so for ' gentem ' in xi 25, 3.

§ 2. proscriptum : not apparently in the proscription of 43 B. C., since it appears he was praetor in 41 B. C. ; but the term describes his condition after the fall of Perusia, when he fled to Sext. Pompeius.

introiit : on the death of his father in 33 B. C.

aemulis : rivals for succession to the imperial throne.

prosperiore, &c., ' enjoyed a stronger measure of popularity '.

§ 3. in lubrico, ' in peril '.

inpudicitiam, &c., ' when he must needs submit to, or withdraw before, his wife's unfaithfulness '. Tiberius was forced to marry Julia in 11 B. C., and went into retirement at Rhodes, owing to her adulteries, from 6 B. C. to 2 A. D.

§ 4. vacuos, &c. : Tacitus reckons from 2 A. D., but Augustus' house was not strictly devoid of heirs till 4 A. D., the date of Gaius Caesar's death.

§ 5. morum, &c., 'his character, too, passed through varied phases' (as well as his life).

egregium : with this, as with 'occultum ac subdolum', supply 'tempus' ; 'first came a period of noble life and honour', &c., 'then dissimulation and an hypocritical assumption of virtue '.

fingendis virtutibus : probably dative, cf. ch. 24, 4.

Germanicus died in 19 A. D., Drusus (Tiberius' son) in 23 A. D.

§ 6. idem : supply ' erat', as also with 'obtectis libidinibus'.

suo tantum ingenio utebatur, 'he was following solely his own disposition'. On Tacitus' estimate of Tiberius' character see Intr. IV.

BOOK XI

1   Chapter 1, § 1. * * nam, &c. : the subject of ' credidit' is ' Messalina ', and ' eius' refers to Poppaea (see ch. 2, 1). Poppaea was the daughter of Poppaeus Sabinus (v 10, 3), and mother, by T. Ollius (xiii 45, 1), of the Poppaea who became Nero's wife. Messalina was prompted to this attack on Poppaea by the latter's adultery with her own paramour Mnester (ch. 4, 2 ; 28, 1).

bis consulem : he was cos. suff. some time before the death of Gaius, and ordinary consul in 46 A. D.

hortis inhians : so ' inhiare dominationi ', iv 12, 5. The gardens of Lucullus were the chief ornament of the Pincian Hill.

coeptos, ' laid out'. extollebat, ' was beautifying'.

P. Suillius Rufus had accompanied Germanicus as his quaestor (iv 31, 5), but was exiled for a time by Tiberius for judicial corruption. Under Claudius he carried on the trade of accuser and enjoyed the imperial favour ; but in the reign of Nero was tried under the 'lex Cincia' and banished in 58 A. D. (xiii 42, 43).

immittit, 'sets on'. accusandis : dative; Intr. II 11.

§ 2. educator = παιδαγωγός. He was probably a freedman. His death was contrived by Agrippina soon after her marriage with Claudius (Dio lx 32, 5).

Britannici : son of Claudius and Messalina, born in 41 or 42 A. D.: his murder by Nero, in 55 A. D., is described in xiii 15–17.

moneret cavere : so 'monet . . . petere', xiii 37, 2 ; Intr. II 31.

praecipuum auctorem : he had not himself taken part in the conspiracy against Gaius, but had publicly glorified the act of

the assassins, and had been regarded as an aspirant to the principate (Josephus). He was, therefore, seriously compromised, but
had participated in the amnesty granted by Claudius on his
accession to all except the actual murderers.

didita fama: abl. of quality, parallel with ' clarum '.

Vienna (Vienne in Dauphiné) was the chief town of the
Allobroges of Gallia Narbonensis. It is thought to have been made
a colony, probably with Latin rights, by Augustus ; and subsequently,
probably under Claudius, it became a Roman colony, but even before
this many individual citizens of Vienna had received full 'civitas ',
as was the case with Asiaticus.

gentiles, ' of his fatherland '.

promptum haberet, ' he had ready means '.

§ 3. **citis** = ' cito agmine ductis ' : so xii 31, 2.

opprimendo: dative; Intr. II 11.

Rufrius Crispinus was colleague in the ' praefectura praetorii'
with Lusius Geta, xii 42, 1. He was the first husband of Poppaea
(afterwards wife of Nero), xiii 45, 4. An account of his exile and
death under Nero is given in xv 71, 8 ; xvi 17, 1.

Chapter 2, § 1. senatus copia, ' access to the senate ', i. e. the **2**
privilege of trial before it ; cf. ' tui copia ', i 58, 6.

Private trials before the princeps were very frequent under
Claudius, and Nero at his accession promised to abolish them,
xiii 4, 2. (Under Tiberius a report of the proceedings used to be
sent to the senate who were expected to pass sentence ; cf. vi 47, 4.)
Such trials had occurred even under Augustus, and arose from the
emperor's privilege of holding 'proconsulare imperium ', involving
power of life and death over his subjects, even within the
' pomerium '.

coram: probably here predicative, as in vi 42, 6 ; Intr. II 49.

corruptionem militum: according to Dio (lx 29, 5) this part
of the accusation utterly broke down.

obstrictos, ' bound to his service ' ; so in xii 25, 1.

§ 2. **victo silentio:** breaking through his resolution to keep
silence ; so 'victo gemitu', iv 8, 3 = suppressing any outburst of
sorrow.

§ 4. **quibus:** dative ; Intr. II 11.

L. Vitellius: consul in this year for the third time, and colleague with Claudius both in that office and in the censorship. He
would on this occasion be sitting with the emperor as ' assessor '
with him in the trial. See also vi 28, 1.

§ 5. **subditis qui:** Intr. II 21, c.

terrore carceris: i. e. of being strangled by the executioner in the
common dungeon.

adeo ignaro: for this trait in his character cf. Intr. V, p. xlvi.

Scipionem: mentioned as a 'legatus legionis' in Africa in
22 A. D., iii 74, 2 ; he was afterwards consul, and is mentioned again
in xii 53, 3.

Chapter 3, § 1. Sed: resuming the account of Asiaticus' trial. **3**

consultanti: dependent on the notion of speaking or answering latent in 'permisit'.

flens, &c.: Vitellius affected to believe that Asiaticus was doomed, and begged for him permission to choose the mode of his death, as if this would be a great favour; Claudius was thus diverted from his inclination to pity (ch. 2, 3), and he granted Vitellius' request, as if the permission to commit suicide were an act of mercy.

Antonia: the younger daughter of Augustus' sister Octavia by Antonius the triumvir. She married Drusus, brother of the Emperor Tiberius, and was mother of Germanicus, Livia (or Livilla), and the Emperor Claudius. Antonia received the title of Augusta on the accession of her grandson Gaius, but soon afterwards died or was put to death.

observavissent: perhaps refers to the honours paid to her after her death, not only to acts of respect during her lifetime.

recenti militia: he had probably been on the personal staff of Claudius.

conciliandae misericordiae: a genitive of quality; Intr. II 26, b.

permisit = 'permittendum censuit'.

in eandem clementiam: as if with 'spectantia'; 'the words of Claudius which followed bestowed mercy in that very shape'.

§ 2. **inediam et lenem exitum:** the latter expression is applied to self-starvation as not less painful but less violent than other forms of suicide, and more resembling a natural death.

remittere, 'declined the favour', i. e. of any extension of time; he would kill himself at once. For omission of 'se' cf. Intr. II 3.

exercitationibus, 'gymnastics'.

periturum: sc. 'fuisse'.

quam quod, &c., 'instead of falling a victim to', &c.

partem in aliam: sc. 'hortorum'.

vapore, 'heat', as constantly in Lucr.

securitatis novissimae, 'composure at his last hour'; cf. 'novissimis', v 7, 1.

4   Chapter 4, § 1. **equites inlustres** = men of senatorial census (1,000,000 sesterces), who remained within the equestrian rank from choice. To such men were given important posts conferred directly by the emperor, as the great 'praefecturae' in Rome, and that of Egypt.

quibus Petra cognomentum: more usually the gentile name of such persons is given as well. Possibly Tacitus here drew his information from some unofficial narrative in which no other name was given.

§ 2. **at:** the real cause of the accusation is contrasted with the professed charge.

Mnester: a famous pantomimist, and a favourite of Gaius and then of Messalina. His death is recorded in ch. 36, 1.

§ 3. **nocturnae quietis species,** 'a dream'.

tamquam, 'on the ground that'. The subjunctive does not necessarily imply that the allegation was false. Intr. II 50.

spicea corona: such a garland was an attribute of Ceres, and was worn by the Fratres Arvales. The inversion of the ears would be regarded as an evil omen.

ea imagine, 'on the ground of that vision'.

§ 4. visam: i.e. on the head of Claudius.

interpretatum: this should be taken in an active sense, with 'eum' supplied. (Intr. II 3.)

§ 5. qualicumque insomnio, 'by his dream, whatever it was'.

quindeciens: sc. 'centena millia'.

insignia praeturae: a senatorial distinction, noteworthy as given to one who was not a senator. So Seianus received 'praetoria ornamenta' from Tiberius, and Laco, the 'praefectus vigilum', received 'quaestoria ornamenta'. Tacitus also records the gift of 'quaestoria insignia' to Narcissus the pantomimist, ch. 38. See also xii 21, 2.

These honorary distinctions gave the recipient the distinctive dress and place at festivals, &c., accorded to senators, but not the right to a seat in the senate.

§ 6. adiecit = 'adicienda censuit'; cf. 'permisit', ch. 3, 1.

consiliis: alluding to ch. 2, 5.

§ 7. admissis = 'delictis'.

eleganti temperamento, 'making a graceful compromise between'.

necessitatem: a senator was under compulsion to answer the question officially put to him; this was the case also under the Republic (Livy xxviii 45, 5).

Chapter 5, § 1. continuus, 'incessantly occupied with criminal accusations'; cf. iv 36, 1 'postulandis reis continuus annus fuit'. 'Reis' is probably ablat. of respect. [Cf. Cicero, *Rep.* ii 20, 32 'equis assignandis . . . diligentes'.]

munia, 'functions'.

§ 2. nec quicquam, &c., 'nor had any wares in the public market so brisk a sale as the treachery of advocates' bribed to betray a case committed to them.

insignis: probably = 'inlustris'. Cf. 4, 1.

praevaricatio strictly denotes a corrupt agreement entered into by an accuser not to make the most of his case for the prosecution; it can, however, also be used of collusive advocacy on either side. Here Samius had probably retained Suillius, for the sum named, for his defence, and had then discovered that he meant to let his case fail.

§ 3. C. Silio: see ch. 12, 2. His father, a distinguished 'legatus' in Upper Germany, had been forced to suicide in 24 A.D. (iv 18 and foll.).

consule designato: cf. ch. 28, 1 'propinquo consulatu'. His downfall occurred before he held this office, and it is not known at what date he was to hold it. As cos. design. he would be asked his opinion first on whatever question was brought before the house, and on this occasion he took the opportunity to make this speech 'per egressionem' (i.e. the senator's right 'egredi relationem', to treat of other questions of public interest apart from that on which he was actually consulted).

memorabo: ch. 12, 12; 26 and foll.

lex Cincia, a plebiscite carried by M. Cincius Alimentus, tribune of the plebs 204 B.C., with the intention of freeing the people from bondage to the great 'patroni' who were senators. Its provisions were evaded by means of voluntary gifts and legacies from clients to their advocates. Augustus revived it in 17 B.C. [Dio liv 18, 2], but evasions were still continued. See also ch. 7, 8 and note.

Suillius was tried under this law in 58 A.D., xiii 42.

6 **Chapter 6, § 1. contumelia,** 'reprimand'.

famam et posteros: an expression similar to 'testamenta et orbos velut indagine eius capi', xiii 42, 7, in which the general term is followed by a specific one.

§ 2. **pulcherrimam alioquin,** &c.: these words give the substance of Silius' argument. 'A talent which would otherwise be the noblest . . . was degraded by services given for gain.'

§ 3. **negotia,** 'litigation'.

inimicitias, &c., 'feuds and prosecutions, hatred and the practice of injustice were encouraged, that just as the prevalence of sickness brings profit to physicians, so advocates may derive wealth from the corruption of the courts'.

§ 4. **Asinii**: ch. 7, 5 shows that this is the Asinius Pollio of Augustus' reign, the 'insigne maestis praesidium reis' of Hor. *Od.* ii 1, 13.

Messallae: see v 3, 4.

L. Arruntius: see vi 5, 1.

Aeserninus Marcellus: son of the consul of 22 B.C., and grandson, on his mother's side, of Pollio. He was a prominent senator and pleader of the latter part of Augustus', and throughout Tiberius', reign. He was at some time 'curator riparum et alvei Tiberis', 'praetor peregrinus' probably in 19 A.D., and at some time cos. suff.

§ 5. **parabatur sententia**: i.e. the consul was preparing to make a formal motion to express the feeling of the house.

lege repetundarum tenerentur: i.e. that pleaders who exacted a fee should be liable to prosecution under the statute 'de rebus repetundis'.

Cossutianus Capito: notorious afterwards as one of the accusers of Thrasea (xvi 28, 1; 33, 4).

manifestos, 'plainly guilty', oftener with genitive of the crime, as ii 85, 3 'delicti manifesta'.

ante acta deprecantes, 'asking pardon for the past' (equiv. to 'poenam ante actorum deprecantes'. So 'facti deprecatio' in Cic.).

7 **Chapter 7, § 1. quem illum,** &c. = 'quem illum esse qui'; cf. xii 36, 2 'avebantque visere quis ille tot per annos opes nostras sprevisset'. [So Cic. *Ac.* ii 22, 69 'quis iste dies inluxerit quaero'.]

spe praesumat, 'anticipate in hope'.

§ 2. **usui et rebus**, 'to meet the requirements and business of life assistance is provided (by professional advocates), that none may be at the mercy of the powerful for lack of men to defend him'. Cf. xv 6, 5 'ex rerum usu', 'in accordance with the requirements of events'.

§ 3. **gratuito contingere**, 'is attained without cost'.

ut quis, 'in order that a man may devote himself to the affairs of others'. 'Ut quis' may also mean 'according as one', &c.; cf. iv 23, 6 'ut quis fortuna inops . . . promptius ruebant'.

§ 4. The two pursuits open to senators (who were debarred from ordinary trade) are mentioned.

exercere agros: so used in xii 43, 4, and elsewhere in Tac. So often in Verg., e.g. *Aen.* vii 798 'exercent vomere colles'.

tolerare vitam (also in xv 45, 6) is also a Vergilian phrase; *Aen.* viii 409.

nihil, &c., 'no calling in life is adopted by any man without the prospect of some remuneration from it'. (Lit. 'except that of which he has foreseen emoluments'.)

§ 5. **magnum animum induisse**, 'assumed a lofty spirit' (in not accepting fees for pleading).

§ 6. **P. Clodius, C. Curio**: not creditable examples, for the former is stated to have been bribed to commit 'praevaricatio' by Catiline (Cic. *de Harusp. Resp.* 20, 42), and the corruption of the latter by Julius Caesar is attested by Lucan (iv 819) and Suetonius (*Iul.* 29).

§ 7. **modicos**, 'of moderate means', with little more than the bare senatorial census. Cf. 'modicis equitibus', i 73, 1.

In reality Suillius (see xiii 43, 6) was very wealthy, and so probably were the others.

quieta re publica: i.e. while the State enjoyed freedom from civil war, with its attendant confiscations and enrichment of partisans of the victors.

cogitaret, &c., 'he should think of the plebeians who won distinction by practice in the courts'.

toga, the emblem of peaceful civic life, may sometimes specifically denote the pleader's dress and functions; cf. 'cedant arma togae', Cic.; 'in toga negotiisque versantur', Pliny, *Ep.* i 22, 6; Martial and Quintilian, 'Romanae gloria magna togae'.

§ 8. **haud frustra**, 'not without grounds'.

dena sestertia: a considerable reduction. Samius had given four times as much to Suillius (ch. 5, 2).

A further change was made at Nero's accession, xiii 5, 1, when apparently an advocate was forbidden to make a bargain for his fee before the trial. These regulations, however, did not stop the payment of advocates, and men like Eprius Marcellus and Vibius Crispus made enormous fortunes (*Dial.* 8, 2).

repetundarum tenerentur: the genitive is used on the analogy of that with 'arguere', 'manifestus', and the like. Intr. II 24.

8   Chapter 8, § 1. Sub idem tempus: loosely expressed, since the date of the return of Mithridates, determined by the contemporary Parthian history (see below) and by that of Vibius Marsus (see note on ch. 10, 1), can hardly have been later than 43 A.D.

Mithridates: this prince had become king of Armenia by the aid of Tiberius; see vi 32, 5.

memoravi: in the lost part of the *Annals* dealing with the times of Gaius.

vinctum: so Dio, ὃν ὁ Γάιος μεταπεμψάμενος ἐδεδέκει (lx 8, 1). During this period Armenia had fallen under Parthian influence.

Pharasmanis: see vi 32, 5.

§ 2. Hiberis: see vi 32, 5 ; and for the case see Intr. II 9.

summa, &c., ' the throne itself was in dispute ; whatever was less important was treated carelessly'.

§ 3. Gotarzes, son of the Parthian king Artabanus III ; see vi 31, 1 and Intr. VI, p. lx.

Vardanes was another son of Artabanus III.

§ 4. ausis: substantival, a Vergilian use.

biduo tria milia stadiorum: i. e. nearly 350 English miles in 48 hours, a rate of progress impossible for a whole army even if consisting of horsemen.   If he came with a few followers, and by relays of horses, the rate is the same as that of Hannibal from Zama to Adrumetum (App. *Pun.* 47), and less than that of Tiberius when travelling to his brother Drusus (Pl. *N. H.* vii. 20, 84).

invadit, ' traverses', ' covers'.

praefecturas, ' provinces'; cf. 10, 1 ; vi 42, 5.   These are the great viceroyalties of the Parthian Empire (eighteen in number according to Pliny ma.), corresponding somewhat to the satrapies of the Persian Empire.   The viceroys were called βίστακες or ' vitaxae '.   ' Praefectura' is also used of the military subdivisions of Armenia, xiii 37, 2.

Seleucenses: Seleucia on the Tigris; see vi 42, 1.

§ 5. defectores: cf. Intr. II 51, a.

ira magis, &c., 'inflamed with anger rather than proceeding according to the immediate needs of the case'.   Cf. 7, 2.

§ 6. The Dahae and Hyrcani were Scythic races, south-east and east of the Caspian. See vi 36, 5.

Bactria: between the Upper Amoo (Oxus) and the Hindoo Koosh (Paropamisus); after the fall of its Greek dynasty its possession was disputed between Parthians and Scythians.

9   Chapter 9, § 1. Tunc : the narrative of the events of Armenia is resumed from ch. 8, 1.

incertis: not ' hesitating', but = ' de quibus incertum erat'; cf. Livy xxx 35, 9 'Italicos, incertos socii an hostes essent, in postremam aciem summotos'.

So xiii 19, 1 ' nemo adire praeter paucas feminas, amore an odio incertas '

vi: instrumental abl., varied in the next clause to abl. abs.; cf. Intr. II 64.

Hibero exercitu: mostly cavalry; vi 34, 2.

§ 2. **proelium ausus:** the accus. with 'audere', common in Tac., e.g. *Ann.* xii 28, 1, is also found in Livy, and earlier in poets.

praefecto: the Parthian viceroy; cf. ch. 8, 4.

§ 3. **paululum, &c.:** i.e. he delayed the acceptance of Mithridates by forming a party who supported his own pretensions.

Cotys: son of a king of Thrace of the same name. This Cotys had in 39 A.D. received his kingdom from Gaius (Dio lix 12, 2). It was a small strip of country west of the Upper Euphrates, previously for some time forming part of Cappadocia.

illuc, 'towards him'. So 'illuc cuncta vergere', i 3, 3.

atrociorem, 'less conciliatory', not necessarily in a very bad sense.

§ 4. Here Parthian events are resumed from ch. 8, 6.

foedus iaciunt: if the reading (that of Med.) is right, it must mean 'sermones iaciunt de foedere'; cf. 'terminos iaciebat', vi 31, 2. Another reading is 'iciunt', and some emend to 'faciunt'.

complexi dextras: cf. xii 47, 3.

pepigere . . . ulcisci: a similar construction is used in xiv 31, 4.

ipsi inter se concedere, 'waive opposing claims'.

§ 6. **septimo . . . anno:** i.e. in 43 A.D. The revolt from Artabanus began in 36 A.D., vi 42, 1.

This date is confirmed by the mention of Vibius Marsus as legatus in Syria, in ch. 10, 1, and by the date of the death of Vardanes, ch. 10, 5.

Chapter 10, § 1. invisit, 'inspects'.

Vibius Marsus: see also vi 48, 1. He probably became legatus of Syria about 42 A.D., succeeding P. Petronius (iii 39, 2), and was succeeded by C. Cassius not later than 45 A.D. (xii 11, 4).

reciperare avebat . . . ni cohibitus foret: Intr. II 38.

§ 3. **Erinden:** unknown, perhaps the Charindas mentioned by Ptolemy (vi 2, 2), one of the streams flowing into the south of the Caspian.

multum certato: impersonal abl. abs.; Intr. II 21.

Sinden: unknown. The campaign took place between the Caspian and Herat. The Arii here are probably not the tribe of that name who lived south-west of Bactria, but the word is probably a corruption for the name of a people north or east of the Dahae in the region of the Oxus or Iaxartes. Vardanes boasts in his inscr. below that he penetrated beyond the established limits of the Parthian Empire.

disterminat: only here used in Tac., but found in Pliny ma.

§ 4. **aspernabantur,** 'detested'.

§ 5. **monimentis:** nothing is now known of these.

nec, &c., 'and declared that he had exacted from those races tribute never yet rendered by them to any of the Arsacidae'.

45

composito, 'concerted'.

paucos inter, 'to be named with only a few of even long-lived monarchs (although his reign had been so short), i.e. 'equalled by few'. Cf. Livy xxii 7, 1 'inter paucas memorata populi Romani clades', of the battle of Lake Thrasymene. For the anastrophe cf. Intr. II 55.

perinde . . . quam: so vi 30, 4.

§ 6. nece Vardanis: the following sentences give a brief summary of events to the end of 48 A.D. The subject is resumed in xii 10.

inter ambiguos = 'cum ambigui essent'.

§ 7. Phraatis: see xii 10, 1.

obsidio: predicative dative of a word (found only here) derived from 'obses'.

§ 8. potitus regiam: the accusative with 'potior' is an archaic use (e.g. it occurs in Lucretius).

adegit mittere: cf. Intr. II 31.

permitti ... orabant: cf. Intr. II 31. 'Petitioned that he should be let go to assume the sovereignty of his fathers' (cf. vi 32, 1).

11 Chapter 11, § 1. Isdem consulibus: Claudius and Vitellius, the consuls of the year, 47 A.D., are meant, though they had by this time probably given place to 'suffecti', and had themselves entered on their censorship (ch. 13, 1).

ludi saeculares: these were now held by Claudius to mark the seventh centenary of the traditional date of the foundation of Rome (753 B.C.), but they had been instituted by Augustus in 17 B.C. to mark a 'saeculum' of a different sort, namely the inauguration of a 'new age', which, according to a tradition partly Greek partly Etruscan, opened upon the expiration of four great periods of 110 years (see below, on 'rationes').

The ceremonies of this festival were modelled on the 'ludi Terentini' believed to be of great antiquity and regular recurrence, of which however the earliest authenticated celebration took place in 249 B.C. (Varro ap. Censorinum), when, on the occurrence of a great number of unfavourable prodigies, 'ludi Terentini in campo Martio' were ordered in honour of Dis and Proserpina, with sacrifices of 'hostiae furvae', and their repetition 'centesimo quoque anno' was enjoined. The festival had been repeated in 146 B.C., but its next centenary lapsed as it fell in the time of the civil war of Pompeius and Julius Caesar. The 'ludi Terentini' were not originally a Roman festival, and the gods honoured were not Roman; hence its celebration outside the 'pomerium'; but Augustus' festival included sacrifices to the Roman state divinities, Jupiter, Juno Lucina, Apollo, Diana, and Latona, as well as to Demeter, the Fates, Dis, and Proserpina.

quarto et sexagensimo: sc. 'anno'; 17 B.C. marked the expiration of the first decade of Augustus' rule, when the 'imperium' conferred on him in 27 B.C. was renewed for five years more.

§ 2. rationes: the 'saeculum' was taken by the 'quindecimviri' to be 110 years ('undenos decies per annos', Hor. *C. S.* 21), and celebrations of the festival were attributed by them to the years 456, 346, 236, 126 B.C., so that 17 B.C. was the closing year of the last 'saeculum' in the series.

libris: the *Histories*, of which the extant portion (Books I–IV and part of V) does not go beyond 70 A.D.

§ 3. **is quoque,** &c.: in 88 A.D.; Domitian followed Augustus' view of the 'saeculum', but anticipated the full amount of the time from Augustus' celebration by six years.

intentius adfui, 'I was particularly interested in them'.

sacerdotio quindecimvirali: see vi 12, 1.

§ 4. **iactantia:** causal ablative.

ea cura, 'the quindecimviri (as a body) had of old the charge of these games, and such of them as happened to be magistrates were selected by preference (rather than others of the body) for the (public) performance of the religious duties'. Cf. Hor. *C.S.* 70 'quindecim Diana preces virorum curet'. In Augustus' time, and so also probably in that of his successors, there were five 'magistri' among the 'quindecimviri', of whom the emperor was one, and it was in that capacity that he held the 'ludi saeculares'. With these 'magistri' were also associated such others of the 'quindecimviri' as were holding one of the higher magistracies.

§ 5. **circensibus ludis:** held on one of the days of the 'ludi saeculares'.

ludicrum Troiae: evolutions such as those referred to in Vergil, *Aen.* v 545 and foll. They were probably of very ancient origin, and were taken up by the earlier Caesars because of the claims of the Iulii to Trojan descent.

pueri nobiles: most of the authorities describe the boys taking part in these evolutions as divided into two 'turmae' of 'maiores' and 'minores', namely those under sixteen and eleven respectively. Princes of the imperial house took part in this show at a very early age: Nero was now only nine, and Britannicus six years old.

adoptione, &c., 'by his adoption soon afterwards accepted as the emperor's heir and entitled Nero'.

§ 6. **dracones:** so Suet. (*Ner.* 6) reports a story of persons sent by Messalina to kill the child being frightened away by a serpent.

externis miraculis: such as the story that Alexander the Great was begotten by a god in the form of a serpent.

Chapter 12, § 1. supererat, 'was a survival'. Germanicus, son of Tiberius' brother Drusus, had died in 19 A.D., and Nero and his mother were the only surviving members of that family.

commotior, 'roused to greater fury'.

quo minus, &c., 'was too much engrossed with . . . to make up charges and suborn accusers'. 'Quo minus' follows the notion of prevention in 'distinebatur'. For the zeugma with 'strueret' cf. 'molitur crimina et accusatorem', xii 22, 1.

§ 2. **Caius Silius:** see ch. 5, 3.

47

exarserat, 'had formed so violent a passion for '.

Iunia Silana: perhaps daughter of L. Silanus, cos. suff. in 27 A.D. She is mentioned subsequently as the friend, and afterwards the enemy, of Agrippina ; xiii 19, 2 ; xiv 12, 8.

vacuo: left without a wife, 'she secured undisputed possession of her paramour'.

§ 3. **certo exitio:** abl. abs., so also 'non nulla spe'; Intr. II 22, a.

fallendi, 'of escaping detection'; like λανθάνειν.

opperiri futura, 'to wait for the future', i. e. 'to let events take their course' Some editors give 'operire', 'to cover, shut his eyes to'

§ 4. **egressibus:** Intr. II 57, a.

honores: such as that of 'consul designatus', ch. 5, 3, and perhaps elevation to the patriciate, ch. 25, 3.

fortuna: so also of the rank and dignity of the princeps, ch. 30, 3; vi 6, 3.

paratus: cf. ch. 30, 3, 'pomp'; Dio (lx 31, 3) says that Messalina transferred to his house πάντα τὰ τιμιώτατα τῶν τοῦ Κλαυδίου κειμηλίων.

13   **Chapter 13,** § 1. **matrimonii:** here probably = conjugal relations, generally, ' his married life ', i. e. the dishonour done to him as a husband. So 'addidit pauca Drusus de matrimonio suo', iii 34, 11. The word might also possibly be used as abstract for concrete, in the sense of ' coniugis ', as in ii 13, 3 'matrimonia ac pecunias hostium praedae destinare '.

munia censoria usurpans, 'now exercising the functions of censor'. The most important powers of the censor had always been vested in the princeps (Intr. p. xxix) ; but no actual censors had been appointed since 23 B.C., until the office was assumed by Claudius and Vitellius, on laying down their consulship in this year.

theatralem lasciviam, ' misbehaviour in the theatre '.

P. Pomponium: cf. v 8, 4.

§ 2. **lege lata:** probably carried by him in his capacity of tribune in the form of a plebiscitum. It is to such laws that 'plebiscitis', in ch. 14, 5 (if the reading is accepted), must refer.

in mortem, 'with a view to the death ', i. e. to be repaid on the death of their parents.

filiis familiarum, persons still ' in potestate patris '.

fontesque aquarum: Claudius, as censor, imitated the great work of his ancestor, Appius Claudius Caecus, who, as censor in 312 B.C., constructed a great aqueduct, the Aqua Claudia, bringing water to the city from the Sabine Hills.

The 'Simbruini colles' contained the three lakes, formed by the Anio, from which the neighbouring 'Sublaqueum' (now Subiaco) derived its name. The great aqueduct referred to here had been begun by Gaius in 38 A.D., and when completed consisted of two parts, the 'Aqua Claudia' and 'Anio Novus', both of which streams entered the city together, one above the other, by the arches, two of which form the present ' Porta Maggiore '. An inscription on it is extant, recording the completion and dedication of the work by Claudius in 52 A.D., and subsequent restorations by Vespasian and Titus. The length of the ' Claudia ' is stated by the inscription to be thirty-five, and that of the Anio Novus sixty-two, Roman miles. Pliny says the water was brought to a level from which all the hills of Rome could be reached (*N. H.* xxxvi 15, 24, 122). The date of the work given by Tacitus does not agree with that in the inscription. Either Tacitus records the inception of the work in the first year of Claudius' censorship, and the inscription records its completion at the end of his office; or, if 'urbi intulit' denotes the completion of the work in this year, 47 A.D., it must be supposed that the introduction of the Aqua Claudia into the city was first accomplished, and that the date in the inscription records the subsequent connexion of the Anio Novus with it.

§ 3. **novas litterarum formas** : see ch. 14, 5.

comperto : Intr. II 21.

litteraturam, ' system of letters ', ' alphabet '.

Chapter 14, § 1. Primi, &c., ' the Egyptians were the first to **14** represent ideas, which they did by means of the shapes of animals (such primitive records of human history are to be seen engraved on rocks ', and they declare that they were the inventors of the alphabet '. Tacitus ignores the fact that in the hieroglyphics other symbols besides the forms of animals are employed. As to their alphabet, two systems were developed, the 'hieratic' and 'demotic' characters, both cursive forms into which the hieroglyphics were modified, the former dating from the eighteenth or nineteenth dynasty, and the latter from the seventh or ninth century B.C. Another tradition, which Pliny ma. follows (*N. H.* vii 56, 57, 192), makes Assyrian the primitive alphabet: this is derived from the Accadian, which again was developed from hieroglyphics.

tamquam reppererint : Intr. II 50.

§ 2. **fama est** : so Hdt. v 58. Pliny ma. also gives this legend, and says that Cadmus' alphabet originally consisted of sixteen letters, to which Palamedes in the time of the Trojan War added four, and later Simonides of Ceos added another four. He quotes also, on the authority of Aristotle, another tradition, making the original number eighteen, and substituting an addition of two by Epicharmus for that of four by Palamedes.

§ 3. **quidam** : the legend which puts Cecrops for Cadmus is only found here.

Linum : so Diodorus and Suidas.

Palamedem : so Stesichorus and Euripides.

sedecim . . . mox alios : this tradition embodies the truth that the Greeks modified the original Phoenician alphabet by dropping the characters to which they had no corresponding sound, and adapting other symbols so as to represent their vowel sounds.

§ 4. **Demaratus,** according to Livy (i 34, 2), was the father of Tarquinius Priscus, so that the tradition Tacitus follows makes the use of letters in Etruria later than in Latium. It is far more likely in fact that the alphabet existed in both districts from a very early date ; see Mommsen, *Hist.* i, ch. 14.

Aborigines: this name is given to the early Latins by Livy (i 1, 5) and other writers.

Evander: mythical founder of the ancient 'Pallanteum' on the Palatine (Verg. *Aen.* viii 81 and foll.). The art of writing was no doubt introduced among the Italians by the Greeks, and Evander is to Latium, as Demaratus to Etruria, the representative in legend of prehistoric Greek influences.

Cumae, colonized as early as the eighth century B.C., is a probable source of the spreading of writing.

forma, &c.: so also Pliny (*N. H.* vii 58, 210).

paucae primum: an overstatement. The known additions are not numerous. Cicero (*N. D.* ii 37, 93) speaks of the alphabet in his time as consisting of twenty-one letters. Of these, *g* (existing in the earliest Scipionic inscription (*circ.* 290 B.C.)) is said by Plutarch to have been introduced by Sp. Carvilius; this would be in the time of the First Punic War. Also *x*, though found in the earliest extant writing, was not in universal use, and *cs* was often used for it. Its position at the end of the proper Roman alphabet suggests that it was added to the earliest system, or perhaps restored after a period of disuse. In Cicero's time *y* and *z* came into use, but were restricted to Greek words. A passage in Suetonius (*Aug.* 88) shows that *x* was regarded as the last letter of the true alphabet.

§ 5. Claudius' additions were the symbols ꟼ for the semi-consonantal *v*,) (antisigma) for *ps* or *bs*, Ⱶ (the Greek sign for the 'spiritus asper') for the *y* sound intermediate between *i* and *u*. Of these new signs the first was employed fairly frequently for a time, but the last two very seldom.

publico † dis plebiscitis: the reading is questionable, and the fact of 'plebiscita' being passed under the Empire is not undisputed (see ch. 13, 2) ; otherwise 'publicandis plebiscitis' might seem a satisfactory emendation. The doubtful words 'dis' and 'plebiscitis' may be glosses to explain 'per fora ac templa', interpolated from the margin into the text.

15 Chapter 15, § 1. **super collegio,** 'about the establishment of a college'. An 'ordo haruspicum Augustorum', apparently of sixty members, is mentioned in an inscription belonging to this period, and was probably established as a result of this motion. 'Haruspices', though honoured in Etruria, were in Rome much inferior to the augurs, who formed one of the great priestly colleges of men of the highest rank. A magistrate's haruspex ranked only with his apparitors, and Cicero (*ad Fam.* vi 18, 1) considers it an indignity that persons who had been haruspices had in his day become senators.

accitos: from Etruria, the home of the science of 'haruspicina'.
habitas, 'kept up'.
patrum Romanorum impulsu: Cicero mentions a 'senatus

consultum' prescribing that six 'principum filii', sons of the highest Etruscan families, should be trained in each Etruscan community to the study (*de Div.* i 41, 92).

publica, &c., 'owing to the general apathy of the citizens in regard to noble accomplishments'.

externae superstitiones: i. e. the Egyptian and Jewish (possibly also the Christian) religions, and the practice of astrology and magic.

§ 2. **ne:** giving the effect of showing gratitude, 'thus preventing', &c.

inter ambigua, 'in times of peril'; so vi 21, 4.

§ 3. **quae,** &c., 'what was to be kept up or strengthened in the institutions of the haruspices'; the establishment of the new 'collegium' would be made in accordance with this resolution. For the omission of 'essent' see Intr. II 27.

Chapter 16, § 1. Cheruscorum gens: they lived north-east of the Chatti, between the Weser and the Elbe. They are mentioned in Caesar, *B. G.* vi 10,5, as neighbours and possible rivals of the Suevi; and after Varus' disaster (9 A. D.) they were prominent in the resistance of the Germans to Rome (9-17 A. D.). By the time of Tacitus they had been overwhelmed by the Chatti (*Germ.* 36, 2) and had become quiescent.

apud urbem habebatur: as son of a prince professing alliance with Rome. So also princes of Eastern kingdoms were brought up in Rome; vi 31, 4; 32, 5.

§ 2. **Arminius** was the chief of the Cherusci who prompted the rebellion in which Varus lost his life and three legions were annihilated (9 A. D.). He had received 'civitas' with equestrian rank for previous services to Rome. His brother Flavus is mentioned in ii 9, 2 as 'insignis fide (erga Romanos) et amisso per vulnus oculo paucis ante annis duce Tiberio'.

Chattorum: the Chatti are described in *Germ.* 30, 1 as inhabiting the 'Hercynius saltus', a term of wide import in most ancient authors. Their name survives in the modern 'Hessen', which, with part of Nassau, represents their locality at this time.

§ 3. **hortatur . . . capessere:** see Intr. II 31.

gentile: so in ch. 1, 2.

primum, &c., 'he was the first prince, born at Rome, and no hostage but a Roman citizen, to proceed to a foreign kingdom'.

civem: his father Flavus had probably received the 'civitas' as had Arminius (see note above).

§ 4. **laetus,** 'welcome'.

§ 6. **adeo,** &c., 'had they absolutely no one born in the same land as themselves to occupy the supreme position'?

exploratoris: mounted scouts, natives of the district in which they served, were used especially in frontier service. Flavus may have been 'praefectus alae exploratorum'.

§ 7. **frustra,** &c., 'in vain is the name of Arminius put forward'; i. e. Italicus is being recommended as his nephew.

posse, &c., 'he might well be received with apprehension, demoralized as he would be by his education, enslavement, and mode of life, all of them foreign'.

§ 8. **at si**: the argument is, ' If he had been a son of Arminius, he would have become demoralized ; while if he takes after his father, he will be a traitor to the Germans'.

17   **Chapter 17, § 2. inrupisse**: supply 'se'; cf. Intr. II 3.

§ 3. **rubori**: so xiv 55, 7 ' mihi rubori est'.

volentibus: Italicus refers to the acquiescence of the Germans in Roman rule before the rising against Varus.

§ 4. **privatim**, &c., 'base in their private life, mischievous in their public activities '.

§ 5. The Langobardi are first heard of on the south side of the Elbe next to the Chauci, and are thought to have been among those driven across that river by the Roman advance under Tiberius. Their importance in South Germany dates from the middle of the fifth century, and their kingdom in Italy lasted for two centuries from 568 A. D. The name is derived by some as = ' long beards ', and by others as 'long axes', cf. 'halberd'.

res, &c., ' brought misery on the Cherusci'; the remark sums up the character of his reign as a whole.

18   **Chapter 18, § 1. Per idem tempus**: probably here, as in ch. 10, the events of more than one year are brought together.

Chauci: they occupied a large space, apparently on each side of the Lower Weser. Those along the coast between the Weser and Ems were under Roman control (i 38). A previous rebellion of theirs is mentioned in Suet. (*Cl.* 24).

nulla, &c. : Intr. II 22, a.

Sanquinii: see vi 4, 4. His death, and the appointment of Corbulo to succeed him, were probably mentioned in the lost books.

Cn. Domitius Corbulo, probably son of the person mentioned in iii 34 as attacking, under Tiberius, the corruption of the contractors for the roads in Italy, was half-brother of Suillius (ch. 1, 1) and Caesonia wife of Gaius ; he was consul in 39 A. D., and proconsul of Asia in 51–52 or 52–53 A.D. Under Nero he was appointed in 54 A. D. to the command in the East, which he held till recalled and forced to suicide in 67 A. D.

Canninefas: living in the ' insula ' of the Rhine adjoining the Batavi.

§ 2. **cui**: this refers to ' gloria'.

triremes : a fleet of sea-going ships was kept on the Rhine in the early Empire. It was used in 5 A. D. by Tiberius in his expedition to the Elbe, and again by Germanicus in 15 A. D. (i 60, 3).

aestuaria : tidal marshes.

fossas: the best known of these was the 'fossa Drusiana', connecting the Rhine with the Yssel at Doesburg.

ut quaeque habiles, ' according to their various capabilities', i. e. as their draught adapted them for shallow water.

praesentia, ' affairs on the spot'.

operum ... ignavas : Intr. II 24, c.

ne, &c. : explaining 'veterem morem', 'the ancient discipline, forbidding', &c.

stationes: pickets on guard, on duty both by day and night.

vigiliae: on duty at night only.

§ 5. **vallum foderet,** ' was digging earth for the rampart'.

iacta, ' rumoured '. **intentum,** ' strict '.

Chapter 19, § 1. **is terror,** 'the dread inspired by him ', into his **19** soldiers by his strictness and into his enemies by his prompt suppression of Gannascus.

nos, &c., 'our spirit was heightened, the barbarians completely lost heart '. So 'auget vires ', iv 24, 1. The idea might more naturally be expressed by a passive construction, but the use of the active is determined by Tacitus' fondness for variety. (Intr. II 64.)

§ 2. **natio Frisiorum :** occupying most of the north of Holland. Their name survives in the modern Friesland. Their rebellion in 28 A. D. is described in iv 72 and foll.

L. Apronius, propraetor of Lower Germany, suffered severe loss in repressing the revolt of 28 A. D. The siege of the fortress ' Flevum ' was raised, but no subjugation of the country was effected.

consedit, &c.: in the same way the Ubii had been granted a reservation in Lower Germany ; see xii 27, 2.

apud = ' in ' : Intr. II 46.

§ 3. **praesidium immunivit,** ' established a fortress and garrison among them ' ; a Graecism like φρούρια ἐντειχίζειν, Xen. *Cyr.* iii 1, 27.

maiores : separated from their western neighbours, the 'minores' Chauci, by the Weser.

§ 4. **degeneres,** ' unworthy ' (of Romans) ; cf. xii 19, 1.

violatorem fidei : see ch. 18, 1.

§ 5. **semina,** &c., ' was acting so as to provoke rebellion ' ; for the metaphor cf. vi 47, 1.

ut laeta, &c. : abl. abs., ' the news of his doings being hailed with joy by many, though viewed with disfavour in certain quarters '. Cf. ' laeti . . . nuntii ', i 5, 6.

§ 6. **formidolosum,** &c., ' a military hero, being an object of dread to a feeble ruler, was a menace to peace'.

(If there were losses, the State, not the general, would suffer ; if he succeeded, Claudius would be jealous of him, and this would drive him into rebellion.)

novam vim, ' any forward movement'.

§ 7. **Germaniae :** this plural, properly denoting the two Roman provinces, as distinct from ' Germania ' the general name of the country, seems sometimes to be used also of those parts beyond the Rhine which were regarded as properly belonging to Rome, though they had either lapsed from allegiance or had not so far been brought under effective control. Cf. i 57, 2.

Chapter 20, § 1. **eae litterae,** ' letters to that effect '. **20**

offunderentur, ' were crowding into his mind'. Intr. II 40.

quondam: Med. has' quosdam '. The correction is supported by the words in Dio lx 30, 5 ὦ μακάριοι οἱ πάλαι ποτὲ στρατηγήσαντες.

§ 2. **fossam**: probably the 'Vliet', leaving the old Rhine at Leyden, and passing by Delft to the Maas.

The purpose of the canal was to enable ships to get from the Rhine to the Maas without having to encounter the perils of the open sea, so disastrous to Germanicus; see i 70; ii 23–4.

incerta Oceani: Intr. II 23.

spatio, 'in length'.

§ 3. **insignia triumphi**: both Claudius and Nero gave this distinction on very light grounds, cf. xii 5; xiii 53, 1 'pervulgatis triumphi insignibus'. Augustus (and probably Tiberius) only gave this honour in cases where, under the Republic, a general would have secured a triumph or ovation.

A person honoured with these 'insignia' had the right to appear at public spectacles wearing a laurel wreath, and, in exceptional cases, the 'vestis triumphalis'; his name was enrolled in the 'Fasti triumphales' and his statue set up in the 'forum Augusti'; and he might decorate the entrance of his house with trophies and set up a laurel-wreathed statue in a triumphal car in his own vestibule.

§ 4. **Curtius Rufus**: legatus of Upper Germany, probably father of the historian.

agro Mattiaco: the district of which Aquae Mattiacae (Wiesbaden) was the centre. The tribe, a branch of the Chatti, seems to have submitted to Rome after the time of Tiberius, and was still faithful in the time of Tacitus (*Germ.* 29, 3).

quaerendis venis: dat. with the force of final clause. Intr. II 11.

cum damno, because the work was unhealthy and involved destruction of their clothes, which they had to pay for themselves, and there was no booty to compensate.

effodere rivos: i. e. to dig channels to drain the mines. If Med. 'et fodere' is read, 'et' = 'both', and this clause would refer to Corbulo's undertaking, § 2.

quae ... gravia, 'what would be hard work above ground'.

§ 5. **subactus**, 'broken down'.

nomine exercituum: this single army wrote as on behalf of all

ut, &c.: i. e. so that generals who had no opportunities of war might not try to earn these honours by works of this kind.

21 Chapter 21, § 1. **neque**, &c., 'I would not publish a false account, and do not care to state the truth in detail'.

exsequi: cf. xii 58, 1.

§ 2. **sector**: 'in the train of', a lower term than 'comes'. Pliny (*Ep.* vii 27, 2) speaks of him as belonging to the 'cohors' of the proconsul.

medium diei: this expression and 'sero diei' both occur in Livy.

§ 3. **degressus**: the verb is used in the sense of 'decedere'.

principis suffragio: i. e. by his 'commendatio'. (Intr. p. xxxi.)

natalium, 'ancestry'.

ex se natus, 'the son of his own achievements'; so Cicero.

referring to his own elevation, although he was a 'novus homo', says of himself 'quem vos *a se ortum* hominibus nobilissimis . . . praetulistis', *Phil.* vi 6, 17.

§ 4. **longa . . . senecta :** abl. of description, followed, for variety, by nominatives 'adrogans', 'difficilis '; note also the dat. 'minoribus' following 'adversus superiores' for the same reason. Cf. Intr. II 64.

tristi adulatione, 'flattering with affected surliness'.

minoribus here = 'inferiors'.

difficilis, 'ungenial', 'brusque'.

consulare imperium = 'consulatum'. The date of this is unknown.

fatale praesagium implevit, 'fulfilled the presage of his destiny'.

Chapter 22, § 1. nullis palam causis: Intr. II 49.   **22**

reperitur : according to Suetonius (*Cl.* 35), persons seeking audience of the emperor at the morning 'salutatio' were searched before admission.

§ 2. **nam :** this explains 'neque cognitis' above.

§ 3. **isdem consulibus :** see ch. 11, 1.

P. Dolabella : prominent as a servile senator under Tiberius ; consul in 10 A.D., and procos. of Africa in 24 A.D. His 'sententia' was evidently taken up by Claudius, for the enactment is referred to as among the 'acta Claudii' in xiii 5, 2, and is ascribed to him by Suetonius (*Cl.* 24).

eorum, &c. : i. e. the 'quaestores designati '; they were relieved of the obligation to give these shows in 54 A.D. (xiii 5, 2).

§ 4. **id :** i.e. appointment to an office of state.

cunctis civium : Intr. II 23. This statement disregards the considerable period of time during which the plebeians, though part of the community, were disqualified from holding any magistracy.

ne aetas quidem : the 'lex Villia annalis ', of 180 B.C., fixed the 'aetas legitima ' for the magistrates ; by its regulations the minimum age for quaestors was thirty-one, for aediles thirty-seven, for praetors forty, and for consuls forty-three. These limits were reduced under Augustus, and the ordinary age for holding the quaestorship was then twenty-four or twenty-five.

§ 5. **regibus imperantibus :** the accounts of the establishment of the quaestors vary and are difficult to harmonize. It seems that the first quaestors under the kings were the 'quaestores parricidii '. Plutarch says that Valerius Poplicola established the treasury in the first year of the Republic, and gave the people the right to choose two quaestors to manage it. It seems then that the 'quaestores parricidii' of the royal period acquired under the Republic additional functions as 'quaestores aerarii ', and in time came to exercise the latter functions only.

lex curiata : this was the act by which 'imperium' was conferred on magistrates after election. The 'comitia centuriata ' very early took over the legislative functions that had belonged originally to the 'comitia curiata ', and the functions of the latter became merely formal, one of them being this bestowal of the 'imperium' on the elected magistrates. In the later times of the Republic the 'comitia curiata' was represented by thirty lictors, with three augurs present.

ab L. Bruto repetita, 'dating back to L. Brutus'. Tacitus ascribes the form of words used at the ceremony conferring imperium on the consuls to the original law of the traditional founder of the Republic, by which the election of the first consuls was ratified and their powers defined; and it is implied in the next sentence that this old 'lex' empowered the consuls to appoint quaestors, as the kings had done before them.

§ 7. **sexagensimo tertio anno:** 447 B.C. The quaestorship had been in abeyance under the Decemvirate, and now upon its re-institution was transferred from consular nomination to popular election in the 'comitia tributa'.

ut, &c.: i.e. to accompany the consuls to war, and take charge of the military chest. 'Res militaris' is analogous to 'res familiaris'.

§ 8. **duo additi, &c.:** according to Livy (iv 43, 4), the quaestors were originally appointed for urban functions, and two additional quaestors were instituted in 421 B.C. to accompany the consuls to war.

mox duplicatus numerus: in 267 B.C., when the subjugation of Italy was completed. The four new quaestors, called 'quaestores classici', administered departments ('provinciae') in Italy. It is possible that one of these was transferred to Lilybaeum after the annexation of Sicily, and that Tacitus refers to this in the words 'et accedentibus provinciarum vectigalibus'. (For this expression cf. Intr. II 23, c.)

stipendiaria, &c., 'when Italy was now subject'. The Italians could not ever have been called 'stipendiarii' in the sense in which the provincials were; most of their communities, however, would naturally pay 'tributum' (a tax on landed property) until its abolition in Italy after the conquest of Macedonia in 168 B.C.

§ 9. **lege Sullae:** in 81 B.C. Some addition to the number of quaestors had probably been made already, as the number of provinces rose.

viginti: Julius Caesar subsequently raised their number to forty, but Augustus seems to have reduced it to twenty again.

supplendo senatui: Sulla made the quaestorship the qualification for entrance into the senate, the numbers of which he had enlarged.

iudicia tradiderat: see xii 60, 4.

cui, 'to whose members'.

§ 10. **et quamquam, &c.:** i.e. the recovery by the equites of a share in the 'iudicia' made it unnecessary to have so large a senate and consequently so many quaestors to keep up its numbers; however, the people did not wish to make that office harder to obtain.

ex dignitate, &c., 'on account of worthiness in the candidates or through the complaisance of the electors'.

venundaretur, 'was thrown open to purchase', because only the rich could afford to give the necessary shows.

Chapter 23, § 1. A. Vitellius: subsequently emperor for part 23 of 69 A.D., until deposed by Vespasian. He was son of the consul of the preceding year. He is only once mentioned again in the *Annals,* in xiv 49, 1, where an instance of his servile deference to Nero is recorded.

L. Vipstanus Poplicola: not otherwise known.

de supplendo senatu: Claudius was about to carry out the 'lectio senatus' in virtue of the censorship, upon which he and his colleague entered on laying down their consulship (ch. 13, 1).

primores: a deputation of young chiefs; cf. 'tot insignes iuvenes quot intueor', *Orat. Claud.* ii 22.

Comata, 'long-haired'; the term denotes the newer provinces, Aquitania Lugdunensis and Belgica, as distinguished from the Romanized Gallia Narbonensis.

foedera et civitatem. These chiefs belonged to clans, such as the Aedui, Remi, and Lingones, which had a 'foedus' with Rome, and themselves possessed Roman citizenship, a privilege which had been freely bestowed by Julius Caesar and Augustus on Gauls of rank.

ius adipiscendorum in urbe honorum: it should be noted that no Roman citizen was, under the rules laid down by Augustus, eligible for a magistracy, unless he was a senator or a member of the senatorial order. These Gaulish chiefs had not this qualification, but were not under any disability not felt by other ordinary 'cives'.

super = 'de'. Cf. vi 15, 4.

rumor, 'talk'.

§ 2. studiis . . . certabatur: there was a conflict of opinions among the advisers of Claudius in a private conference ('apud principem'), and the arguments of those opposed to the granting of the petition of the Gauls occupy the remainder of this chapter. Claudius combated their objections ('statim', ch. 24, 1), but, failing to convince them, convened the senate and there re-stated his view of the case. Tacitus seems to combine the two utterances of Claudius in his paraphrase.

§ 3. consanguineis populis: dative. 'The rule of native-born Romans had once sufficed for (i. e. been acquiesced in by) kindred peoples'.

olim: when Latins, Sabines, &c., had not yet full equality with citizens living on 'ager Romanus'.

ad: sc. 'spectantia'. 'Nay, still deeds were quoted as the product of the Roman character under the old way of life, exemplifying heroism and winning renown.'

§ 4. Veneti et Insubres: quoted as typical of the Transpadani, who received the citizenship from Julius Caesar in 49 B. C.

nisi, &c., 'unless the semblance of captivity is to be inflicted on us through the crowd of aliens introduced '. The reading of Med. is 'coetus'; 'unless a crowd of aliens is to be imposed on us, bringing as it were captivity upon us'.

§ 5. ultra: to be taken predicatively, supplying 'fore', 'would be left', i.e. if Roman aspirants to office were crowded out by an influx of provincial candidates.

aut si quis, &c., 'any poor senator from Latium', i.e. any 'novus homo' from one of the 'municipia'. (To 'si quis' supply an antecedent in the dative case.)

§ 6. divites illos : cf. ch. 18, 1.

duces, in apposition with 'avi proavique'.

apud Alesiam : where Vercingetorix made his last stand, 52 B.C. The site is identified with Alise Sainte Reine, in the Côte d'Or.

obsederint: for a time Caesar was besieged as well as besieger.

§ 7. oreretur . . . sint: emended from Med. 'moreretur qui Capitolio et ara Romana manibus eorundem per se satis'. 'eorum' refers to the Romans, and 'eorundem' to the Gauls. The allusion is to the capture of Rome by the Senones in 390 B.C.

24 Chapter 24, § 1. ita exorsus est : the speech here given, as well as the fragments of Claudius' actual speech which have been preserved, show reminiscences of the speech of Canuleius in Livy iv 3-5.

Clausus : Attus Clausus, according to the most generally accepted version of tradition, migrated with his followers from Regillus to Rome, 504 B.C. (Livy ii 16).

hortantur uti : so in ch. 16, 3 ; Intr. II 31.

in re publica capessenda, 'in my political action '; cf. xvi 26, 8 'quod . . . capessendae rei publicae iter ingrederetur'.

Iulios Alba : Romulus himself was one of the royal house of Alba and descended from Iulus. The transference of the inhabitants of Alba Longa to Rome was attributed to Tullus Hostilius, the third king of Rome.

§ 2. Camerium, or Cameria, one of the Latin cities, was destroyed at so early a date that its site is doubtful.

Coruncanios : according to Cicero, Ti. Coruncanius, the famous jurist, consul 280 B.C., came from Tusculum.

Porcios : M. Porcius Cato, 234–149 B.C., consul 195 B.C., censor 184 B.C., would be the best known of this family.

Etruria Lucaniaque : abl. Intr. II 13.

accitos, sc. 'homines'; cf. similar ellipse in ch. 14, 4.

The allusion is to the general admission of the Italians to citizenship after the Social War, 89 B.C.

ipsam = Italiam.

ad Alpes promotam : though the Transpadani had been granted 'civitas' in 49 B.C., the province of Cisalpine Gaul was not formally abolished till 41 B.C., owing to the disturbances of the Civil War.

§ 3. quies : referring to the peace secured by Augustus.

tunc . . . cum does not refer to the actual year of the enfranchisement of the Transpadani, 49 B.C., which was immediately followed by civil war and disturbances of all sorts, but to the period, generally, when all Italy had become Roman.

specie, &c., 'under colour of providing settlements about the world for our legions (i. e. veterans), the failing strength of our empire was recruited by the admission of the finest of our provincials'. When colonies of veterans were planted, provincials were admitted into them and received 'civitas'. Such settlements naturally became valuable as outposts of Empire and recruiting grounds.

§ 4. **L. Cornelius Balbus** obtained citizenship from Pompeius, but afterwards joined Julius Caesar. His consulship in 40 B.C. was the first ever obtained by a foreigner. His nephew (of the same name) won a triumph for successes as proconsul in Africa, 19 B.C. He built a theatre in the Campus Martius near the river, dedicated 13 B.C.

nec minus insignes : natives of Gaul had been admitted into the senate by Julius Caesar (Suetonius, *Iul.* 80).

§ 5. **victos pro alienigenis arcebant,** 'excluded (from political privileges) as men of alien birth'. For this use of 'pro' cf. iv 38, 2 'pro sepulchris spernuntur' (said of temples built to personages who were deified after death and subsequently became unpopular).

arcebant: for the facts, cf. the treatment of the Messenians by the Spartans, and of their maritime allies by the Athenians.

§ 6. **nostri:** cf. xii 37, 4.

plerosque = 'permultos'. Romulus was said to have admitted the men of Antemnae and Crustumerium into the State, and to have shared his power with Tatius and the Sabines (Livy i 11 and 13).

§ 7. **advenae :** e. g. Numa, Tarquinius Priscus, and Servius Tullius.

libertinorum : the term denotes 'freedmen' as a class, 'libertus' being used of a freedman in relation to his late master, as 'libertus Pompeii'. Suetonius (*Cl.* 24) says that in the time of Appius Claudius, censor in 312 B.C., 'libertinus' meant 'son of a freedman', and that Claudius ignored that fact ; but the use of the word by other Roman authors does not bear out that view.

magistratus : Cn. Flavius, son of a freedman, obtained the curule aedileship owing to the influence of Appius Claudius in 304 B.C., and the son of a freedman was tribune in 100 B.C. (App. *B. C.* i 33).

repens : here = 'recens'. Cf. vi 7, 4.

priori: in the time of the Republic.

§ 8. **Senonibus :** the Gauls who captured Rome, 390 B.C.

Vulsci et Aequi : the chief enemies of Rome in the early days of the Republic, with whom Rome and the cities of the Latin League had to contend during the fifth and part of the sixth centuries B.C.

§ 9. **Tuscis :** alluding to the conquest of Rome by Porsena.

Samnitium iugum subiimus : after the disaster at the 'Caudine Forks', 321 B.C. (Livy ix 1-6).

breviore spatio: the completion of the conquest of Gaul by Julius Caesar in the period 58–50 B.C. suggests a contrast with the long resistance of Spain and the failure to subdue Germany; some of the Eastern conquests were much more quickly achieved.

continua ac fida pax: the rising of Iulius Florus in 21 A.D. (*Ann.* iii 40) is ignored.

§ 11. **plebeii**: the allusion is to the admission of plebeians to the magistracies which at first were monopolized by the patricians.

Latini: an instance is afforded by Ti. Coruncanius (a native of Tusculum), who was consul in 280 B.C.

[Magistracies would only be open to a few of the Latin towns whose citizens had the full rights of Roman citizens; not to those who possessed merely the 'Caerite franchise'.]

Italiae: i. e. after the Social War. Thus, Ventidius Bassus, a native of Picenum, taken prisoner in the Social War in his infancy, subsequently became consul and was awarded a triumph in 38 B.C.

25 **Chapter 25, § 1. primi**: it is not clear whether Tacitus means that the Aeduan chiefs were taken first among those admitted to the new privilege, or that the privilege was at first limited for a time to these ancient allies of Rome. Their admission into the senate was probably effected by the direct 'adlectio' of the princeps in his censorial capacity.

§ 2. **foederi**: the date of this treaty is unknown, but the Aedui are called 'socii' as early as 121 B.C. (Livy, *Epit.* lxi).

fraternitatis nomen: Caesar speaks of the Aedui as 'fratres consanguineosque saepenumero ab senatu appellatos' (Caes. *B. G.* i. 33, 2).

§ 3. **in numerum patriciorum adscivit.** When Julius Caesar and Augustus added to the patricians, they acted by special law (see below); Claudius, and after him Vespasian and Titus, confer patrician rank by virtue of their censorial powers. Such grants were made to individuals (e. g. L. Salvius Otho, father of the emperor, P. Plautius Pulcher, brother of the emperor's former wife Plautia Urgulanilla, and possibly C. Silius, were thus ennobled at this time). Anciently when addition was made to the 'patricii', the honour would be conferred on whole families, not merely on individuals, and would be effected by co-optation by the existing patrician 'curiae'.

vetustissimum quemque, 'senators of longest standing'.

quas Romulus, &c. According to Livy (i 8, 7) the 100 senators of Romulus were the founders of the original patriciate. Besides these the houses supposed to have come in with the Sabines under Tatius, or on the destruction of Alba, were still 'maiorum gentium'. Those styled 'minorum gentium' are represented by all authorities except Tacitus as the families derived from the 100 senators added by Tarquinius Priscus (Livy i 35, 6). Tacitus seems to have confused the tradition about Tarquin with that about Brutus, who is said (Livy ii 1, 10) to have made up the senate, weakened by the last king, to 300, by adding 'conscripti' from the 'primores equestris

60

gradus'. (This enrolment of new members into the senate must not be confused with admission of new members into the patriciate; these senatorial ' conscripti ' remained plebeians.)

lege Cassia : this law is nowhere else mentioned, but was doubtless the law by which Caesar in 45 B.C. admitted into the patriciate numerous ex-consuls and ex-magistrates of other grades (Dio xliii 47, 3). Among those then added to the patricians were the Octavii (Suet. *Aug.* 1).

lege Saenia : Augustus says in the *Monumentum Ancyranum* (ii 1) ' patriciorum numerum auxi consul quintum (29 B.C.) iussu populi et senatus '.

L. Saenius was ' consul suffectus ' towards the end of 30 B.C., and doubtless gave his name to the measure passed in the popular assembly enabling Augustus to add to the patricians.

§ 4. in rem publicam : equivalent to ' in publicum ', similarly associated with ' laetus ' in xii 8, 3.

' These measures, gratifying to the public, were undertaken with great pleasure on the part of the censor.'

§ 5. recens repertam : in 29 B.C. Augustus had induced fifty senators to resign their rank voluntarily, and had obliged 140 others to retire from the senate. This was to ' purify ' the order, after the indiscriminate additions made to it by Julius Caesar. Cf. also xii 52, 4.

quam : understand ' magis '. Intr. II 47.

peteret ius, &c. : senators could not resign their rank without the emperor's leave. Cf. i 75, 5, where a senator requested leave to · resign through poverty, and was presented with the sum of HS 1,000,000 by Tiberius to enable him to maintain his position.

§ 6. propositurum, ' he would publish '.

permixta : neut. plur., as agreeing with words of different gender; ' so that the avoidance of distinction between a sentence of the censors and the modesty of voluntary retirement might relieve their dishonour '.

§ 7. promiscum, ' given to others ', viz. to Cicero, Julius Caesar, and Augustus.

§ 8. condidit lustrum : the phrase technically denotes the closing of the ceremony of ' lustratio ' with the sacrifice of ' suovetaurilia ' (vi 37, 2).

censa sunt civium : the total, 5,984,072, comprises only the adult male citizens.

noscere . . . adactus : sc. ' est '; for the infin. cf. Intr. II 31.

nuptias incestas : with Agrippina his niece.

Chapter 26, § 1. facilitate, &c., ' through the easiness of her **26** adulteries passing to distaste for them '.

profluebat = ' prolabebatur ', ' began to sink '.

fatali vaecordia, ' blinded by destiny '.

an : unusual as introducing an alternative after ' sive '; it may indicate a preference for the second explanation.

urgebat : here alone used with acc. and infin.; Intr. II 31.

61

§ 2. **non eo ventum ut**, 'they were not in a position to

consilia: contrasted with 'audacia'. 'Innoxia' is predicative. 'To the innocent deliberate plans were safe, but for detected crime security must be sought from a bold stroke.'

§ 3. **caelibem**: he had divorced his wife, ch. 12, 2.

§ 4. **insidiis**: probably dative, 'unsuspicious of any plot'; cf. '(Seianus Tiberium) sibi uni incautum (effecit)'.

irae properum: cf. 'oblatae occasionis propera', xii 66, 2 and Intr. II 24.

§ 5. **amore**: causal abl. Intr. II 19.

ne, 'from fear lest'.

§ 6. **nomen matrimonii**, 'name of wife'.

cuius, &c., 'a pleasure which with the abandoned outlasts all others'.

prodigos: the adj. is found only here in this sense, ἄσωτος.

§ 7. **expectato**: see Intr. II 21.

Ostiam proficisceretur: Claudius had carried out great works at Ostia to improve the harbour. His visit on this occasion is said by Dio (lx 31, 4) to have been πρὸς ἐπίσκεψιν σίτου. The sacrifice mentioned by Tacitus may have been one for the safe arrival of corn from abroad.

27   Chapter 27, § 1. **securitatis**, 'recklessness'.

nedum, 'much more'. So xiii 20, 5 'cuicumque, nedum parenti, defensionem tribuendam'. This use, in an affirmative clause, seems to occur first in Livy (ix 18, 4).

consulem designatum: ch. 5, 3.

qui obsignarent, 'who were to sign the marriage contract'.

velut suscipiendorum liberorum causa: words to this effect would form an essential part of the marriage contract.

velut: used like ὡς with a participle, Intr. II 50, a.

auspicum verba: cf. 'missi auspices' (to the bride), xv 37, 9; 'veniet cum signatoribus auspex', Juvenal, *Sat.* x 336. The signing of the marriage contract, and the announcement by 'auspices' that the omens were favourable, would form part of the marriage ceremony held at the bride's house, before the 'deductio' to the bridegroom's home. Anciently nothing of any importance was done without taking auspices, but by this time the taking of auspices was ordinarily represented at the marriage ceremony by the repetition by some of the friends present of a formula pronouncing good luck.

subisse: the word seems to refer to some phrase used in the course of the marriage ceremony, perhaps that for entering the door of the husband's house; cf. '*subi* forem', Catullus lxi 168 (161).

discubitum: sc. 'ab ipsis', 'they took their places'.

oscula complexus: sc. 'fuisse'

§ 2. **senioribus**: dat. of agent. Intr. II 10.

The description of Messalina's marriage with Silius should be compared with Juvenal, *Sat.* x 329 and foll.

Chapter 28, § 1. quos, &c. = the chief freedmen, named in the **28** following chapter.

si res verterentur, 'if a revolution ensued '.

histrio = Mnester, ch. 4, 2 ; 36, 1.

excidium: sc. 'principis'.

dignitate formae, vi mentis: brachylogical ablatives of quality. Intr. II 18.

consulatu: ch. 5, 3.

adcingi, 'was arming himself'.

§ 3. facilitas, 'pliability'.

sed in eo, &c., 'the crisis turned on the chance whether she would get a hearing, and on the necessity of closing his ears even against a confession'. 'Si' and 'ut' carry on the force of 'in eo', and the expression is greatly compressed; 'utque'='et quod efficiendum esset ut'.

Chapter 29, § 1. ac primo . . . § 2. dein: these particles mark **29** the change of purpose on the part of the three powerful freedmen when they came to take definite steps to carry out their resolution, stated in the last chapter, to attack Messalina.

Callistus: his full name was C. Iulius Claudius Callistus, showing that he took names from both his patrons, the Emperor Gaius as well as Claudius. His department under Claudius was 'a libellis'; that is, he dealt with petitions addressed to the emperor.

mihi narratus: in a portion of the lost books, where his complicity in the assassination of Gaius was no doubt described.

For 'mihi' see Intr. II 10, and for the use of 'circa' Intr. II 46.

Appianae caedis: the murder of Appius Iunius Silanus, consul in 28 B.C., who had become second husband of Messalina's mother, Domitia Lepida, in 42 A.D., and lost his life through a plot concocted with Narcissus by Messalina in her anger at Appius' rejection of her advances.

Narcissus: the emperor's secretary ('ab epistulis'). On Nero's accession, he fell a victim to Agrippina's resentment (xiii 1, 4), in consequence of his opposition to her on various occasions ; e.g. xii 57, 4 ; 65, 2.

Pallas: a freedman of Antonia (mother of Claudius), whose brother Felix was the governor of Judaea mentioned in the Acts. He was Claudius' treasurer ('a rationibus'). He is said to have been poisoned by Nero for the sake of his wealth, in 62 A.D. (xiv 65).

flagrantissima . . . gratia, 'who at that time was at the height of his pernicious influence'; abl. of description.

dissimulantes, 'concealing their knowledge of all else', i.e. the conspiracy (ch. 26, 2).

§ 2. ultro: i.e. fearing that they would not only fail, but themselves incur destruction.

prioris regiae=the court of Gaius.

63

haberi: dependent on 'peritus', applying to the second clause, by zeugma, in the sense of 'expertus'.

perstitit, solum id immutans: i.e. Narcissus adhered to the original determination to proceed against Messalina, rejecting the method, suggested in § 1, of turning her from her adultery by a protest addressed privately to herself.

§ 3. **longa mora**: abl. abs.

paelices, 'concubines'.

perpulit ... subire: Intr. II 31.

30   Chapter 30, § 1. **secretum**, 'private interview'.

genibus provoluta: for the more usual 'ad genua'. So also xii 18, 3.

§ 2. **cieri postulat**: Intr. II 31.

§ 3. **quod**, &c., 'for having concealed from him his knowledge of the adulteries of such men as Vettius and Plautius' (see ch. 31, 6; 36, 5). The circumstances had probably been made familiar to his readers by Tacitus in the lost portion of the *Annals*.

nedum: the subject of 'reposceret' is Claudius, and the sentence is bitterly ironical, 'still less must the emperor think of demanding back his establishment, his slaves, and the other accompaniments of imperial rank'.

§ 4. **tabulas nuptialis**: the tablets on which the marriage contract was inscribed.

§ 5. **discidium tuum**, 'her repudiation of her marriage with you'.

31   Chapter 31, § 1. **potissimum quemque**: so 'potissimos amicorum', xiii 18, 1.

Turranium: he is mentioned as 'praefectus annonae' at the beginning of Tiberius' reign, 14 A.D. (i 7, 3), thirty-four years previously. [The charge of the corn supply was one of the great 'praefecturae' open to a Roman knight in the emperor's service.]

Lusius Geta: criticized unfavourably in ch. 33, 1; later on Agrippina was able to remove him and his colleague Rufrius Crispinus from their command, and appoint Burrus in their stead, 51 A.D., xii 42.

§ 2. **castra**: the praetorian camp, into which the 'cohortes' forming the emperor's bodyguard had been concentrated by Seianus in 23 A.D. (iv 2, 1). The camp was outside the 'agger Servii' between the Viminal and Colline gates.

§ 3. **offusum**, 'overpowered'. ('Offunditur luce solis lumen lucernae', Cic. *Fin.* iii 14, 45.)

privatus, 'a subject'.

§ 4. **non alias**, &c., 'more wildly profligate than ever'.

adulto = ἀκμάζοντος.

The usual period of the vintage was marked by an opening sacrifice on the 19th Aug., and the 'vindemialis feria', lasting from Aug. 22 to Oct. 15.

simulacrum, 'a representation of a vintage festival'.

domum: that of Silius.

§ 5. **lacus,** 'the vats', into which the juice of the grapes was received.

pellibus, 'fawnskins'. The νεβρίς was a characteristic feature in the garb of a Bacchante.

fluxo = 'fluitante'.

hedera vinctus: probably in assumption of the character of Bacchus.

§ 6. **Vettius Valens:** mentioned by Pliny as a famous physician and a favourite of Messalina (*N. H.* xxix 1, 4, 8).

lascivia, 'in his gaiety'.

sive, &c., 'whether the signs of storm had really arisen, or a chance utterance of his was taken as prophetic'.

Chapter 32, § 1. **gnara** = 'nota'. See Intr. II 51.　　　**32**

§ 2. **Lucullianos in hortos:** cf. ch. 1, 1.

metu: probably dative (of purpose); Intr. II 11.

§ 4. **quamquam,** &c., 'although the imminence of peril deprived her of time for deliberation'. For the mood, cf. Intr. II 40.

intendit, 'made up her mind to'. For this, and 'oravit' (§ 5), with infin., cf. Intr. II 31.

misit, 'sent orders'.

§ 5. **vetustissimam:** she was the chief of the Vestal Virgins, the lady abbess of the order, 'virgo vestalis maxima'. The intercession of a Vestal Virgin for a criminal might not be disregarded.

aures adire, 'to obtain audience'.

§ 6. **id … solitudinis** = 'tanta solitudo'.

spatium urbis, 'the whole breadth of the city'; from the gardens on the Pincian Hill to the gate where the 'via Ostiensis' left the city.

praevalebat, 'had more weight in their minds'.

Chapter 33, § 1. **a Caesare:** possibly = 'on Caesar's side', re-　**33** ferring not merely to the emperor's feelings but to those of his supporters; cf. 'ab Romanis', iv 25, 3. This interpretation makes the plural 'fidebant' natural.

levi, 'unstable', 'unreliable'.

ad, 'in respect to', so often; see Intr. II 46.

iuxta, 'alike': so in xii 10, 1.

§ 2. **adsumptis quibus:** Intr. II 21, c.

ius militum, 'the control of the soldiers'; so 'iura libertorum', *Hist.* ii 92, 5.

§ 3. **L. Vitellius:** see xi 2, 4.

C. Largus Caecina was consul with Claudius in 42 A.D., remaining the whole year in office. He owned the house which had once belonged to the orator Crassus. [Dio and Pliny.]

gestamine: used elsewhere by Tacitus with a defining genitive, as 'lecticae' or 'sellae'. Here, a carriage capable of holding four persons must be meant. 'Gestari' and 'gestatio' are used of taking a drive in a carriage, as well as of other modes of conveyance.

34   Chapter 34, § 2. instabat, &c., 'was pressing him to explain his ambiguity, and permit them to know his real meaning'. For the construction cf. 'hortantur (me) uti', xi 24, 1 and Intr. II 31.

non ideo, 'for all that, he did not', &c.

non pervicit quin: an unusual phrase; but Livy has 'nec . . . valuit quin', iv 44, 2.

suspensa, &c., 'hesitating expressions, capable of bearing whatever meaning was assigned to them'; cf. 'in crimen duci', 'to be distorted into a ground of accusation', vi 5, 2.

§ 3. cum obstrepere: for historic infin. after a conjunction see Intr. II 34.

§ 4. communes liberi: Octavia and Britannicus, as contrasted with Antonia, Claudius' daughter by Paetina, xii 2, 1.

offerebantur, nisi iussisset: Intr. II 38.

§ 5. invidia, 'reproachful language'; cf. xv 19, 2 'magna cum invidia senatum adeunt'.

35   Chapter 35, § 1. ignaro propior, 'resembled one unconscious'.

§ 2. patris: cf. ch. 12. His trial for 'maiestas', and condemnation, is recounted in iv 18-20, but nothing is there said of any decree ordering the destruction of his statues.

Statues of condemned ancestors were usually not shown in funeral processions, but it was a measure of rather unusual severity to prohibit their possession within doors.

quidquid, &c., 'how all the heirlooms of the Nerones and Drusi had gone to swell the reward of infamy'. Cf. 'in pretium belli cessurae', *Hist.* i 11, 4. The names of Nero and Drusus are thus coupled to denote the union, in the reigning house, of the families of the Claudii Nerones and the Livii Drusi; see v 1, 1.

§ 3. praemonente Narcisso, 'after a preliminary admonition from Narcissus', addressed to the soldiers. Cf. xii 69, 1 'monente praefecto'. For the tense cf. Intr. II 42.

etsi: to be taken closely with 'iustum', like 'quamvis'. 'Nam' explains 'pauca'.

§ 4. tribunali: the seat of judgment, one of the features of the officers' quarters ('principia') in the camp.

§ 5. inlustres equites: see vi 18, 4; xi 4, 1.

§ 6. The names cited in this section are perhaps those of the 'equites' just mentioned, although Proculus could not have been said to show the same 'constantia' as Silius. Vettius Valens is mentioned in ch. 30, and a 'Helvius' (not 'Saufeius') Trogus in Seneca, *Lud.* xiii 4; otherwise these persons are unknown.

custodem: husband and wife sometimes assigned a 'custos' to each other, to ensure fidelity. 'Custodes das, Polla, viro, non accipis ipsa', Mart. x 69, 1. 'Quis custodiat ipsos custodes'? Juv. vi 347.

indicium offerentem: he hoped by this means to secure his own acquittal. Cf. vi 3, 5.

iubet: supply 'Claudius' as subject.

§ 7. **vigilum praefectus.** The command of the 'vigiles' was an important equestrian office; cf. vi 18, 4; xi 4, 1.

ludi procurator, 'superintendent of a school of gladiators'. An imperial institution for the training and supply of gladiators existed as early as in the time of Gaius (Pliny, *N. H.* xi 37, 54, 144). Its procurators were of equestrian rank.

Iuncus Vergilianus, perhaps the same as the person called 'Iunius praetorius', mentioned in the list of victims by Seneca (*Lud.* xiii 4).

Chapter 36, § 1. Mnester: see ch. 4, 2.   36
verberum: stripes, for resisting Messalina's will.

vocis, &c.: Dio states (lx 22, 5) that Messalina procured from Claudius a general injunction that Mnester was 'to obey her in all things'.

obnoxium = 'under the dominion of', 'liable to'.

§ 2. **largitione . . . magnitudine:** causal ablatives.

§ 4. **ultro:** by Messalina, without any advances on his part.

paribus, &c., 'her disgust being as capricious as her desire'.

§ 5. **Suillius Caesoninus** was a son of the Suillius of ch. 2. His cognomen seems to be taken from the wife of Gaius, Caesonia, who was his father's half-sister.

Plautius Lateranus was nephew of A. Plautius Silvanus, the commander of the great invasion of Britain. Intr. p. lxi. His restoration to the senate by Nero, in 55 A.D., is mentioned in xiii 11, 2, and his participation in Piso's conspiracy, and consequent death, in 65 A.D., in xv 49, 2 and 60, 1.

tamquam = ὡς. See Intr. II 50.

Chapter 37, § 1. Lucullianis in hortis: ch. 1, 1. She had   37
gone thither after her interview with Claudius, ch. 34, 3.

componere preces, 'draws up a petition'.

non nulla spe, &c.: Intr. II 22.

ni properavisset, verterat: for the moods cf. Intr. II 38. For the intransitive use of 'verterat' cf. ch. 31, 6.

§ 2. **tempestivis,** 'beginning early'. In the Augustan age, to dine 'de die', before sunset, was luxurious; Hor. *Od.* i 1, 20. Martial (iv 8, 6) mentions the 'hora nona' as the proper time in his day. In xiv 2, 1 Nero is mentioned as feasting 'medio diei'.

§ 3. **languescere . . . redire:** historic infin., with 'ubi'; Intr. II 34. The variation of construction after 'ubi' should be noticed.

denuntiat, 'commands'; so 'nuntiat patri abicere spem', xvi 11, 1. The officers mentioned here would be those on duty at the emperor's palace; cf. xii 69, 1.

§ 4. **exactor:** sc. 'supplicii'.

e libertis: sc. 'Caesaris'.

praegressus, 'going on before them'.

Lepida: Domitia Lepida, daughter of L. Domitius and the elder Antonia. See also xii 64, 4 and foll.

38   **haud concors:** Messalina had caused the death of her second
husband, Appius Silanus ; ch. 29, 1.
    § 5. **ducebantur,** ' were being prolonged '.
    per silentium : Intr. II 46.
    Chapter 38, § 1. introspexit, 'looked in the face'.
    transigitur: cf. 'gladio eum transigit', ii 68, 1.
    § 2. **non distincto :** Intr. II 21, a.
    nec ille quaesivit: cf. a similar case of such indifference in
ch. 2. 5.
    solita convivio, 'what was customary at a banquet'; ' convivio '
seems to be ablative.   So 'proelio solita', xii 56, 2.   Intr. II 15.
    § 3. **filios,** 'his son and daughter'.   So ' fratrum ' = ' brother and
sister ', xii 4, 2 ; ' soceros ' = ' parents-in-law ', Verg. *Aen.* ii 457.
    § 4. **nomen :** her name was to be erased from public inscrip-
tions.   Similar measures were taken against Livia (Tiberius' niece),
vi 2, 1.
    § 5. **quaestoria insignia :** it was an innovation to give such a
distinction to a freedman.
    honesta quidem, &c. : this concluding sentence is corrupt, and
may best be regarded as the note of a reader, introduced by a
copyist into the text.   ' Honesta ' refers generally to the punishment of Messalina and her accomplices, and ' deterrima ' to Claudius'
subsequent marriage with Agrippina and its evil consequences.
' Tristitiis multis ' may be part of the ' epigraph '; running ' tristitiis
multis Cornelii Taciti Liber Undecimus explicit.   Incipit xii '.

BOOK XII

1   **Chapter 1, § 1. convulsa,** 'was upset', 'shaken to its foundations '.   So vi 40, 3.   The freedmen, who had hitherto held
together, were now divided.
    apud = 'inter'.   Cf. Intr. II 46.   So iii 39, 2 'dissensione orta
apud obsidentis '.
    caelibis vitae intoleranti. He had contracted three marriages,
besides two betrothals in early life.   Intr. p. xlvii.
    obnoxio : as in xi 36, 1.
    § 2. **nec,** &c., ' among the women, too, broke out an equally fierce
rivalry '.
    contendere, 'brought into comparison' (with those of others).
So, ' vetera et praesentia contendere ', xiii 3, 3.
    ac digna, &c., ' urged their claims to so grand a match '.
    § 3. **Lollia Paulina :** she was granddaughter of M. Lollius,
famous in the time of Augustus.   He was the first governor of
Galatia, in 25 B.C. ; consul in 21 B.C. ; legatus in Germany in 16 B.C.

He was an enemy of Tiberius and intrigued against him, encouraging Gaius Caesar in opposition when Tiberius was under a cloud. Pliny and Velleius describe him unfavourably ; Horace eulogizes him, *Od.* iv 9, 34-44. He committed suicide on losing Gaius' favour. For Lollia's subsequent history see ch. 22.

M. Lollii consularis : sc. ' filiam ', a rare ellipsis. The younger Lollius is not known to have ever been consul, hence Madvig's suggestion that ' M. Lollio filio ', constructed with ' genitam ', has dropped out from before ' M. Lollii '.

Agrippina : see note on ch. 2, 3.

Aelia Paetina had already been married to Claudius, and had been divorced, after the birth of a daughter, Antonia (ch. 2, 1).

Tuberonum : the most famous of these was the jurist Q. Aelius Tubero, possibly her grandfather.

Narcisso : dat. Cf. Intr. II 10.

§ 4. **promptus :** inclined to favour. Cf. iv 60, 5 ' mater Agrippina promptior Neroni erat '. [This Nero was son of Germanicus, not the emperor.]

Chapter 2, § 1. **communem :** cf. ' communes liberi ', xi 34, 4. **2**
' Filiam ' is corrected for ' familiam ' of Med.

nihil . . . novum, ' the absence of any change ' ; cf. iii 9, 3 ' celebritate loci nihil occultum ' and Intr. II 2.

proxima suis : next to her own, in affection.

pignora, ' pledges of affection ', a word common in Augustan poets, and adopted by Tacitus to express children, or near relatives ; cf. xv 17, 3 and *Germ.* vii 4.

§ 2. **improbatam,** ' disqualified '.

privignis : cf. note on ' filios ', xi 38, 3.

§ 3. **Germanici nepotem :** young L. Domitius (Nero).

dignum, &c., ' fully worthy of imperial position ' ; Pallas does not mean to recommend him as successor to Claudius, but as worthy to be an adopted member of his family.

stirpem, &c., ' let him unite to himself a noble race, the posterity of the Julii and the Claudii '.

' Et . . . posteros ' is explanatory of ' stirpem nobilem ', and refers to the lineage of Agrippina and her son. She was of the Julian house, on her mother's side, and of the Claudian house, on her father's side. See Genealogical Tree, Intr. p. lxv.

[The reading of Med., ' et familiae Claudiae quae posteros coniungeret ', might perhaps mean, ' Her offspring (viz. Nero) was a noble one, and (a scion) of the house of Claudius, and would be a bond uniting their (Claudius' and Agrippina's possible) issue ' ; i.e. Nero would remain in Claudius' family, and be merely one of his possible new children ; he would help to keep the imperial family together, by being adopted by the emperor instead of remaining outside. The argument is of course far-fetched and unnatural.—H. P.]

expertae, ' proved '.

integra iuventa. She was about thirty-three years old.

claritudinem Caesarum, ' the illustrious name of the Caesars '.

3   **Chapter 3, § 1. per speciem necessitudinis,** 'on the plea of her relationship', as his niece.

§ 2. Cn. Domitius Ahenobarbus, first husband of Agrippina, consul 32 A. D., see vi I, I.

Octavia: Claudius' daughter by Messalina.

L. Silanus: great-great-grandson of Augustus. His mother, Aemilia Lepida, was daughter of L. Aemilius Paulus and Julia the granddaughter of Augustus; see Genealogical Tree, Intr. p. lxv. From a Greek inscription we learn that he had filled the offices of 'praefectus urbi ob ferias Latinas', 'triumvir monetalis', and 'quaestor Caesaris'. From Dio we learn that he was given the privilege of holding magistracies five years before the legal age, and that he became praetor πολὺ πρὸ τοῦ καθήκοντος χρόνου [lx 31, 7]. He was not more than twenty-five years old at the time of his death.

desponderat Octaviam. This betrothal was apparently arranged in the first year of Claudius' rule [Dio lx 5, 7], when Octavia was a mere infant. She was twenty at the date of her death, 62 A. D., xiv 64, I.

et alia clarum = τά τ' ἄλλα λαμπρόν. Cf. Intr. II 4.

insigni triumphalium: cf. xi 20, 3. The occasion on which he received this honour was probably the British triumph of Claudius in 44 A. D., when he was only nineteen or twenty years old, and had filled no magistracy. This was a great departure from ancient practice.

gladiatorii muneris: a show given by Silanus as praetor, at the cost of Claudius [Dio lx 31, 7].

protulerat, 'had put forward', 'recommended'.

§ 3. nihil arduum, &c., 'no change seemed too hard to bring about in the inclination of a prince', &c.

iudicium: favourable opinion. So Cic. *ad Fam.* xiii 46 'patroni iudicio ornatus'.

erat . . . indita: Intr. p. xlvi.

4   **Chapter 4, § 1. nomine censoris:** cf. xi 13, 1.

fallacias, 'falsehoods'. **serviles:** cf. vi 32, 7; xi 34, 1.

provisor: here in the unusual sense of 'one who foresees'; in Hor. *A. P.* 164 = 'a provider'.

ferre = 'proferre'. So vi 49, 3.

sane: to be taken with 'decora' and 'procax' concessively, as showing colour for the charge. 'Procax' = 'merry', 'lively'; here not in a bad sense.

Vitellii nurus: as wife, probably, of L. Vitellius, brother of the future emperor.

§ 2. hinc: i. e., he took up the charge of incest as a matter affecting his son's household, and grounded on information coming from this source.

fratrum, 'brother and sister'; cf. xi 38, 3.

traxit, &c., 'put a foul construction on the innocent but unconcealed affection existing between brother and sister'.

§ 3. **accipiendis**: dat. with 'promptior'; so 'faciendis sceleribus promptus', xv 67, 5.

§ 4. **per edictum**: the censorial power of expelling senators was usually exercised at this time by the princeps, or by the senate in its judicial capacity. For other acts of the censorship in which Claudius and Vitellius were colleagues see xi 13, 1 ; 23, 1 ; 25, 3.

lustroque condito: this ceremony should properly have marked the expiration of the powers of the existing censors.

§ 5. **adfinitatem**: his espousal to Octavia.

eiurare = 'iurando abdicare'. The magistrate, on laying down his office, swore 'se nihil contra leges fecisse' (Plin. *Pan.* 65).

reliquus praeturae dies: he was forced to resign on Dec. 29 (Suet. *Cl.* 29).

Eprius Marcellus, the famous 'delator' of Nero's times. He is mentioned again in xiii 33, 4 as escaping, by corrupt influence, a charge of extortion brought against him after his government of Lycia (58 A.D.) ; and in xvi 22 and foll. he figures as one of the accusers of Thrasea (66 A.D.). He was also three years proconsul of Asia (70-3 A.D.). He conspired against Vespasian, and was forced to suicide in 79 A.D.

Chapter 5, § 1. C. Pompeius: possibly the grandson of the 5 Pompeius who was consul at the beginning of Tiberius' reign (i 7, 3).

Veranius is also mentioned in xiv 29, 1 as successor to A. Didius in the government of Britain. It appears from *Agr.* 14, 3 that he died in the first year of his command in Britain (58 A. D.).

firmabatur, 'was cemented'.

fama: i.e. it was so talked of that it was difficult to draw back from it.

nullo exemplo: for the abl. cf. Intr. II 22.

deductae in domum: a regular phrase for marriage ; so also in xiv 63, 4.

§ 2. **quin et**, &c., 'to be sure it was an unhallowed union, and if that consideration was disregarded, disastrous results to the State were to be feared'.

With 'incestum' supply 'esse' ; as subject of 'sperneretur' understand 'metus incesti'.

id refers back to 'celebrare sollemnia'.

§ 3. **consensui imparem**, 'ready to bow to the general will'.

§ 4. **summamque**, &c., 'protesting that the highest interests of the State were involved'.

§ 5. **censoriae**, 'worthy of a censor', as we speak of 'a judicial mind'.

levamentum: the relaxation of a wifes society. 'What finer solace could there be for a censor's cares than to take a wife, &c.'

luxui, 'debauchery'.

prosperis dubiisque: abl. abs.

6 Chapter 6, § 1. **postquam**, &c., 'after he had introduced the subject in these attractive terms'.

deligi : the report of Vitellius' speech is continued, without any verb of speaking being expressed.

sanctimonia, 'purity'. The word is applied to a Vestal Virgin, ii 86, 1.

§ 2. **anquirendum** : here alone used with the construction of 'dubitare'. Intr. II 51.

congruere artes honestas, 'her virtues corresponded', to her nobility of race.

§ 3. **vidua** : since the death of Domitius she had married the orator Crispus Passienus (see vi 20, 2), whom she was supposed to have poisoned (Schol. on Juv. iv 81).

sua tantum, &c., 'who had been true to his own consorts'; the contrast implied is with the adulteries of Gaius, and perhaps of Tiberius (vi 1).

audivisse : refers to the abduction of Livia from Nero by Augustus (v 1, 3).

vidisse : Gaius' abduction of Drusilla, Livia Orestilla, and Lollia Paulina from their respective husbands. [Suet. *Cal.* 24, 25.]

§ 4. **documentum**, 'an example'. 'Let a precedent be instituted for the bestowal of a wife on the emperor.'

§ 5. **at enim** : anticipating an objection.

in : Intr. II 46.

sollemnia, 'regular'. Such were the marriages of the Spartan kings, Anaxandrides and Leonidas, Hdt. v 39 ; vii 239.

sobrinarum, 'second cousins'. The word is probably here used, loosely, for 'cousins' generally. First cousins, 'consobrini', might not marry till after the enactment of a plebiscitum, passed at some date before 171 B.C., when such a marriage is referred to by Livy xliii 34, 3.

morem, &c., 'custom was adapted as was expedient, and this (viz. marriage of uncle and niece) would also become one of the things usual in the near future'.

7 Chapter 7, § 3. **nec ultra expectato** : a similar phrase occurs in xi 26, 7. See Intr. II 21.

apud = in ; see Intr. II 46.

decretum : such decrees were now the usual orm of legislative enactments, the functions of the 'comitia' having been reduced to a few acts of a merely formal character, such as the ratification of elections.

inter patruos fratrumque filias. This enactment did not permit marriage with a sister's daughter (so Gaius i 62), and it was abolished by Constantine and Constans.

§ 4. **cupitor** : unusual, but also occurring in xv 42, 4. Cf. also 'provisor', xii 4, 1 and Intr. II 51.

Alledius Severus : probably the 'primipilaris' mentioned by Suet. (*Cl.* 26) at whose marriage Claudius and Agrippina were present.

gratia : i.e. the desire to secure her favour; cf. Intr. II 61.

72

non per lasciviam, &c., 'who played with the interests of Rome, though not for immoral purposes, as did Messalina'.

ut Messalina: sc. 'inludebat'.

inludenti: for 'inludere' = treat casually, without respect, cf. inludo chartis, 'I spoil paper' (by scribbling on it), Hor. *Sat.* i 4, 139.

§ 6. **adductum,** &c., 'hers was a strict, almost masculine, despotism'. 'Adducere' = to draw tight, of reins, in contrast with 'remittere' = slacken. Cf. 'adductius regnari', *Germ.* 44, 1.

nisi dominationi expediret, 'except to secure her supremacy'. She was alleged to have purchased Pallas' support by adultery with him (ch. 25, 1).

§ 7. **obtentum habebat quasi,** 'was defended by the pretext that—'. For 'quasi' see Intr. II 50.

regno: the word is also used as the object of Seianus' ambition, iv 1, 4.

Chapter 8, § 1. die nuptiarum: very early in the year 49 A.D. **8**

Silanus: see ch. 3, 2 and foll. His suicide is described by Suetonius as compulsory.

§ 2. **Calvina:** see ch. 4, 1. She was allowed to return ten years later (xiv 12, 5).

Tulli regis: Tullus Hostilius prescribed expiatory sacrifices to be paid by Horatius for the murder of his sister (Livy i 26, 13). These sacrifices are prescribed here by Claudius, as 'pontifex maximus', for the alleged incest (ch. 4, 4).

lucum Dianae: probably that near Aricia (mod. Nemi), where the priest was an escaped slave who won the office by slaying his predecessor (Verg. *Aen.* vii 764).

§ 3. **veniam,** 'remission'. This was probably effected by a decree of the senate (Suet. *Cl.* 12). Seneca, son of a famous rhetorician from Spain, had attained the quaestorship, and by the time of Gaius was a leading senatorial pleader. Messalina procured his relegation to Corsica, in the first year of Claudius' reign, on a charge of adultery with Julia, daughter of Germanicus.

in publicum: cf. xi 25, 7.

studiorum, 'literary works'.

uterentur: the plural refers to Agrippina and her party. So also 'inducunt', ch. 9, 1.

iniuriae: the word implies that the charge on which he was banished was unfounded, though Suillius, his enemy, assumes its justice, xiii 42, 3.

Chapter 9, § 1. designatum consulem: an inscription shows **9** that his full name was L. Mammius Pollio, and that he was consul with Q. Allius Maximus in May, 49 A.D. He was probably designated in March. His 'sententia' was probably pronounced 'per egressionem', i.e. going beyond the limits of the question put to him by the presiding magistrate. He would be asked his opinion first, as consul designate.

inducunt ... oraretur: for the infin. following each of these verbs see Intr. II 31.

aetati utriusque: Nero was now twelve, Octavia seven.

§ 2. **priorem necessitudinem**: he was already stepson and great-nephew of Claudius.

studiis matris, 'thanks to his mother's intrigues'.

quis: dative; see Intr. II 10.

ex filio: Britannicus.

10   Chapter 10, § 1. **ut rettuli**: the narrative is taken up from xi 10, 8. The embassy is there stated to have been sent to the emperor, and this chapter and 11, 1 show that it was received by him in presence of the senate.

foederis: the treaty already made with Augustus in 20 B.C. (Intr. p. lvii) had been renewed with Tiberius through Germanicus, 18 A.D., and again with Gaius through L. Vitellius.

defectione: causal; see Intr. II 19.

iuxta: so in xi 33, 1.

§ 2. **longius sitos**, 'more distant relatives'.

adici, 'were added to his victims'.

§ 3. **publice**, 'nationally'.

virium aemulis, 'our rivals in power'.

11   Chapter 11, § 1. **dissertavere**: Intr. II 51, d.

de fastigio, &c., 'the supremacy of Rome and the homage paid by Parthia'; a reply to the Parthians' claims in ch. 10, 3 end.

obsequiis: referring especially to the restoration of the Roman standards by Phraates in 20 B.C.

petitum . . . regem: Vonones; Intr. p. lix.

Tiberius had sent Phraates, and, after his death, Tiridates (vi 32).

miserat: for a similar omission of object cf. xi 14, 4.

§ 2. **ut . . . cogitaret**, 'to think of himself as a governor among freemen, not as a despot over slaves'; cf. 'tamquam . . . Catonem cogitasset' (*Dial.* 2, 1).

quanto ignota: Intr. II 47, b.

laetiora: an emendation for Med. 'toleratiora'. For 'laetus' in this sense cf. ch. 8, 3.

§ 3. **ad id** = 'ad id temporis'.

ac tamen: even if his character was not perfect, they should obey him as monarch.

§ 4. **Caius Cassius**: for his parentage see vi 15, 3. He became proconsul of Asia in 40 A.D., and succeeded Vibius Marsus as governor of Syria not later than 45 A.D., and was succeeded by Ummidius Quadratus some time before 51 A.D. (ch. 45, 6). He was exiled by Nero in 65 A.D. (xvi 9) on a charge of disloyalty.

deducere: cf. vi 12, 4 and Intr. II 31.

12   Chapter 12, § 1. **ceteros praeminebat**: the accusative after this verb, and after 'praesidere' ch. 14, 7, was also used by Sallust, and is common in Tacitus.

industriosque, &c., 'and peace obscures the difference between the energetic and the unwarlike'. 'Industria', 'ignavia' are often used by Tacitus for soldierly qualities and their reverse, ch. 27, 4.

§ 2. **provisu**: used in ch. 6, 3.

ingrueret: the use of a personal subject with this verb is a reminiscence of Vergil's 'ingruit Aeneas', *Aen.* xii 628. Intr. II 68.

celebrata: C. Cassius, the subsequent conspirator, successfully defended the province of Syria, where he was quaestor, from Parthian invasion, after Crassus' defeat and death.

§ 3. **excitis quorum:** Intr. II 21.

Zeugma. This place, named originally from the bridge made by Alexander, was connected by a bridge with Apameia by Seleucus Nicator, the founder of both towns.

rexque Arabum Acbarus. The 'Arabs' here mentioned were the tribe inhabiting the district of Upper Mesopotamia, opposite to Commagene, and known afterwards as Osrhoene. Its capital was Edessa. 'Acbarus' is a name borne by each reigning prince of this tribe (like the title 'Pharaoh' borne by the kings of Egypt). The correct form of the name, written Ἄκβαρος in Appian, Αὔγαρος in Dio, is shown in coins and inscriptions to be 'Abgarus'.

impetus acres, 'active devotion'.

§ 4. **quod, &c.,** 'this advice was disregarded, thanks to the treachery of Acbarus'.

ignarum, 'unconscious' of Acbarus' treachery. ('In his simplicity.')

summam fortunam, 'royalty'.

luxu, 'sensual indulgence'; so in ch. 5, 5.

apud: Intr. II 46.

Edessa was about forty miles from Zeugma, founded originally in the early times of the Syro-Macedonian dynasty, and at one time known as Antiochia.

§ 5. **Carenes** was evidently governor of Mesopotamia, and is spoken of here as though known to the reader (presumably from mention in the lost portion of the *Annals*).

comminus, 'by a direct route'. **flexu,** 'by a detour'.

importunam, 'unfavourable'; so in ch. 33, 2.

Chapter 13, § 1. Exim. The ensuing narrative seems to **13** belong to the following year (50 A.D.). The mountains are those at the south of Armenia, viz. the ranges of Taurus and Masius.

campos propinquabant. Elsewhere Tacitus uses dative with 'propinquare'. The verb is not found in earlier prose authors, except Sallust, who uses accusative with it.

Adiabene is properly the northern part of Assyria, which lies between the Tigris and the Lycus (Greater Zab), and the mountains of Kurdistan. The name is sometimes used, loosely, for the whole of Assyria; and the district, as containing Ninus, may be regarded as the cradle of Assyria.

Izates: mentioned in Josephus (*Ant.* xx 2–4); he was son of Monobazus and Helena, and became a Jewish proselyte. He had helped Artabanus to recover his throne, but was at variance with his successors.

75

palam induerat, &c., 'made public profession of alliance with Meherdates, but had a secret understanding binding him to the support of Gotarzes'.

§ 2. **Ninos.** This passage attests the existence, at this time, of an inhabited town upon the site of Nineveh, though references to it in other authors (Pliny, Strabo, and Lucian) seem to imply that it had wholly perished.

postremo . . . proelio: the battle known as that of 'Arbela', 331 B.C., though it took place many miles from that town.

castellum. A fort was probably built by one of the Macedonian kings on the site of the battle.

§ 3. **Sanbulos.** The name seems to be preserved in the modern 'Sunbulah', a considerable offshoot of Mt. Zagros (between the plains of Ghilan and Deira).

praecipua religione Herculis, 'the especial worship being that of Hercules'. For the abl. cf. Intr. II 22. The deity in question was probably the Assyrian god Ninip or Nin, worshipped as giving the king success in hunting and in war, and identified by the Greeks with 'Heracles', as resembling him in many attributes.

tempore stato, 'at regular intervals'.

per quietem, 'during their sleep'.

14 **Chapter 14, § 1. Corma:** an unknown river, perhaps the 'Kara-su', or river of Kermanschat.

The campaign must have taken place in 'Chalonitis', between Mt. Zagros and the Tigris.

per insectationes et nuntios, 'by insulting messages'. Intr. II 54.

emercari, 'bought over'; cf. ch. 45, 1.

§ 2. **Adiabeno:** sc. 'cum exercitu'.

levitate gentili, 'with the treachery characteristic of their race'.

For 'gentilis'= 'gentis suae' cf. ch. 17, 3; xi 1, 2.

§ 3. **rem in casum dare,** &c., 'to face the risk and try the fortune of war'.

§ 4. **ferox,** 'confident, emboldened'.

§ 5. **paterni clientis,** 'a vassal of his father'.

§ 6. **non propinquum,** &c., '(treating) him not as a kinsman, but upbraiding him as of alien birth'. Intr. II 60.

ostentui . . . dehonestamento: Intr. II 12. The mutilation would deprive Meherdates of his chance of the crown.

§ 7. **dein,** &c. Evidence from coins points to the death of Gotarzes about 51 A.D., and to the succession of Vologeses late in that year after his father had reigned little more than two months. The account of Vologeses' relations with Rome is resumed in ch. 44.

Medos tum praesidens: cf. ch. 12, 1.

15 **Chapter 15, § 1. Mithridates Bosporanus:** so named to distinguish him from the king of Armenia (xi 8, 1).

Tacitus is here, no doubt, resuming the account of events in this part of the world given by him in the lost portion of the *Annals*. This Mithridates is stated by Dio to have been a descendant of the great Mithridates, and to have received his kingdom from Claudius (41 A. D.) in succession to Polemo, who was transferred to Cilicia. Subsequently Claudius deposed him, and set up his brother Cotys in his stead (46 A. D.); cf. ch. 18, 1.

This kingdom, having Panticapaeum for its capital, and extending over most of the Crimea, with an undefined supremacy over the tribes east of the Cimmerian Bosporus, had been annexed by the great Mithridates and retained by his son Pharnaces, after whose death it became dependent on Rome.

Didium : A. Didius Gallus, acting perhaps as legatus of Moesia. He was afterwards governor of Britain (ch. 40, 1), and is called a consular in *Agr.* 14, 3 ; but the date of his consulship is unknown.

cohortium : sc. 'auxiliarium'.

Iulius Aquila is known from inscriptions to have been 'procurator Caesaris' in Bithynia in 58 A. D., and to have made a road there by order of Nero.

Dandaridarum : a Sarmatian tribe living near the Hypanis.

§ 2. **invasurus habebatur :** cf. 'Piso . . . dolo caesus habetur , iv 45, 5.

Siraci. These, and the Aorsi, who adjoined them on the south, were Sarmatian races living between the Tanais, the Euxine, the Caspian, and the Caucasus (Strabo). Both were offshoots of the great nation of the more distant Aorsi, who lived further north-east, on the Caspian.

hostilia resumpserat : cf. 'hostilia facere', xv 13, 4.

§ 3. **in arduo :** so also 'spes in arduo', iv 7, 2 ; 'in levi habendum ', iii 54, 6. So οὐκ ἐν ἐλαφρῷ, Theocr. xxii 213.

'(To secure) an alliance was a matter of no difficulty for a power that could display on its own side the might of Rome.'

Chapter 16, § 1. composito agmine : here probably = 'with 16 combined forces'. Elsewhere the phrase often means ' with orderly ', or ' well disciplined, forces '.

nostris in armis : to be taken especially with ' Bosporani '.

§ 2. **Soza,** and also **Uspe,** and the river **Panda,** below, are nowhere else mentioned ; but the line of march may be understood to have been in a direction north-east from the straits (ch. 17, 3).

popularium, 'the inhabitants', 'native population'; not here, 'the countrymen' of Mithridates.

ob, &c., explains 'obtineri visum', rather than 'desertum '.

§ 3. **editam loco :** cf. 'rudem iuventa ', ch. 15, 1, and Intr. II 17.

nisi quod : cf. vi 24, 2.

'Well protected by wall and moat, only that the walls, not being made of stone but of hurdles and wickerwork with earth between, were not proof against a storming party.'

moenia non saxo sed cratibus : for this abl. of description, without an adj., cf. xi 28, 1 'iuvenem nobilem dignitate formae, vi mentis', and Intr. II 18.

17   Chapter 17, § 1. **postero**: 'die' is easily supplied, from the proximity of 'eundem intra diem' just above.

servitii: cf. 'e servitio Blaesi', i 23, 2 and Intr. II 1.

quod, 'this offer'; and from what follows we see that no other terms were entertained. 'Belli potius', &c., gives the substance of the answer made to the envoys, or the thought in the mind of the officers who gave the 'signum caedis'.

evaserant: sc. 'in moenia'.

§ 2. On the style of this sentence see Intr. II 64, viii.

iuxta = 'pariter'; so xi 33, 1.

§ 3. **pensitato**: cf. Intr. II 21, a.

gentilis: cf. note on ch. 14, 2.

procubuit, 'prostrated himself before the effigy of Caesar', which was carried with the standards.

magna gloria: abl. abs. 'To the great glory of the Roman army, which was generally known to have come within three days' march of the river Tanais without loss and victoriously.' The Tanais was regarded by the ancients as at the extremity of the known world.

§ 4. **Taurorum.** Herodotus represents this people as inhabiting the Crimea (iv 99, 3), and refers to their savage worship of the goddess (to whom they sacrificed strangers), iv 103, 1.

plerisque = 'permultis'; so usually in Tacitus.

auxiliarium: the soldiers of the cohorts, ch. 15, 1.

18   Chapter 18, § 1. **nullo . . . subsidio**: Intr. II 22.

proditor olim: a Byzantine writer, Petrus Patricius, states that Mithridates had meditated revolt, but to keep up the appearance of fidelity sent to Rome his brother Cotys, who there informed against him, and received the kingdom as his reward.

id auctoritatis: an expression modelled on 'id temporis', frequent in Cicero. Here it is attached attributively to 'nemo'; so 'id aetatis corpora', v 9, 3; 'cum ceteris idem aetatis nobilibus', xiii 16, 1. The Roman commander at hand was only an 'eques'; ch. 15, 1.

§ 2. **convertit**: intrans.   **propriis**, 'personal'.   **recens**: adv.

§ 3. **genibus provolutus**: so in xi 30, 1.

Romanis: Intr. II 10.

prole magni Achaemenis: his ancestor, the great Mithridates, claimed descent on his father's side from Cyrus and Darius. Achaemenes is represented as great-grandfather of Cyrus (Hdt. vii 11, 3), and founder of the Achaemenidae, the family to which all the Persian kings belonged (Hdt. i 125, 5).

'Treat as you will one who boasts descent from the great Achaemenes, the sole possession not taken from me by my foes.'

quod: not constructed in grammatical connexion with 'proles', but with the idea of 'ancestry' suggested by it. For other phrases where the full meaning is not explicitly stated, see Intr. II 61.

Chapter 19, § 1. degeneri, 'undignified'; cf. xi 19, 4.   **19**
dextram, 'plighted friendship'; cf. 'renovari dextras', ii 58, 1,
of renewing a compact.
petendae veniae: Intr. II 11.
§ 2. primam . . . amicitiam, 'friendship originates'. For
'fortuna' in the sense of rank cf. xi 30, 3.
   § 3. **quotiens,** &c., 'whenever the matter is ended by a pardon '.
So, 'cum spe votoque uxoris semel transigitur', *Germ.* 19, 3.
   § 4. **precari:** supply ' se '; Intr. II 3, a.
ne triumpharetur, 'that he should not be led in triumph'. The
use of the passive of this verb in this sense occurs in Vergil,
Horace, and Ovid.
   poenas expenderet : the phrase occurs in Vergil, *Aen.* x 669.
   Chapter 20, § 1. nobilitatibus: abstr. for concrete. 'Nobili- **20**
tas' and 'nobilis' are also applied to royal descent elsewhere ; so
ch. 37, 1 and 53, 3.
   accipere . . . pacto salutis, 'to get him into his hands as a
prisoner by a promise to spare his life'; 'accipere pacto' corresponding to ' armis repetere'.
   repetere, 'recover'.
   § 2. **hinc,** 'on the one hand'.
   iniuriarum : his intended rebellion (18, 1) and hostile attitude,
15, 1 and 2.
   adigebat : so also, without explanatory subordinate clause,
xv 33, 1.
   suscipi: translate as though = ' suscipiendum ', 'that it involved
a war ', &c.
   avio itinere, inportuoso mari : Intr. II 22.
   ad hoc, ' besides '; so ch. 34, 1.
   § 3. **quin arriperet oblata,** 'why not seize the offer?' The
phrase represents the direct ' quin arripe '.
   servaret, ' keep him alive '.
   § 4. **novissima,** 'the uttermost'; so vi 50, 8.
   exempla: used of punishments ; so in Caes. *B. G.* i 31, 12
'omnia exempla cruciatusque edere' ('punishments of the most
exemplary severity').
   ita, &c., 'our ancestors had adopted this principle, to show
clemency to suppliants no less than ruthlessness towards the enemy'.
   integris : either ' whole ' peoples, as opposed to individuals, or
' unimpaired ', as opposed to the state of Mithridates' kingdom.
   Chapter 21, § 1. procuratorem Ponti : he was 'procurator **21**
Caesaris' in Pontus.
   elata in vulgum, ' became publicly known '.
   dimitte et quaere, 'set me free and catch me if you can '.
   § 2. **rostra iuxta:** Intr. II 55.
   consularia insignia, &c. : cf. xi 38, 5.
The bestowal of the higher honour upon Cilo, who had not really
done so much as Aquila, may have been due to the influence of
Narcissus, of whom Dio tells a story (lx 33, 5), representing him as

using his interest with the emperor in Cilo's favour when he was accused of extortion.

22 Chapter 22, § 1. **atrox odii**, 'relentless in her hatred'. Intr. II 24, c.

Lolliae : cf. ch. 1, 3.

molitur, with 'accusatorem', by zeugma, as well as with ' crimina '; Intr. II 60. 'Worked up charges, and inspired an accuser.'

Chaldaeos, magos, 'astrologers and magicians'. The practice of consulting astrologers was common in the early Empire (cf. Hor. *Od.* i 11; ii 17, &c.). Augustus and Tiberius both patronized astrologers, and the latter was himself a student of their science (vi 20). In 16 A. D. astrologers were expelled from Italy by a decree of the senate (ii 32, 5), and two were actually executed ; and a similar order of expulsion was made in 52 A. D. (xii 52, 3). The charge of consulting astrologers about the future of the reigning emperor, or members of the royal house,—as an act indicating intention of conspiracy,—often appears in the account of prosecutions; cf. iii 22, 2 ; xii 52, 1 ; xvi 14, 4.

magos : dealers in philtres, spells, and incantations. Their art was so old in Italy as to have fallen under the ban of the laws of the Twelve Tables (449 B. C.). The witchcraft practised in the Augustan age may be illustrated from Verg. *Ecl.* viii ; Hor. *Od.* i 27, 21 ; *Epod.* 5 ; *Sat.* i 8.

Apollinis Clarii simulacrum : the famous oracle near Colophon (consulted by her through persons sent for the purpose). Tacitus gives a short account of it in ii 54, 4.

§ 2. **L. Volusius :** his death in 56 A. D., at the age of ninety-three, is mentioned in xiii 30, 4. He is known to have been legatus of Delmatia under Tiberius and Gaius, and for a long period towards the close of his life was' praefectus urbis'. He is said by Tacitus to have enjoyed 'praecipuae opes bonis artibus' (wealth secured by no corrupt methods) and 'inoffensa tot imperatorum amicitia '.

maiorem patruum, 'great-uncle'.

Cotta Messalinus : see vi 5, 1.

Memmius Regulus : see note on v 11, 1.

perniciosa : supply ' esse', or perhaps some such word as ' prohibenda' by zeugma from ' detrahendam '.

materiem sceleri, 'her means for criminal enterprise', i. e. her wealth.

cederet Italia : this sentence denotes 'relegatio', which might not involve confiscation of property, as did 'exilium '.

§ 3. **quinquagiens sestertium :** supply centena millia, 5,000,000 sesterces, about £42,000.

inlustris femina : these words distinguish her from the Calpurnia of xi 30. She was recalled under Nero, in 59 A. D. ; xiv 12, 5.

pervertitur : cf. ch. 59, 1.

ira, &c., 'Agrippina's resentment stopped short of the extreme penalty'. Cf. 'citraque necem tua constitit ira', Ovid, *Tr.* ii 127.

§ 4. **Cadius Rufus :** the evidence from coins shows that he was proconsul of Bithynia in, or before, 48 A. D. He seems to have been expelled from the senate, to which he was restored twenty years later by Otho (*Hist.* i 77, 6).

Chapter 23, § 1. Gallia Narbonensis was under senatorial 23 rule, and was now completely Romanized ('Italia verius quam provincia', Pliny).

ut senatoribus, &c. Under the Republic, senators who desired leave of absence from the capital to attend to their property, could often obtain it under a 'libera legatio' conferred by the senate Augustus, shortly after Actium, forbade senators to reside out of Italy without his permission; those, however, who had estates in Sicily might go there when they pleased. A similar concession was now extended by Claudius to senators coming from Narbonese Gaul.

iure quo, &c., 'under the privilege applying to Sicily'.

§ 2. Ituraea had been subdued by Pompeius Magnus in 63 B.C., and made part of the dominions of Herod the Great, after whose death it passed to his son Philip.

Sohaemus: made king of Ituraea by Gaius, in 39 A. D.

Agrippa: grandson of Herod the Great. He had received the northern tetrarchies of Palestine, with the title of king, from Gaius, and for his assistance to Claudius at his accession was rewarded by the addition of Judaea and Samaria, so that his kingdom was as extensive as that of Herod the Great, and 'Iudaei' here should be taken in a wide sense, covering all his dominion. His death (Acts xii 23) may be referred to 44 A. D. Tacitus perhaps deferred mention of it till now, so as to record together the incorporation of Judaea and Ituraea.

provinciae Suriae additi: these districts would be under 'procuratores', subordinate to the legatus of Syria.

§ 3. Salutis augurium. A ceremony in which the will of the gods was sought by divination by the augurs as to whether public prayers might be offered for the general health of the State. This might only be done on an occasion of absolute immunity from war or warlike preparation.

lxxv annis omissum: the ceremony had been revived by Augustus in 29 B. C., having lapsed for many years owing to the constant civil and foreign wars of the latter period of the Republic.

continuari, 'to be made annual'.

§ 4. pomerium: Gellius' definition of this, drawn from the books of the augurs, describes it as a belt of ground marking the circumference of the city, defined by fixed boundaries on the inner side of the city wall, and marking the limit of 'urbani auspicii' (the space within which auguries for the city could be taken). The traditional derivation is from 'post murum' (so Varro, Plutarch, and Livy). The outer limit of this consecrated belt came to be regarded as of more importance than the inner: beyond it the powers of the urban magistrates ended. The emperor's 'proconsulare imperium' and 'tribunicia potestas' were however independent of such limitation.

auxit, 'extended'. One feature of this extension was the inclusion of the Aventine.

more prisco: from a passage in Seneca we learn that it was only the acquisition of Italian territory that justified an enlargement of the pomerium. Claudius' action therefore is to be regarded as the result of some enlargement of the bounds of Italy, possibly the incorporation of the Amauni (near Trent), rather than of his conquest of Britain.

§ 5. **nisi L. Sulla et divus Augustus.** Seneca and Gellius attest Sulla's extension, but not any extension by Augustus. Nor does the *Monumentum Ancyranum* record any such act by Augustus; and so it is possible that Tacitus and Dio (lv 6, 6) were misled on this point, perhaps by the accounts they followed of Augustus' work in dividing the city into 'regiones', in the course of which a definition of the city's boundaries would have to be made.

24 **Chapter 24, § 1. Regum,** &c., 'there are various accounts of the pretensions or the renown of kings in that matter'; i. e. some of the kings extended the pomerium through vanity in respect of pretended conquests, others to record the glory of real ones. Livy mentions no extension of the pomerium except that by Servius Tullius (i 44, 3), though both Tullus and Ancus enlarged the city (i 30 and 33).

§ 2. **forum boarium:** near 'San Giorgio in Velabro', between the Tiber and the western corner of the Palatine.

aereum tauri simulacrum: a statue forming part of the plunder brought from Greece, and the chief specimen in Rome of Aeginetan bronze. It was placed in the cattle-market as the most appropriate site. 'Quia', &c., gives the reason for taking this as the starting-point of the line, 'sulcus'.

designandi oppidi: see Intr. II 26.

sulcus: the line so traced was the outer limit of the pomerium, within which the wall of defence was built afterwards. [See Ov. *Fast.* iv 821 and foll] The ceremony is stated to have been of Etruscan origin, and, if so, was probably not observed when Rome was first founded as a primitive Latin town.

Herculis aram. The 'Ara Maxima', near the northern end, or 'carceres', of the Circus. The deity to which it was originally erected was probably the Italian Hercules, the presiding spirit of the homestead and of property, the god of good faith ('Deus Fidius') Tradition, however, made it belong to the worship of the Greek Heracles, instituted by Evander to commemorate the slaying of Cacus (Verg. *Aen.* viii 179 and foll.).

§ 3. **lapides,** 'boundary stones', 'cippi pomerii'. It seems these were left to mark out the course of the Luperci when they ran round the site of the ancient city on the Palatine at the festival held annually on the 15th of February.

ad aram Consi: this, and the next two places enumerated, were probably turning points in the line, and marked by terminal 'cippi'

This 'ara defossa', near the 'meta' of the Circus, was exposed to view only during the 'Consualia', a festival held with games in the Circus in August, said to have been instituted by Romulus and to have been the occasion of the rape of the Sabines. The name 'Consus' is probably connected with 'condere', denoting the god of the stored-up harvest, and the festival was a celebration of 'harvest-home'. The god was identified by some ancient authors with Neptune (Poseidon Hippios), because horse-races were a feature of the festival.

curias veteres: supply 'ad', from the context, and also with 'forum Romanum'. The site of the 'curiae veteres', the original meeting-place of the 'curiae', is not known for certain, but was probably near the place where the arch of Constantine now stands.

sacellum Larum: generally supposed to be the 'aedes Larum in summa sacra via', built or rebuilt by Augustus (*Mon. Anc.* iv 7), and dedicated to the Lares 'gemini qui compita servant', the legend of whose birth is given in Ov. *Fast.* ii 599 and foll.

inde, &c.: i.e. the pomerium skirted the Forum, without including it. The temple of Vesta, between the Palatine and Forum, although belonging to the worship of the primitive settlement at Rome, lay outside its original fortified limits ('Roma Quadrata') The Capitol was originally the citadel of the Sabines settled on the Quirinal, and the 'Forum' a market-place between them and the Roman inhabitants on the Palatine.

Tacitus says nothing of the line of the pomerium from the Forum to its starting-place, probably because in ancient times the ground over which it ran was usually inundated and so unsuitable for 'cippi'.

pro fortuna, 'according to acquisitions made'.

§ 4. publicis actis: probably means public inscriptions.

Chapter 25, § 1. C. Antistio M. Suillio: their full names were **25** C. Antistius Vetus and M. Suillius Nerullinus. The former was probably son of the Antistius who was consul in 23 A.D., and related to the Antistius who was Nero's colleague in the consulship in 55 A.D. (xiii 11, 1). The latter was son of the Suillius of xi 1, 1 and brother of the Caesoninus of xi 36, 5. From the evidence of coinage he is known to have been proconsul of Asia under Vespasian.

adoptio in Domitium: cf. 'in fratrum filias coniugia', ch. 6, 5 and Intr. II 46.

obstrictus, 'pledged to the service of'; cf. xi 2, 1.

robore circumdaret: a metaphor from fortification by palisade; 'that he might secure Britannicus in his boyhood by a strong defence'.

§ 2. subnixum, 'supported by'. nepotibus: Gaius and Lucius, the sons of Julia. privignos: Tiberius and Drusus, sons of Livia.

propriam stirpem: Drusus Caesar, his son by Agrippa's daughter Vipsania, born 13 B.C.; associated with Tiberius in the 'tribunicia potestas', 22 A.D.; poisoned by Seianus in 23 A.D. (iv 8).

Germanicum: Tiberius' nephew (son of Drusus his brother).

83   Q 2

accingeret: metaphor from girding on a sword; 'let him attach to himself a youth', &c.

§ 3. **biennio maiorem natu**: so Med.; but it is known that Nero was born in Dec., 41 A.D., so that 'triennio' would be correct.

filio anteponit: by adoption, Nero became Britannicus' equal in position, and would then naturally take precedence as the elder. The relations of Germanicus and Drusus in the family of Tiberius were similar.

§ 4. **periti** = 'docti', 'experts'.

patricios: the term distinguishes them from the plebeian branch of the family, the Claudii Marcelli. Tiberius had already become one of the 'Iulii' when he adopted Germanicus, and so received him into that house.

Atto Clauso: xi 24, 1. 'And they had persisted in an unbroken line from Attus Clausus.'

26   Chapter 26, § 1. **quaesitiore**, &c., 'specially elaborate compliments being paid to Domitius'.

rogata lex. This was a 'lex curiata', passed in the presence of the pontiffs, the proper form whereby an adoption of a person 'sui iuris' was effected. For this the concurrence of the people, assembled in 'curiae', was supposed to be requisite, but this division by 'curiae' had long become obsolete, and the 'curiae' were represented by some lictors (properly thirty in number).

nomen Neronis. His name from this time till his accession is 'Ti. Claudius Nero Caesar', or 'Nero Claudius Caesar Drusus Germanicus'.

augetur, 'is exalted'. Cf. 'honoribus augebantur', vi 8, 4.

Augustae. Livia had become 'Augusta' by Augustus' will, Antonia after the accession of her grandson (Gaius), Messalina only by provincial adulation; Agrippina is the first to receive the title in her husband's lifetime and to treat it as conferring a substantial share of power. Nero gave the title to Poppaea, and from Domitian's time it was generally borne by emperors' wives.

§ 2. **desolatus**: poetical = 'privatus'. [So Statius, *Theb.* ix 672 'desolatumque magistro agmen'.] The removal of his attendants is further described in ch. 41, 8.

perintempestiva, 'extremely ill-timed'; a new word, see Intr. II 51.

falsi = 'fraudis'. For the case cf. 'intellegentem humani divinique iuris', iv 38, 3.

§ 3. **sive,** &c., 'whether this was really so, or, winning sympathy by his peril, he has retained the credit (of ability) without being put to the proof of it'.

27   Chapter 27, § 1. **oppidum Ubiorum**, 'the capital of the Ubii', where Agrippina was born in 15 A.D. The colony of veterans here planted was named 'Colonia Agrippinensis' (or 'Agrippinensium'), sometimes 'Colonia Claudia Augusta Agrippinensium', or Colonia Claudia Ara'. It is the modern Cologne (Köln).

veteranos coloniamque: Intr. II 54.

impetrat: Intr. II 31.

§ 2. **ac forte**: i. e. there was this further reason for the name. The Ubii were transported to the western bank with their own consent, and the date was probably 38 B. C., when Agrippa is mentioned by Dio as having crossed the Rhine (48, 49, 3).

§ 3. **Chattorum**: the most formidable enemies of Rome, beyond the Rhine, at this period. Their district formed part of the extensive ' Hercynius saltus', and their name is thought to survive in ' Hessen', which with part of Nassau, represents their locality.

Pomponius: see v 8, 1.

Vangionas ac Nemetas: situated on the left bank of the Rhine in ' Germania superior'.

equite alario, ' allied cavalry ', ' force of mounted allies '.

anteirent, ' get before them ', on their line of retreat.

§ 4. **industria**: used of soldierly vigour; cf. ch. 12, 1.

recens: adv., so in ch. 18, 2.

clade Variana: the defeat of Varus in 9 A. D.

Chapter 28, § 1. qui dextris, &c. This body had probably **28** operated along the valley of the Main, while the other division (ch. 27, 4) had proceeded along the Lahn.

compendiis: sometimes accompanied by ' viarum '.

aciem auso: cf. xi 9, 2

Taunum: i. e. to the Roman fort, established on the lower slopes of Mt. Taunus to guard the communications up the valley.

si, 'in case that '. **casum**, ' opportunity'.

§ 2. **Cherusci**: xi 16, г.

aeternum: adv. So in Verg. and Hor. Intr. II 2.

triumphalis honos: i. e. the ' ornamenta triumphalia ' ; cf note on xi 20, 3.

carminum: see v 8, 4.

gloria: probably nominative.

Chapter 29, § 1. Vannius is mentioned in ii 63 as of the race **29** of the Quadi, and was set up as king over some of the subjects of the deposed Maroboduus by Drusus Caesar (Tiberius' son), in 19 A. D. This kingdom, called here Suebic, seems to have included the whole territory of the Marcomani and Quadi (Bohemia and Moravia), as the enemies of Vannius are Hermunduri and Lugii, who were on the west and north of what is now Bohemia, while his allies are the Iazuges (§ 4), who bordered on the Quadi to the east.

mox, &c., ' but subsequently, through the long duration (of his rule), lapsing into tyranny '.

mutans: here intrans., as in ii 23, 4, and often in Livy. Cf. the use of ' vertere ', vi 46, 3 ; ' ferre ', ii 23, 4.

odio: with ' circumventus '.

§ 2. **Vibilius** is mentioned as chieftain of the Hermunduri in 19 A. D. (ii 63, 7).

85

Hermunduri: described in *Germania* xli 1 as a friendly and privileged people adjoining Raetia, between the Marcomani and Chatti.

Palpellio Histro: this name, corrupt in the MS., is restored from an inscription, which states his full name and the offices held by him.

Pannoniam praesidebat: for the case cf. ch. 14, 7. Pannonia was one of the most important Caesarian provinces, and its 'legatus' was always of consular rank. It extended along the Rhine, from Carnuntum (below Vienna) to Belgrade, its western boundary from the Danube to the Drave being nearly that of the modern Hungary.

auxilia: here, not the regular auxiliaries attached to the legions, but levies specially called out, 'tumultuariae catervae' (i 56, 1).

componere: see Intr. II 31.

pro ripa, 'along the bank', of the Danube.

subsidio . . . et terrorem: notice the variation of the cases, both words expressing the effect of ' legionem . . . componere '.

§ 3. **Lugii.** Med. reads 'ligii'; the Greek form is Λύγιοι (Dio) or Λούγιοι (Strabo). The name seems to be connected with 'lug', an old German word for a marsh or wood; the tribe, Suebic with many subdivisions, lived north of Bohemia, in what is the modernSilesia and part of Poland.

fama: causal abl. Intr. II 19.

vectigalibus: by duties on merchandise. There was a considerable traffic across the Danube in those quarters (ii 62, 4).

§ 4. **Iazygibus:** the Iazyges had driven out the Dacians from the tract between the Danube and Tibiscus, and were thus on the frontiers of Pannonia. We hear of them on the Lower Danube in Ov. *ex P*. iv 7, 9 ; *Trist*. ii 191 ; and other branches of the race were on the Euxine and Palus Maeotis (Strabo and Ptolemy).

impar: to be taken as referring to the whole army. ' His own force consisted of infantry, while his cavalry were composed of Sarmatian Iazyges, an army inferior ', &c.

ducere, 'to prolong'; so 'lacrimae . . . ducebantur', xi 37, 5.

30 Chapter 30, § 1. **necessitudinem,** &c., 'made a battle unavoidable', because they were attacked, and Vannius was obliged to bring them help.

ingruerant: cf. ch. 12, 2.

§ 2. **rebus adversis:** abl. abs.

§ 3. **classem:** the squadron called ' classis Pannonica ', stationed on the Upper Danube. There was also a squadron, ' classis Moesica ', on the Lower Danube.

clientes: his ' comitatus '; cf. *Germ*. xiii 14.

§ 4. **Vangio ac Sido.** The latter was still reigning in 69 A. D., when he joined Vespasian, as did also Italicus, who had succeeded Vangio. (*Hist*. iii 5, 4 ; 21, 3.)

partivere. This active form is archaic. The past participle is however used in passive sense by Caesar and Livy.

egregia . . . fide: abl. of quality, as is also 'multa caritate' and 'maiore odio'. 'Subiectis' is dative, parallel with 'adversus nos', above. 'Displaying towards us an admirable loyalty, whilst by their subjects,—owing either to their own (fickle) temperament, or to the character produced by enslavement (abl. of cause),—they were viewed with warm affection until they won their kingdom, and with still warmer hatred after they had won it '.

dominationis: for the case, cf. 'rerum adeptus est', iii 55, 1.

Chapter 31, § 1. At in Britannia, &c.: the narrative here goes **31** back to the date of the appointment of Ostorius, who succeeded Plautius Silvanus in 47 A. D. P. Ostorius Scapula is known to have been consul suffectus with a certain Vellius Rufus (perhaps the Suillius Rufus of xi 1, 1) in Claudius' reign.

§ 2. **primis eventibus,** 'by the first results of measures taken'.

rapit, 'hurries' (by forced marches).

caesis qui: Intr. II 21.

permitteret, following 'ne'. ' In case a peace, formed without friendly feelings or loyal intentions, should afford no security to general and army alike.'

cunctaque castris Antonam et Sabrinam: so Med. The passage is unintelligible without some alteration. The reading 'cunctaque cis Trisantonam et Sabrinam' involves the change of one letter only [cis for cas-]. Τρισαντών occurs in Ptolemy as the name of a British river flowing to the south coast ; this is not taken to be the one referred to here, but the name may well be one applied, like 'Avon', to several rivers. ' Trannonus' occurs as the name for the Trent in the ninth century, and this may be the form into which Trisanton, or Trisantona, passed. This interpretation suggests, then, that Ostorius, engaged in protecting the friendly tribes of south Britain from attacks from the north, prepared to bring into subjection a large tract of the Midlands, here described as east of the Severn and south of the Trent, and his operations provoked risings from the Iceni on the east, the Brigantes on the north, and the Welsh tribes on the west.

§ 3. **quod:** i. e. Ostorius' operations.

Iceni: the name occurs on coins as 'Eceni', probably = 'swordsmen'. Their territory extended over the present counties of Cambridgeshire, Norfolk, and Suffolk. Their town, Venta Icenorum, may be Norwich, or Caistor.

abnuere, 'rebelled against'.

accesserant: Intr. II 5.

§ 4. **aggere.** A portion of the strong earthworks thrown up by the Iceni for protection on their western frontier survives in the 'Devil's Dyke', crossing the road from Cambridge to Newmarket.

§ 5. **perrumpere adgreditur:** Intr. II 35.

peditum: to be taken with 'munia'.

§ 7. **filius**: his death, on a charge of conspiracy against Nero in 66 A. D., is described in xvi 15.

servati civis decus: the 'civica corona'.

32   **Chapter 32, § 1. compositi**, 'were quieted'; so in ch. 40, 1.

bellum inter: Intr. II 55.

in Decangos. Med. has 'inde cangos'.

Tacitus' account, that the army reached a point near the Irish Channel, and the indication that its operations provoked the hostility of the Brigantes (who lived north of the Mersey and the Humber as far as the Solway and Tyne), suggests that this tribe lived somewhere in the North of Wales. Pigs of lead have been found in Cheshire and Staffordshire engraved DECEA, DECEANG, and DECE-ANGI, and these are thought to have come from the lead-producing districts of Flintshire, probably on both sides of the Dee ; i. e. from among the tribe here called 'Decangi'. It is a disputed point whether DE, on the pigs, is part of the name, or a preposition. The reading of Med. is in favour of the latter interpretation ; but the Welsh name Tegenigl, still applied to the district between the Dee and Clwyd, makes it probable that DE is the first syllable of the name.

§ 2. **ausis aciem**: cf. ch. 28, 1.

carpere, 'to harass'; so also in Caesar and Livy.

temptarent: subj. of repeated action, in a dependent clause.

§ 3. **destinationis certum**, 'unwavering in his resolution'; Intr. II 24.

§ 4. **arma coeptabant**: so 'coeptare seditionem', i 38, 1.

Silures. These, with the kindred tribe Demetae west of them, held a territory nearly corresponding to South Wales, Monmouthshire, and Herefordshire.

quin: following on the idea of 'prevention' suggested by 'mutabatur'.

§ 5. **veniret** = 'eveniret'. Intr. II 28.

Camulodunum: Colchester, a town of the 'Trinobantes'. The name is derived from the Celtic war-god 'Camulos'. Tacitus does not mean that a colony at Colchester would overawe rebel tribes in the West ; but, to facilitate the transfer of the legions from Essex westwards, a military colony was established at Colchester, which now ceased to be a camp.

valida manu: abl. of quality.

inbuendis: dat. Intr. II 11.

33   **Chapter 33, § 1. Caratacus**, one of the sons of Cunobelinus, had no doubt been already mentioned by Tacitus in his account of the invasion of Britain under Claudius. The name is connected with the Celtic 'carat' (= beloved), whence 'Caradog', 'Carthach', 'McCarthy'. The form 'Caractacus' is erroneous.

ambigua: the adjective is similarly contrasted with 'prospera' in xi 15, 2. 'A long career, of varied peril and success.' [The ordinary meaning 'battles indecisive in result', as contrasted with decisive defeats, is also possible.]

praemineret: with accus. ; cf. ch. 12, 1.

§ 2. **astu locorum fraude**: 'fraus loci' or 'locorum' is a poetical expression, occurring in Verg. *Aen.* ix 397 and Ov. *Tr.* iv 2, 33; it is added to explain the more general word 'astu'. 'Getting the advantage by stratagem through the difficulty of the country, although inferior in military strength, he shifted the seat of war.' The Ordovices occupied the chief part of Central and North Wales, and their name is thought to be derived from the Celtic word for their characteristic weapon, the axe-hammer.

pacem nostram: the 'pax Romana', of which Calgacus is represented, in *Agr.* 30, 5, as saying 'ubi solitudinem faciunt, pacem appellant'.

novissimum, 'extreme', 'uttermost', as in vi 50, 8. 'Risked the ultimate decision of Fortune.'

abscessus, 'means of escape', 'outlets'.

inportuna: so in ch. 12, 5.

montibus arduis: abl. abs. ; Intr. II 22. The site of the battle is described too vaguely to be identified.

si qua: nom. plur., subj. to 'accedi poterant'.

clementer, 'by an easy ascent'; cf. 'colles clementer adsurgentes', xiii 38, 5.

praestruit: here takes direct obj. 'saxa'. More usually the word means 'to block up'.

§ 3. **vado incerto**, 'of shifting depth'.

pro munimentis, 'along the fortifications'. Cf. 'pro ripa', ch. 29, 2.

Chapter 34, § 1. Ad hoc, 'besides'; as in ch. 20, 2.   **34**

§ 2. **enimvero**: emphasizes Caratacus as the principal figure among the chieftains who were delivering exhortations. Cf. ch. 64, 6.

§ 3. **pepulissent**: an exaggeration. [Of Caesar's invasion of Britain Tacitus says 'quamquam prospera pugna terruerit incolas ac litore potitus sit, potest videri ostendisse (Britanniam) posteris, non tradidisse', *Agr.* 13, 2.]

§ 4. **obstringi** = 'obstringere se'; 'each swore by his tribal gods'. On the ellipse of 'se' before 'cessuros' see Intr. II 3, a.

Chapter 35, § 1. nihil nisi atrox, &c., 'the forbidding aspect   **35** of the whole position, crowded with defenders'. Cf. 'nihil . . . novum', ch. 2, 1.

§ 2. **praefecti**: the commanders of the auxiliary cohorts and 'alae'.

intendebant = 'augebant' ; so often in Tacitus.

§ 3. **circumspectis quae**: Intr. II 21.

infensos, 'eager for the fray'.

evadit, 'passes through'. So also in v 10, 4.

§ 4. **in nos**: cf. 32, 4 and Intr. II 46.

pleraeque = 'plurimae'.

'The greater number of casualties fell on our men, who lost heavily.'

§ 5. **rudes et informes saxorum compages**: cf. Intr. II 57, b.

par comminus acies, 'the lines met close together on equal terms'.

decedere, 'left their position'. (The word often indicates the departure of a provincial governor from his sphere of administration.)

§ 6. **ferentarius**: the auxiliaries, just as 'gravis miles' means the legionaries. The word is applied, according to Varro, to 'equites . . . qui ea modo habebant arma quae ferrentur, ut iaculum'. Vegetius speaks of foot-soldiers so called, 'apud veteres', who were light-armed and stationed with the slingers on the wings, and opened the battle by skirmishing. The word is used, in a figure, by Plautus, and occurs in Sallust, probably as an archaism. As such, Tacitus seems to have adopted it from Sallust.

conferto gradu, 'in close order'.

resisterent . . . verterent: frequentative, as in ch. 32, 2 'temptarent'.

spathis: 'gravis armatura . . . habebant . . . gladios maiores, quos spathas vocant'; Vegetius.

36   **Chapter 36**, § 1. **ut**, &c., 'as adversity generally brings insecurity'.

nono post anno, &c.: 51 A. D., reckoning inclusively from 43 A. D.

§ 2. **unde**: i. e. from this prolonged resistance.

evecta insulas: so 'evadere' (ch. 35, 3) and 'egredi' (i 30, 2) are followed by accusative in Tacitus.

insulas: naturally plural, as a Roman would think of Ireland, 'Mona', 'Vectis', and the islands north and west of Scotland as forming one group with Britain.

quis ille = 'quis ille esset qui . . . '; cf. xi 7, 1.

§ 4. **in armis**: usually, in the city, the soldiers were 'togati' (*Hist*. i 38, 5).

campo: Intr. II 14.

castra: the praetorian camp. (Instituted by Seianus, 23 A. D.)

praeiacet: with accus.; cf. 'praesidere', ch. 14, 7; 'praeminere', ch. 12, 1.

§ 5. **phalerae**: plates or bosses of chased metal worn on the breast.

torques: a specially Celtic ornament.

externis: from the Roman point of view, 'in British wars'.

traducta, 'were led in procession'.

§ 6. **dégeneres**: cf. ch. 19, 1.

at non: the negative belongs only to 'aut . . . aut'.

in hunc modum. The speech is probably Tacitus' composition. It is hardly likely that Caratacus knew enough Latin to deliver a public address. On the other hand, it is not impossible that he should have learnt a speech by rote, for this ceremony.

37   **Chapter 37**, § 1. **fortuna**, 'rank'; cf. ch. 19, 2.

rerum prosperarum moderatio, 'moderate use of', 'humility in, prosperity'.

dedignatus esses . . . accipere: so ii 45, 2 'fratris filio patruus parere dedignabatur'. ['Dedignor' is usually confined to poets.]

pluribus gentibus. The sovereignty inherited from his father Cunobelinus had extended over many tribes (Intr. p. lxi), and even after this was broken up, he had been accepted by the Silures and Ordovices as their leader.

§ 3. sequitur, 'does it follow?' The omission of an interrogative particle adds energy to the question.

§ 4. si statim deditus traderer, 'if I had been delivered to you after making prompt submission'. 'Deditus' refers to his possible action in Britain, 'traderer' to his arrival at Rome; the latter word does not merely repeat the idea already expressed by the former.

mei: cf. 'sui', vi 7, 4.

§ 5. ad ea, 'in reply to this'.

suggestu = 'tribunali'.

isdem . . . venerati, 'paid the same expressions of honour and gratitude'.

gratibus: elsewhere the nom. and acc. of this word are alone used. (Intr. II 51.)

§ 6. signis Romanis praesidere: i. e. to sit, like the emperor, on a 'tribunal', surrounded by the standards.

parti a maioribus. She was great-granddaughter of Augustus, and granddaughter by adoption of Tiberius.

semet ferebat, 'displayed herself as'.

Chapter 38, § 1. Syphax, king of Numidia, was led in triumph **38** by Scipio Africanus, 201 B. C. Perses appeared at the triumph of L. Aemilius Paulus in 167 B. C.

si qui alii, &c. Jugurtha appeared at the triumph of Marius, 104 B. C., and Vercingetorix at Julius Caesar's in 45 B. C.

neque minus, &c., 'declared that it was no less glorious an event than the exhibition of Syphax by P. Scipio, of Perses by L. Paulus, or (the success of) any other generals who had displayed kings in chains to the Roman people'. [*Or*, 'the display by any other generals of kings in chains shown to the Roman people'.]

§ 2. triumphi insignia: cf. xi 20, 3.

ad id, 'up to that time'.

§ 3. praefectum castrorum. This officer was usually one promoted from the rank of centurion, as a reward of long and good service. Even in a camp containing more than one legion, a single 'praefectus castrorum' would be appointed in charge of it. Cases occur in Tacitus of a praefectus castrorum taking charge of a legion in the absence of the 'legatus'. After Domitian ordered that each legion should have a separate camp, this officer is called 'praefectus castrorum legionis', and in the second century becomes 'praefectus legionis', and ultimately takes the place of the 'legatus legionis' (*Ann.* ii 20).

exstruendis praesidiis: dat. of purpose. Intr. II 11.

circumfundunt: the earlier usage, of the passive with dative, also occurs in Tacitus; e. g. ch. 27, 3.

§ 4. ni nuntiis, &c.: the text of this passage is uncertain, and it is therefore doubtful whether its construction is correct. It appears from the early part of the next chapter that the main body came to the support of the beleaguered troops, so that 'ex castellis' may be connected with 'nuntiis', though strictly for this purpose the phrase requires the addition of some such participle as 'missis'. 'Had not help, in consequence of a message dispatched from the nearest forts, been sent to the beleaguered forces, they would have been absolutely wiped out.' ('Obsidio', dative from 'obsidium'.)

obsidio copiarum = 'copiis obsessis'. Intr. II 57.

39 Chapter 39, § 1. sistebat, ni . . . excepissent: Intr. II 38.

pro meliore fuit, 'was equivalent to a success'. Cf. 'pro firmato stetit magistratus eius ius', Liv. iv 7, 3.

§ 3. in modum latrocinii, 'after the fashion of guerilla fighting'.

ut cuique, &c., 'taking place, according to the opportunity or valour of each party, on the spur of the moment, or from prearranged design'. 'Proviso' does not occur elsewhere in this sense = 're ante provisa', but is probably formed on the model of 'improviso', common in Cicero.

(For the change from asyndeton to connexion by particles cf. Intr. II 64.)

§ 4. imperatoris: i. e. Ostorius.

Sugambri. The destruction of part of this tribe and the settlement of the rest of them on the west side of the Rhine seems to have been carried out by Tiberius in 8 B.C. [References to their conquest are made by Horace in *Od.* iv 2, 34; 14, 51.]

in Gallias: i. e. on to the Gallic side of the Rhine. It was on this side that the two German provinces lay, but the west side of the Rhine continued to be spoken of as 'ripa Gallica', even after the two German provinces had been constructed along it.

§ 5. avaritia: causal ablative.

tamquam: Intr. II 50.

40 Chapter 40, § 1. A. Didium: see ch. 15, 1. The date of his appointment is generally taken to be 52 A.D., and he seems to have held it for rather more than five years.

integras: i. e. in the state in which the death of Ostorius had left them.

Manlius Valens: mentioned in *Hist.* i 64, 7 as legatus of a newly-raised legion in 69 A.D. He was consul in 96 A.D. at the age of ninety (Dio lxvii 47, 5).

auctaque, &c. The sentence is awkward. 'Et apud hostes' seems to be answered by 'atque illo augente'. 'The account of the affair was magnified, both on the part of the enemy who thus sought to intimidate the approaching commander, while he too exaggerated the report, that he might procure the greater honour from their subjection and have a better excuse if they maintained their resistance.'

compositi: so Med. The participle may be taken as nom. pl.,

with 'forent' understood; 'that their pacification might be the greater credit'. Some editors prefer 'compositis', to be taken as a concise abl. abs.

§ 3. **Venutius:** mentioned in *Hist.* iii 45 and also in the lost part of the *Annals* ('ut supra memoravi'). He may have been one of the princes who made terms with the Romans in the campaigns of Plautius. (Intr. p. lxii.)

discidio, 'divorce'.

In *Hist.* iii 45 it is stated that the wealth and prosperity which Cartimandua gained from her service to the Romans in the betrayal of Caratacus led her to reject Venutius, and to take in his stead his 'armiger' Vellocatus; but the nation took the side of the injured husband, and she was reduced 'in extremum discrimen'.

§ 5. **feminae.** Elsewhere Tacitus states that the Britons had no objection to the rule of a woman. ('Neque enim sexum in imperiis discernunt', *Agr.* 16, 1.) Cf. also Boudicca's declaration: 'solitum quidem Britannis feminarum ductu bellare', xiv 35, 1.

armis: abl. of respect.

lecta = 'insignis' or 'praestans'.

§ 6. **initio ambiguo,** &c. In the *Histories* nothing is said about the employment of any legion, and the auxiliary forces are stated to have accomplished no more than the rescue of Cartimandua herself, leaving Venutius master of the situation. The Brigantes were still in arms under him in 69 A.D., and were only partially reduced by Cerialis in the time of Vespasian (*Agr.* 17, 2).

§ 7. **multa copia honorum:** abl. of quality, parallel with, and not dependent on, 'gravis'.

§ 8. **plures per annos:** viz. 47–58 A.D. (The treatment of affairs in Britain is resumed in xiv 29.)

haud perinde, 'not as well as they should'.

Chapter 41, § 1. **Servio Cornelio Orfito.** He is mentioned **41** again in xvi 12, 3 as author of the proposal for changing the names of the months May and June into 'Claudius' and 'Germanicus', in honour of Nero, 65 A.D., in addition to the previous alteration of April to 'Neroneus'. He appears to have perished in the last years of Nero (*Hist.* iv 42, 1).

maturata, 'was hastened'; i.e. bestowed earlier than usual. Nero had just completed his thirteenth year; the 'toga virilis' was usually not assumed before the completion of the fourteenth year.

capessendae rei publicae. The phrase is applied to imperial functions in xi 24, 1, but here refers rather to those attached to the office mentioned in § 2.

§ 2. **vicensimo aetatis anno,** &c. This privilege, with the exemption from passing through the lower magistracies, and also the title 'principes iuventutis', had been granted to Gaius and Lucius Caesar, the grandsons of Augustus. Other members of the imperial house, as Tiberius and his brother Drusus, had been allowed to take the quaestorship five years before the usual age, passing on to praetorship and consulship after the ordinary interval. (Thus they held the

93

consulship at about the age of thirty. The ordinary age for the consulship at this period is put by Mommsen at thirty-five.)

interim: this word goes closely with 'designatus', and does not imply that he was to lay down his proconsular power on becoming consul.

extra urbem: these words distinguish Nero's proconsular power from that held by the emperor, which extended within the 'pomerium' as well.

princeps iuventutis: the title is analogous to that of 'princeps senatus', and appears to have been new when conferred on Augustus' grandsons. The *Monumentum Ancyranum* speaks of it as an honour conferred by the 'equites'.

§ 3. **donativum**: this word is always specially used of largess to soldiers (cf. ch. 69, 3).

congiarium: a present of money to the populace. Originally the word denoted a present of wine, oil, or salt,—from 'congius' the vessel in which it was stored (Livy xxv 2). In this case Suetonius states (*Ner.* 7) that Nero himself announced these gifts, as well as a public parade ('decursio') of the praetorians.

§ 4. **adquirendis**: Intr. II 11.

triumphali veste: this, comprising the 'tunica palmata', 'toga picta' (embroidered with gold), and laurel wreath, was not confined to persons who had triumphed, but was also worn by the chief magistrates of the Republic on certain solemn occasions, and after their example by the emperor, whence it is called below 'habitus imperatorius', and was no doubt assumed by Nero in virtue of his proconsular imperium.

spectaret: indirect jussive, expressing the thought of Agrippina and her party, 'let the people see'. Some insert 'ut' after 'sunt', or in its place.

perinde, 'correspondingly'. (So too in Livy and Sallust.)

§ 5. **centurionum tribunorumque**: viz. of the praetorian cohorts.

et alii, 'most on false charges, and some on pretence of promotion'. The expression is not quite identical with 'alii ... alii', but distinguishes a smaller body from the larger; so xv 54, 2 'libertate et alii pecunia donati'.

tali occasione, 'by taking an opportunity of the following sort'. This interpretation is supported by 'commotus his' in § 8.

§ 6. **ille Domitium**: Britannicus ignored Nero's adoption as Claudius' son, and his change of name. Suetonius makes him use the name 'Ahenobarbus' on this occasion (*Ner.* 7).

§ 7. **quae iusserit populus**: referring to the 'lex curiata', which formed part of the ceremony of adoption, ch. 26, 1. This had been preceded by a decree of the senate, ch. 25, 3.

nisi, 'unless a check were put on the evil influence of those who prompted such offensiveness, it would break out with fatal results to the State'.

eruptura: a subject may be supplied from 'infensa'.

§ 8. **morte**: Sosibius (xi 1, 2) suffered this (Dio lx 32, 5). Dio adds κἀκ τούτου παραδοῦσα αὐτὸν οἷς ἤθελεν, ἐκάκου ὅσον ἐδύνατο, καὶ οὔτε τῷ πατρὶ συνεῖναι οὔτε ἐς τὸ δημόσιον προϊέναι εἴα, ἀλλ' ἐν ἀδέσμῳ τρόπον τινὰ φυλακῇ εἶχεν.

Chapter 42, § 1. cura, and 'curare', are often used of military **42** command by Tacitus.

audebat, ni . . . exsolverentur: Intr. II 38.

Lusius Geta: cf. xi 31, 1.

Rufrius Crispinus: cf. xi 1, 3.

§ 2. **ambitu**, 'rivalry' in courting the soldiers. The partition of this command between two praefects is ascribed by Dio (lii 24, 1) to Maecenas' advice to Augustus. This was not, however, invariably followed; thus Seianus had had sole command, under Tiberius. After the death of Burrus, in 62 A. D., the praetorians were again put under the command of two men, viz. Faenius Rufus and Sofonius Tigellinus (xiv 51, 5).

Burrus: the name is an old synonym for 'Rufus'; 'Burrus' or 'Purrus' is Ennius' form for 'Pyrrhus'. An inscription found at Vaison records his previous career. He was a native probably of the Gallic Vasio, of equestrian rank, served as 'tribunus militum' in a legion not specified, and was then agent ('procurator') in succession to Livia, Tiberius, and Claudia. He was consequently already a trusted servant of 'the household of Caesar' when promoted to the praetorian prefecture, and like Seneca was a provincial. His 'nomen' Afranius may indicate that an ancestor had served under the Pompeian general of that name, and had received Roman citizenship from him.

§ 3. **fastigium**, 'dignity'.

carpento: a two-wheeled carriage with an ornamental cover. A similar privilege was allowed to magistrates and priests on solemn occasions: it was the ordinary privilege of Vestals, and had been accorded to Messalina, who was drawn in such a carriage at the triumph of Claudius (Suet. *Cl.* 17).

sacris: objects of worship, such as the Palladium kept in the temple of Vesta, and perhaps the images of the Penates of Rome.

imperatore: her father Germanicus had received this title from Tiberius in 15 A. D., after his campaign in Germany against the Chatti.

sororem: of Gaius.

quam . . . fuisse unicum . . . exemplum est: equivalent to 'quam . . . fuisse solam . . . tradunt'. 'Who was the only instance so far of one who, herself an emperor's daughter, was sister, wife, and daughter of the ruler of the world.'

§ 4. **Vitellius**: cf. xi 2, 4 and vi 28, 1.

§ 5. **maiestatis**: trials under this offence, so common under Tiberius, had been discontinued by Claudius at the beginning of his reign (Dio lx 3, 6), and were revived under Nero first in 62 A. D. (xiv 48, 3).

aqua atque igni interdiceret: this sentence was one of 'exilium', involving loss of property.

hactenus, 'thus far' (and no more). 'Vitellius pressing for no further penalty.'

43   **Chapter 43, § 1. prodigia**: the mention of portents does not occur in the earlier books of the *Annals*, but from this point is fairly common. Tacitus does not state what evils he regards these occurrences as foreshadowing; the famine is recorded as itself another portent; perhaps we are to infer that they presaged the troubles in the East and the evils arising from the supplanting of Britannicus by Nero.

diris avibus, 'birds of ill-omen'. The sight of an owl in the daytime was regarded as a specially bad sign.

dum latius metuitur, 'as the panic spread'.

obtriti: the plural is thus used after 'quisque' in several passages in Tacitus; e.g. xiv 18, 2 'agrorum quos . . . proximus quisque possessor invaserant'.

§ 2. **iura reddentem**: cf. Intr. pp. xxix, lii.

turbidis, 'disorderly', 'tumultuous'.

§ 3. **modestia**, 'mildness'; a rare word, but 'aquarum modestia' occurs in Pliny (*N. H.*). Cf. also 'saevitia annonae', ii 87, 1.

§ 4. **nec nunc infecunditate laboratur**, 'its troubles are not even now due to any lack of fertility'. The decay of farming in Italy, ascribed by Varro to the preference by the peasantry of an idle life in Rome, by Pliny to the prevalence of 'latifundia' and slave labour, was perhaps principally due on the economic side to the fact that grain imported from Africa and Sicily cost less than that raised in Italy.

Africam et Aegyptum: Josephus represents Herod Agrippa as saying that Rome was supported by Egypt for four months in the year and by Africa for eight (*B. I.* ii 16, 4).

exercemus: cf. xi 7, 4.

navibusque: Tiberius makes a similar reflection, iii 54, 6.

44   **Chapter 44, § 1. Hiberos**: see xi 8, 2.

§ 2. **Vologeses**: ch. 14, 8.

fratrum: Tiridates (ch. 50, 1) and Pacorus (xv 2, 1).

Pharasmanes . . . Mithridates: see xi 8, 1.

§ 3. **patrias**, 'native' accomplishments, i. e. riding and archery.

§ 4. **modicum**, 'inconsiderable as it was', implying that if only it was in his hands he would extend it.

detineri, 'was being kept from him'; cf. xiv 65, 1 (where Nero is stated to have brought about the death of Pallas) 'quod mmensam pecuniam longa senecta detineret'.

§ 5. **potentiae promptum**, 'ready to grasp power'; cf. 'promptum ultioni', xi 32, 1.

accinctum: cf. ch. 25, 2.

a semet: cf. vi 32, 5; 33, 1.

memorando: Intr. II 22, b.

§ 6. **multa,** &c., 'treated with every courtesy, like a son' (lit. = 'so as to give him the appearance of one of his own children').

ornante, 'strengthening his power'. 'Cultus' refers to his treatment at his first arrival, 'ornante' to Mithridates' continued kindness while Radamistus was engaged in intriguing against him.

Chapter 45, § 2. proelianti, &c.: this clause gives the sub- **45** stance of Pharasmanes' professed grounds for hostilities.

Albanorum: see vi 33, 3. The war alluded to here is unknown; in vi 33 the Albani are mentioned as in alliance with Pharasmanes.

§ 3. **exutum campis,** 'driven from the open country'; so 'hostem exuere sedibus', xiii 39, 3.

Gorneas. Probably one of the strong fortresses (γαζοφυλάκια) mentioned in Strabo (xi 14, 6, 529). Kiepert identifies it with some ruins still called 'Garhni', east of Erivan.

militum: sc. 'Romanorum'. That Mithridates had been aided by Roman troops in reducing rebel strongholds has been mentioned in xi 9, 1. **Praefectus:** sc. 'cohortis', as in ch. 39, 5.

Casperius: mentioned again xv 5, 2; perhaps the Casperius Niger of *Hist.* iii 73, 3.

§ 4. **ignarum** = 'ignotum'; so also below, 'gnaram'='notam'; cf. xi 32, 1.

machinamenta, &c., 'engines and devices of siege work'. The following clause, implying in the Romans skill in repelling as well as conducting a siege, attributes Radamistus' failure to the ability of the defenders as well as the incapacity of the besiegers.

§ 5. **obsidium,** 'a blockade'. (The word occurs in the dative in ch. 38, 4.)

emercatur: cf. ch. 14, 1.

avaritiam praefecti: Intr. II 57.

verterentur: for 'everterentur'; cf. Intr. II 28.

§ 6. **abscedit:** sc. 'Casperius'. **ut:** expresses Casperius' purpose (not the terms of the 'indutiae').

Ummidius Quadratus: from an inscription we learn that he was quaestor in the last year of Augustus' and the first of Tiberius' reign, praetor in 18 A. D., governor of Lusitania in 37 A. D., consul suffectus probably under Gaius (or at the beginning of Claudius' reign); he succeeded Cassius (ch. 11, 4) in Syria, which he held till his death in 60 A. D. (xiv 26, 4), when he was succeeded by Corbulo.

praesidem: this title for the legatus of a province begins after the first century A. D., and before long is found as the regular term. It is used in vi 41, 1.

Chapter 46, § 1. coniunctionem fratrum, 'the tie of brother- **46** hood'; implying Mithridates' duty to defer to the wishes of his elder brother.

necessitudinum nomina, 'titles of connexion'; these are explained in the two following clauses.

§ 2. **in tempore:** here, very unusually,= 'at the present moment'. Usually, as in ch. 50, 4, it means 'at the right time' (ἐν καιρῷ).

ne, &c., 'he should not choose to try the uncertain fortune of war rather than accept a bloodless settlement'.

§ 3. in omnem, &c., 'one who could be bought over to any wickedness'.

§ 4. propalam, &c., 'while openly returning vague answers, usually of a pacific tendency'.

et saepius, 'and usually'. So 'ac saepius', ch. 7, 6.

monet celerare: cf. xi 1, 2 and Intr. II 31.

§ 6. qua necessitate: causal abl.; cf. Intr. II 19.

47 Chapter 47, § 1. effusus, 'rushing into his embrace'. 'Effundi' is used in a middle or reflexive sense of giving way to a feeling; and 'effusus', of the feeling thus indulged in, as 'effusae clementiae' vi 30, 3.

adlaturum: for omission of reflexive cf. Intr. II 3.

§ 2. sacrificii paratum, 'the necessary furniture for the sacrifice'; cf. Livy x 41, 3 'occulti paratus sacri'. (The reading of Med. is 'sacrificium imperatum'.)

§ 3. in societatem coeant, 'meet to form an alliance'. The subjunctive is that of action often repeated; Intr. II 41.

arcanum, 'mystical'.

§ 4. decidisse: supply 'se' (rather than 'vincla'), as this pronoun is often omitted by Tacitus (cf. Intr. II 3, a), and 'ipsum' in the next clause, distinguishing Mithridates from the subject of the verb, suggests this meaning.

concursu plurium = 'pluribus concurrentibus'; cf. Intr. II 57.

§ 5. mox quia, &c.: supply 'vulgus' a second time, as subject to 'intentabat'. On Mithridates' rule cf. xi 9, 3.

intentabat: Intr. II 60.

§ 7. visui tamen, &c., 'he spared his eyes the actual sight of their execution'; cf. 'aspectui pepercit', xv 61, 7. For 'consulere' nearly = 'parcere' cf. xi 36, 3.

§ 8. sororem: cf. ch. 46, 1.

48 Chapter 48, § 1. Quadratus, &c. The narrative illustrates the control exercised by the legatus of Syria, in virtue of his authority over the commanders of troops in Cappadocia and other eastern provinces, over the administration of the provinces and dependent kingdoms towards the Parthian frontier.

cognoscens: aoristic present; cf. 'respondens', ch. 46, 4, and 'praemonente', xi 35, 3. (Intr. II 42.)

consilium: the persons thus consulted would be taken from the principal persons in his suite, to which might be added any Roman citizens of senatorial or equestrian rank who happened to be in the neighbourhood. The actual decision on the point under discussion rested with the governor.

§ 2. tuta disserunt, 'recommend avoidance of danger'.

cum laetitia habendum, 'must be received with joy'. So 'nec cum hostili odio ... nomen ... habebatur', xv 28, 1. 'Cum', with noun, is equivalent to an adverb of manner, such as often accompanies 'habere' in this sense; cf. 'civiliter habuit' (iv 21, 2).

98

ut saepe, 'as Roman emperors have often, under pretext of bestowing the kingdom, set this very Armenia as a cause of disturbance among the barbarians'; i. e. set up some prince, who, as their nominee, would be unpopular and provoke disturbances. (Cf. vi 32, 5; xi 8, 1; and 'donum populi Romani', ch. 45, 5.)

turbandis: Intr. II 11.

§ 3. **dum,** 'so long as he became hated and infamous'; 'dum', taken in the sense of 'dummodo', with 'esset' supplied from 'foret' at the end of the sentence. 'Esset' is also supplied with 'quando', which is here causal; so also in ch. 62, 2; 67, 2.

itum: the phraseology applying to the Roman senate is here used, although the decision in this case was not really reached by voting but lay with the governor. See note on § 1.

§ 4. **adnuisse facinori:** cf. 'adnue coeptis', Verg. *G.* i 40.

Chapter 49, § 1. Cappadocia: its organization as a province 49 in 18 A. D., under Tiberius, is mentioned in ii 56, 4. It became a Caesarian province under a praefectus or procurator, who was subordinate to the legatus of Syria, but in Vespasian's time it was put under the legatus of Galatia, and a legion was stationed there.

deridiculo, 'absurdity'; i.e. deformity. The word is also used thus as a substantive in vi 2, 2.

conversatione, 'society'.

iners: the word means what is detached from practical life, e.g. rhetoric and philosophy as contrasted with actual work in the forum or business of any sort; cf. xiii 42, 4, where Seneca's accomplishments are called 'studia inertia', as contrasted with the 'vivida eloquentia' of the advocates who practised in the courts.

§ 2. **auxiliis provincialium:** not the regular auxiliary forces attached to a legion, but local levies raised for this particular purpose.

tamquam: with fut. participle, like ὡς, as in vi 36, 1.

abscessu suorum: see Intr. II 57. The departing force was perhaps that under Pollio.

ultro, 'actually'; so far from preventing, even encouraged him.

regium insigne: the tiara and diadem.

cohortatur: with infin.; cf. xi 16, 3 and Intr. II 31.

§ 3. **turpi:** the epithet applicable properly to the fact reported is attached to the report itself; cf. 'maesta fama', *Hist.* ii 46, 1; 'atroces nuntii', *Hist.* i 51, 8.

ne ceteri, &c., 'lest all Romans should be regarded as of Paelignus' stamp'; cf. 'ex vero statuere', iv 43, 4.

Helvidius Priscus: not the famous person of that name, prominent in the *Histories* (iv 5); for he was not quaestor till the time of Nero, and the 'legati legionum' were drawn from senators of praetorian rank.

mittitur: i. e. 'a Quadrato', there being no legions in the East at this time except those in Syria.

pro tempore, 'as suited the occasion'.

§ 4. **Taurum**: he would cross a part of this chain, in coming from Syria through Commagene to Cappadocia.

rediret ... iubetur: cf. xiii 15, 3 'Britannico iussit exsurgeret'.

50 Chapter 50, § 1. The chronology of these events is not clear. In xiii 6, 1 we read that the second occupation of Armenia by the Parthians (after the 'atrox hiems' of ch. 50, 3) did not become known at Rome till the end of 54 A. D.; it presumably happened in the earlier part of that year; so that the 'atrox hiems' would be that of 53–54 A. D. The events of chs. 44–49 may well have extended over a longer period than the year 51 A. D., to which they are ascribed (ch. 44, 1).

casum, 'opportunity'; so in xi 9, 1.

a maioribus suis. In recent times Vonones (ii 4, 3) and Arsaces son of Artabanus (vi 31, 2) had been at least nominal kings of Armenia, and Parthians had ruled it during the captivity of Mithridates (xi 8, 1); but the expression here points rather to the Arsacid kings of the second and first century B.C., who claimed to be of the same stock as the Parthian royal race.

pars domus, 'member of his family'. His other brother, Pacorus, held Media (xv 2, 1).

§ 2. **Artaxata**: on the Araxes, near Erivan. The word is sometimes treated as a neut. plur., sometimes as fem. sing.

Tigranocerta: ascribed by Kiepert to the site of ruins known as Tell-Ermen, a little south-west of Mardin, thirty-seven miles from Nisibis, and in the extreme south of Armenia.

§ 3. **tabes**, 'pestilence'. **omittere praesentia**, 'abandon affairs on the spot'. Cf. xi 18, 2.

§ 4. **defectores**: so in xi 8, 5.

in tempore: cf. ch. 46, 2 note.

§ 5. **patientiam abrumpunt**: cf. 'abrumpi dissimulationem', xi 26, 1.

51 Chapter 51, § 2. **utcumque**: to be taken with 'toleravit', 'endured somehow'. So Livy xxix 15, 1 'quae ... utcumque tolerata essent'.

festinatione continua: causal abl.

§ 3. **adlevare**: the word is proper to the action of raising a petitioner from a suppliant's position; 'adlevat supplicem', ch. 19, 1. Perhaps Zenobia had dismounted and knelt in entreaty. [Otherwise the word is used metaphorically = 'encouraged'.]

§ 4. **violentia**: causal abl., co-ordinated with adj.; cf. Intr. II 64; 'carried away by his love, and accustomed as he was to violence'.

acinacen: a short sabre.

ripam ad: anastrophe; see Intr. II 55.

Araxes: this river passed under the walls of Artaxata, where was the 'regia' (50, 5) from which he was escaping.

Hiberos: if the text is sound this must be taken in apposition with 'regnum'. 'Made his way to his father's kingdom, the 'Hiberi'. The construction is unusual, and 'Hiberos' may be a gloss.

§ 5. **vitae manifestam**: Intr. II 24.

advertere = 'animadvertere'.

dignitate, &c., 'owing to the grandeur of her appearance thinking that she was no ignoble sufferer'.

ad Tiridaten: the words imply that he retook Armenia, upon the general rising against Radamistus.

cultu regio habita, 'was treated in the style of a queen'.

Chapter 52, § 1. Faustus Sulla was husband of Antonia 52 daughter of Claudius, and was accused, under Nero, of plotting to make himself emperor, first in 55 A. D., when the charge broke down (xiii 23), and again in 58 A. D., after which, although the charge was not proved, he was banished to Massilia (xiii 47), where he was put to death by Nero's orders in 62 A. D. (xiv 57, 6).

Salvius Otho was brother of the subsequent emperor, and is often mentioned in the *Histories* (e. g. i 75, 77, 90; ii 23, 33, 39, 50, 60). He was proconsul of Asia, with Agricola as his quaestor, in 63-64 A. D.

Furius Scribonianus: son of the consul of 32 A. D.; ch. vi 1, 1.

quasi, 'on the ground that '; see Intr. II 50.

Chaldaeos: see notes on xii 22, 1; vi 20, 3.

ut: to be taken with ' inpatiens ', like ὡς with participle.

§ 2. **arma . . . moverat**: this refers to the conspiracy of 42 A. D. Cf. Intr. p. liii.

Delmatia: bounded by Pannonia on the north, and in other directions by Moesia and Epirus. (It is also known as 'superior provincia Illyricum ' and ' maritima pars Illyrici '.)

ad clementiam trahebat, 'claimed it as an act of clemency '.

iterum: he might have executed him for his father's guilt, as had been done to Seianus' children (v 9, 1), and he might now put him to death for his own offence.

§ 3. **morte fortuita an**, &c. The sentence is so compressed as to produce an anacoluthon; after 'esset ' some such words as ' parum constitit ' are expected, but instead of this the clause of indirect question is immediately followed by the statement that the reports were coloured by people's preconceived ideas. ' His end, whether natural or due to poison, was variously described, according to the beliefs of the speakers.'

de mathematicis: for other such decrees see note on ch. 22, 1.

atrox et inritum, 'severe, yet futile '. ['Et' = 'and yet '; so ' neque' = ' but not ', in vi 37, 3.]

§ 4. **ob angustias**: i. e. from not possessing the senatorial census.

motique: the power of revising the list of senators rested at all times with the princeps, apart from his occasional tenure of the censorship.

Chapter 53, § 1. ut, &c., 'that those who thus degraded themselves without the knowledge of the slave's master must remain among his slaves, but if the master's consent had been obtained, they should be treated as his freedwomen '. ' Haberentur ', with 'in servitute', has the sense of 'tenerentur', but with 'pro libertis = 'should be treated'.

§ 2. **praetoria insignia**: cf. xi 38, 5.

centiens quinquagiens: supply ' centena milia '.

consul designatus: he was one of the 'consules suffecti' of this year. He is said to have shown 'iustitia et industria' as governor of Asia in 61–62 A.D., and to have been one of Nero's victims in 66 A.D. (xvi 23).

censuit: as cos. design. he had to speak first on the motion.

§ 3. **Cornelius Scipio**: see xi 2, 5.

regibus Arcadiae ortus: Scipio claims for him descent from Pallas, ancestor of Evander, after whom the original Pallanteum on the Palatine Hill was named (Verg. *Aen.* viii 54). ' Pallas ' was the name which he bore when a slave in Antonia's household (xi 29, 1), and on his liberation he probably took the name ' M. Antonius Pallas '.

§ 5 **fixum**, &c.: this inscription is quoted at length by Pliny, *Ep.* viii 6. It was set up near the statue of Julius Caesar in the Forum Iulii.

sestertii ter miliens: 300,000,000 sesterces.

54   **Chapter 54, § 1. Felix**: he also, like Pallas, bore the name Antonius (*Hist.* v 9, 5), and (according to Suidas) Claudius. Suetonius mentions him among the most influential freedmen, ' quem cohortibus et alis provinciaeque Iudaeae proposuit, trium reginarum maritum '. Of these three wives one was Drusilla, daughter of Herod Agrippa I ; another, a granddaughter of Antony and Cleopatra, is named Drusilla by Tacitus (*Hist.* v 9) ; the third is unknown.

pari moderatione: said ironically.

iam pridem: this expression harmonizes with the view that he was contemporary with, not successor to, Cumanus (see below), whose appointment dates from 48 A.D. (Jos.).

impune : predicatively ; sc. 'futura '.

potentia: that of Pallas.

§ 2. **postquam** : the occasion was that of the command of Gaius to erect his effigy in the Temple (*Hist.* v 9), which Tacitus probably described in a part of the lost books of the *Annals*, and here referred to with a few words that have dropped out.

obtemperatum esset: the subj depends on some such word as ' quamquam ', which has been lost in the lacuna between 'postquam' and ' cognita' ; 'though, on news of his death, the command was not executed '.

§ 3. **intempestivis**, &c., ' by ill-timed repression infuriated them to worse crimes'.

aemulo, 'while V. C. vied with him in misgovernment '.

Ventidius Cumanus: Tacitus' account is at variance with that of Josephus (*Ant.* xx 5), who makes Cumanus sole governor, from 48–52 A.D., and represents Felix as not appointed until Cumanus was deposed and banished, 52 A.D., an account in accord with the usual

practice whereby the province of Judaea was under a single procurator resident at Caesarea and governing all parts of Palestine
except those under native princes. The divergence between the two
historians on this point can only be reconciled by supposing Felix
to have held at this time a post of administration in Samaria, under
Cumanus; but there is no independent evidence for this.

cui : dative of agent ; Intr. II 10.

divisis : supply 'provincialibus' from the context.

§ 4. latronum globos : Josephus describes this as a retaliation
on the part of the Galilaeans and other Jews for the molestation by
the Samaritans of those going up from Galilee to Jerusalem to
festivals, for which justice had been refused by Cumanus.

§ 6. adversus, 'in regard to'.

cunctationem adferebant, 'the case of Cumanus and Felix
caused him embarrassment'.

quia : this does not explain the reason of his embarrassment, but
why he had to deal with them as well as the Jewish insurgents.

ius . . . dederat: even without such a special enactment,
the legatus of Syria had a general authority over these procurators.

§ 7. damnatus . . . Cumanus: Josephus (*Ant.* xx 6, 2, 3) says
that Cumanus was sent to Rome for trial, and there sentenced to
banishment.

Chapter 55, § 1. agrestium, 'wild'.　　　　　　　　　　　**55**

Clitarum : see vi 41, 1.

decursu in litora = 'decurrendo in litora'; Intr. II 57.

vim . . . audebant: cf. 'non ausis aciem hostibus', ch. 32, 2.

§ 2. Anemurium: a town on the most southerly point of Asia
Minor, opposite Cyprus ; now the cape, and castle, of Anamur.

duri: explained by 'montis asperos' above.

§ 3. Antiochus Epiphanes IV, restored by Gaius to Commagene,
and further enriched with this portion of Cilicia, was afterwards
deposed by him, and then restored by Claudius. He rendered help
to the Romans during Corbulo's campaigns in the East, under Nero,
and to Vespasian in the Civil War and against the Jews. In 72 A. D.
he was deposed on a charge of disaffection, and his kingdom
became a province. He himself ended his days at Rome.

composuit : as in ch. 40, 1.

Chapter 56, § 1. perrupto monte. The construction of this **56**
tunnel, originally contemplated by Julius Caesar, was undertaken
to relieve the surplus waters of the lake, for which there was
no sufficient natural outlet. Its completion increased the area of
cultivable land in the neighbourhood and rendered the Liris more
navigable. The length of the tunnel was about three miles ; and
the work was very difficult and expensive, and is said by Suetonius
(*Cl.* 20) to have occupied 30,000 men for eleven years. Under Nero
the tunnel became choked, but it was cleared again by Hadrian. In
Dio's time it had again become useless. In modern times the outlet from the lake was again brought into use (1874), in consequence

of which 40,000 acres have been brought into cultivation and a pestilential district rendered healthy.

levibus navigiis : the *Monumentum Ancyranum* gives the number of vessels that fought in Augustus' naval spectacle as thirty ' triremes aut biremes', with more of lesser size.

minore copia : the *Mon. Anc.* gives the number of combatants as ' tria milia ', not counting the rowers.

§ 2. **cincto,** &c., ' having formed a ring by means of a circle of rafts, so as to give no chance of escape to stragglers, while at the same time he enclosed a space fully sufficient for ', &c.

ad : cf. xi 23, 3.

proelio solita : cf. ' solita convivio ', xi 38, 2.

§ 3. **tenderentur,** ' might be directed ', against any who tried to escape. These precautions were necessary as the combatants were armed criminals.

classiarii : apparently here = the naval gladiators. [The word usually means ' marines ', so that this clause might mean rather that an additional guard of ships manned by marines was placed to command that part of the lake not occupied by the ' rates ' of the praetorians or required for the spectacle.]

tectis navibus, ' with decked ships ' ; ναυσὶ καταφράκτοις.

§ 4. **montium edita :** Intr. II 23.

officio, ' by way of attention ', ' in compliment to '.

§ 5. **paludamentum :** the ' sagum purpureum', worn by a Roman general when on active service. Such a cloak became a regular feature in the dress of a Roman emperor. In shape it resembled the Greek ' chlamys ', and in fact the cloak worn by Agrippina on this occasion, here termed ' chlamys aurata ', is described by Pliny as a ' paludamentum' of cloth of gold (*N. H.* xxxiii 63).

sontes : they were θανάτῳ καταδεδικασμένοι (Dio).

multum vulnerum : Intr. II 23.

57   Chapter 57, § 1. **haud satis depressi,** ' which had not been carried down to a low enough level '.

ad lacus ima vel media : (1) ' to the lowest, or even the medium depth of the lake ', or (2) ' to the lowest part or even the middle of the lake ', implying that the greatest depth would naturally be found in the middle.

§ 2. **eoque,** ' and therefore '.

specus, ' the tunnel ', ' the excavations '. [Plural for singular.]

contrahendae multitudini : Intr. II 11.

inditis pontibus, ' pontoons having been placed on the water ' (left in the lake).

§ 3. **quin et,** &c., ' moreover, a banqueting room had been constructed close to the outlet of the lake, and this gave rise to a great panic among all there '.

convivium : so in xv 37.

proxima, ' the nearest parts ' of the structure, which was probably a temporary one, of woodwork ; **ulterioribus,** ' the more distant parts ', including the persons on it ; ' while, the more distant parts feeling the shock, much terror was caused by the crashing and roaring'.

§ 4. **Narcissum:** he was obnoxious to her as having supported a rival (ch. 2, 1), and now becomes her pronounced enemy (ch. 65, 2).

cupidinis, 'avarice'. His fortune is stated by Dio to have amounted to 400 million sesterces (Dio lx 34, 4), the largest on record of the great fortunes of that age [over £3,000,000].

§ 5. **inpotentiam,** 'imperiousness'; cf. 'mater inpotens', v 1, 5. The word denotes absence of restraint on one's inclinations.

Chapter 58, § 1. Decimus Iunius Silanus Torquatus was **58** one of the great-great-grandsons of Augustus (see Genealogical Tree, Intr. p. lxv). He committed suicide in 64 A. D., on being charged with conspiring against Nero.

Q. Haterius Antoninus was son of D. Haterius Agrippa, mentioned in ii 51 as 'propinquus Germanici' (owing to his father's marriage with a daughter of Agrippa).

sedecim: he had really only just entered on his sixteenth year, see ch. 25, 3.

Octaviam: see ch. 3, 2.

Iliensium: the Ilium of this date was the town restored by Sulla, after an almost complete destruction by Fimbria in 85 B. C. In spite of the privileges already accorded to it, it was of insignificant power and wealth.

Romanum, 'the Roman people', as 'Samnis', 'Poenus', &c., in Livy.

demissum: so Vergil, *Aen.* i 288.

haud procul, 'not far removed from'; adjectivally used, as 'palam' in xi 22, 1.

omni publico munere: Ilium had been declared a free city by the Romans even before the time of Sulla, who confirmed the privilege anew. Julius Caesar confirmed it in the ἐλευθερία καὶ ἀλειτουργησία (freedom, and immunity from contributions in money or service) once bestowed by Alexander (so Strabo). This immunity had perhaps come to be disregarded, and required to be affirmed anew.

§ 2. **eodem oratore** = 'eodem orante'; these words apply to all the three decrees mentioned.

Bononia: a Latin colony established in Cisalpine Gaul in 189 B. C. Originally it was an Etruscan town, Felsina.

haustae: applied metaphorically to destruction by fire; so in iii 72, 4.

Rhodiis: the Rhodians had gained a privileged position as allies of Rome in the Macedonian and Mithridatic wars ('bellis externis'), but had been deprived of their freedom by Claudius nine years before this date for having crucified some Roman citizens (Dio lx 24, 4). The island was subsequently reduced to a province by Vespasian.

Apamensibus: their town was Apamea Cibotus, in Phrygia, close to Celaenae, on the Marsyas. Its position on the road of traffic gave it commercial importance second only to that of Ephesus. A similar remission of tribute to cities in Asia Minor on the occasion of an earthquake in 17 A. D. is described in ii 47. Such remissions of tribute were usually granted by means of a decree of the senate, 'auctore principe'.

59 Chapter 59, § 1. At contrasts the odious part forced on him with the popular part assigned to Nero.

promere adigebatur: Intr. II 31.

eiusdem: the word implies that Agrippina had prompted Nero's actions in the preceding chapter.

Statilius Taurus: son of the consul of 16 A. D., and himself consul in 44 A. D. He was perhaps the brother of Statilius Taurus Corvinus, who was consul in 45 A. D., and was implicated with Asinius Gallus in the abortive conspiracy of 46 A. D.

hortis inhians: cf. xi 1, 1.

pervertit: cf. ch. 22, 3.

Tarquitius Priscus was himself subsequently convicted of extortion, in Bithynia, in 61 A. D. (xiv 46, 1).

§ 2. imperio proconsulari: this denotes the power of a governor of a senatorial province (Intr. p. xxxii). Such an officer was colleague rather than servant of the emperor.

ceterum, 'but especially'.

magicas superstitiones: the practice of sorcery, or consultation of astrologers, against the emperor. Cf. ch. 52.

§ 3. sordes: the mourning attire put on by an accused person. So vi 8, 4.

vim . . . attulit: he thus hoped to save the confiscation of his property; cf. vi 29, 2. In this case the charge broke down, as the accuser was punished, in Agrippina's despite, § 4.

§ 4. curia exactus: this expulsion was effected by sentence of the senate itself. Tarquitius seems to have been restored by Nero, as he was subsequently proconsul of Bithynia (xiv 46, 1).

quod . . . pervicere, 'a point which the senators carried'; cf ch. 60, 5 'quae vicerant'.

60 Chapter 60, § 1. rerum . . . a procuratoribus . . . iudicatarum: the regulation now introduced referred to the 'procuratores' of the emperor's private estates, wherever situated. Their powers hitherto had been strictly limited, and in enforcing claims for the princeps' dues in respect of such estates they had formerly been compelled to sue in the ordinary courts, as claimants not as judges (cf. iv 6, 7). Actual jurisdiction no doubt had already belonged to the procurators of the highest rank, those in charge of the lesser Caesarian provinces, and perhaps also to the second class of procurators, those who held in each Caesarian province a position under his 'legatus' corresponding to that of the quaestors in the senatorial provinces. (See Intr. p. xxxiii.)

§ 2. prolapsus: sc. 'in eam sententiam'.

senatus quoque, &c., 'a further extension and fuller definition of their powers was effected by a decree of the senate'. The terms of the decree are not known; but at a later date we find the civil jurisdiction of the procurator, in cases between the 'fiscus' and private persons, concurrent with and practically superseding that of the proconsul.

§ 3. **equestres**: here equivalent to 'equites'. The 'praefectura Aegypti' and 'praefectura praetorii' were the two most important offices open to knights. The former involved the command of two legions, and other troops. The language of the section marks the difference between even the highest of the emperor's 'praefecti' and the elected magistrates.

concessa sunt: sc. 'praefectis'.

praetoribus: the word applies to the governors in the provinces as well as the praetors at Rome.

noscebantur: for 'cognoscebantur', cf. Intr. II 28.

§ 4. There is a confusion of thought in this passage. The privilege at issue in the contests of 'equites' and senate under the Republic was that of furnishing the jury in the criminal 'quaestiones perpetuae'; the question now dealt with is that of the jurisdiction of an individual procurator, usually of equestrian rank, without a jury, in civil actions between the princeps and individuals.

omne ius, &c., 'put into their hands the whole jurisdiction which had been so often the cause of party-strife or civil war'.

Semproniis rogationibus: pl. for sing.; the reference being to the law of Caius Gracchus in 122 B. C.

Serviliae: probably also pl. for sing. The law of Servilius Caepio, consul in 106 B.C., which aimed at restoring to the senate the control of the 'iudicia', does not seem to have been carried. His proposal had been vehemently opposed by another Servilius, namely Glaucia, who was tribune in 106 B.C., and a few years later the confederate of Saturninus.

Marius et Sulla: Tacitus' account is here misleading. The question upon which these two came into conflict was that of the command against Mithridates, in 88 B.C., when the tribune P. Sulpicius Rufus carried a measure in the comitia giving it to Marius, although the senate had already appointed Sulla. Of course, the parties to which Marius and Sulla belonged held opposing views as to the constitution of the 'iudicia', and in his dictatorship Sulla ordained that the 'iudices' should be taken from the senators instead of equites. It may be noticed that Tacitus omits mention of the 'lex Aurelia' of 70 B.C., passed in the consulship of Pompey and Crassus, by which 'iudices' were to be taken from senators, equites, and 'tribuni aerarii', and of the final constitution of the 'iudicia' by Augustus.

§ 5. **sed**, &c., 'but in those days the rivalry was one of whole classes, and what either side carried had the force of constitutional practice'; whereas now the power of the freedmen was a matter of personal influence and the pleasure of the princeps.

C. Oppius et Cornelius Balbus: for the latter cf. xi 24, 4. His career as 'eques', before promotion to consulship and the senate.

is here referred to. Balbus and Oppius acted as Julius Caesar's financial agents during his absence in Gaul, and were also his confidants in his overtures to Pompeius before the Civil War.

§ 6. **C. Matius** is often mentioned in Cicero's letters. He was 'ex equestri ordine, divi Augusti amicus', Pliny, *N. H.* xii 2, 6, 13.

Vedius Pollio was the 'eques' infamous for throwing live slaves to his lampreys; his house was demolished, after his death, by Augustus.

cetera: such as Maecenas, Sallustius Crispus (iii 30), Seianus.

rei familiari: this, and 'res suae', are earlier expressions than 'fiscus', for the emperor's privy purse.

61   **Chapter 61, § 1. Cois**: the inhabitants of Cos, or Cous, a small island to the north of Rhodes, famous for its temple of Ἀσκληπιός (Aesculapius) with its caste of physician priests, 'Asclepiadae', of whom the most famous was Hippocrates.

Argivos: the island was colonized by Epidaurians (Hdt. v 99, 4), not strictly Argives.

Coeus: one of the Titans, son of Uranus and Gaea.

adventu Aesculapii: the worship of this god seems to have been introduced into Cos from Epidaurus, the original seat of the cult.

posteros: the 'Asclepiadae'.

§ 2. **Xenophontem**: this physician, credited afterwards with having poisoned his master (ch. 67, 2), is known from inscriptions to have borne the name C. Stertinius Xenophon, to have been 'tribunus militum', and also 'praefectus fabrum' in the British invasion of Claudius, to have been secretary 'ab epistulis Graecis', and to have filled priestly offices in his native island, which paid honour to his memory as ἥρωι τῷ τᾶς πατρίδος εὐεργέτα.

ministram: probably a translation of νεωκόρος.

§ 3. **multa merita**: they had supported Roman interests as early as 190 B.C. (Livy xxxvii 16, 2), had resisted those who would have drawn them to the side of Perseus, and had joined Rome in the great Mithridatic war. On the occasion last mentioned, Roman citizens found a safe asylum in the temple of Aesculapius, when the massacre of Romans in Asia Minor and the islands of the Aegean was ordered by Mithridates in 88 B.C.

§ 4. **facilitate solita**: to be taken with 'uni concesserat'; 'did not excuse an indulgence made with his usual compliance to one individual by adducing any grounds apart from his own wish.'

extrinsecus: cf. 'nullis palam causis', xi 22, 1.

62   **Chapter 62, § 1. At**: in contrast with the previous sentence. They had to plead their own cause, and therefore made the most of their services to Rome.

apud senatum: the claim was addressed to the senate because the city, though called 'Thraecia urbs' in ii 54, 2, did not belong to the Caesarian province of Thrace, but to the then senatorial province of Bithynia.

cuncta repetivere, 'recounted all their past services'.

§ 2. **foedere**: Byzantium originally joined Rome as a 'civitas

foederata ', and in the time of Cicero it was both 'libera' and
'immunis'. The present passage shows that it had become tribu-
tary; it is called a free state by Pliny (*N. H.* iv 11, 18, 46), but
lost its freedom under Vespasian (Suet. *Vesp.* 8).

ut degeneri, 'as one meanly born'. This was Andriscus, the
son of a fuller of Adramytium, who claimed to be Philip, son of
Perseus. He gained possession of Macedonia for about a year, but
was conquered and taken prisoner by Q. Caecilius Metellus in
148 B.C.

posthac: to be taken with 'memorabant'.

Antiochus: defeated by L. Scipio at the battle of Magnesia,
190 B.C.

Perses: defeated at Pydna, 168 B.C., by L. Aemilius Paulus.

Aristonicus: the claimant for the throne of Pergamus after the
death of Eumenes. The war with him lasted from 131 to 129 B.C.,
when the consul M. Perperna defeated and captured him.

Antonius: son of the orator and father of the triumvir. He was
commissioned to put down the pirates in 74 B.C., but was wholly
unsuccessful.

quaeque . . . obtulissent: referring to services rendered in the
wars against Mithridates; possibly also in Pompeius' campaign
against the pirates in 67 B.C.

recentia: in the Thracian and Bosporan wars (ch. 63, 3).

quando: causal, 'occupying as they did a position which was of
vital importance to leaders and armies making their passage either
by land or sea, as well as serviceable for the conveyance of
supplies '.

terra marique: the passage from Thrace to Asia Minor, and
that from the Aegean to the Euxine.

commeatu: dat. here. The endings *-ui* or *-u* seem to be used
indifferently by Tacitus for the dative of words of the fourth
declension.

Chapter 63, § 1. artissimo . . . divortio, 'where the strait is **63**
narrowest'.

divortium: the word denotes a point of separation, and elsewhere
is used of a bifurcation of roads and a watershed.

posuere Graeci: probably from Megara. The traditional date
is 657 B.C.

Apollinem: Tacitus here follows Strabo (vii 6, 2, 320). The
saying is attributed to the Persian general Megabazus by Hdt.
(iv 144).

§ 2. ambage, 'riddle'. Cf. vi 46, 6.

Chalcedon had been founded by Megarians seventeen years
before the colonization of Byzantium, on the other side of the
strait.

praevisa, 'though they had seen first' (but had not noticed).
The sense is different to that of the word in ch. 40, 6.

vis piscium: shoals of the πηλαμύς, or 'thynnus'. Pliny (*N. H.*
ix 15, 20, 50) says that the harbour of Byzantium (called Κέρας by

Strabo from the similarity of its ramifications to a stag's horn) had already in his time the name of the Golden Horn, from the wealth flowing into it.

Pontum erumpens : cf. ' erumpere nubem ' Verg. *Aen.* i 580.

§ 3. **quaestuosi,** &c., 'this was originally the source of their traffic and wealth.' In xiii 35, 3 ' nitidi et quaestuosi ' = luxurious and profit-mongers, eager traders.

finem aut modum, 'remission or abatement'.

Thraecio, &c. The Bosporan war is that of which the later part is related in chs. 15–21. The ' Thracian war ' probably refers to some hostilities which occurred at the time when Thrace became a province, in 46 A.D.

64   **Chapter 64, § 1. M. Asinius Marcellus,** great-grandson of Asinius Pollio, Augustus' contemporary, is mentioned again in xiv 40 as one of the accomplices in a case of the forgery of a will in 61 A.D. ; although guilty, he was excused punishment on the score of his noble descent and at Nero's intercession.

M'. Acilius : subsequently proconsul of Asia, 65–66 A.D., probably son of the Acilius Aviola mentioned in iii 41, who as legatus of Gallia Lugdunensis was active in the suppression of the first beginnings of the revolt in Gaul instigated by Sacrovir and Florus, in 21 A.D.

igne caelesti : lightning, or the phenomenon called St. Elmo's fire.

fastigio, 'on the pediment'. The accus. is usually found with the verb ' insido ', in Tacitus ; the dative however is supported by Verg. *Aen.* vi 708 ' floribus insidunt '.

§ 2. **biformes,** 'monstrous', whether referring to duplication of organs, or to half-human, half-bestial forms.

editum : the change to indirect speech is very abrupt. The reading of Med. ' ediditum ' may be a corruption for ' editum esse creditum ', or a verb such as ' memorabant ' has dropped out before ' numerabatur '.

§ 3. **defunctis :** none of these are known ; the consul must have been a ' suffectus ', as both those given above are known to have been living after.

§ 4. **vocem :** Suet. (*Cl.* 43) adds that other expressions led Agrippina to fear that Claudius meant to restore Britannicus to the position from which he had been ousted in favour of Nero.

Domitia Lepida : cf. xi 37, 4.

minore : the same mistake has been made here as in iv 44. She was really daughter of the elder Antonia.

avunculo, ' great-uncle '. The construction is abl. abs.

sobrina prior, ' first cousin once removed '. Domitia was grand-daughter of Octavia, sister of Augustus ; Agrippina was Augustus' great-granddaughter.

Gnaei : Gnaeus Domitius Ahenobarbus, father of Nero ; cf. vi 1, 1.

§ 5. **quam :** supply ' eis ' before ' si qua '.

§ 6. **enimvero**: laying stress on the strongest point of rivalry ; cf. ch. 34, 2. Lepida had taken the boy into her house in his infancy when his father died and his mother was in exile, and had evidently been in close intimacy with him ever since that time.

dare: sc. 'quibat', supplied from 'nequibat'; so 'potest' is supplied from 'non potest' in xiii 56, 3 'deesse nobis terra in vitam, in qua moriamur, non potest'.

Chapter 65, § 1. obiecta sunt: the trial appears to have **65** taken the form of one conducted before the family by Claudius as its head. A trial of this nature is described in xiii 32, §§ 3, 4. 'Mors indicta' points to an autocratic decree rather than a judicial sentence.

devotionibus, 'with incantations'. 'Devotio' was accomplished by piercing or burning an effigy of the person practised against, or by inscribing the name, with appropriate curses, on a tablet which was then dedicated to the infernal deities.

parum coercitis, &c. : troops of armed and mounted herdsmen were maintained by the great proprietors on their extensive grazing grounds ('saltus') in Apulia and Calabria. These were always liable to take to brigandage ; they had provided Catiline with recruits in 63 B. C. ; and under Tiberius a quaestor was stationed in South Italy to superintend police measures against them.

§ 2. **prompsisse,** 'to have declared'.

seu Britannicus, &c. : he had destroyed the mother of the former, and opposed the mother of the latter (ch. 2, foll.), so that he was sure of the disfavour of both.

§ 3. **convictam,** &c. : xi 26-38.

pares, &c., 'there were equally strong grounds for bringing an accusation (of conspiring against Claudius) a second time, should Nero become emperor ; but if Britannicus were the successor, the emperor need have no fear'. The Latin is generally regarded as unsatisfactory, as the sense seems to be spoilt by the clause 'si Nero imperitaret'; the object of bringing an accusation against Agrippina and Nero would naturally seem to be to frustrate their schemes against Claudius and Britannicus ; if Nero were on the throne, the time for denunciation would be gone. Most commentators propose to delete either the whole, or some part of the words from 'si' to 'at'; but 'novercae' follows more naturally if 'Britannico' is retained, and a removal of any part of the sentence 'si . . . metum' destroys the balance of the whole. Perhaps the confusion of thought in the sentence as it stands is due to the excitement under which Narcissus is represented as speaking ; or perhaps we may take it that Narcissus meant, 'If Nero were to become emperor, then there would be justifiable cause for another prosecution (against those guilty of conspiracy against Claudius)'; such a prosecution would indeed be too late to save Claudius' life, but Narcissus naturally would not emphasize that fact too strongly out of deference to the emperor.

maiore flagitio: abl. abs., 'while the outrage would then be more horrible than it would have been if he had not exposed the sin of his former consort' (cf. xi 29, 2 foll.).

§ 4. **ne quis**, &c., 'so that no one can doubt'. With 'habere' supply 'eam'. (Cf. Intr. II 3.)

§ 5. **maturrimum**: the superlative adj. is not elsewhere found. The adv. 'maturrime' is common.

adolesceret: indirect command, suggested by 'precari' above.

66 Chapter 66, § 1. **corripitur**: the subject is 'Narcissus'.

Sinuessam: on the coast, just north of the mouth of the Vulturnus. Dio states that Narcissus suffered from gout, and that the springs of Sinuessa were a cure for that complaint (lx 34, 4).

§ 2. **sceleris**: in the specific sense of 'poisoning'; so in vi 33, 1.

certa, 'resolved upon'; so, 'relinquendae vitae certus', iv 34, 2; 'certus eundi', Verg. *Aen.* iv 554.

oblatae occasionis: for the genit. cf. xi 26, 4. The opportunity lay in the removal of the vigilance of Narcissus.

consultavit: from this verb supply the idea of 'metuens' with the two following clauses.

praecipiti: immediate in its action.

tabidum: causing slow decay, 'wasting'.

admotus supremis, 'when brought near to his end' (cf. vi 50, 3).

§ 3. It may be noticed that the actual narrative of Claudius' end does not corroborate what Tacitus says of the assassins' intentions.

§ 4. **vocabulo** = 'nomine'; so often in Tacitus.

Locusta: in Suet. and Juvenal the name is written 'Lucusta'. The scholiast on Juvenal says that she was a native of Gaul. She was again employed to poison Britannicus (xiii 15, 4), continued as 'one of the tools of despotism' ('inter instrumenta regni') through the reign of Nero, and was put to death by Galba.

§ 5. **ingenio**, 'inventiveness'. So, 'obtulit ingenium Anicetus' (xiv 3, 5), when Nero desired to murder his mother.

Halotus: he survived Nero, and was promoted to a wealthy procuratorship by Galba (Suet. *Galb.* 15). The 'praegustator' was one of the officials of the court even under Augustus, and in the time of Claudius there were several of them, forming a 'collegium' under a procurator.

67 Chapter 67, § 1. **scriptores**: the authorities told the story with several discrepancies (see Suet. *Cl.* 44), and Josephus (*Ant.* xx 8, 1) merely says λόγος ἦν παρά τινων that Claudius was poisoned. Many Latin authors, however, including Suet., Pliny ma., and Juvenal, affirm that poison was administered to him in a mushroom; and both Suet. and Dio report Nero's jest in speaking of mushrooms as 'deorum cibus' (referring to Claudius' apotheosis).

delectabili, 'served as a delicacy'.

socordia: it is not clear whether Tacitus means 'owing to the dullness of those near him' or 'owing to Claudius' usual lethargy'.

The account in Dio states that he at once collapsed and was carried away, dying that same night ; but that he had so often been removed intoxicated that no suspicion was at the time excited in those present.

§ 2. **et**: this couples ' exterrita' to the abl. abs. **quando**: cf. note on ch. 48, 3.

ultima, 'the uttermost penalties' (as 'novissima' in vi 50, 8), which were dreaded if he recovered.

provisam ... conscientiam, 'the complicity already secured'.

§ 3. **nisus evomentis**, ' his efforts to vomit'.

faucibus : probably ablat., equivalent to ' per fauces'.

Chapter 68, § 1. dum, &c., ' while the necessary arrangements **68** for securing Nero's accession were being organized'.

firmando imperio : Intr. II 12.

§ 2. **iam primum**, ' to begin with'.

§ 3. **ire in melius**, ' was proceeding favourably'.

miles : the palace guards (ch. 69, 1).

tempus, &c., 'the auspicious moment as revealed by the astrologers' ; cf. vi 22, 6. (The next sentence shows that this favourable moment was midday.)

Chapter 69, § 1. medio diei : cf. xi 21, 2. **69**

tertium ante Idus : a variation from the more usual ' ante diem tertium Iduum'.

Burro : naturally present, as being ' praefectus praetorio'.

cohortem : cf. xi 37, 3.

excubiis : dative. Cf. Intr. II 11.

monente : cf. 'praemonente Narcisso', xi 35, 3.

faustis vocibus, ' with acclamations'. They probably saluted him as ' imperator', and the general body of praetorians confirmed the salutation soon afterwards, § 3.

inditur lecticae, &c.: in the same way Claudius, after the murder of Gaius, was hailed ' imperator' by a party of soldiers who found him in the palace and then carried him off to the praetorian camp, where he was accepted as the new emperor.

§ 2. **nullo**, &c., ' as no one suggested a contrary course, they accepted the choice presented to them '.

§ 3. **praefatus** : his speech was composed for him by Seneca, according to Dio.

paternae largitionis : so Claudius had bought the support of the praetorians by promise of fifteen sestertia to each (Suet. *Cl.* 10).

secuta patrum consulta : decrees confirming him in all the powers held by the emperor. There would also be a ' lex' to the same effect passed in the ' comitia'.

apud provincias : referring to the armies there.

§ 4. **caelestesque honores** : these, and the funeral honours, are spoken of again in xiii 2, 6, where we see that the apotheosis was not decreed till some time after the funeral.

§ 5. **testamentum,** &c. The will of Augustus, on the other hand,

had been read in the senate (i 8, 1).   Dio (lxi 1, 2) states that Nero
destroyed Claudius' will, and Suetonius (*Cl.* 44) implies that the
will was in Britannicus' favour. Tacitus expressly states the contrary,
and the fact that the will was not made public sufficiently accounts
for the prevalence of the other view.

   iniuria et invidia, 'sense of wrong and resentment'.   Cf. xi 6, 3
'odia et iniurias', and Verg. *Aen.* iii 604 ' si sceleris tanta est iniuria
nostri '.

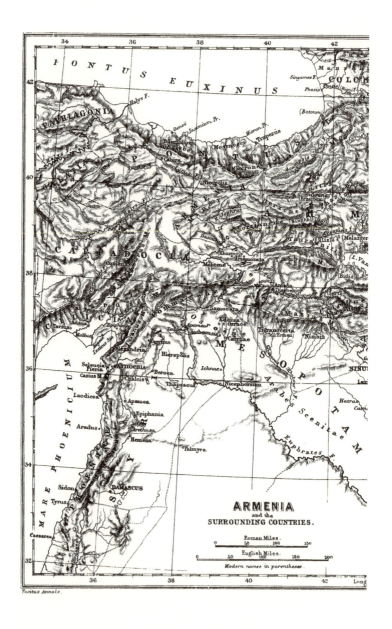

ARMENIA
and the
SURROUNDING COUNTRIES.

Roman Miles.

English Miles.

Modern names in parentheses.

Tacitus Annals.

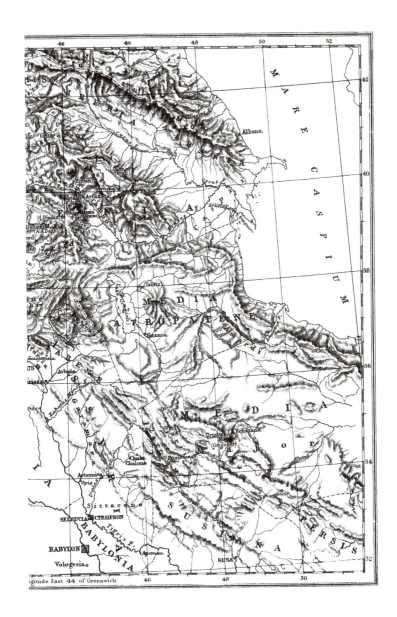

For EU product safety concerns, contact us at Calle de José Abascal, 56–1°,
28003 Madrid, Spain or eugpsr@cambridge.org.

www.ingramcontent.com/pod-product-compliance
Ingram Content Group UK Ltd.
Pitfield, Milton Keynes, MK11 3LW, UK
UKHW010345140625
459647UK00010B/835